The Ethical Turn

MW00984488

Levinas (1969) claims that "morality is not a branch of philosophy, but first philosophy" and if he is right about this, might ethics also serve as a first *psychology*? This possibility is explored by the authors in this volume who seek to bring the "ethical turn" into the world of psychoanalysis. This phenomenologically rich and socially conscious ethics has taken centre stage in a variety of academic disciplines, inspired by the work of philosophers and theologians concerned with the moral fabric of subjectivity, human relationships, and socio-political life. At the heart of this movement is a reconsideration of the other person, and the dangers created when the question of the "Other" is subsumed by grander themes.

The authors showcased here represent the exceptional work being done by both scholars and practitioners working at the crossroads between psychology and philosophy in order to rethink the foundations of their disciplines. *The Ethical Turn: Otherness and subjectivity in contemporary psychoanalysis* guides readers into the heart of this fresh and exciting movement and includes contributions from many leading thinkers, who provide fascinating new avenues for enriching our responses to suffering and understandings of human identity. It will be of use to psychoanalysts, professionals in psychology, postgraduate students, professors and other academics in the field.

David M. Goodman is the Associate Dean at the Woods College of Advancing Studies at Boston College, the Director of *Psychology and the Other* and a Teaching Associate at Harvard Medical School/Cambridge Hospital. He has written over a dozen articles, a book titled *The Demanded Self: Levinasian Ethics and Identity in Psychology* (Duquesne University Press, 2012) and has co-edited several books on the intersection of psychology and philosophy. Dr. Goodman is also a licensed clinical psychologist and has a private practice in Cambridge, MA.

Eric R. Severson is a philosopher specializing in the work of Emmanuel Levinas. He is author of the books *Levinas's Philosophy of Time* (Duquesne University Press, 2013) and *Scandalous Obligation* (Beacon Hill Press, 2011), and editor of several other works. He currently teaches for both Seattle University and Seattle Pacific University.

RELATIONAL PERSPECTIVES BOOK SERIES

LEWIS ARON & ADRIENNE HARRIS
Series Co-Editors

STEVEN KUCHUCK & EYAL ROZMARIN
Associate Editors

The Relational Perspectives Book Series (RPBS) publishes books that grow out of or contribute to the relational tradition in contemporary psychoanalysis. The term *relational psychoanalysis* was first used by Greenberg and Mitchell[1] to bridge the traditions of interpersonal relations, as developed within interpersonal psychoanalysis and object relations, as developed within contemporary British theory. But, under the seminal work of the late Stephen Mitchell, the term *relational psychoanalysis* grew and began to accrue to itself many other influences and developments. Various tributaries—interpersonal psychoanalysis, object relations theory, self psychology, empirical infancy research and elements of contemporary Freudian and Kleinian thought—flow into this tradition, which understands relational configurations between self and others, both real and fantasied, as the primary subject of psychoanalytic investigation.

We refer to the relational tradition, rather than to a relational school, to highlight that we are identifying a trend, a tendency within contemporary psychoanalysis, not a more formally organized or coherent school or system of beliefs. Our use of the term *relational* signifies a dimension of theory and practice that has become salient across the wide spectrum of contemporary psychoanalysis. Now under the editorial supervision of Lewis Aron and Adrienne Harris with the assistance of Associate Editors Steven Kuchuck and Eyal Rozmarin, the Relational Perspectives Book Series originated in

1 Greenberg, J. & Mitchell, S. (1983). *Object relations in psychoanalytic theory.* Cambridge, MA: Harvard University Press.

1990 under the editorial eye of the late Stephen A. Mitchell. Mitchell was the most prolific and influential of the originators of the relational tradition. He was committed to dialogue among psychoanalysts and he abhorred the authoritarianism that dictated adherence to a rigid set of beliefs or technical restrictions. He championed open discussion and comparative and integrative approaches, and he promoted new voices across the generations.

Included in the Relational Perspectives Book Series are authors and works that come from within the relational tradition, and extend and develop the tradition, as well as works that critique relational approaches or compare and contrast them with alternative points of view. The series includes our most distinguished senior psychoanalysts, along with younger contributors who bring fresh vision.

The Ethical Turn

Otherness and subjectivity in
contemporary psychoanalysis

Edited by David M. Goodman
and Eric R. Severson

 Routledge
Taylor & Francis Group

LONDON AND NEW YORK

First published 2016
by Routledge
2 Park Square, Milton Park, Abingdon, Oxon OX14 4RN

and by Routledge
711 Third Avenue, New York, NY 10017

Routledge is an imprint of the Taylor & Francis Group, an informa business

British Library Cataloguing in Publication Data
A catalogue record for this book is available from the British Library

Library of Congress Cataloging in Publication Data
Names: Goodman, David, 1980- editor. | Severson, Eric R., editor.
Title: The ethical turn : otherness and subjectivity in contemporary
    psychoanalysis / edited by David M. Goodman and David R. Severson.
Description: 1 Edition. | New York : Routledge, 2016. | Series: The relational
    perspectives book series
Identifiers: LCCN 2015046122| ISBN 9781138813274 (hardback) |
    ISBN 9781315748252 (ebook) | ISBN 9781138813281 (pbk.)
Subjects: LCSH: Psychoanalysis. | Subjectivity. | Other (Philosophy) |
    Psychology.
Classification: LCC BF175 .E796 2016 | DDC 150.19/5—dc23
LC record available at http://lccn.loc.gov/2015046122

ISBN: 978-1-138-81327-4 (hbk)
ISBN: 978-1-138-81328-1 (pbk)
ISBN: 978-1-315-74825-2 (ebk)

Typeset in Times New Roman
by Swales & Willis Ltd, Exeter, Devon, UK

To Philip Cushman, whose mentorship, friendship and calling
invite moral encounter

Contents

Contributors

Judith Alpert – New York University

Lewis Aron – New York University Postdoctoral Program

Peter August – Private Practice

Sam Binkley – Emerson College

Doris Brothers – TRISP Foundation

Elizabeth Corpt – Massachusetts Institute for Psychoanalysis

Christina Emanuel – Institute of Contemporary Psychoanalysis

David M. Goodman – Boston College

Susannah Heschel – Dartmouth College

Claire Katz – Texas A&M

Lynne Layton – Harvard Medical School

Michael Oppenheim – Concordia University

Donna Orange – New York University Postdoctoral Program

Jill Salberg – New York University Postdoctoral Program

Donna San Antonio – Lesley University

José Saporta – Harvard Medical School

Eric R. Severson – Seattle University

Brian Smothers – Wisconsin School of Professional Psychology

Esther Sperber – Studio ST Architects

Acknowledgements

Coordinating interdisciplinary conversations is a gratifying and challenging endeavor. Remarkable possibilities can emerge from any discourse that inhabits the liminal space between experiences, expertise, and wisdom traditions. At the same time, interdisciplinary conversation can quickly make us aware of the gaps and limitations of language. The crucial ingredient in such conversations is surely humility. Our first acknowledgment, at the outset of this collection, is a word of gratitude for the humble and open approach of each partner in this collaborative project.

This type of effort involves many hands, many people sharing in the risk and investing themselves in a type of vulnerability of exchange. We hope to express our gratitude to those very people whose hands shaped the creation of the second *Psychology and the Other* conference, which provided the original catalyst for this volume. The many people involved in bringing this to life—the speakers, families, students, mentors, editors, steering committee members, scholars, administrators and institutions—are too numerous to mention, but we want to speak to at least several individuals whose labors generously carved out the spaces for these exchanges. We are profoundly grateful to each of them.

First, a small group of students and colleagues met every week for the two years preceding this event to create the vision for its life and to carry the logistical weight of a gathering that brought over four hundred and seventy people from over forty-two countries around the world. It was a team dedicated to learning with one another through readings, sharing with one another in the struggles of life, sweating with one another in the untenable set of responsibilities that they all carried and dreaming up a type of playground that would invite a hospitable and creative space for discourses to play. This group comprised Ben Arcangeli, Jacqueline Aug, Brian Becker,

Abigail Collins, Adeline Dettor, Samuel Gable, Katie Howe-Goodman, Heather Macdonald, David House, Cacky Mellor, Danielle Moreno and Kimm Topping. With no remuneration each of them dedicated themselves to creating a conference to hold the tensions, energies and hopes of inter-disciplinary engagement. Their care and total dedication still moves us in ways that are impossible for us to describe.

Several mentors also provided encouragement, guidance, coura-geous modeling through their scholarship and life paths, and continuous reminders about the true needs that our professions face. They are Philip Cushman, Al Dueck, Mark Freeman, Sue Grand, Richard Kearney, Lynne Layton and Donna Orange. These individuals have been the pioneers who have forged the paths on which this conference walks.

Three close friends and colleagues generously tethered themselves to the formation of this event and have been living reminders of the work we are trying to accomplish. Brian Becker, Heather Macdonald and Ann Pellegrini have constantly restored the purpose and heart of this move-ment in our conversations and these times together were the bedrock upon which this conference was built.

We are grateful to Lew Aron for encouraging the formation of this vol-ume in the first place. Our editor, Steven Kuchuck, provided a keen eye, a supportive spirit, and an attuned sense of the *Relational Book Series* readership. Steven is a brilliant scholar in his own right, which made this editorial process a pleasure and greatly strengthened the volume. Alexandra Rabasco, our graduate research assistant at Boston College, spent months indexing the various chapters and providing detailed copyediting and ref-erence work. Christopher Schuck's comprehensive view of the work was instrumental in shaping the Introduction as well.

Our authors and their expressive, brilliant and receptive approaches have inspired us to believe that these types of conversations, though messy, can yield field-changing and character-forming possibilities. We are deeply appreciative of their openness and excellent work.

The conference and this volume would not have the seen the light of day without the financial and institutional support of several individu-als and departments. Lesley University provided space, personnel and resources that nurtured this bourgeoning conversation. Provost Selase Williams, Elizabeth Chambers and the Graduate School of Arts and Social Sciences shared the vision for this event and were wonderful partners.

The Continuing Education Units were generously and masterfully administered by The Danielsen Institute at Boston University, Lauren Kehoe and George Stavros in particular. Lastly, Boston College, more specifically its Woods College of Advancing Studies under the leadership of Father James Burns, was a dedicated and generous ally in the formation of this conversation and graciously invited the ongoing life of this community to exist at Boston College. This is a gift that will allow this interdisciplinary movement to gain continuous momentum and impact mainstream conversations in the clinical world.

Chapter 1

Introduction

Ethics as first psychology

David M. Goodman and Eric R. Severson

According to Elie Wiesel, "Madness is the result not of uncertainty, but certainty" (Wiesel, 1992). Thought does not begin with knowledge. Knowing and understanding arise from exchange, address, and a person in front of me – always saturated with the ethical. Said differently, it is our very boundedness to one another, our vulnerability of living in this world as fleshly and small, and the calling and address made by one another's vulnerabilities that are the starting points of rationality, personhood, and subjectivity. Emmanuel Levinas makes the assertion that ethics precedes ontology and that "ethics is first philosophy" (Levinas, 1989). We begin with the encounter and then theory, systems, and ontological paradigms stagger forward into words, definitions, and institutions. This is a radical notion, which upsets knowledge claims and foundational rubrics that frequently guide conceptualizations about the human subject. It is this type of assertion, one among many, that has fueled an *ethical turn* in the humanities during the second half of the 20th century. A phenomenologically rich and socially conscious ethics has taken center stage in a variety of academic disciplines, inspired by the work of philosophers and theologians concerned with the moral fabric of subjectivity, human relationships, and socio-political life.

Throughout the modern era, and particularly since the enlightenment, the Western idea of the "self" has leaned heavily on autonomy, self-sufficiency, and individualism. This masterfully bounded and rationally consolidated self has lost significant ground in the second half of the 20th century (Cushman, 1995; Cushman & Gilford, 1999).[1] Problematic on many levels – political, social, economic, religious, familial, and psychological – this hegemonic paradigm has been unsettled by new paradigms of intersubjectivity, social constructivism, hermeneutical theory, gender studies, and ethical phenomenology which have forced a more sophisticated approach to understanding the self's origins – origins that are inescapably bounded to Others (Butler, 2005), always and inevitably ethical. Though called by many different names, this recognition is at the heart of the *ethical turn* that has impacted a variety of academic disciplines.

A "turn" implies unresolved transition – a movement that has not yet reached a destination, yet also cannot return to the security of its origin. A "turn" of any sort moves both *toward* and *away* from something. The ethical turn is a movement *away* from a situation that has dominated the history of thinking, across the disciplines, across the centuries. From the earliest stirrings of philosophy, ethicists have derived the principles of morality from grander principles and universal paradigms. Ethics has been secondary, and rarely primary, for philosophy. Thinkers such as Levinas express considerable concern about the ways that the relation to the other person has, therefore, always been conditioned by larger frameworks of philosophical ideas. Propositions, abstractions, conceptualizations, and detached inquiry become foundations for truth and morality. They are several steps removed, distant and untouched by the ethical imperatives resident in sensate encounter. Levinas goes so far as to link this paradigmatic propensity to the *Shoah* (Levinas, 1982).

In the ethical turn, however, philosophy has moved *toward* relation to the other person as an origin point from which notions and conceptualizations emerge. It is from the encounter in the face-to-face relation with the particular other, the one who is before me, that philosophy has its origins. Theories and systems take shape in the wake of this encounter; they are not the origin of philosophy but the efforts of philosophers to come to grips with a responsibility that begins before thinking has initiated (Levinas, 1998). Hannah Arendt (1998) directed attention to political theory, for instance, pointing out the great distance between the grand notions of the human condition and the lived experience of human beings. She wrote: "men, not Man, live on the earth and inhabit the world" (p. 7). Arendt points to the experiences of a person in the singular, and demonstrates the abstractions and complications that arise when the encounter with the singular other is conditioned by political theories. The ethical turn is not a matter of positioning some theory of ethics at the forefront of philosophy; this movement is about the primacy of the suffering other. It is a turn toward the one who sufferings, along with the awareness that this suffering calls into question any philosophical framework that might make sense of it.

As philosophy re-directs itself to examine and question these founda-tions for the relation to the other person, a similar awakening has taken place in other disciplines. There is a lot more to this "turn" – more history, nuance, and diversity – than we can touch upon here. In this volume our concern lies with the impact of the ethical turn upon mental health dis-ciplines, psychoanalysis more specifically. Psychology, psychiatry, and social work have had a complex relationship to the ethical turn. On the one hand, no professions are ostensibly more concerned with the dynam-ics of interpersonal relationships than these. On the other hand, mental health disciplines have longstanding commitments to grand psychological theories and philosophies of science that problematize Levinas's conten-tion that "ethics is first philosophy." The literature on "evidence-based practice" is illustrative of the many entanglements that prevent a dimen-sional ethics from serving as the starting point of clinical formulations and decision-making (Hoffman, 2009; Wachtel, 2010, 2014). Ethics remains a consideration for mental health practitioners, but for the most part this simply means concern about professional liabilities, accreditation, and a discipline's reputation [i.e., procedural ethics] (Birrell, 2006; Brown, 1997). There are occasional forays into eruptive moral issues, such as the involvement of psychologists in torture practices (Soldz, 2010). Yet for the most part, the ethical turn we are describing goes beyond these under-standings, and threatens the stability of a system that requires practitioners to be first and foremost scientists, clinicians, or evidence-informed techni-cians. The proximity of mental health practice to the medical community further complicates any turn toward fundamental ethics. Allured by the placements, appointments, titles, funding, and legitimizations inherent in medicine, the mental health disciplines have often been seduced by its metrics and forms of epistemological authority. However, inasmuch as psychology conforms to a medical model, it is pushed toward quantifica-tion, diagnosis, and generalization, and away from the unique encounter with the other person (Conrad, 2007). So while the mental health profes-sions seem poised to participate in the ethical turn, there has not been much epistemological or practical space to allow a substantive response to this movement.

Ethics has, however, made something of a comeback in particular quar-ters of psychoanalytic theory and practice. The rise of attachment and mentalization research, neuroscientific emphasis on our "social" brains, and the "relational turn" in several dominant theoretical models have all contributed to an emphasis on moral considerations in human identity, development, and relationships. Relationality has become the occasion for ethics to be considered anew.

This volume provides a granulated analysis of this burgeoning trend in psychoanalysis, and the conceptual lineage that contributed to its formation.

The ethical turn in psychoanalysis: three dimensions

What created the ethical turn in psychoanalysis and what was the "clearing" that allowed it to take shape? The *relational* turn surely laid the foundation for the *ethical* turn (Mitchell & Aron, 1999; Corpt, this volume; Orange, 2010, 2011), but there is more to it than that. There are, no doubt, widely diverse entry points and angles from which to approach the turn to ethics within the psychoanalytic tradition. We propose that there are three cross-pollinating dimensions, which we will name and briefly describe. The main braids that interweave include: (1) attachment, mentalization, and evolutionary biological research (e.g., Bowlby, Bucci, Fonagy, Slavin, Target), (2) scholarship related to critical theory and political positioning (e.g., Benjamin, Dimen, Harris, Layton), and (3) phenomenological, hermeneutical, social constructionist, and dialogical literatures (e.g., Butler, Cushman, Foehl, Gergen, Hoffman, Orange, Stern, Saporta, Summers). These three strands do not serve to demarcate separate aspects of this ethical turn as much as demonstrate a diverse set of tributaries feeding into this conversation. Each brings a different angle, unique voices, and a possibility of new ethical insights emergent from human boundedness.

The inextricable field of two: neuroscience, attachment, and the social bond

The ethical turn points, unrelentingly, to the encounter with the specific other. This movement has also been known as the "relational" turn in psychoanalysis because it has directed attention to the central role of relationality in psychoanalytic approaches. We have come to realize that we are biologically, anatomically, and developmentally structured in such a way that ties us to one another. This realization is reflected by trending emphases on the dynamics of attachment, mentalization research, infant-caretaker studies, and neuroscientific principles regarding our "social" brains. We are not rational beings, first and foremost. We are beings whose psyches are shaped and linked to the maintenance of connection, love, recognition, and attachment (Brandchaft, Doctors, & Sorter, 2010; Brandchaft, 2007; Stolorow, Atwood, & Brandchaft, 1994). These needs frame the very shape of moral subjectivity. Rather than a collection of drives pressing for discharge, as Freud might have it, we are first of all creatures in relation. Relationality precedes rationality, drives, and passions. It frames them and gives them the meaning that they come to have (Mitchell, 1988). The implication, then, is that morality and ethics are defined through notions of empathic response, our ability to recognize others' cognitive and emotional states (mentalization), and the formation of developmental pathways that lead to or away from integrative and open responsiveness to the world around us.

These discourses are enticing and exciting because they provide new and credible ways of thinking about the intersubjective realm. These avenues are also sexy from both political and academic standpoints, because they can be legitimized by research and by apparent connections to science. Beautiful and compelling claims can be made about the ways we are bound together, socially constituted by a relational dynamic that is easily overlooked in atomistic culture (Frie & Orange, 2009). By leaning on research, this avenue of psychoanalytic development tends to point toward developmental processes and hard-wired psychological tendencies. Rendering the relational turn in scientific terminology has the added benefit of maintaining contact with the language and culture familiar to the discipline of neuroscience, along with all the funding, reimbursement, and credibility privileges this entails.

Jessica Benjamin (1988) has presented a striking and compelling rendition of Hegel's master-slave dialectic as it relates to gender norms and caretaking practices. She then uses neuroscientific findings and affective research to show how these insights are verified in evolutionary principles. Through poetry, literary references, dream interpretations, and gorgeous case studies, Philip Bromberg (2006) walks us through the multiplicity and complex range of human subjectivity and intersubjectivity. Then, the "open" circuitry of infant brains and core attributes of mentalizing frameworks are invoked to legitimize such insights (see also Baraitser, 2008).

These examples, however, underscore a clear problem: before ethical and relational insights can impact the discipline of psychoanalysis, they must first make solid contact with some ontological, naturalistic, or scientific foundation. This problem has severely hamstrung developments in the ethical turn in psychoanalysis, for we are left with the impression that ethics remains *second* psychology. The beautiful claims about sociality, boundedness, and connectedness must first be established on the basis of a developmental theory, or some hardwiring of the human psyche. If we are to think of ethics as first psychology, it will be necessary to suspend the requirement that all findings be restricted to that which can be legitimized by ontology and science.

We are implicated: political positioning, definitional violence, and disavowed otherness

Roger Frie and Donna Orange (2009), in their edited book *Beyond Postmodernism: New Dimensions in Clinical Theory and Practice*, chronicle the many ways that the relational schools of thought have taken on a version of deconstructionism and critical theory inspired by philosophers like Jacques Derrida and Michel Foucault. Through these thinkers, along with the influences of feminist, multicultural, and postcolonial movements, the psychoanalytic community has found its way into a deep awareness of the ethical and political significance of culture, class, race, sexual preference, gender identification, and a variety of practices that "position" the subject in an oppressive manner (both within the consulting room and in larger social contexts; Altman, 2010; Aron & Starr, 2013; Benjamin, 1988; Cushman, 1995; Dimen, 2011; Grand, 2009; Harris & Botticelli, 2010; Layton, 2009). Furthermore, this group of psychoanalysts has grown concerned with its own historical trends and preoccupations. A growing awareness has emerged of implicitly sexist theoretical claims, ethnocentrism, and even some of the problematic ways that psychoanalysis took shape out of a traumatized, post-holocaust Europe (Aron & Starr, 2013; Aron, this volume).

More broadly, psychoanalysis has become more ethically attuned because of its growing awareness of our inescapable implication in the suffering of others – whether our shared buy-in to neoliberalism (Layton, 2009, 2015), our definitions of masculinity and femininity (Harris, 2008), the limits of our language and imposition of ideologies in the consulting room, and so forth. We are all caught in what Lynne Layton (2015) describes as "normative unconscious processes" that drive our theories, our definitions, our clinical practices, and our values. We are inevitably ethical agents in such a world, though there is no guarantee we are operating ethically. Each person is a subject already caught in power structures, already situated in history and its political tangles. Michael Foucault, Judith Butler, members of the Frankfurt school, and a variety of other thinkers are frequently invoked to advance this trend in the discipline. Ethics, then, becomes about interrupting the motions of normative life and calling into question the ways that one's subjectivity, practices, and commitments uphold the status quo.

We see here the fingerprints of critical theory, feminist writings, multiculturalism, social constructionism, and the input of several significant political and activist movements. This dimension of the ethical turn in psychoanalysis has carried the movement into the world, or has at least invited the world to affect psychoanalytic ideas and practices. A good example of this appears in this volume, where several authors consider overlooked phenomena in the transmission of trauma. Scientific and ontological approaches to trauma studies have taken little notice of the notion of transgenerational trauma. In her chapter, Judie Alpert explores the surprising, subtle, and haunting way that trauma can move across generations. Transgenerational trauma is difficult to quantify and research. Thinkers in this movement, including Alpert, refuse to confine psychoanalysis to that which can be quantified scientifically.

The ethical weaving of mind: phenomenology, hermeneutics, and the intersubjective

Freud was a "reluctant philosopher" (Tauber, 2010), conflicted about his relationship to the philosophical precursors and foundations of psychoanalysis. But many of those that followed him did not have the same reticence, and the relational turn has created even more space for their voices. Daniel Burston and Roger Frie (2006), in their book *Psychotherapy as a Human Science*, show us how Laing, Boss, Binswager, Fromm, and other psychoanalytic thinkers maintained a rich dialogue with philosophical traditions throughout the middle of the 20th century even while much of mainstream, American psychoanalysis increasingly defined itself in relationship to the medical profession. At the same time, Freud, a "reluctant moralist" as well (Rieff, 1979, 1987, 2006; Tauber, 2010), engaged the subject in such a way that centers around moral and ethical inquiry. There is no way around it: Freud's approach revolved around the question of *who I am* and how reality is represented to myself and lived (Tauber, 2010). This very question is saturated with ethical meaning. How I represent the world to myself and respond to the world around me – the very construction of my existence – is at first an ethical question. It implicates me in this world.

In recent decades, relational and intersubjective schools have carved out a greater openness to the rich philosophical resources in phenomenology and hermeneutics (Summers, 2013). This has contributed to some of the recent emphases on embodiment, language, ethics, dialogical theory, and creative models of intersubjectivity in contemporary scholarship and discussions. These days, it is not terribly uncommon to hear psychoanalysts bringing Levinas, Heidegger, Hegel, Kristeva, Gadamer, Ricoeur, Lacan, Zizek, and many others into their clinical conceptualizations (e.g., Rozmarin, 2007). Continental philosophy – including ethical phenomenology, existentialism, and the like – has become a conversation partner that leads to a concern with the Other: a recognition of ethical questions at the core of answering the question "Who am I?" (Goodman, 2012; Goodman & Freeman, 2015), and an awareness that the origins of the mind are intersubjective, narrative, dripping with moral implications.

One can find in the literature debates between Judith Butler and Jessica Benjamin on the appropriate ways of reading Hegel and how this has bearing on our understanding of how the Other marks, shapes, and determines the self (Butler, 2000; Benjamin, 2000). The clinical formulations surrounding healing that emerge from this dimension can no longer get away with the same assumptions about an agentic, masterfully bounded, thinking subject. The critique of an invulnerable and discretely knowable subject in continental philosophy is a constant haunting in contemporary psychoanalytic thought. Judith Butler (2005) writes: "Full articulability should not be deemed the final goal of psychoanalytic work in any event, for that goal would imply a linguistic and egoistic mastery over unconscious material that would seek to transform the unconscious itself into reflective, conscious articulation – an impossible ideal" (p. 58). Coburn, Corpt, Cushman, Foehl, Frie, Margulies, Orange, Rozmarin, and Shabad are all current voices who are bringing forward these philosophical sources, and changing how subjectivity and the subject are understood – with ethics forever at the front.

In nearly any interpretation regarding clinical process, there is an emphasis on the two persons present in the room and the intersubjective activities at work. Singular interpretations that orient around an internal process of a single person have a more difficult time finding passage in this dialogic and intersubjectively defined space (Mitchell & Aron, 1999; Stolorow, Atwood, and Orange, 2002). Donna Orange's (2010) description of fallibilism is an exemplar for this type of ethical concern and awareness in psychoanalytic process.

Most of our discussion thus far has focused on the central presence and influence of the ethical turn in psychoanalysis, as witnessed in several emerging bodies of thought and innovations within this field. Now, we examine in closer detail how these more ethically informed perspectives are contributing to newer and richer psychoanalytic understandings that can be applied in the therapeutic context.

Psychology and the other: a conversation

Levinas (1969) claims that "morality is not a branch of philosophy, but first philosophy" and if he is right about this, might ethics also serve as a first *psychology*? How might this come about? We have noted that the ethical turn is somewhat irreverent; it respects few, if any, of the foundations and boundaries that have been taken so seriously by traditional mental health disciplines. Psychoanalysts interested in this "turn" have demonstrated a unique willingness to listen to other disciplines, to engage the cutting edge of gender studies, aesthetics, theology, literary studies, and much more. The authors showcased in the coming chapters represent some of the diverse conversations taking place in psychoanalysis' ethical turn, and also inspire the possibility of informing its geography in such a manner that calls it to its fullest potential. These authors share a common irreverence for the tendency, in psychoanalysis, to ground ethics in scientific naturalism and essentialism. The fact that they do not partake in the contemporary trends toward essentialist theories does not mean that each chapter starts in the same place. The ethical turn, across many disciplines, defies the myth of monogenesis, the idea that to approach psychoanalysis rightly we must first pledge allegiance to some foundational theory. As Elizabeth Corpt will show in her chapter, psychoanalysis might actually be uniquely suited to overcome this problem.

Throughout this volume, many of the following questions guide and orient the discussion: How do the "relational" and "ethical" turns relate? What is meant by the "ethical turn" in psychoanalysis and what is meant by "ethical subjectivity"? What ethical demand does the "Other" make on one's subjectivity and how does this play out and relate to the psychoanalytic encounter? How do ethics, of the Levinasian, Gadamerian, Ricoeurian, or Derridian type, relate to human development, healing, and identity? How do contemporary questions regarding intersubjectivity, enactment, multiplicity, vulnerability, empathy, desire, mutuality, and the "third" relate to these questions? More broadly, how are psychoanalysis' assumptions challenged and enriched by philosophical and theological traditions that speak about subjectivity and its relationship to the Other in radically different ways? In what ways is psychoanalysis uniquely situated and able to attend to these complicated questions, perhaps more so than many other clinical orientations?

Pointing back to the Wiesel quote that began this Introduction, we contend that psychoanalysis has the potential of holding uncertainty in a way that much surrounding theory and practice is unable to do. It, however, remains susceptible to the pull toward certainties and conceptual territories. We are concerned about its susceptibility to contemporary intoxication with neuroscience, which effectively reverses Levinas's prescription and makes ethics *second* psychology at best. In neuroscience, all too often, ontology actually precedes ethics and sets its parameters. In the chapters that follow, another way is proposed: an *otherwise* than ontological psychoanalysis. The road forward is not terribly clear, and the authors below do not all agree on which way we must turn. But they do share a common suspicion that we have much work to do to hear and see the other, in psychoanalysis and beyond. Their efforts move us forward, tentatively, and promise to enliven the work of psychoanalysts.

As Esther Sperber's chapter takes time to point out, there is much to be learned in the awkward exercise of cross-disciplinary conversation. The chapters in this volume have their genesis in the 2013 *Psychology and the Other* conference.[2] These gatherings are eclectic, exciting, and surprising, and the discourses that follow exemplify the dynamic results of these daring conversations. The authors' contributions represent an ongoing calling to this recognition and to the uncertain face and needs of the other person, as they address the intersection of psychoanalysis and the ethical subject – an intersection considered from a plurality of positions within the psychoanalytic community. This volume features a grouping of scholars and clinicians who are representative of diverse entry points and angles into this conversation.

Contents of the volume

Lewis Aron has taken profound and lasting leadership in this movement, and we are delighted to include some of his latest work in this volume. There is a significant trend among philosophers to ground the philosophy of ethics in the experience of vulnerability, and in Chapter 2, he extends that insight to the underlying ethos of the clinical situation. Aron argues that by acknowledging one's own permeability and vulnerability, the psychoanalyst no longer projects all of the conflict, splitting, shame, disgust, animalistic embodiment, penetrability, and vulnerability onto the patient. He points to a reclamation of the bedrock "femininity" that Freud repudiated.

In Chapter 3, Esther Sperber provides both a response to and engagement with Aron's chapter, and a unique articulation of the value of interdisciplinary conversation. Sperber demonstrates the power and scope of the ethical turn by elaborating the dynamic connections between Aron's insights into vulnerability and the discipline of architecture. She points to a similar resistance in the field of architecture to any acceptance of the mutuality and vulnerability inherent in the work of the architect.

Donna Orange is also a key figure in this burgeoning field. Her contribution, in Chapter 4, explores an important objection to the ethical turn. If we follow Emmanuel Levinas and begin to think of ethics as first philosophy, and first psychology, does this situation not make the demands of the other person, the destitute other, a tremendous burden on some patients? Does not Levinas's philosophy valorize the already over-accommodative and masochistic patient who, if anything, needs to become more agentic and to develop a stronger ego? Orange uses distinctions borrowed from Emmanuel Ghent and Stephen Mitchell, as well as some careful examinations of relevant Levinasian texts, to explain the difference between compulsive submission to others and genuine ethical response.

The themes of vulnerability and dependency take center stage in Lynne Layton's work. In Chapter 5 Layton points out that our current social conditions of increasing income inequality, downsizing, outsourcing, and high unemployment have created a significant amount of anxiety about class status and well-being across all classes. This has led to a splitting between states of immense vulnerability and insecurity on the one hand, and on the other, to public hatred of any signs of vulnerability and dependency. Dependency has come to signify "poor" and "failure." From a psychological perspective, however, we know that denying dependency leads to a kind of grandiose sense of omnipotence. As a result, it becomes hard to see how rich and poor, powerful and vulnerable, are in fact connected to each other, how we are all part of the same social system and thus mutually interdependent. Grandiose states tend to be unstable and crash, precisely because we do need others. Layton connects this tension to the individual and large-group psychological effects of neoliberal social and economic policy. Her chapter demonstrates how the resulting tension between domination and submission is eroticized, and leads to sadomasochistic and instrumentalized relational scenarios.

In Chapter 6, Sam Binkley provides both a response to Layton's thesis and a creative interpretation of Michel Foucault on similar themes. Binkley highlights one of the key ideas of this book when he points out that psychoanalysis is not "disciplinary technology" but a kind of counter-science, a discipline that cuts against the "hegemonic discourse of neoliberalism itself." Following Foucault, Binkley argues convincingly that the psychological professions are fundamentally social in character.

According to Levinas, the call from the other is what brings me into subjectivity; I am called to open the door to the "widow, the orphan, and the stranger." In her powerful contribution to this volume, Elizabeth Corpt uses this metaphor as a stepping-off point from which to explore the complications of caring within a psychoanalytically informed relationship. Acutely aware of the scope of the ethical turn across many disciplines, Corpt focuses the seventh chapter of this volume on what this means for psychoanalysts. What does it mean to be infinitely responsible to one's patient whose developmentally younger self longs to be completely cared for, as she never had been as a child? How does one know when it is ethically more responsible to metaphorically open a door, close it, or wait and reflect upon one's decision before speaking to or taking action with a patient in our care? What does it mean and how does it feel to cause a patient to suffer in the moment for potentially greater gains down the road? Corpt explores these and other questions at the heart of the complex dynamic of psychoanalytic care.

The complex ways in which uncertainty and ethics are interrelated emerge in sharp focus when they are considered with respect to trauma. In Chapter 8, Doris Brothers suggests that trauma is a relational phenomenon and therefore always marked by uncertainty. She points out that for Levinas, "the ethical demand is a traumatic demand," and then examines trauma from the standpoint of the "economic" metapsychology that Freud elaborated in *Beyond the Pleasure Principle*. Brothers argues that traumatic experience involves the destruction of the certainties that organize selfhood as well as efforts, at times extreme, to restore a sense of certainty about psychological survival.

Several chapters in this volume relate the ethical turn to religious experience, and especially the traumatic experiences of modern Jews. In Chapter 9, Claire Katz offers her considerable expertise in the work of Levinas to explore what it means to have history, in particular, the meanings that inform the approach to Jewish education proposed by Levinas as an answer to rampant 20th-century anti-Semitism. Using the analysis of anti-Semitism by Jean-Paul Sartre, but especially Levinas's confessional Jewish writings, Katz asks: is one to be Jewish in a manner that is not simply a reaction to the anti-Semite's construction of Jewish identity? She then examines Levinas's writings on Jewish education and the problem of assimilation. In these essays, Katz finds a plea to the French Jews to reclaim Judaism, but specifically to return to a Judaism that is pre-modern, pre-secular, and pre-anti-Semitism – in short, a Judaism possessing a history and an identity that Levinas believes is its own. Katz is acutely aware of the implications of the pressure of anti-Semitism for psychoanalysis, and in his response to her chapter, in Chapter 10, Lewis Aron makes these connections explicit, pointing to parallel problems in Freudian psychoanalysis. Aron points to the dangers of privileging the individual over the social, the intrapsychic over the interpersonal, and civilization over primitivity, which brings us back to the interrelated and entangled problems of racism, anti-Semitism, misogyny, and homophobia.

In Chapter 11, Judith Alpert provides an unforgettable introduction to transgenerational trauma, with a personal and powerful exploration of her own Jewish family history and especially the violence experienced by her grandmother in the Russian pogroms. Occluded by the larger atrocity of the Holocaust, the pogroms seem like a disappearing fragment of Jewish history. As with all atrocities, one monstrosity readily absorbs and displaces another, and so the specificity of human suffering is lost, and its victims are rendered nameless. In the recent transgenerational turn of psychoanalysis, those ghosts emerge from namelessness, and enhance our knowledge of ourselves. In tracing the history of her grandmother's trauma, and the unspoken history she retained, Alpert begins to witness herself. In tracing her own story, in turn, she illuminates the intersubjectivity of our conversations with the ghosts of transgenerational trauma.

Jill Salberg explores the way gender binaries appear and are reinforced in psychoanalysis. In Chapter 12, Salberg points out that such binaries are a legacy of patriarchy, which has deep streams both within Judaism and within Freud and psychoanalysis as a whole, and still continues to infuse fantasy life. While gender has always had a primary position within psychoanalysis, it has been in the past twenty-five years that there have been substantial reformulations. Salberg points out that relational psychoanalysis has recast Freud's singular ego, the seat of self-awareness, as multiple self-states each carrying affects, memories, and desires. She uses the insights of Adrienne Harris to suggest that gender emerges to solve some intrapsychic, interpersonal, or intersubjective problem. As a consequence, there may be within one person both girl and boy self-states, each authentically true within certain family configurations and experiential contexts. Salberg's essay demonstrates these tensions through an intriguing exploration of the Jewish stories of Beruriah and Yentl.

Chapter 13 provides a response to both Judith Alpert and Jill Salberg's chapters by Susannah Heschel. With her characteristically keen insight, Heschel points out that both Alpert and Salberg narrate the manner in which traumatic experiences are encapsulated in women's bodies. Heschel explores the openings created by Alpert and Salberg to rethink memory, Jewishness, and the surreptitious limitations imposed on women in male-dominated societies.

Michael Oppenheim, in Chapter 14, offers a study on the complicated relationship between Martin Heidegger's Nazism and *Being and Time*, focusing on the view of responsibility and the wider purview of human relations. He then turns to discussions of the complex responses to Heidegger seen through Loewald's psychoanalytic understanding of intersubjectivity and responsibility, and through Levinas's philosophic rendering of these themes. He uses these conversations to underscore the importance given to responsibility by some post-Freudian psychoanalysts.

José Saporta takes us into the work of Mikhail Bakhtin, and suggests a model for how dialogue and context shape meaning and meaning-making in psychodynamic psychotherapy. In Chapter 15, Saporta considers some of Bakhtin's important concepts as they apply to dialogue in psychotherapy, including: the theory of the utterance, addressivity and positioning, the importance of difference and the excess of meaning for the outside other, monological vs. dialogical ways of relating, authoritative vs. internally persuasive discourse, and stability vs. indeterminacy of meaning. Saporta points out that psychotherapy mobilizes dialogical processes within the self and between self and others, which leads to more complex and flexible meaning-making that is more responsive to unique local contexts. Rather than a limited number of fixed positions from which to make meaning, rigidly and universally applied to all contexts, Saporta suggests that we develop a richer variety of positions from which to generate this meaning in varied relational contexts.

Donna San Antonio uses philosophical hermeneutics to explore the implications of the ethical turn for cultural identity, beginning with her own experiences as an Italian-American. In Chapter 16, she points out that cultural identity is socially influenced, nuanced, and unstable, even more so when we let ourselves consider the multiplicity of our identities, rejecting some aspects of cultural ideals that we previously embraced. Psychoanalysis, San Antonio points out, is in part an iterative process of undermining the cultural ideals with which we identify ourselves.

Chapter 17 turns our attention to creativity and hospitality. Brian Smothers suggests that empathy and understanding are two essentials of psychoanalytic inquiry, yet there are patients encountered in clinical practice for whom these interventions appear to cause greater distress than relief. Smothers wonders: what are we to do when our patients desire to become known, yet the act of being known reminds them of traumatic intrusions? For such patients, being known represents a paradox, as each encounter with another is full of both exciting and horrifying potentials. Using the concepts of enactment and traumatic impingement as points of investigation, Smothers seeks to explore a stance of hospitality that is comfortable moving within the medians of the known and unknown without seeking foreclosure. An attitude of hospitality toward emerging developments within the therapeutic dyad has the potential to allow for the co-creation of novel possibilities for the paradoxes of knowing and being known, while restoring a sense of creativity that is often lost in moments of enactment or impingement.

Christina Emanuel's contribution, Chapter 18, provides an unforgettable exploration of the ethical turn as it relates to disability studies. She movingly introduces us to her own work with autistic individuals, and suggests some reasons for the paucity of work on disability in the psychoanalytic literature. Although psychoanalytic writers commonly theorize race, class, and gender, they have not theorized disability, with the disabled comprising a group of most othered others. Emanuel makes suggestions about what might be gained by adding a Disability Studies sensibility to psychoanalytic theory and practice. Bringing in themes from the Disability Studies literature, we can better theorize the body that shows up in psychoanalytic discourse.

In Chapter 19, Peter August demonstrates the powerful way that play is opened up by the ethical turn. In play, the seriousness and solemnity of psychoanalytic discourse are undermined by the invitational quality of playful discourse. August uses the ideas of Maurice Blanchot and D.W. Winnicott to show that psychoanalysis is less about explanation than it is about invitation. Those who "play" are unburdened of the demand to communicate univocally. Play, August argues, is free to respond to what fascinates polysemously. Every idea is relentlessly dismantled and meanings are eliminated by "infinite degree," leaving us, in the end, at the beginning.

August's vision of psychoanalysis as playful and circular rather than abstract, explanatory, and linear might likewise describe our vision for the experience of reading this book as a whole: a journey of sorts that is unfolding yet circuitous, which takes the reader back to the "beginning" even as it suggests uncharted territories and possibilities. Amidst the disparate chapters and topics outlined above, one can nevertheless find patterns and connections, reflecting the writers' shared project of unearthing and elaborating fresh understandings and meanings for the endlessly rich and mysterious phenomenon of otherness. Exactly how these understandings and meanings connect to one another, and where they might stimulate further dialogue, we leave to the playful insight and exploration of the reader.

Notes

1 It is important to add here that critiques of neo-liberalism assure us that this self is alive and well – healthfully fed and perpetually upheld by late capitalist economic systems that require this enterprising subjectivity to function as its engine (Binkley, 2011; Layton, 2009, 2015; Rose, 1989, 1998).

2 The *Psychology and the Other* conference is a biannual, international meeting in Cambridge, MA. The first meeting was in October 2011 (7th–9th), the second meeting in October 2013 (4th–6th), and the third meeting in October 2015 (9th–11th).

References

Alford, C. F. (2002). *Levinas, the Frankfurt school, and psychoanalysis.* Middletown, CT: Wesleyan University Press.

Alford, C. F. (2007). Levinas, Winnicott, and therapy. *Psychoanalytic Review, 94*, 529–551.

Altman, N. (2010). *The analyst in the inner city: Race, class, and culture through a psychoanalytic lens, 2nd ed.* New York: Routledge.

Arendt, H. (1998). *The human condition, 2nd ed.* Chicago: University of Chicago.

Aron, L., & Starr, K. (2013). *A psychotherapy for the people: Toward a progressive psychoanalysis.* New York: Routledge.

Baraitser, L. (2008). Mum's the word: Intersubjectivity, alterity, and the maternal subject. *Studies in Gender and Sexuality, 9*, 86–110.

Benjamin, J. (1988). *The bonds of love: Psychoanalysis, feminism, and the problem of domination.* New York: Pantheon.

Benjamin, J. (2000). Response to commentaries by Mitchell and by Butler. *Studies in Gender and Sexuality 1,* 291–308.

Binkley, S. (2011). Psychological life as enterprise: Social practice and the government of neo-liberal interiority. *History of the Human Sciences, 24,* 83–102.

Birrell, P. J. (2006). An ethic of possibility: Relationship, risk, and presence. *Ethics & Behavior, 16,* 95–115.

Brandchaft, B. (2007). Systems of pathological accommodation and change in analysis. *Psychoanalytic Psychology, 24,* 667–687.

Brandchaft, B., Doctors, S., & Sorter, D. (2010). *Toward an emancipatory psychoanalysis: Brandchaft's intersubjective vision.* New York: Routledge.

Bromberg, P. (2006). *Awakening the dreamer: Clinical journeys.* Mahwah, NJ: Analytic Press.

Brown, L. (1997). Ethics in psychology: *Cui Bono?* In D. Fox and I. Prilleltensky (Eds.), *Critical psychology: An introduction* (pp. 51–67). Thousand Oaks, CA: Sage Publications.

Burston, D., & Frie, R. (2006). *Psychotherapy as a human science.* Pittsburgh, PA: Duquesne University Press.

Butler, J. (2000). Longing for recognition. *Studies in Gender and Sexuality, 1,* 271–290.

Butler, J. (2005). *Giving an account of oneself.* New York: Fordham University Press.

Conrad, P. (2007). *The medicalization of society: On the transformation of human conditions into treatable disorders.* Baltimore, MD: The Johns Hopkins University Press.

Cushman, P. (1995). *Constructing the self, constructing America: A cultural history of psychotherapy.* Garden City, NY: DaCapo Press.

Cushman, P., & Gilford, P. (1999). From emptiness to multiplicity: The self at the year 2000. *Psychohistory Review, 27,* 15–31.

Dimen, M. (Ed.). (2011). *With culture in mind: Psychoanalytic stories (Relational Perspectives Book Series).* New York: Routledge.

Frie, R., & Orange, D. (Eds.). (2009). *Beyond postmodernism: New dimensions in clinical theory and practice.* London: Routledge.

Goodman, D. (2012). *The demanded self: Levinasian ethics and identity in psychology.* Pittsburgh, PA: Duquesne University Press.

Goodman, D., & Freeman, M. (Eds) (2015). *Psychology and the Other.* New York: Oxford University Press.

Grand, S. (2009). *The hero in the mirror: From fear to fortitude.* New York: Routledge.

Harris, A. (2008). *Gender as soft assembly.* New York: Routledge.

Harris, A., & Botticelli, S. (2010). *First do no harm: The paradoxical encounters of psychoanalysis, warmaking, and resistance.* New York: Taylor and Francis.

Hoffman, I. Z. (2009). Doublethinking our way to "scientific" legitimacy: The desiccation of human experience. *Journal of the American Psychoanalytic Association, 57,* 1043–1069.

Layton, L. (2009). Who's responsible? Our mutual implication in each other's suffering. *Psychoanalytic Dialogues, 19,* 105–120.

Layton, L. (2015). Beyond sameness and difference: Normative unconscious processes and our mutual implication in each other's suffering. In D. Goodman and M. Freeman (Eds.) *Psychology and the Other* (pp. 168–188). New York: Oxford University Press.

Levinas, E. (1969). *Totality and infinity: An essay on exteriority* (A. Lingis, Trans.). Pittsburgh, PA: Duquesne University Press. (Original work published 1961.)

Levinas, E. (1982). Useless suffering. In *Entre Nous: Thinking of the Other*, translated by Michael B. Smith and Barbara Harshav (pp. 159–177). New York: Columbia University Press.

Levinas, E. (1989). Ethics as first philosophy. In S. Hand (Ed.), *The Levinas Reader*. Cambridge, MA: Blackwell.

Levinas, E. (1998). *Otherwise than being: Or beyond essence* (trans. A. Lingis). Pittsburgh, PA: Duquesne University Press.

Mitchell, S. A. (1988). *Relational concepts in psychoanalysis: An integration*. Cambridge, MA: Harvard University Press.

Mitchell, S. A., & Aron, L. (1999). *Relational psychoanalysis: The emergence of a tradition*. Hillsdale, NJ: Taylor & Francis Group.

Orange, D. M. (2010). *Thinking for clinicians: Philosophical resources for contemporary psychoanalysis and the humanistic psychotherapies*. New York: Routledge.

Orange, D. M. (2011). *The suffering stranger: Hermeneutics for everyday clinical practice*. New York: Routledge.

Rieff, P. (1979). *Freud: The mind of a moralist.* Chicago: University of Chicago Press.

Rieff, P. (1987). *The triumph of the therapeutic: Uses of faith after Freud.* Chicago: University of Chicago Press.

Rieff, P. (2006). *My life among the deathworks: Illustrations of the aesthetics of authority.* Charlottesville: University of Virginia Press.

Rose, N. (1989). *Governing the soul: The shaping of private life, 2nd ed.* London: Free Association.

Rose, N. (1998). *Inventing ourselves: Psychology, power and personhood.* Cambridge: Cambridge University Press.

Rozmarin, E. (2007). An other in psychoanalysis: Emmanuel Levinas's critique of knowledge and analytic sense. *Contemporary Psychoanalysis, 43,* 327–360.

Soldz, S. (2010). Psychologists defying torture: The challenge and the path ahead. In A. Harris and S Botticelli (Eds.) *First do no harm: The paradoxical encounters of psychoanalysis, warmaking, and resistance* (pp. 67–105). New York: Routledge.

Stolorow, R. D., Atwood, G. E., & Brandchaft, B. (1994). *The intersubjective perspective.* Northvale, NJ: Jason Aronson Inc.

Stolorow, R. D., Atwood, G. E., & Orange, D. M. (2002). *Worlds of experience: Interweaving philosophical and clinical dimensions in psychoanalysis.* New York: Basic Books.

Summers, F. (2013). *The psychoanalytic vision: The experiencing subject, transcendence, and the therapeutic process.* New York: Routledge.

Tauber, A. (2010). *Freud, the reluctant philosopher.* Princeton, NJ: Princeton University Press.

Wachtel, P. L. (2010). Beyond "ESTs": Problematic assumptions in the pursuit of evidence-based practice. *Psychoanalytic Psychology, 27,* 251–272.

Wachtel, P. L. (2014). On the limits of theoretical fundamentalism. *Journal of Psychotherapy Integration, 24,* 95–98.

Wiesel, E. (1992, April). When passion is dangerous. *Parade Magazine* (pp. 153–154).

Chapter 2

Mutual vulnerability

An ethic of clinical practice

Lewis Aron[1]

In our book, *A Psychotherapy for the People* (2012), Karen Starr and I trace a genealogy, an architecture, a deep binary structure embedded in the history of psychoanalysis along the fault lines of the split between psychoanalysis and psychotherapy, especially psychoanalytic psychotherapy. We trace this history to a two-stage, *nachträglich* development of psychoanalysis, first in Europe and then in post-Second World War America, by founding analysts who were on the margins of their society, at most second-generation immigrants: Jews repeatedly fleeing persecution, poverty, prejudice, and anti-Semitism, people who were traumatized and vulnerable. To summarize, we argue that psychoanalysis repeatedly arose out of traumatic circumstances. The discipline of psychoanalysis therefore suffers from a traumatic history that accounts for its lack of history, its disrupted narrative, its tendency toward splitting and fragmentation, and its structure of reversal and manic defense in which all vulnerability is projected, displaced, denied, and dissociated.

My earlier study of "the third", developed with Jessica Benjamin (Aron & Benjamin, 1999; Aron, 2006), led me to focus on impasses and stalemates in analytic therapy by recognizing the ways in which patient and analyst became polarized around certain issues and for one reason or another could not negotiate those polarities. Hence Benjamin's (2004) brilliant explication of "doer-done to", "push me-pull you", "see-saw" or "one up/one down", "my way or the highway", sadomasochistic relations. My examination of these dynamics led to the recognition that not only did analysts get caught up in these clinical interactions with patients, but that there was something about psychoanalysis itself, its history, its institutionalization, and its social and economic structure that actually contributed to enacting these configurations socially and professionally. Psychoanalysis had defined itself in opposition to, and hierarchically elevated above, suggestion and psychotherapy along the lines of a set of binaries in which psychoanalysis was always on top. Furthermore, the very structuring of the analytic process lent itself to the analyst and the analytic functions being viewed as hierarchically elevated relative to the patient. Hence, only a search for some form of "the third" could free us from the various clinical and cultural impasses in which psychoanalysis has been trapped.

According to Derrida (1976), Western thought, especially metaphysics, is based on dualistic oppositions that are often value-laden and ethnocentric, and that create a hierarchy that inevitably privileges one term of each pole. Derrida's (1976) deconstructive strategy does not rest with reversing dichotomies, but rather aims to undermine the dichotomies themselves, and to show that there are "undecidable" items that do not belong on either side of a dichotomy. These "undecidables" are "third" terms. Deconstruction contends that in any text there are inevitably points of "undecidability" that betray any stable meaning an author might seek to impose upon his or her text. According to Derrida (1976), the dominance of reason, the logos, is allied with the archetypically male will to dominate society, which he described as "phallogocentrism". One can easily see how feminists such as Derrida's close friend and colleague Hélène Cixous (2004) could use Derrida's concepts to develop a deconstructive approach to the usual binaries by which men and women, as well as stereotypical male and female characteristics, were polarized. The male term, as Derrida suspected, is almost always hierarchically superior to the female term, dominating it and reinforcing a male domination of women. Cixous (2004) argues that masculine sexuality and masculine language are phallocentric and logocentric, fixing meaning through such binary oppositions as father/mother, intelligible/sensitive, and logos/pathos, which rely for their meaning on the primary binary opposition between male and female, phallic/castrated, all reproducing patriarchy and the subordination of women. Benjamin (1988) demonstrated that gender was socially constructed by repudiating and splitting off all that was weak and dependent to create femininity. Applying deconstructive principles to relational psychoanalysis, Muriel Dimen (2003) writes:

Dualism's separate-but-equal masks a hierarchy: the one behind the two is always on top. In the table of opposites that have been around since the pre-Socratics – for example, male-female, light-dark, reason-emotion, mind-body, nature-culture – one term is always implicitly better or higher than the other. Hence the usual deconstructive reading: a binary always conceals a hierarchy.

(p. 7)

Let me add here a "link" to the work of Bion (1989/1977) and to more contemporary post-Bionian psychoanalytic thought (Levine & Brown, 2013). Freud (1959/1926) had indicated that there was much greater continuity between intra-uterine life and earliest infancy than "the impressive caesura of the act of birth would have us believe" (p. 138). Building on Freud's remark, Bion (1989/1977) used the term "caesura" to signify that which both unites and separates simultaneously, difference and continuity, presence and absence, the proto-mental and the mental, non-symbolic and symbolic, life and death. The caesura is, for Bion, a link between what seem to be independent categories but which are in fact connected with the caesura being the indicator and regulator of their connection. Trachtenberg (2013) spells out that the caesura signifies the undecidability of categories and that each "link" is a point in which one cannot decide what belongs to one category or the other, subject or object, mother or baby, analyst or patient. In short, Bion's link, the caesura, serves the same function in Bionian theory that the "undecidable" serves for Derrida's deconstruction. From this perspective, Bionian theory stresses process and paradox. Trachtenberg (2013) notes: "Bion says that, when he talks of hate, he is referring to a pole of love, since there cannot be shadow without the presence of light" (p. 235). Bionian theory, from this vertex, is radically dialectical, and his link or caesura serves the function of "the undecidable" or thirdness (Benjamin, 2004), that space that regulates the tension between opposites and permits us to move beyond binary dualities and complementarity.

An understanding of these dichotomies and how they have structured psychoanalysis is a radically liberating insight. Once we see how these dualities undergird psychoanalytic thought, we are in a much better position to recognize and correct trouble spots in the theory and practice of psychoanalysis. The process involves finding "undecidables" or "thirds" and using them to break down polarized thinking. One must be careful to clearly keep in mind that deconstructing a polarity does not mean eliminating difference. As you think through my deconstruction of the psychotherapy/psychoanalysis binary, keep in mind that the point is to critique the polarization and hierarchization, rather than to eliminate all difference. For example, I am not contending that seeing a patient once a week or four times a week are equivalent. Rather, the issue is whether to think of psychotherapy and psychoanalysis as dichotomous and hierarchical, and much of the literature in our field has worked with that fundamental assumption, much to our detriment.

The argument I am making is that psychoanalysis has always defined itself in opposition to something else. At first, in Freud's work, that something else was suggestion. Later, in America, it was psychotherapy. From its inception, psychoanalysis identified itself and the analyst with what was masculine, autonomous, rational, scientific, and objective, as opposed to what it viewed as feminine, relational, irrational, unscientific, and subjective – all characteristics that were later attributed to psychotherapy, which was then devalued. In Freud's age, a viciously anti-Semitic era in which Jewish men were "othered", debased as effeminate, immoral, and concrete, Freud projected these debased characteristics onto the other "other": women (Gilman, 1993; Boyarin, 1997). For example, where Jewish men had been regarded as of low moral character and possessing poor abstract abilities, Freud would view women as having weaker superegos and as more concrete. Likewise, in America in the 1950s, psychoanalysis projected the devalued qualities of dependency and relationality onto psychotherapy, keeping itself at a distance from these contaminating effeminate and primitive qualities. Most psychoanalytic institutes would not even teach psychotherapy, as it might contaminate the purity of analytic training.

Genius that Freud was, he was nevertheless caught in a matrix of binaries that permeated his culture and his very existence. As a Jewish man in Austria, he was regarded by his anti-Semitic countrymen as circumcised and thus as effeminate, perverse, and homosexual. In this virulently anti-Semitic milieu, Jews were viewed as immoral, degenerate, and perverse, tied to the concrete and the body, and incapable of rationality and science. Like all colonized and oppressed people, Freud, to some degree, internalized these attributes (Gilman, 1993; Boyarin, 1997). Freud and his creation, like all Jews and their productions, were freakish, monstrous, and perverse. Larry Friedman (2006) celebrates psychoanalysis as being freakish, weird, bizarre, and unnatural – a monster. The salient characteristic of a monster is precisely that it does not fit neatly into natural categories. As a monster, psychoanalysis is neither art nor science; not quite a method of research or a medical treatment. To insist that psychoanalysis is one thing or another is to tame the beast. Similarly, ghosts are not quite alive but not thoroughly dead. Psychoanalysis is haunted – *heimlich* and *unheimlich* – and, as Freud proclaimed, could only have been invented by "a Godless Jew" (as cited in Gay, 1987, p. vii), that is, by a monster, someone who never fit neatly into standard categories, always already "Other", as Derrida, also a "Godless Jew", wrote: "the undecidables". The development of psychoanalysis required the subjective position of one who was "optimally marginal", neither this nor that, in or out. Optimal marginality creates the necessary conditions for optimally observing-participation, or thirdness.

According to Philip Reiff (1966), "a tolerance of ambiguity is the key to what Freud considered the most difficult of all personal accomplishments" (p. 57). Fortunately for psychoanalysis, Freud's thinking was always more complex and nuanced than the binaries in which he was culturally caught. Freud's very place on the boundaries as both insider and outsider, and as neither insider nor outsider, is precisely what allowed him to appreciate ambiguities. Freud was neither Austrian nor German nor Jewish. Neither was he white or black, as Jews were regarded as mulattos. He was a doctor, but not a real university doctor, as Jews could not obtain those positions. While in some ways conventionally straight and even patriarchal, Freud was not a phallic man from the point of view of his anti-Semitic surrounding, since he was circumcised and therefore castrated and effeminate. Nor was he a woman, onto whom he would project all dependency, shame, and inferiority. Rather, according to the anti-Semitic trope, Freud, like all Jewish men, was in some ways effeminate and perverse; Jewish men were a third sex. Boyarin (1997) writes: "Gilman has provided a vitally important piece of information by observing how thoroughly Jewishness was constructed as queer in *fin de siècle* Europe" (p. 214). He continues: "the Jew was queer and hysterical – and therefore, not a man" (p. 215). Freud had been in love with a male friend, Fliess, with whom he championed bisexuality, had regular "congresses", and compared menstrual cycles. In short, Freud was a monster: a ghost, queer, undecidable, mulatto, circumcised, *unheimlich*, a third. Who else could discover such a monster as psychoanalysis? Janus-like in its doubleness (Boyarin, 1997, p. 244), always on the boundary's edge, Freud's writing can serve as a basis for drawing diametrically opposed conclusions. His work is the basis for both conservative and radical projects. Freud longed to be culturally German, civilized, cultured, but was always vulnerable to prejudice, to castration.

Before moving on I would like to add a word to clarify that as Starr and I explain in our book, we are not reducing patriarchy and misogyny to anti-Semitism, but rather we are exploring the intersection of misogyny, racism, anti-Semitism, and homophobia. Feminism has exposed the inherent relationship between patriarchy and misogyny, and postcolonial studies have investigated the interrelations between racism, misogyny, and homophobia. A psychoanalytic study of the intersection of anti-Semitism, racism, homophobia, and misogyny enriches and usefully complicates the findings of feminism. I want to add that our focus on anti-Semitism in understanding Freud's disavowal, displacement, projection, or dissociation of his vulnerability is also not meant to ignore or displace personal biographical understandings. Hence it seems clear that Freud's aversion to helplessness, to childishness, and to human vulnerability was rooted in his personal childhood, familial experiences as the eldest son of a narcissistic mother, his later disillusionment with his father, and family tragedies like the loss of his brother. All of these personal factors of his biography would shape his personal reactions to anti-Semitism.

Here I will argue that a central binary underlying the dichotomization of psychoanalysis and psychotherapy is vulnerability and invulnerability. In its "halcyon days", psychoanalysis viewed the analyst as well enough analyzed, so as not to be vulnerable to the patient's efforts to dislodge the analyst's neutrality and equanimity. In the classic debates about psychotherapy and psychoanalysis of the 1950s, Leo Rangell (1954) said that in psychoanalysis the analyst sits at the margins like a referee in a tennis match, while in psychotherapy the therapist is on the court interacting with the patient. Similarly, Fenichel (1941) had written that the principal goal in the management of transference is "not joining the game" (p. 73). Well, if you are off the field, not playing the game, then you cannot get scored on. You are not likely to get hurt, and if you call the ball out, then it is out; you are invulnerable.

There is a significant trend among philosophers to ground the philosophy of ethics in the experience of vulnerability. In my view, the ethics and practice of psychoanalysis also need to be grounded in the experience of vulnerability. I am suggesting that the ethos of psychoanalysis be rooted not in neutrality and objectivity, but rather in our acceptance and acknowledgment of mutual vulnerability. In *Precarious Life* (2004), Judith Butler builds on Freud's discussion of mourning to argue that mourning entails an acceptance that one is changed by the loss, that mourning depends on our acceptance of or submission to being transformed by the loss, a transformation that we cannot fully control, predict, or determine. The languages of the law and legal rights are argued in terms of bounded individuals and groups, delineated subjects before the law. But Butler (2004) suggests that while this language establishes our legitimacy within a legal framework, "it does not do justice to passion, grief, and rage, that tear us from ourselves, bind us to others, transport us, undo us, implicate us in lives that are not our own, irreversibly, if not fatally" (p. 25). In other words we are joined in the game, not off the field in the margins, and ethics is grounded in our shared human vulnerability.

Donna Orange (2011) articulated a hermeneutic, intersubjective approach to psychoanalysis, which devotes exquisite attention to our receptivity to human suffering. For Orange, following Gadamer, understanding is constituted by receptivity and suffering. Elaborating on Gadamer, Orange (2011) writes:

> Not only are we required to witness and to participate emotionally in the suffering of our patients, but, in addition, the process of understanding itself means that we place ourselves at risk and allow the other to make an impact on us, to teach us, to challenge our preconceptions and habitual ways of being, to change us for their sake, even to disappoint and reject us.
>
> (p. 23)

In Orange's (2011) psychoanalytic application of Gadamerian hermeneutics, analytic listening means listening in a truly open way, "holding oneself open, vulnerable, to the conversation" (p. 64). Employing the contributions of Emmanuel Levinas, Orange goes even further in placing vulnerability at the center of psychoanalysis. Levinas's philosophy emerged from his experiences in the Holocaust and was rooted in the experience of trauma, persecution, and suffering. Orange cites Michael Kugel, an authority on Levinas, who argues that: "This reevaluation of vulnerability is the basic task of Levinas's thinking . . . a phenomenology grounded in an optical situation established in Auschwitz, established not by Levinas but by Hitler" (as cited in Orange, 2011, p. 60). For Levinas, the suffering of the face of the other places you in contact with the infinite, the sacred, or the holy. With this view of listening to the suffering stranger, the psychoanalytic vocation itself becomes something of a sacred calling.

Levinas claims that the Western proclivity to conceive the subject in terms of freedom and rationality mistakenly obscures and distorts our humanity by hiding the significance of human vulnerability and dependence, or what Freud called helplessness. As Hilary Putnam (2008) put it, "In Levinas's image of man, the *vulnerability* of the other is what is stressed, in contrast to what Levinas sees as the Enlightenment's radiant image of the human essence" (p. 83). The Jewish view of ethics that Levinas paradoxically champions and universalizes is based not on reason and rationality but on human vulnerability seen face-to-face.

Drawing on Levinas, Katz (2012) argues that the rabbinic commentary on the Hebrew Bible, the *midrash*, fills in the gaps in the text and hence focuses on alterity. *Midrash* thus gives voice to those whose voices were left out of the text and thus opens us to the presence of the Other. What is most uniquely original and of value in Levinas is his call for an ethics free of narcissism and egocentrism. A non-egocentric ethics must recognize and engage the other as other, not as a like-subject but as Other. My ethical obligation must not depend on my recognition of similarity or even on comprehension of the other, or on abstract, rational, and universal principles, or on an expectation of reciprocity. Rather, my obligation is grounded on the direct perception of the other person as other. To respond to the other only as a like-subject similar to you and therefore arousing sympathy is to be trapped in one's own egocentricity. That many believe Levinas carried this ethical asymmetry too far is irrelevant for our purposes today. Even while Levinas's contribution may be criticized, it can be appreciated for his dramatic and powerful charge to respond to the suffering of the other as other.

Freud and psychoanalysts following him have long differentiated the primitive from the civilized, primitive versus mature defenses or psychic mechanisms, primitive populations versus those that are better structured, higher in the development of sophisticated mental operations. Celia Brickman (2003) has suggested that what analysts mean by "primitivity" is essentially "vulnerability". For Freud, this was thematically expressed throughout his work in terms of penetrating and being penetrated. To penetrate was to be phallic, whole, and firm, whereas to be penetrated was to be castrated, permeable, and vulnerable.

Drawing on the French tradition of interest in the monstrous, Julia Kristeva (1982) developed the idea of the abject as that which is rejected by and disturbs social reason. Abjection is done to the part of ourselves we exclude: the mother. We must abject the maternal, the object that has created us, to construct an identity – that is, our identity requires boundaries in place of fluidity. The corpse, as well as bodily fluids, exemplifies Kristeva's concept since it literalizes the breakdown of the distinction between subject and object, which is crucial for the establishment of identity. Luce Irigaray (1985) also describes the privileging of solid over fluid mechanics, which she attributes to the association of fluidity with femininity. Whereas men have sex organs that protrude and become rigid, women have openings that leak menstrual blood and vaginal fluids. Although men too emit fluids, this aspect of their sexuality is deemphasized. It is the rigidity of the male organ that counts, not its fluid flow which is devalued. Martha Nussbaum (2010) demonstrates in *From Disgust to Humanity* that misogyny is rooted in "projective disgust" (p. 15). Males distance themselves from bodily, animal vulnerability by associating women with bodily fluids, and dissociating themselves from their own corporeality. Homophobia is structured along the same lines as misogyny. Nussbaum (2010) writes:

> What inspires disgust is typically the male thought of the male homosexual, imagined as anally penetrable. The idea of semen and feces mixing together inside the body of a male is one of the most disgusting ideas imaginable – to males, for whom the idea of nonpenetrability is a sacred boundary against stickiness, ooze, and death.
>
> (p. 18)

Jonathan Schofer (2010), in *Confronting Vulnerability*, argues that vulnerability is the bedrock of classic Jewish, that is rabbinic, ethics. It is striking that Freud (1950/1895) too attributed ethics to the condition of human vulnerability. He wrote, "the initial helplessness of human beings is the primal source of all moral motives" (p. 318). Schofer (2010) provides a series of studies of how vulnerability organized the structure of rabbinic law. He begins with a symbol quite similar to Nussbaum's (2010) imagery of bodily fluids, quoting an ethical maxim from Mishna Avot: "Know from where you come . . . from a putrid secretion" (as cited in Schofer, 2010, p. 2). The image of humans emerging from semen is humbling and captures precisely the bodily fluidity that Nussbaum highlights. "Ethics cannot presume a continually healthy, strong, independent agent who encounters weak, needy others" (Schofer, 2010, p. 3). The rabbis, according to Schofer, emphasize a variety of forms of vulnerability, old age, persecution, drought, poverty, widowhood, orphanhood, being a stranger, and especially death, precisely because we have a tendency to deny our vulnerability. Schofer (2010) explains: "Confronting vulnerability becomes central to ethical cultivation" (p. 4). While of course the analyst's personal analysis should help the analyst be in touch with vulnerability, too often it is used as a rationalization to deny vulnerability and thus to project all vulnerability onto the patient.

As a 19th-century European man, Freud believed the height of civilization was the achievement of individual autonomy, later theorized as "ego autonomy". Having clear and firm boundaries meant that you were independent and whole, phallic and impenetrable. To be merged with another, to experience the "oceanic feeling", fluidity, was to be penetrable, vulnerable to the influence of the other, susceptible to infection. This was primitivity (Brickman, 2003), and as Nussbaum (2010) argues, it signified vulnerability and mortality. It was the primitive who was suggestible – the hysteric, the woman, the African, Asian, or Jew, the poor and uneducated. For the Western Jew, it was the Eastern Jew. Primitivity was vulnerability to penetration, contamination, and death. Gilman (1993) noted that non-Jewish men were viewed as phallic while the clitoris was referred to as the Jew and female masturbation as "playing with the Jew" (p. 39). Boyarin (1997) points out that where non-Jews referred to Jews as both the pinky and the clitoris, Jews returned the favor by referring to the non-Jews as the thumb. Here we see so clearly the inter-digitation of racism, anti-Semitism, homophobia, and misogyny as the clitoris, the circumcised penis, and the Jew regarded as primitives. In Freud's day, Jews were regarded as smelly, contaminated, and contagious. This ideology culminated with Hitler, for whom Jews were "maggots inside a rotting body" (as cited by Nussbaum, 2010, p. 23). As circumcision was the embodied mark of the Jew as feminine and castrated, castration anxiety took on a central role in Freudian clinical theory and practice. This explains why Freud (1964/1937) believed that the bedrock of psychoanalysis was "the repudiation of femininity" (p. 403). This was not just a slip or passing sentiment – it was at the core of his values. The repudiation of femininity – that is, castration anxiety – was essential to patriarchy. Phallic/castrated and masculine/feminine were binaries running in parallel with Aryan/Jew, white/black, heterosexual/homosexual, civilized/primitive, health/illness, and life/death. Carol Gilligan (2011) defines patriarchy as constituted by those attitudes and values, moral codes and institutions that create separations between men and boys as well as between men and women, and divide women into the good and the bad. Gilligan (2011) links patriarchy with trauma and psychic fragmentation, writing: "As long as human qualities are divided into masculine and feminine, we will be alienated from one another and from ourselves" (p. 178). Gilligan's (2011) call is for the recognition that "Vulnerability, once associated with women, is a characteristic of humans" (p. 43). I would add that it is a characteristic of analysts as well as patients, and characteristic of senior analysts as well as of our students. Compassion, being with suffering, with our patients and co-participants, requires the acceptance and acknowledgment of our own vulnerability.

From the classical perspective, helping a patient get better using suggestion could only reinforce the patient's primitivity, even if it helped them in other ways (so-called transference cures), or was necessary due to practical circumstances, such as limited resources. Psychoanalysis proper had to eliminate suggestion; porousness was to be replaced by firm ego boundaries. Certainly it did not eliminate all "influence", for how else could you help someone? Freud (1921) distinguished between two types of influence. He objected to the kind of influence based on interpersonal effect – the force of one's personality or subjectivity. Rather, as an enlightenment science, analysis influenced the patient through rational means. To be influenced by accepting a rational argument means you have used your own reason to evaluate the influence, and so you remain independent and autonomous – that is why in its later formulation, psychoanalysis was supposed to work by interpretation alone (Gill, 1954). In contrast, in hypnotic influence, you are subject to the direct interpersonal influence of the other person. Hypnotic suggestion relies on dependence and merging with the will of the other – penetration and passivity – homosexual submission to the father, and hence is thought to reinforce dependence and "primitive" lack of differentiation.

Celia Brickman, in her brilliant 2003 book, *Aboriginal Populations in the Mind*, demonstrates that the origins of psychoanalysis coincided with European colonialism. She makes use of postcolonial studies to show the influence of evolutionary anthropology on Freud's thinking. The racialized "primitive, savage, and barbarian", together with the religious "heathen, infidel, pagan" (Brickman, 2003, p. 19), were the outsiders, the "not-us". Much to Freud's credit, he demonstrated that primitivity is universal:

each of us has a "primitive" part of our minds. That was quite an achievement at a time when those around him saw themselves as civilized. Freud showed that we each have an ego and an id, an ego and a "Yid", a German and a Jew. The id, the unconscious, is primitive, unstructured, timeless, unbound, incapable of reason or delay, dark and feminine. This is consistent with Freud's championing of bisexuality – we each have male and female characteristics. We all have unconscious perverse and homosexual inclinations. This was a revolutionary idea. However, by arguing that we all have a "primitive" mind, with "primitive" drives, Freud reinforced the duality of civilized/primitive. While that duality might now be understood to be universal, it remains a duality and a hierarchy.

In the Middle Ages religion was dominant, and the duality was Christian/heathen. With the advent of the Enlightenment, the human mind "matured" into "rationality" and there was a "simple reversal", by which in "civilized" circles, to be religious was to be primitive, superstitious, or magical. In the operation of any binary, one can flip the power relations but maintain and even reinforce the binary structure. Hence while Christian/heathen was originally lined up with right/wrong, Heaven/Hell, mature/immature, the hierarchy was then reversed, such that the binary became secular/Christian, lined up with rational/irrational, mature/immature. With increasing industrialization, the value of delayed gratification, considered by evolutionary theorists to be the mark of the civilized man, became more prominent. To be "civilized" and adult was to be disciplined, while "primitives" were thought to be impulsive, seeking immediate gratification. Adult/child lined up with civilized/primitive, conscious/unconscious, white/black, responsible/irresponsible, and culture/nature. To be civilized was to have a history, to live in time. To be primitive was to be pre-historical, out of time. The unconscious, being primitive, does not know time.

All these polarities were mapped onto male/female. Men were considered civilized and adult, while women were regarded as more like children – irrational, concrete, immoral, and impulsive. What Freud (1964/1937) called the "bedrock" answer for both sexes was to "repudiate femininity"; for men, the fear of castration, and for women "penis envy" (p. 252). Freud noted that in his culture masculinity was active, while femininity was passive. To be a woman (or male homosexual) is to be passively penetrated. The feminine-masochistic wish is to be penetrated, just as it is the wish of the "primitive" to be dominated. To be phallic is to be the active one who does the penetrating/dominating. To be phallic and not penetrable is to be solid, bounded, invulnerable, and autonomous. To be female is to be penetrated, porous, vulnerable, submissive, masochistic, dependent, embodied, oozing bodily fluids and therefore porous, contaminating, and associated with death. Ultimately, to be primitive is to be subject to domination and penetration – to actually long to be dominated to give up autonomy. In analysis, this dichotomy positions the patient as primitive and the analyst as civilized. The analyst, of course, was to be "opaque", impenetrable, and courageous, even heroic. The patient is childish, pathological, out of time and history. The dark, feminine, oozing unconscious is penetrated by the analyst's interpretations – "the firm analytic instrument". While this phrase is strongly associated with Otto Isakower (1963), he based it directly on Freud (1912), p. 116.

Let's now return to contemporary relational theory, which is an attempt to move beyond binary oppositions by emphasizing "both/and" rather than "either/or" conceptualizations, culminating in the conceptualization of the intersubjective third. Benjamin (2011) has described the "moral third" by referring to the sense of lawfulness and trust in reestablishing connection after disruption. Patient and therapist (like mother and infant) establish a rhythm, some ongoing regulation that facilitates predictability and that allows each of them to feel sensed and known by the other, thus come to know the other and to know themselves (Lachmann & Beebe, 1996; Beebe et al., 2012). At some point this rhythm inevitably breaks down, and the difference between the two is highlighted. Then comes repair and reestablishment of connection. This is "the law" of intersubjective life; it is about the co-creation and breakdown of patterns of mutual regulation and mutual recognition. This is not paternal Oedipal law, but rather as Benjamin quips, it is more like the law of gravity, just the way things work. We move between collisions and acknowledgment. Analysis is a study of these configurations as they are relived, reenacted, and reworked while being examined and articulated. Benjamin credits Tronick as well as Beebe and Lachmann, who, following Kohut, described this cycle of rupture and repair. We have traced the origins of this approach back to Ferenczi. Ferenczi and Dupont (1988/1932) were explicit in arguing that the analyst would inevitably repeat (we would say "enact") the traumatic experiences of childhood with the patient, but unlike the earlier objects who denied their participation in the crime, analysts had to take responsibility and acknowledge their participation and guilt.

The analyst acknowledges the rupture, and through this non-defensive validation reestablishes the ongoing regulation, leaving the patient with a feeling of having been recognized, a moment of meeting, a meeting of minds and hearts. The analyst's acknowledgment shows that the injury is perceived as a violation of an expectable pattern, "the law", and thus it relieves the felt emotional abandonment. Both patient and therapist "surrender" to the trust that exists between them, trust in the process, trust in love, in faith – some call it God – in something beyond them to which they both surrender. Thus, they are not submitting to the other so much as surrendering to thirdness, to a moral law, to lawfulness itself – the law that all relationships are inevitably constituted by rupture and repair, and can then go on being or be resurrected into new life.

The surrender being described here must be differentiated from submission. If the analyst too quickly takes all the responsibility, takes all the "bad object" (Davies, 2004) experience onto him or herself, or simply apologizes to the patient for the disruption of attunement and failure of mutual regulation, then this hardly lends itself to the creation of thirdness. That would more precisely be an enactment of a simple reversal in which the "hot potato" has been thrown from one person to another. In other words, the good and bad objects have simply been reversed rather than transformed. Self-disclosure of the analyst's bad object feelings and the confessional "mea culpa" prayer, "through my fault, through my fault, through my most grievous fault", can be too easily mistaken for an intersubjective psychoanalytic process that only slowly and step by step leads beyond cycles of mutual blame, accusation, confession, and forgiveness which can perpetuate complementarity good/bad, God/sinner, or victim/victimizer relations. The analyst's acknowledgment of participation in collisions must include an analytic process that allows such acknowledgment to take place in a space that transcends these binary good/bad splits, and this can only happen intersubjectively, between patient and analyst as they work together to find a way to a third position, beyond kill or be killed, doer–done to polarities. If done explicitly, self-disclosures are not technical maneuvers or confessions, but are rather undertaken as part of a disciplined relational process of exchanging relevant, mutually generated clinical data in the service of opening up space for both greater "relational freedom" (Stern, 2013) and intersubjective reflection, which together reestablish thirdness – that is, they move us beyond binary dualities.

If this sounds suspiciously religious, it is. Benjamin (1988, 2004, 2011) absorbed German idealism, particularly Hegel. It reverberates with Christian theology, the trinity, the one in three and the three in the one. As Marie Hoffman (2011) has so persuasively elaborated, think here of incarnation, crucifixion, and resurrection. Yet the idea can also be traced very clearly to prominent themes in the Hebrew Bible. God recognizes and loves "his" people, Israel. The people sin and lust after foreign gods and are punished; Israel returns and is forgiven. Think ongoing regulation, heightened affect moments, disruption and repair – it's the main theme throughout the biblical narrative.

Undoubtedly most of us can associate the theme of thirdness with the many centuries of Christian theological controversy concerning the Trinitarian Creed, especially the first 400 years from the Apostles to the Church Fathers, culminating by the end of the fourth century in the doctrine of the Trinity. God exists as three *persons*, or *hypostases*, but is one being having a single divine nature: one in the third and the third in the one. But many of us are less familiar with this theme in Jewish scholarship. Consider one example from medieval Jewish theology that illustrates how closely Benjamin's ideas are to traditional themes in the Jewish tradition. The pre-rabbinic schools or houses of Hillel and Shamai were known for their heated disputes regarding the law, and though they disagreed and at times argued for diametrically opposite conclusions, nevertheless Jewish tradition has it that a voice from Heaven proclaims "these and these are the words of the Living God". How can opposites both be true? Rabbi Judah Loew, widely known as the Maharal of Prague, was an important 16th-century Talmudic scholar, Jewish mystic, writer, and philosopher. In his work *Tif'ereth Yisrael* ("The Glory of Israel") he describes the mystical power of the number three. Drawing on Loew, Kolbrener (2011) writes: "In three, two separate lines are transformed into 'one' through a third line that joins them. Through the Maharal's geometry, three is at the same time *less* and *greater* than two" (p. 77); three represents the paradox of both unity and division.

When patient and therapist are in an enactment or impasse, it often takes the form of a clash, a tug of war, a push me–pull you, doer–done to, or sadomasochistic enactment. This is precisely where Benjamin (1988) began in *The Bonds of Love*, looking at gender relations in terms of sadomasochism. When in these states, we are often dealing with binaries. Either I am guilty or I am a victim, either you started it or I did, either it's your fault or mine, either you really are withholding from me or I am too demanding, either you really let me down or I expect too much, either you are the best therapist in the world or you suck, either you are crazy or I am. Each of these is a binary, and we are talking about splitting, or more specifically two people who both get caught in splitting. This is why it is called complementarity – it is complementary splitting or enactment resulting from mutual defensiveness and dissociation.

Following collisions, the therapist needs to acknowledge, implicitly if not always explicitly, the way in which he or she has hurt the patient, broken the trust or the rhythm, recognize how they were un-attuned. We are predominantly focusing on analysts acknowledging to themselves their own participation in enactments, and also their validating the patient's sense of having been injured by them. Previously, I suggested (Aron, 2006) that the therapist needs to open space within herself to reflect on how she is conflicted or torn, how she can think or feel more than one way about something, and how she can open up to differences within herself: "stand in the spaces" (Bromberg, 1996), or "build bridges" (Pizer, 1998) to her own multiple self-states. For example, the therapist may be both angry with the patient and also blaming himself for something. In creating some room for difference within the self, a "dialectics of difference" as Bollas (1989) called it, one creates a triangular space or thirdness, perhaps something like what Bion (1962) meant by "binocular vision" (p. 86). Rather than being stuck in a polarization, there is some room within which to think/feel.

What I am adding today is the simple clarification (simple to say, not so easy to do) that a psychoanalytic ethic of mutual vulnerability facilitates the creation of such triangular space and helps free us from such blaming and self-blaming polarizations. The mistaken and inhuman ideal of being so thoroughly analyzed that one is impervious to the patient's transference, capable of not being caught up in the game, was and remains a great impediment to acknowledgment (even to oneself) of analytic ruptures, of splits in the analyst's self, of shared anxieties, defenses, and conflicts, of mutual resistances and regressions. In sum, what Benjamin and I are each calling for in conceptualizing the third is a change in analytic sensibility, from analytic opaqueness and impenetrability toward greater inter-penetrability and mutual recognition of shared vulnerability. Stated in the more contemporary language that has become associated with relational psychoanalysis and especially with the contributions of

Jody Davies (2004), Philip Bromberg (1996), and Donnel Stern (2013), the analyst's acknowledgment of her participation in enactments involves a form of mentalization or self-reflective awareness that creates room for multiplicity and dialog among multiple self-states, within the analyst, the patient, and intersubjectively in co-created shared space between patient and analyst. This is an analytic ethos rooted in the assumption of mutual vulnerability.

It should not be surprising that psychotherapy and psychoanalysis, contemporary secularized derivatives of religious guidance and moral wisdom traditions, incorporate and recirculate these principles. As we increasingly recognize the influence of our own subjectivity on our theories and practice, our religious and spiritual subjectivity is inevitably relevant. As an illustration of this inspiration, I (2004) have previously highlighted the connection between my psychoanalytic vision and my religious ethos. Mutual vulnerability is a concept at the heart of the particular Jewish philosophy that inspired me. Abraham Joshua Heschel, in his classic 1962 study of *The Prophets*, suggested that we have to understand the prophetic God as a God of pathos, a feelingful God who cares about the world and about people. This led his student, and my teacher, Neil Gillman to articulate a vulnerable God whose vulnerability is in our hands. The mutual vulnerability between God and humanity becomes the cornerstone of Gillman's theology. Gillman (2013) frequently illustrates God's vulnerability with the *midrash*, a classic rabbinic story; when the Temple was destroyed and Jerusalem burned, God sat and wept over the fate of the people. The angels insisted that God not cry. "You must not cry, you are God!" After several pleas God replied to the angels: "If you don't let me cry, I'm going to go into my private bedroom, close the door, lock it, and cry by myself" (Gillman, 2013, p. 33). This particular word picture of a tearful God is only one of many diverse metaphors, but I am suggesting that to the degree that our religious values affect our interpersonal relationships, this model offers a useful ideal for the humanity and vulnerability of the analyst.

And while crediting teachers who have influenced me, I want to add here that I believe many of us learned this clinical approach directly from Stephen Mitchell. In my view, this was at the heart of Mitchell's clinical approach, and it is characteristic of Mitchell's methodology both to clinical practice and to comparative psychoanalysis. I can only hint at this fascinating argument here.

Mitchell (1988), who had learned a good deal of this approach from Edgar Levenson's (1983) formulation of "resisting transformation", repeatedly emphasized that patient and analyst had to get caught up in an impasse and that therapeutic action consisted in working our way out of such gridlocks. He wrote about one case in 1991: "We seemed trapped in the closed world of these two relational configurations in which he was either cruelly deprived or lovingly crippled. This was, in my view, precisely the sort of trap in which we needed to be caught" (p. 168). Notice here that Mitchell was describing precisely what Benjamin (2004) calls "push me–pull you" or "doer–done to" configurations. Mitchell (1988) continues:

> Perhaps there was a way for us to acknowledge both and thereby work our way out of the trap we had created. The collaborative, interpretive delineation of the impasse itself began to provide a way out, an alternative way for us to engage each other which broadened the constrictive grasp of the old relational configurations.
>
> (p. 169)

I am suggesting that deconstructing binaries, finding thirds, opening up triangular space was characteristic of Mitchell's methodology, whether he was solving theoretical or clinical dilemmas. (For a more detailed exegesis of this aspect of Mitchell's clinical and theoretical methodology, see Aron, 2003.)

The dialectics of difference requires permeability; the therapist implicitly or explicitly reveals something about being moved by the patient. The therapist is not masochistic or without boundaries, but is penetrable, movable, reachable. As Adrienne Harris has emphasized, analytic vulnerability needs to be accompanied by self-care, including bodily self-care, as well as by analytic responsibility (Harris & Sinsheimer, 2008). Neither patient nor therapist need be phallic or castrated, civilized or primitive. Meanings and interpretations are not given and received as much as negotiated and co-created. Empathy and even acknowledgment are not given by the therapist but are mutual and bi-directional, even if the therapist tries to lead in some areas of conflict. Thirdness means moving beyond binary oppositions and the inevitable hierarchy that accompanies splitting, thus opening up space to think/feel.

It has been said that there are two types of people – those who divide the world into two categories and those who do not. The very opposition of binary thinking versus moving beyond binaries is itself a binary; contrasting split complementarity with the third may be read as yet another binary even when it is intended to be dialectical. If it seems that while deconstructing various binaries that I have myself become stuck in binary thinking or created new oppositions, that is inevitable. It is the law, the law of rupture and repair, of deconstruction as an ongoing and always unstable activity, of the third not as some final resolution but as a fleeting moment in an ongoing process. Binaries (and the associated splitting) do have their usefulness, providing stability and structure until such time as integrations of greater complexity can be achieved.

In *A Meeting of the Minds* (1996) I presented relational psychoanalysis as characterized by a variety of forms of mutuality including mutual influence, mutual recognition, mutual resistances, mutual empathy, the mutual generation of data, many other dimensions of mutuality, as well as by some aspects of asymmetry in role, function, and responsibility. Here I want to add an explicit emphasis on mutual vulnerability but again want to be clear that mutuality does not mean equality, nor does it imply symmetry. Patient and analyst are mutually vulnerable, but the analyst has a different role and distinct responsibilities, and in some respects the therapist holds power over the patient, often leaving the patient with greater exposure and less protection. In acknowledging one's own permeability and vulnerability, however – one's embodiment, mortality, and humanity – one does not need to project all of the conflict, splitting, shame, disgust, animalistic embodiment, penetrability, and vulnerability onto the patient. By owning one's own vulnerability, the analyst reduces the patient's shame and thus allows the patient to face vulnerability with less pain and dread. In their *Clinical Diary* Ferenczi and Dupont (1988/1932) wrote:

> Should it ever occur, as it does occasionally to me, that experiencing another's and my own suffering brings a tear to my eye (and one should not conceal this emotion from the patient), then the tears of doctor and patient mingle in a sublimated communion, which perhaps finds its analogy only in the mother-child relationship. And this is the healing agent, which like a kind of glue, binds together permanently the intellectually assembled fragments, surrounding even the personality thus repaired with a new aura of vitality and optimism.
>
> (p. 65)[2]

This is the image of mutual vulnerability and bodily fluidity (that is, as we have seen, so often associated with feared, devalued, and contagious femininity) that leads not to disgust and shame but is rather transformed, sublimated, and spiritualized into healing.

The Yom Kippur: "*Selichot*", a penitential liturgy, includes the prayer "*Mol Levavenu*", "Circumcise our hearts", based on the biblical phrase "And the LORD your God will circumcise your heart, and the heart of your offspring, to love the LORD thy God with all your heart, and with all your soul, that you may live" (Deut. 30:6). The prayer includes the commentary, "Circumcision creates a wound, and the one who is wounded is vulnerable" (Teutsch, 1999). Here we see that in Jewish tradition, not only is circumcision viewed positively, as a symbol of the desired covenant with God, but also that vulnerability is acknowledged, even valued, as a necessary prerequisite for relationship and connection. Intersubjective methodology might help analysts not only with clinical impasses and stalemates, but also with professional, theoretical, sexual, cultural, and historical deadlocks as well. Not only in the clinical interaction, but as a profession and discipline, by owning our vulnerability, attachment, and dependency, by not refuting femininity, psychoanalysis need not split itself off from psychotherapy as its inferior, shameful other. The discipline of psychoanalysis and the psychoanalytic practitioner, in touch with vulnerability and not needing to split off and project it onto others, is capable of mutual recognition, empathy, and moral responsibility.

No longer invulnerable, we cannot remain safely behind the couch in our private practices. We must become socially, politically, and environmentally active and bring complexity, depth, dialectics, and dynamic understanding to problems in our communities and in the wider world, as legitimate psychoanalytic praxis. We would invoke Levinas's Biblical call to serve the poor, the orphaned, and the widowed, and apply it to Freud's (1912) vision of making psychoanalysis "a psychotherapy for the people" (p. 168). No longer dissociating our vulnerability, and without disclaiming our agency, we will move toward a progressive psychoanalysis.

Notes

1 This chapter is an elaboration and further development of ideas first published together with Karen Starr in our book: Aron, L., & Starr, K., *A psychotherapy for the people*, New York: Routledge. It is with much appreciation that I acknowledge her contribution.

2 Even before Ferenczi, Carl Jung was the first to emphasize the mutuality inherent in psychotherapy. He proposed that the analyst had to be open and responsive to change for the patient to change and therefore psychotherapy required mutual vulnerability. The patient transference is understood as the transfer of their unconscious demons into the analyst, a psychic infection, contagion. Vulnerability means, literally, "woundability", and Jung and post-Jungians consider analysts as "wounded healers" (Sedgwick, 1994).

References

Aron, L. (1996). *A meeting of the minds: Mutuality in psychoanalysis.* New York: Routledge.

Aron, L. (2003). Clinical outbursts and theoretical breakthroughs: A unifying theme in the work of Stephen A. Mitchell. *Psychoanalytic Dialogues, 13*(2), 259–273.

Aron, L. (2004). God's influence on my psychoanalytic vision and values. *Psychoanalytic Psychology, 21,* 442–451.

Aron, L. (2006). Analytic impasse and the third: Clinical implications of intersubjectivity theory. *International Journal of Psychoanalysis, 87,* 349–368.

Aron, L., & Benjamin, J. (1999). *The development of intersubjectivity and the struggle to think.* Paper presented at the spring meeting of *Division 39 (Psychoanalysis) of the American Psychological Association.* New York.

Aron, L., & Starr, K. (2012). *A psychotherapy for the people: Toward a progressive psychoanalysis.* New York: Routledge.

Beebe, B., Lachmann, F. M., Markese, S., Buck, K. A., Bahrick, L. E., Chen, H., Cohen, P., Andrews, H., Feldstein, S., & Jaffe, J. (2012). On the origins of disorganized attachment and internal working models: Paper II. An empirical microanalysis of 4-month mother–infant interaction. *Psychoanalytic Dialogues, 22*(3), 352–374.

Benjamin, J. (1988). *The bonds of love.* New York: Pantheon.

Benjamin, J. (2004). Beyond doer and done to. *Psychoanalytic Quarterly, 73*(1), 5–46.

Benjamin, J. (2011). Beyond doer and done to: An intersubjective view of thirdness. In L. Aron & A. Harris (Eds.), *Relational psychoanalysis, 4,* 91–130. New York: Routledge.

Bion, W. R. (1962). *Learning from experience.* London: Tavistock.

Bion, W. R. (1989). Caesura. In F. Bion & M. Patterson (Eds.), *Two papers: 'The grid' and 'caesura'* (pp. 35–59). London: Karnac Books. (Original work published in 1977)

Bollas, C. (1989). *Forces of destiny.* London: Free Association Press.

Boyarin, D. (1997). *Unheroic conduct: The rise of heterosexuality and the invention of the Jewish man.* Berkeley: University of California Press.

Brickman, C. (2003). *Aboriginal populations in the mind.* New York: Columbia University Press.

Bromberg, P. M. (1996). *Standing in the spaces.* Hillsdale, NJ: The Analytic Press.

Butler, J. (2004). *Precarious life.* London: Verso.

Cixous, H. (2004). *Portrait of Jacques Derrida as a young Jewish saint.* (B. B. Brahic, Trans.). New York: Columbia University Press.

Davies, J. M. (2004). Transformations of desire and despair. In J. Salberg (Ed.), *Good enough endings* (pp. 83–106). New York: Routledge.

Derrida, J. (1976). *Of grammatology.* (G. C. Spivak, Trans.). Baltimore: Johns Hopkins University Press.

Dimen, M. (2003). *Sexuality, intimacy, power.* Hillsdale, NJ: The Analytic Press.

Fenichel, O. (1941). *Problems of psychoanalytic technique.* Albany, NY: Psychoanalytic Quarterly.

Ferenczi, S., & Dupont, J. (Ed.). (1988). *The clinical diary of Sandor Ferenczi* (M. Balint & N. Jackson, Trans.). Cambridge, MA: Harvard University Press. (Original work published in 1932)

Freud, S. (1912). Recommendations to physicians practising psychoanalysis. *The standard edition of the complete psychological works of Sigmund Freud 1911–1913: The case of Schreber, papers on technique and other works volume XII* (pp. 109–120). London: Hogarth Press.

Freud, S. (1921). Group psychology and the analysis of the ego. *The standard edition of the complete psychological works of Sigmund Freud 1920–1922: Beyond the pleasure principle, group psychology and other works volume XVIII* (pp. 65–144). London: Hogarth Press.

Freud, S. (1950). Project for a scientific psychology. In J. Strachey (Ed. and Trans.), *The standard edition of the complete psychological works of Sigmund Freud volume I* (pp. 281–391). London: Hogarth Press. (Original work published in 1895)

Freud, S. (1955). Lines of advance in psychoanalytic therapy. In L. Strachey (Ed. & Trans.), *The standard edition of the complete psychological works of Sigmund Freud volume 17* (pp. 157–168). London: Hogarth Press. (Originally published in 1919)

Freud, S. (1959). Inhibitions, symptoms and anxiety. In J. Strachey (Ed. & Trans.), *The standard edition of the complete psychological works of Sigmund Freud volume XX* (pp. 75–176).London: Hogarth Press. (Original work published in 1926)

Freud, S. (1964). Analysis terminable and interminable. In J. Strachey (Ed. & Trans.), *The standard edition of the complete psychological works of Sigmund Freud volume XXIII,* (pp. 216–253). London: Hogarth Press. (Original work published in 1937)

Friedman, L. J. (2006). What is psychoanalysis? *Psychoanalytic Quarterly, 75,* 689–671.

Gay, P. (1987). *A godless Jew: Freud, atheism, and the making of psychoanalysis.* New Haven, CT: Yale University Press.

Gill, M. M. (1954). Psychoanalysis and exploratory psychotherapy. *Journal of the American Psychoanalytic Association, 2,* 771–797.

Gilligan, C. (2011). *Joining the resistance.* Cambridge, UK: Polity Press.

Gillman, N. (2013). *Believing and its tensions.* New York: Jewish Lights Publishing.

Gilman, S. L. (1993). *Freud, race, and gender.* Princeton, NJ: Princeton University Press.

Harris, A. E., & Sinsheimer, K. (2008). The analyst's vulnerability. In F. S. Anderson (Ed.), *Bodies in treatment.* (pp. 255–274). New York: The Analytic Press.

Heschel, A. J. (1962). *The prophets.* New York: Harper & Row.

Hoffman, M. (2011). *Toward mutual recognition: Relational psychoanalysis and the Christian narrative.* New York: Routledge.

Irigaray, L. (1985). *This sex which is not one.* Ithaca: Cornell University Press.

Isakower, O. (1963, October 14). In minutes of faculty meeting New York Psychoanalytic Institute [Mimeographed].

Katz, C. E. (2012). *Levinas and the crisis of humanism.* Bloomington, IN: Indiana University Press.

Kolbrener, W. (2011). *Open minded Torah.* London: Continuum.

Kristeva, J. (1982). *Powers of horror: An essay on abjection.* New York: Columbia University Press.

Lachmann, F. M., & Beebe, B. A. (1996). Three principles of salience in the organization of the patient–analyst interaction. *Psychoanalytic Psychology, 13,* 1–22.

Levenson, E. A. (1983). *The ambiguity of change.* New York: Basic Books.

Levine, H. B., & Brown, L. J. (2013). *Growth and turbulence in the container/contained: Bion's continuing legacy.* New York: Routledge.

Mitchell, S. A. (1988). *Relational concepts in psychoanalysis: An integration.* Cambridge, MA: Harvard University Press.

Nussbaum, M. C. (2010). *From disgust to humanity.* Oxford: Oxford University Press.

Orange, D. M. (2011). *The suffering stranger.* New York: Routledge.

Pizer, S. (1998). *Building bridges.* Hillsdale, NJ: The Analytic Press.

Putnam, H. (2008). *Jewish philosophy as a guide to life: Rosenzweig, Buber, Levinas, Wittgenstein.* Bloomington, IN: Indiana University Press.

Rangell, L. (1954). Similarities and differences between psychoanalysis and dynamic psychotherapy. *Journal of the American Psychoanalytic Association, 2,* 734–744.

Reiff, P. (1966). *The triumph of the therapeutic.* New York: Harper and Row.

Schofer, J. W. (2010). *Confronting vulnerability: The body and the divine in rabbinic ethics.* Chicago, IL: University of Chicago Press.

Sedgwick, D. (1994). *The wounded healer: Counter-transference from a Jungian perspective.* London: Routledge.

Stern, D. B. (2013). Relational freedom and therapeutic action. *Journal of American Psychoanalytic Association, 61*(2), 227–256.

Teutsch, D. A. (Ed.). (1999). *Kol Haneshana: Prayerbook for the days of awe.* Wyncote, PA: Reconstructionist Press.

Trachtenberg, R. (2013). Caesura, denial, and envy. In H. B. Levine & L. J. Brown (Eds.), *Growth and turbulence in the container/contained: Bion's continuing legacy* (pp. 231–242). London & New York: Routledge.

Chapter 3

Kissing disciplines, relational architecture

Esther Sperber[1]

How do disciplines interact? How does one field affect, question and transform another? Is knowledge from one area of study applicable to others? In this chapter I will explore a potential overlap between relational psychoanalysis and the understanding of the architectural experience, both as a creative design process and the phenomenology of inhabiting and dwelling within the architectural space. Relational psychoanalysis has brought to the fore a new attention to the mutuality of the therapy process, contending that we discover our own minds only through the intersubjective field that is shared with others; a view that exposes the interdependence of the analytic dyad in which analyst and patient together construct the analytic space of healing.

In the field of architecture there has been a long-standing reluctance to see design as anything but the independent creation of the lone architect. In this view of history, the creative process and the reality of the architectural design exclude a wide range of innovative processes which arise from the inevitable messy interaction the architect will have with the building's physical surroundings, the clients and the many other participants in the design and construction process (Sperber, 2013).

In this chapter I use Aron's ideas, raised in his "Mutual Vulnerability: An Ethic of Clinical Practice" (Chapter 2 of this volume), to expose a previously hidden aspect of the architectural practice. I suggest an overlapping sensibility between the psychoanalytic understandings of vulnerability as Aron describes it, and a resistance to accepting the mutuality and vulnerability inherent in the work of the architect and the field of architecture. I also point to a particular manner in which two disciplines – architecture and psychoanalysis – can meet and affect one another, while maintaining their own unique identity. This manner of interaction may be seen as a kiss, an idea influenced but Lavin's book *Kissing Architecture* (2011).

Mutual vulnerability

Aron tells a story that challenges us to reexamine the binary habits that typically characterize the parameters of psychoanalysis: opposites such as woman–man, passive–active, care–cure, Jew–non-Jew and relational theory–drive theory. Aron tells an alternative history of psychoanalysis, one that is akin to the experience of early childhood trauma. This trauma was a result of the anti-Semitism experienced by Freud and his followers, the difficulties of immigration and a general culture of misogyny and homophobia. Like personal trauma that creates dissociation and defensive splitting of painful unformulated affect, so did psychoanalysis split off a part of its own self, limiting its emotional and behavioral range. As Aron explains, the discipline chose to favor the "masculine," rational, scientific, autonomous view of interpretation and cure over what it saw as the "feminine," caring, interpersonal and vulnerable aspects of therapy which it split off. Aron suggests that just as personal health depends on the ability to embrace and accept a wide range of self-states, so, too, the field of psychoanalysis can survive only if a new pluralism of theory and technique is embraced.

Coming from the epicenter of relational psychoanalysis, Aron considers the analytic project as always co-created. This follows Aron's notable and prolific contributions that demonstrate how insight, pain, hope and cure reside in both analyst and patient and flow in and out and around the dyad (1996, 2013). In this chapter I suggest that a relational view of the world can help us better understand other fields such as architecture and their specific dissociated histories.

Over more than a century, psychoanalytic ideas have influenced our cultural vocabulary and permeated many parts of the humanities. Freud's original brilliance extended far beyond inventing a therapy. He created a constellation of structures, myths, ideas and metaphors that, having been stated, frame the way we understand the world. We can use, argue or reject these concepts, such as the unconscious, narcissism, Oedipal strivings or transference, but we can no longer un-think them. Following Freud, other psychoanalytic thinkers have contributed to a general academic discourse. We find Melanie Klein's ideas in art theory and Jacques Lacan's concepts of the "Real" and the gaze in critical theory and film theory. Jessica Benjamin, Julia Kristeva and Judith Butler have all played major roles in shaping contemporary feminism and gender studies.

Relational psychoanalysis developed over the last 30 years in the United States. From a foundation of object relations and interpersonal psychoanalysis, it has developed a language of understanding the inherently relational nature of all human interactions. Contributions from Mitchell (1993), Aron (1996), Benjamin (1998), Davies and Frawley (1992), Bromberg (1998), Ogden (2008) and many others have elaborated a theory of self that is no longer an isolated, fixed entity. Relational psychoanalysis asserts that our experience is always a complex configuration of multiple selves. These selves emerge in the specificity of an interactive matrix between self and other, creating relational moments. This understanding of the human experience has significant technical implications for therapeutic approaches. Relational psychoanalysis rejects the analyst as neutral observer; instead it sees the analyst as an involved participant in the understanding of the interpersonal and intersubjective events of the analysis. This dyad, though not symmetrical (Aron, 1992), co-creates the analytic space. Relational psychoanalysis believes that all social interactions occur within a field of interconnectedness, a web of attachments, and continue the flow of conscious and unconscious communication.

These relational ideas resonate with my architectural design experience. I suggest that these insights, although developed in the protective space of the analytic interaction, and through a close attunement to patient-therapist dynamics, can emerge from the cocooned consulting room and participate in a conversation with other disciplines. I therefore venture to explore what these psychoanalytic ideas of mutuality, intersubjectivity and a co-created relational field add to the understanding of architecture.

Architecture and psychoanalysis

Architecture and psychoanalysis seem to be very different practices at first glance. Architecture is charged with building physical structures to solve complex sets of human and social requirements and needs. The completed project is a building, a physical structure that can be inhabited by the private client or the public organization that commissioned it. To realize an architectural project, the architect needs to manage a large team of collaborating parties which includes consultants, engineers, contractors, project managers, financing institutions and government approval agencies. Budgets, schedules, all-nighters, punch lists, filings, change orders, emails and spreadsheets are the stuff from which an architectural practice is made. At the completion of the project, the architect may proudly show her work to friends and colleagues and publish the beautiful images in glossy magazines and monographs.

Psychoanalysis by comparison is a very private affair, framed by the repetition of time and place unfolding in the interiority of the consulting room, and amidst the minds of the analytic dyad (Sperber, 2014b). Outside information is carefully filtered through the subjectivities of the analyst and patient, entering by way of their verbal and non-verbal styles of communicating. Intellectual and emotional dramas are performed or enacted by them, and for them, in the consulting room theater (Loewald, 1975; Schafer, 1976). The results and effects of this joint analytic work remain ephemeral and "disguise and consent" are required when the analyst presents this work to a wider public.

One notices some other intriguing differences between architects and psychoanalysts. Architects, when presenting their work, tend to focus on the final product, showing photos and plans of the completed project. It has been a long-standing tradition in architectural magazines to publish photos that are not "contaminated" with people so that the pure forms of the building or interior are documented as abstract, uninhabited and uncluttered spaces. Although at times architects may show a sketch or diagram explaining the conceptual background of the design solution, they typically do not dwell on their process of design. The creative method remains hidden, a way of protecting the precious intellectual property of the architect, a trade secret. Rarely do architects present their construction details which reveal the way in which a specific feature of the building was achieved. Technical details are seen as the firm's private, in-house "family secrets," a shared knowledge and mythology that create each firm's identify and legacy.

It is interesting, and perhaps inevitable, that the psychoanalytic literature adopts the opposite method for sharing analytic work. The literature of psychoanalysis discusses in depth the technical methods and intellectual framework in which the analytic process takes place. Not being able to "show" the analytic product or the cured patient, or to demonstrate positive progress in the patient's life, much of the written accounts describe progress through the changes and improvements within the analytic dyad's relationship. The patient's ability to tolerate a wider range of affects toward the therapist, both intimacy and aggression, love and envy, are proof of analytic progress. Without showing the patient, as the product of the years of joint work, the currency analysts use to construct a hierarchy of success and creativity becomes the stories of the analytic technique processes, those same trade secrets that the architect conceals.

Yet there are also many similarities between architecture and psychoanalysis. Both are charged to make life more pleasant and to widen the range of personal and social experience (Sperber, 2014a). Although psychoanalysis is barely over 100 years old while architecture has a history as long as human history itself, both professions as we practice them today evolved a response to the project of modernity and the evolution of the urban metropolis of the 20th century.

Urbanization and the growing density of the 19th and 20th centuries demanded new ways of living within society. New typologies of city dwelling evolved out of the growing urbanization and industrialization, a complex layering of infrastructure, transportation systems and cultural institutions. The high-rise building, the office tower, suburban sprawl, strip malls and school campuses were new typologies for a new time. Public spaces were designed for use by the masses and recreational spaces were reconceived, adding parks and stadiums to the urban fabric to provide respite from the rushed and crowded city environment. The design possibilities created by modern building technologies and computer programs have further accelerated these innovations in architecture.

Psychoanalysis similarly came into being as a reaction to pressures of modernity on the individual (Homans, 1989; Zaretsky, 2004). Changes in family structures and group affiliation, the depersonalized and blasé conditions of city dwelling and the uncertainty of the new capitalistic economy, all join together to destabilize people's inner life. The industrial revolution paired with social isolation and indifference brought much discomfort and unhappiness. Roles were shifting, boundaries were changing, and previously clear social hierarchies, gender expectations and religious and ethical foundations were no longer firmly understood. As architecture struggled to provide light and air, running water, electricity and access to green outdoor space for the ever-growing numbers of city dwellers, psychoanalysis attempted to give them back their ability to "work and love," to find personal space for emotional intimacy and creativity and authenticity within this new human environment.

The architect and the psychoanalyst share not only the influence of a certain moment in history; they also share a dependence on a client to enable them to do the work they love. It is true that Freud discovered the importance of dreams through his own self-analysis, and that similarly some architects get their first opportunity by building a home for their own family (Philip Johnson's Glass House, Frank Ghery's Santa Monica house) or their parents (Venturi's house for his mother – Vanna Venturi), and that architectural competitions offer architects the opportunity to develop their thoughts independent of a specific client. Nevertheless, these forays are the exception and the vast majority of architectural work is done for a client. The success of the design depends on a good interaction, a financial contract and a mutual trust between client and designer. Psychoanalytic treatment similarly depends on a working relationship between analyst and analysand and self-analysis, while often very productive, omits crucial aspects of the analytic process such as the ability to depend, to be vulnerable and intimate with another person. It is be hard to imagine a process of termination in self-analysis.

If current-day architecture and psychoanalysis share a common historical set of circumstances and the goal of making human experience more varied and more pleasant, perhaps these two professions can influence and illuminate one another.

Heroic autonomy

Christine Battersby (1989) in her book *Gender and Genius* traces the origins of the notion of the heroic independent, autonomous, male genius to 18th and 19th-century Romanticism. The heroic artists and architect does it on his own. He conceives and executes his vision despite and in the face of resistance from society and those around him. Heroic autonomy and independence, packaged as neutrality and rationality, were also at the core of the image of early and mid-century psychoanalysis. Aron convincingly shows how aspects of therapy that focused on caring, compassion and mutuality were split off and redefined as psychotherapy of consulting social work. Aron traces this splitting to the traumatic origins of the field of psychoanalysis, much like personal trauma which splits off and dissociates painful affect. The valuation of autonomy and independence is born of an attitude that defends against the mutual dependence and vulnerability of analyst and patient.

Although the major currents of mid-century ego psychology presented ego strength, independence and mastery as the main goals of analysis (Hartmann, 1939), other views can be traced alongside this leading understanding, views that acknowledged and valued the interdependence of patient and analyst and the value of other modalities of thought. Ferenczi (1949) notes that the neutrality, suggested as the correct position of the analyst, might at times re-traumatize the patient who feels yet again alone with his overwhelming pain. Harold Searles (1999/1975) suggests that in treatment there is a point in which the patient heals the analyst, a view that transcends the usual dichotomy in which the analyst is the healer and the patient is the one who needs healing.

This heroic image burdened not only psychoanalysis but the arts and sciences as well. Women are of course the largest group excluded from this version of cultural history, as we are reminded by the haunting words of the 19th-century physician and criminologist Lomborso: "There are no women of genius; the women of genius are men" (Battersby, 1989, p. 4). Battersby illustrates how eccentricities, gender ambiguity and an insatiable need for love or solitude were all celebrated as signs of the creative male genius while these same traits were condemned as madness in woman. Following Aron, one realizes that at the heart of this lone, autonomous genius artist is a similar dissociative resistance to a world that is always anaclitic, mutually enacted and alive in the complex field of relational interactions.

In the title of her seminal paper, art critic Linda Nochlin (1971) asked "Why have there been no great women artists?" (p. 203). Unlike Lombroso, who argued that artistic genius was a form of hereditary insanity, an essentialist view of the artist as a uniquely gifted person, Nochlin sees art as a situated practice that involves both talent and education. She suggests that:

> [A]rt is not a free, autonomous activity of a super-endowed individual, "influenced" by previous artists, and more vaguely and superficially, by "social forces," but, rather, that the total situation of art making, both in terms of the development of the art maker and in the nature and quality of the work of art itself, occur in a social situation, are integral elements of this social structure, and are mediated and determined by specific and definable social institutions, be they art academies, systems of patronage, mythologies of the divine creator, artist as he-man or social outcast.
>
> (p. 203)

There were no great women artists ("nor have there been any great Lithuanian jazz pianists, nor Eskimo tennis players," she notes) because women were excluded from the educational institutions of teaching, supporting and exhibiting art. To rephrase this in the terms used in this chapter, art is a relational practice which happens within personal and cultural social ties, and these ties were denied to women, therefore excluding them from this creative field.

If Nochlin suggested that artistic creativity is a learned part of human culture, Pierre Bourdieu (1993) further expands the situated nature of art by arguing that it originates from a field of artistic productions. This field of production includes the individual artist, the social group, the critic, the historian and the museum curator, who together produce what we define as the work of art. Freud, in *Group Psychology* (1921), makes a similar suggestion. In comparing the mediocrity of group thinking to the higher achievements of the individual, he write that all great progress "in the realm of thought and momentous discoveries and solutions of problems [is] only possible to an individual working in solitude." Yet, he adds, it remains a question of "how much the individual thinker or writer owes to the stimulation of the group in which he lives, and whether he does more than perfect a mental work in which the others have had a simultaneous share" (p. 83).

I want to make clear that while I emphasize the relational nature of creativity, I do not wish to deny or devalue the role of the individual, the personal inventiveness and the power of agency (Slavin, 2010). Many ideas, works of art and scientific discoveries are in fact discovered by gifted individuals. Yet even those individuals who labor in their isolated labs or studios are situated within a historical, political and intellectual network that is ever present. Aron's (1992) well-known insight that mutuality does not equate with symmetry is well taken and appropriate for collaborative creative work as it is in the analytic dyad.

Freud was both a genius and a product of his own time, shaped by turn-of-the-century conventions of autonomy and masculinity. When Freud's fiancée, Martha Bernays, mentioned reading John Stuart Mill, Freud (1883) wrote back to her, stating his view of a woman's role: "I dare say we agree that housekeeping and the care and education of children claim the whole person and particularly rule out any profession" (p. 75).

But we are no longer in the late 19th or even the 20th century and Aron and Starr (2013) provide a new lens through which to bring psychoanalysis up to date. As the authors write:

> No longer invulnerable, we cannot remain safely behind the couch in our private practices. We must become socially, politically, and environmentally active and bring complexity, depth, dialectic and

dynamic understanding to problems in our communities and in the wider world.

(p. 402)

I now turn to explore how the psychoanalytic quest for a less rigidly divided world, one that accepts co-creation and experiences the ever-presence of an intersubjective field, the creativity of mutuality and the ethics of vulnerability, might affect the architectural practice and theory of its production.

Form follows libido

On the continuum between autonomous individuality at one extreme and collaborative vulnerability at the other, the modernist architect can be located on the autonomous side. Typically the image of the architect was of an inventor who imagines bold, new ideas which he then struggles to realize by overcoming the client's resistance, budgetary constraints and the conservative restrictions of approval agencies. The architect oversees and enforces the implementation of his exact vision by the team of contractors and suppliers who follow his instructions.

While this view of the architectural profession was celebrated in the 20th century, it has its origins earlier in the Renaissance. Mario Carpo (2011) traces how Alberti (1404–72), in his classic book *De Re Aedificatoria* (1452, On the Art of Building), created our modern understanding of the architect as the sole creator of the building. The architect produces plans and elevations which form a one-way communication between the architect and the construction team who are expected to follow his vision. Brunelleschi (1377–1446), working around the same time, had a very different approach. Rather than providing plans, Brunelleschi was continuously present on the construction site, engaged in dialogue, negotiation and argument with the site masters and guild laborers. In current architectural practice we continue to struggle with the modernist legacy of architecture as omnipotence, a tradition that enabled Le Corbusier to propose replacing the beauty of medieval Paris with a series of towers in the park and in which Mies van der Rohe's skyscraper heritage evolved into the alienating glass towers of corporate America.

Alongside this view of architecture there have always been other understandings of the profession. In her seminal book *Women and the Making of the Modern House* (1998), Alice Friedman studies a number of iconic modernist buildings, suggesting that the women clients who commissioned these homes played a central role in their design and construction, a role that has been overlooked or perhaps repressed in the telling of the modernist history, which gave all the credit to the male architects. An in-depth exploration of the collaborative nature of the design process can also be found in Lambert and Bergdoll's recent book (2013) on the making of the Seagram building, a masterpiece that came into being because of Lambert's foresight as the client, and a complicated yet fascinating collaboration between the architect Mies van der Rohe and Philip Johnson who was at the time the building's lighting designer.

As it so happened, while I was reading Aron and Starr's (2013) book *A Psychotherapy for the People*, on which Chapter 2 of this volume was based, I finally surrendered to Amazon's algorithm that had long insisted "people like me" would enjoy Sylvia Lavin's (2007) book, Form *Follows Libido: Architecture and Richard Neutra in a Psychoanalytic Culture*.

Richard Neutra is one such architect who does not simply fit the archetype of the heroic creator. In Lavin's book I learned that Neutra and psychoanalysis were born at the same time and place, late 19th-century Vienna. Much like the shifting of the psychoanalytic center from Vienna to the US, so did Neutra immigrate to America in 1923. Interestingly, Neutra was a frequent guest at the Freuds' home, being a close friend of Freud's son Ernst with whom he took a study trip in 1912 to Italy and the Balkans. They had both studied architecture at Adolf Loos's independent architectural school. Neutra worked at the offices of some of the greatest architects of the time, first in Loos's studio in Vienna, then with Erich Mendelsohn in Berlin and briefly with Frank Lloyd Wright in the United States.

Neutra was a prolific architect and a cultural celebrity in his day, widely known for his case study houses; he was on the cover of *Time* magazine in August 1949. After moving to California he promoted a unique style of regional modernism, which was clean and new yet sensual and visually pleasing. Although Neutra is often included in 20th-century architectural narratives, Lavin (2007) argues that:

> he is always cast in a supporting role: helping structure triumph over decoration but doing so less vigorously then Mies; pursuing the social program of the avant-garde but with less engagement than Gropius; and blazing the trail of the New Pioneers but with less clarity than Le Corbusier.

(p. 11)

Neutra wrote extensively, believing that psychological suffering, health ailments and unhappy marriages were all caused by inhabiting deficient environments. He claimed that the architect possesses the power to remedy these sufferings by providing spaces that awaken and enliven the client's senses (Neutra, 1954).

In Neutra's legacy, I find an endearing, if curious, complexity. Neutra was, on the one hand, heir to the Albertian, modernist legacy of the all-too-familiar omnipotent grand master who solves the world's problems with insight and fine design. Yet Neutra was also a humanist. Lavin writes about his "unusual sensitivity to his client and their wishes and needs" (Lavin, 2007, p. 14); he was attuned to the collaborative aspect of design and was sensitive to the delicate relationship of the new house, existing landscape and local climate. In an article about his case study house No. 6 from 1945, Neutra describes his careful interest in the client's ideas: "It is always an interesting story when the clients descend on the expert, who makes himself a sponge to absorb all the weighty information and also those imponderables, which make us know each other as human beings" (Neutra, 1945). Although he designed the Von Sternberg house in 1935, the house in which Ayn Rand lived, his manner of working with clients was not at the least similar to Rand's hero, Howard Roark, the architect in *The Fountainhead*.

Neutra was drawn to the concept of *einfühlung*, a central idea in aesthetic theory of the late 19th century. Translated as empathy, the term was introduced in 1909 by Theodor Lipps (coined originally by Robert Vischer) to explain our capacity to understand the other by mirroring and reflecting their feelings. Through empathy, which literally means "in-feeling," we feel the emotion embedded in an object of art, in space and in the mental states of other people (Mallgrave, 2010). In an unpublished essay Neutra writes that "infeeling" and love are experiences of "being favorably stimulated by the recognition that one is oneself a stimulus to the other individual" (Lavin, 2007, p. 33). Empathy translates perception and sensation into emotional recognition in a reciprocal process. The notion of Einfühlung resonates with the contemporary understandings of mentalization (Fonagy, Gergely, Jurist, & Target, 2002) as a process of understanding oneself through the ability to see and understand the minds of the others (Sperber, 2014a). The mutuality and recognition of empathy also fits well with Aron's understanding of the relational field.

Neutra saw the architect's work as similar to that of the psychoanalyst, a co-created process which is based on the understanding of the client's inner desires and memories:

> An architect producing the proper rapport with the client's aspirations and expressed or half-expressed need is actually acting very closely to the patterns and procedure of a psychiatrist. His analytical searching and retrospections into infantile precedent, conditions, trauma lead to an understanding, supplementary to empathy which so puzzlingly makes co-creativeness as affective mutual attitude and a dynamic phenomenon of the most eminent social and cultural significance.
>
> (as cited in Lavin, 2007, p. 49)

Lavin writes that for Neutra "empathy transforms architecture into a love triangle between the architect, the client and the postwar house" (p. 40) and Neutra "fathered" over 300 homes with his residential clients. Both the architect and client depend on the house to fulfill their needs and hopes. One of Neutra's clients, Constance Perkins, asked him to design a house that "she could love so much that it would make her homesick" (p. 42). Neutra took similar comfort in this house, saying he returned to visit the Perkins house "whenever he felt low" (p. 42). Therefore it was not only a methodology of creating the architectural design that relied on the co-creation of architect and client; rather they also shared the design product as a shared object that brought calm and comfort to both of them.

Kissing architecture

From Sylvia Lavin's book on Neutra, I now free associate to Lavin's (2011) more recent book *Kissing Architecture. Kissing Architecture* explores a new type of hybrid building that incorporates digital art and interactive structures on the static architectural structure. Lavin (2011) regards these interactive systems as disciplines that have come to kiss the fixed architectural discipline. She writes:

> The kiss offers to architecture, a field that in its traditional forms has been committed to permanence and mastery, not merely the obvious allure of sensuality but also a set of qualities that architecture has long resisted: ephemerality and consilience. However long or short,

however socially constrained or erotically desiring, a kiss is the coming together of two similar but not identical surfaces, surfaces that soften, flex, and deform when in contact, a performance of temporary singularities.

(p. 5)

I get a bit excited when I read Lavin's phenomenology of kissing. Not just because kissing is sexy, but because Lavin employs kissing to suggest a way for two disciplines to interact. She continues to describe a process that puts "form into slow and stretchy motion, loosening form's fixity and relaxing its gestalt unities" (p. 5).

The excitement Lavin (2011) describes of "slow stretchy motion" is what I imagine attracts everyone interested in cross-disciplinary work, a place that facilitates "new definitions of threshold that operate through suction and slippage rather than delimitation and boundary" (p. 5). I am excited to envision a place in which the field of psychoanalysis, and its acceptance of the disorganized human mind, can kiss the thoughtful reasoning of philosophy, the wonderment of religion and perhaps even the concrete usefulness of architecture. Kissing, as Lavin writes, is "a union of bedazzling convergence and identification during which separation is inconceivable yet inevitable" (p. 5).

And so kissing brings us back to Aron's "Mutual Vulnerability" because a good kiss depends on surrender, openness, fluidity, relationality and mutuality. In kissing, gender roles soften, age is irrelevant and the dichotomies of "doer and done to" are transcended. It is this call for vulnerability that I adopt from Aron's work and transfer back to my world of architecture, a call that permits, demands, even pleads for us all to occupy the entire spectrum of human behavior from autonomy to dependence. Aron offers an image of mutual vulnerability and physical fluidity leading "not to disgust and shame but transformed, sublimated, and spiritualized into healing" (Chapter 2, p. 38). We would all be enriched, in our various disciplines, from a softening of the boundaries that restrict us to heroic positions of autonomous self-creation, a softening that invites our own disciplines to kiss others.

Note

1 I wish to thank Lewis Aron, Bruce Goldberger, Ruth Kara-Ivanov Kaniel, Danielle Knafo and David Sperber for their helpful comments.

References

Aron, L. (1992). Interpretation as expression of the analyst's subjectivity. *Psychoanal. Dial.*, *2*, 475–507.

Aron, L. (1996). *A meeting of minds: Mutuality in psychoanalysis, 4*. New York: Routledge.

Aron, L., & Starr, K. (2013). *Psychotherapy for the people: Toward a progressive psychoanalysis, 55*. New York: Routledge.

Battersby, C. (1989). *Gender and genius: Towards a feminist aesthetics*. Indiana: University Press.

Benjamin, J. (1998). *The shadow of the other, intersubjectivity and gender in psychoanalysis*. New York: Routledge.

Bourdieu, P. (1993). *But who created the "creators": Sociology in question*. London: Sage.

Bromberg, P. (1998). *Standing in the spaces*. New York: Psychology Press.

Carpo, M. (2011). *The alphabet and the algorithm*. Cambridge, MA: MIT Press.

Davies, J.M., & Frawley, M.G. (1992). Dissociative processes and transference-countertransference paradigms in the psychoanalytically oriented treatment of adult survivors of childhood sexual abuse. *Psychoanal. Dialogue, 2*, 5–36.

Ferenczi, S. (1949). Confusion of the tongues between the adults and the child. *The Language International Journal of Psycho-Analysis, 30*, 225–230.

Fonagy, P., Gergely, G., Jurist, E., & Target, M. (2002). *Affect regulation, mentalization, and the development of self*. New York: Other Press.

Freud, S. (1883). Letter from Sigmund Freud to Martha Bernays, November 15, 1883. *Letters of Sigmund Freud 1873–1939*. 74–76.

Freud, S. (1921). *Group psychology and the analysis of the ego*. Vienna: International Psychoanalytic Publishing House.

Hartmann, H. (1939). *Ego psychology and the problem of adaptation*. New York: International Universities Press, Inc.

Homans, P. (1989). *The ability to mourn: Disillusionment and the social origins of psychoanalysis*. Chicago: University of Chicago Press.

Lavin, S. (2007). *Form follows libido: Architecture and Richard Neutra in a psychoanalytic culture*. Cambridge, MA: MIT Press.

Lavin, S. (2011). *Kissing architecture*. Princeton, NJ: Princeton University Press.

Loewald, H. (1975). Psychoanalysis as an art and the fantasy character of the psychoanalytic situation. *Papers on Psychoanalysis*. New Haven, CT: Yale University Press.

Mallgrave, H.F. (2010). *The architect's brain: Neuroscience, creativity and architecture*. London: John Wiley & Sons.

Mitchell, S. (1993). *Hope and dread in psychoanalysis*. New York: Basic Books.

Neutra, R.J. (1945, October). *Case study house program: Arts & architecture*. Retrieved from www.artsandarchitecture.com/case.houses/houses.html.

Neutra, R.J. (1954). *Survival through design*. London: Oxford University Press.

Nochlin, L. (1971). Why have there been no great women artists. *The feminism and visual culture reader*. New York: Routledge (pp. 229–233).

Ogden, T. (2008). *Rediscovering psychoanalysis: Thinking and dreaming, learning and forgetting*. New York: Routledge.

Schafer, R. (1976). *A new language for psychoanalysis*. New Haven, CT: Yale University Press.

Searles, H.F. (1999). The patient as a therapist to his analyst. *Countertransference and related subjects: Selected papers* (pp. 380–459). Madison, CT: International Universities Press. (Original work published 1975.)

Slavin, J. (2010). Becoming an individual: Technically subversive thoughts on the role of the analyst's influence. *Psychoanalytic Dialogues, 20*, 308–324.

Sperber, E. (2013, Fall). Gender and genius: Revisiting our ideas about collective inspiration. *Lillith Magazine*, *38*(3), 1–10.

Sperber, E. (2014a). Site, incite, and insight: Architecture and psychoanalysis: Commentary on Leanne Domash's paper. *Psychoanal. Perspect., 11*, 122–132.

Sperber, E. (2014b). Sublimation: Building or dwelling? Loewald, Freud, and architecture. *Psychoanal. Psychol., 31*, 507–524.

Zaretsky, E. (2004). *Secrets of the soul: A social and cultural history of psychoanalysis.* New York: Random House.

Chapter 4

Is ethics masochism?

Or infinite ethical responsibility and finite human capacity

Donna Orange

When I speak of Levinasian ethics to clinical colleagues, without fail the apprehensive questions emerge: isn't this radical responsibility, this deference to the other, a disguised masochism? What about the patient, or the clinician, already exploited as a parentified child, who needs to learn to feel *less* responsible? Isn't ethics, of the type you describe, a form of what Bernard Brandchaft (2007) has named pathological accommodation, or what Winnicott (1965) called the false-self? Have we here narcissism hidden behind a mirage of religion? We need only to consult our daily news to see where *that* can lead its hubristic self-deluders. My colleagues who raise these questions do not wish to evade the ethical call; they want to understand how it works, and to be sure it will destroy neither the humanity they feel called to heal, nor their own. Thus, I will use this opportunity to make some distinctions – yes, I will put on my philosophical hat – to help clarify ethics, masochism, accommodation, and subjectivity. Undoubtedly, confronting clinical work with Levinasian ethics *should* arouse worries, but others than those just mentioned.

First, let us look at the ethical demand to live for the other, voiced by various ethical thinkers, by religious traditions, in literary examples, and radically expressed in the work of 20th-century phenomenologist and prophet Emmanuel Levinas. Then let us consider the concept of masochism, primarily as it has been understood in Freudian and relational psychoanalysis, to see where it does and/or does not intersect with forms of ethics that inspire the writers brought together here. Third, let us introduce the work of Bernard Brandchaft and recall that of Winnicott, on pathological accommodation and false-self compliance, respectively, to see whether even if ethics may not be masochistic, living otherwise may still be psychologically dangerous. Along the way, I will introduce careful distinctions, including those made by Emmanuel Ghent, to suggest that it is more than possible to live for the other without losing any kind of subjectivity worth having.

Living for-the-other

What threatening message so worries my readers? Emmanuel Levinas returned from five years in Nazi labor camps to find that his entire family in Lithuania was dead, and to learn, like many others, the scope of the massacre. His philosophy, for his remaining 50 years, challenged us to respond responsibly to the face of the suffering other, not to evade. Solidarity with the other costs me suffering, but so be it. Me voici, hineni.[1] That many others require my care means that social justice, what he called the third party, must come in. But my passive vulnerability to the other (my useful suffering, i.e. suffering accepted for the sake of the other), required to respond to the useless suffering of the vulnerable and devastated other, produces experiences of persecution that never end. In the words Levinas (2001) never tired of quoting (in various forms) from Dostoevsky's *Brothers Karamazov*, "We are all responsible for everything and guilty in front of everyone, but I am that more than all others." My life is not about me; it's about the other. My always-already responsibility never ends. I never sought this responsibility.

A word of context: as *The New York Times* columnist David Brooks (2013) recently noted, egoism and individualism have taken deep root in our everyday talk as well as in our intellectual and political discourse in the past century. He finds the language of community, of the common good, and of solidarity simply disappearing. No wonder, then, that therapeutic work – to appeal to our contemporaries – must be framed in the jargon of self-fulfillment, authenticity, and agency, and that unsurprisingly we may find our thinking upended by someone who proclaims that responding to the other comes first, that human solidarity comes before my own benefit.

Levinasian ethics can be presented in two voices. One is the voice of persecution, substitution, being taken hostage, infinite guilt and responsibility, insistent demandingness. This voice thunders like a biblical prophet: "Thus saith the Lord." This one truly scares clinicians, I think. The second voice sounds warm, inviting, hospitable, slow to classify or to judge. How can I help you? Let me tell you first about this other Levinas. He was a phenomenologist, student of both Husserl and Heidegger. But his phenomenology inverts the intentionality of Husserl; that is, the directionality goes not from the knower to the known, but from the other to me. Before any agreements are made, the concrete need or suffering of the widow, the orphan, and the stranger requires from me a hospitable response, and creates my subjectivity as subjection in what Levinas (1990) called a "curvature of intersubjective space" (p. 291). The other goes first.

Where did Levinas get these strange ideas? Let's back up a bit. He was born in Kovno (Kaunas), Lithuania, in 1906, but threats to the Jewish community moved his family already in 1914 to Ukraine where he attended an excellent secondary school. By his own account, he spoke Russian at home all his life, and his first major influences came from Russian literature – Pushkin, Lermontov, and above all, Dostoevsky – which he credited with leading him into philosophy. These, I note, were strongly ethical influences. Back in Lithuania by the age of 14, re-immersed in the very intellectual Judaism he often described as one of his origins, he left for university in Strasbourg in 1923. There he encountered phenomenology, and wrote as his dissertation a book that introduced Husserl to giants like Sartre and Merleau-Ponty. I tell you all this to emphasize the three-cornered sources of early and late Levinasian thought, which I do not want to prioritize, as others might do: Russian literature (especially the Dostoevskian notion of responsibility), Torah and Talmud, and Western philosophy beginning with Plato. But then, as Primo Levi (Levi, 1988; Levi, 1996) also told us, a radical assault on human dignity occurred.

For our purposes and for those of Levinas, the crucial point is that phenomenology, and its relationship to psychoanalysis, has been turned upside down. It is no longer about me. It is no longer about *my* death, or *my* losses, or *my* trauma, or *my* anxiety, or *my* finitude. Let us listen a bit to this radical discourse, first in its gentler form.

In an interview with philosopher Jean-François Poirier, Levinas (2001) begins as if it is all quite an everyday matter, this reversal:

> Is not the first word *bonjour?* As simple as *bonjour. Bonjour* as benediction and my being available for the other man. It doesn't mean: what a beautiful day. Rather: I wish you peace, I wish you a good day, expression of one who worries for the other. It underlies all the rest of communication, underlies all discourse.
>
> (p. 47)

For-the-other. It's not about me, or about my place in the sun. This simple greeting of welcome, and well-wishing in the elevator or on the street, changes phenomenology from a search from essences and definitions and totalities to a response to the other. But let us hear more. Poirier follows up by asking if he has completed his life project. Well, responds Levinas (2001), I never thought of having a well-written biography. In other words, it wasn't about *me*. Instead, he mused,

> The true, the incontestable value, about which it is not ridiculous to think, is holiness. This is not a matter of privations, but it is in the certitude that one must yield to the other the first place in everything, from the *après vous* before an open door right up to the disposition – hardly possible but holiness demands it – to die for the other. In this attitude of holiness, there is reversal of the normal order of things, the natural order of things, the persisting in being of the ontology of things and of the living.
>
> (p. 47)

So phenomenology's famous intentionality, its directedness always striving, now becomes radically passive and vulnerable to the other. In the words of a famous rabbinic saying, "the neighbor's material needs are my spiritual needs." This non-indifference completely reverses the scientific attitude of Husserl's beloved mathematics. Heidegger made the first reversal, and showed that we are born situated and never able to abstract ourselves from the world and our assumptions in the way that Husserl had hoped. But he could not, preoccupied with his "ownmost" *Eigentlichkeit*, take the next step. A great irony, in my view, lies in the very German word that comes out in English as "authenticity." *Eigen* means own, and both suffixes substantialize it, as if to say, ownnessness. It is really untranslatable, but it is such a cornerstone of Heidegger's philosophy that it is difficult to capture the Levinasian reversal without feeling the impact of this word.

Though Levinas spoke of holiness, he completely agreed with Nietzsche about "the death of a certain god" (Stauffer & Bergo, 2009). Theodicies, arguments that defend a provident god after gulags and holocaust, he found absurd and obscene. But simple holiness, and the unexpected goodness found among ordinary people, these were traces, and he would not stop speaking about them. In his later years Levinas (2001) loved the work of the Russian journalist and novelist Vassily Grossman, and told this story from Grossman's *Life and Fate*:

when Stalingrad has already been rescued, the German prisoners, including an officer, are cleaning out a basement and removing the decomposing bodies. The officer suffers particularly from this misery. In the crowd, a woman who hates Germans is delighted to see this man more miserable than the others. Then she gives him the last piece of bread she has. This is extraordinary. Even in hatred there exists a mercy stronger than hatred. I give to this act a religious significance. This is my way of saying that the mercy of God occurs through the particular man – not all because he is organized in a certain way or because he belongs to a society or an institution. There are acts of stupid, senseless goodness.

(p. 89)

Levinas considered this to be faithful phenomenological description, and ethics.

So what happened to the radical Levinas of *Otherwise than Being*? In my view, as will become clearer below, this capacity for goodness is the same vulnerability that he calls ethical subjectivity, which makes us hostage, traumatized by the other's suffering, infinitely responsible. Levinas (2003) wrote:

The "one" is for the other of a being who lets go of itself [se déprend] without turning into a contemporary of "the other," without taking place next to him in a synthesis exposing itself as a theme; the one-for-the-other. Between the one that I am and the other for whom I answer gapes a bottomless difference, which is also the non-indifference of responsibility, significance of signification, irreducible to any system whatsoever. Non-in-difference, which is the proximity of one's fellow, by which is profiled a base of community between one and the other.

(p. 6)

In other words, you and I are two, in community. We are different, but I can never be indifferent to you. I am my brother's keeper.

Next, let us consider the problem of masochism, usually understood as seeking and enjoying pain.

Masochism: seeking pain

Laplanche and Pontalis (1973) remind us that Richard Krafft-Ebing, an older contemporary of Freud, first described masochism as a sexual perversion in men, an attitude and practice of servility toward dominant women. They provide a more general definition: "Sexual perversion in which satisfaction is tied to the suffering or humiliation undergone by the subject" (p. 245). By 1924, Freud in "The Economic Problem of Masochism" (1924b) had extended, in his usual style, his understanding of psychological masochism far beyond literal sexuality to encompass what he called "moral masochism." He wrote:

> All other masochistic sufferings carry with them the condition that they shall emanate from the loved person and shall be endured at his command. This restriction has been dropped in moral masochism. The suffering itself is what matters; whether it is decreed by someone who is loved or by someone who is indifferent is of no importance. It may even be caused by impersonal powers or by circumstances; the true masochist always turns his cheek whenever he has a chance of receiving a blow.
>
> (p. 164)

Freud's (1924a) reference here, "turns the cheek," to religious people, particularly Christian, makes it clear what a wide net he was casting in describing moral masochism and its motivations. The willingness to receive suffering for the sake of the other he next linked to an unconscious desire to suffer:

> It is very tempting, in explaining this attitude, to leave the libido out of account and to confine oneself to assuming that in this case the destructive instinct has been turned inwards again and is now raging against the self; yet there must be some meaning in the fact that linguistic usage has not given up the connection between this norm of behaviour and erotism and calls these self-injurers masochists too.
>
> (p. 164)

In other words, the Freudian moral masochist, referred to by implication in my title and in the questions so often put to me, unconsciously *enjoys* the suffering taken on from what Freud explained in this same essay as guilt resulting from some indefinite crime, never identified and never adequately expiated. The masochist *unconsciously seeks to suffer and owns the suffering as deserved.* Freud (1924a) continued:

The fact that moral masochism is unconscious leads us to an obvious clue. We were able to translate the expression "unconscious sense of guilt" as meaning a need for punishment at the hands of a parental power. We now know that the wish, which so frequently appears in phantasies, to be beaten by the father stands very close to the other wish, to have a passive (feminine) sexual relation to him and is only a regressive distortion of it. If we insert this explanation into the content of moral masochism, its hidden meaning becomes clear to us. Conscience and morality have arisen through the overcoming, the desexualization, of the Oedipus complex; but through moral masochism morality becomes sexualized once more, the Oedipus complex is revived and the way is opened for a regression from morality to the Oedipus complex.

(p. 169)

So the puzzle is resolved: the conscious goodness of the moral masochist masks a sadistic superego punishing the psychic apparatus for our universal Oedipal crimes. In Freud's view, the Kantian requirement to treat others so that the maxim of our actions would be universalizable is heir to the Oedipus complex. It imposes a harsh requirement to seek punishment for crimes of parricide we must all commit (Loewald, 1979) to become ourselves and internalize our parents. We, patients and therapists alike, want to suffer and we enjoy it because we know we deserve to suffer.

It is precisely this moral masochism, in patients and therapists alike, that concerns many who question me about Levinasian ethics. Are we simply, in our welcoming response to the other – especially when it stretches us, as working in the service of the other often must – living out unanalyzed moral masochism? Should we be setting better limits, for our own sakes and – as many theorists would argue – for that of the patient as well? Better limits according to whom? How do we decide which phone call not to take, which extra session to refuse, which patient not to take? How do we decide what is service to the other, and what is masochism?

But some have also understood masochism otherwise. Bernhard Berliner (1958) described it already in the 1950s most thoroughly and passionately as a relational matter:

the other person does not enter into the picture only after the passive aim is established. The other person is a reality from the very beginning and is instrumental in bringing about the whole masochistic process . . . . Masochism I do not consider an instinctual phenomenon like sadism or aggression. Masochism is a defensive reaction, motivated by libidinal needs, to the sadism of *another person* . . . . The experience of hate and ill-treatment is repressed. The child, in its imperative need for love, accepts this hate and ill-treatment as if they were love and is not conscious of the difference. Suffering thus libidinized is introjected.

(pp. 39–44)

So masochism results from internalized mistreatment, much like Ferenczi's (1949) identification with the aggressor. It only superficially resembles the seeking of pain. Instead, it reenacts the childhood situation, where the masochist acts both roles of perpetrator and victim, just as Primo Levi (1988) described among the more privileged "guests," as he ironically called them, of Auschwitz, who inhabited a gray zone. Berliner (1958) continued:

The masochistic patient appears in a double light: he is the *victim* of a traumatic childhood, and he is a *troublemaker* who entangles himself in actual conflicts by which he continuously makes himself the victim again. He is sinned against and sinning, to paraphrase Shakespeare. We [should] give the analysis of the victim priority over the analysis of the troublemaker.

(p. 53)

So we see that already among Freudian psychoanalysts existed the possibility for genuine empathy with the plight of the patient who seemed forever doomed to a life of suffering, even when to the observer life seemed to offer exits from purgatory. They could mention identification with the aggressor – the patient's absorbing of the point of view of the perpetrator – even if they could not dare to mention Ferenczi, just as they could speak of object relations without mentioning Fairbairn or Winnicott.

Not only our patients, but also we clinicians who attempt an ethical hospitality – always only an attempt, of course – live this double life. Does this mean we seek pain? If our own history as the "wise babies" Ferenczi (1949) described brings us to clinical work, are we moral masochists? Meanwhile, we have a few more thinkers to help us along.

Next came Harry Stack Sullivan, who called the idea of masochism "foggy thinking" (Sullivan & Perry, 1953, p. 352). But of course, as Ruth Imber (1995) notes, he could not avoid the clinical phenomena that the word so badly connotes. Sullivan described what he called a "malevolent transformation," understood at least as empathically as Berliner (1958) was understanding "moral masochism" in the same years. In Imber's paraphrase:

> there were people who had learned, as children, the futility or even danger of seeking love or tenderness from their uncaring and rejecting caretakers. Rather than continue to suffer the hurt and disappointment of trying to get what was not available, such a child would instead learn to change his or her *behavior* from tenderness-seeking to angry rejection or mischievousness. While the need for tenderness went unmet, the malevolent transformation *did* protect against the pain and anxiety of being rejected or punished for seeking what was not to be had. And if the "malevolence" was met with punishment, that at least was under one's control. The child could thus salvage some sense of security by acting as if to say "If I am the architect of my own misery, I need not fear being at someone else's mercy."
>
> (pp. 581–582)

This interpersonalist interpretation points to the effort, in some instances, of seizing one's human dignity, if only by causing one's own pain. Such suffering is sought, not for its own sake, but for its crucial *no* to the domination by the other.

But soon came Heinrich Racker (1958), unafraid to mention the early subversives Fairbairn and Winnicott, and much concerned about the masochism of the analyst, our particular concern. He believed that "psychoanalytic cure consists in establishing a unity within the psychic structure of the patient. Most of what is ego alien must be relinquished or reintegrated in the ego" (p. 555). He was working here not with ego as substructure (id, ego, superego) but with what Freud called the *Gesamt-Ich*, or whole I, or the personality as a whole. Insofar as the analyst was holding parts of the patient, by projection or through various forms of unconscious countertransference, the cure would be held back.

Racker (1958) assumes masochism – understood as developmental residue – in every analyst/therapist, but also that each of us has a particular "countertransference characteropathy" or character pathology with which we need to be deeply familiar. He warns:

> It should be stressed, first of all, that the analyst's masochism aims at making him fail in his task. We should, therefore, never be too sure that we are really seeking success and must be prepared to recognize the existence of an "inner saboteur" (as Fairbairn says) of our professional work. We must likewise reckon with an unseen collaboration between the masochism of the analyst and that of the patient.
>
> (p. 558)

Racker uses, we see, a concept of masochism that differs from Freud's "seeking suffering" and also from Berliner's (1958) "inner victim." Here we have Fairbairn's "inner saboteur" – the bad internal object making trouble for both therapist and patient, and obstructing our work. In the Fairbairnian world no longer punished for Oedipal crimes, we remain forever unlovable because we could not get our mothers to love us. We need not seek pain, but we must work forever to become lovable. The internal saboteur will never let us rest. Racker (1958) continued:

> it predisposes the analyst to feel persecuted by the patient and to see mainly the patient's negative transference and his aggression. Masochism and paranoid anxiety act like smoked glasses, hindering our perception of the patient's love and what is good in him, which in turn increases the negative transference. Our understanding becomes a partial one; while we clearly perceive the present negative transference, we easily become blind to the latent and potential positive transference.
>
> (p. 559)

In my experience the precise opposite partial understanding – missing the negative and aggressive transference – can also blind and mislead, with painful results.

The word masochism blames. Perhaps it would be more accurate to say, given our survey, in classical as well as more relational accounts of masochism, that the word tends to blame. Psychoanalysis, having originated among the people of the book, understands well that words have power. In classical psychoanalysis, this word implied that the masochist, whether patient or analyst, sought and enjoyed suffering. In relational accounts, by contrast, masochistic relating requires engagement with relational trauma. Perhaps also to be noted (Lansky, 1994; Morrison, 1999; Wurmser, 1991), greater – and generally extremely helpful – attention to shame in recent years has shifted our focus away from masochism. Vulnerability understood as intersubjectively constituted by patterns of humiliation and violent subjugation brings a different focus, in which what seems a desire to suffer may now seem an automatic assumption of a familiar role. Judith Lewis Herman (2011) recently wrote of posttraumatic stress as a shame disorder. Instead of a disparaging "this patient wants to suffer," we now think: "how does one escape this miserable prison?" No matter the understanding, we do not idealize this suffering. It is, like all suffering in the other, as Levinas would have clearly said, useless suffering. It becomes useful suffering only when accepted for the other's sake (Levinas, 1998).

As part of his critique of "obscene" theodicy (the defense of belief in a god both all-good and all-powerful), common to many post-Holocaust writers, Levinas (1990) developed a strong distinction between useless and useful suffering: meaningful in me but absurd in the other, unutterable. He wrote:

> There is a radical difference between *the suffering in the other to me*, where it is unforgivable to *me*, solicits me and calls me and suffering *in me*, my own experience of suffering, whose constitutional or congenital uselessness can take on a meaning, the only one of which suffering is capable, in becoming a suffering for the suffering (inexorable though it may be) of someone else.
>
> (p. 94)

But what of the person who takes on suffering for the sake of the other, the Levinasian (1998) "useful suffering"? This is the trickier question. Now we seem to be in the territory of the ethical, the territory where each of us lives every day in our therapeutic work. Is this moral masochism, the unconscious self-punishment that Freud described? If we take on the suffering of the other too much, we quickly burn out or get into boundary violations. If we avoid and evade the other's suffering, we abandon the other to die alone and reduce our profession to a technology. To complicate matters further, many of our patients come to us as compulsive caregivers (altruists on autopilot) who cannot say no even when they are being grossly, let alone subtly abused.

Here the "is ethics masochism?" question becomes practical. Most reasonably wise therapists of all persuasions would respond that they want to help these patients discover (and model for them) a life that is reasonably generous, but does not consist in being a doormat. How can we conceptualize the difference between false-self (as contrasted with the creative true self in Winnicott) compliance and the kind of holiness that Levinas described?

Compliance, accommodation, and ethical subjectivity

Beyond concerns about moral masochism lie related worries that our ethical vulnerability, emotional availability (Orange, 1995), or compassion (Orange, 2006), our tent flaps as open as we are able to keep them – as in the story of Abraham and the Arab angels so much discussed by Talmudic commentators, then in Talmudic readings by Levinas (1990) – may involve us in massive false-self compliance. Worse, we may model such a false-self for our patients, or fail to help them grow beyond this half-life.

Winnicott (1965) described the false-self in his early writings, later writing more simply of compliance, as the infant's effort to survive impingements. In the good-enough situation, the need to develop such a compliant social self, unfortunately named "false" to distinguish it from what feels spontaneous and originating from oneself, i.e. true, remains minimal. Depending on the extent of impingements, ranging from displacements due to war, family separation, and bombing to all kinds of parental pathologies, the need for development of a protective social false-self could be more or less extreme, even amounting to experiential eclipse of true selfhood altogether. His compassionate understanding that many symptoms resulted from very early deprivation and impingement allowed forms of therapeutic engagement that sought and welcomed the creativity and spontaneity, as well as the extreme suffering, within the patient into the transitional space of the treatment room. But many, seeing Winnicott as a moral masochist, worried that it was his overwork, rather than his smoking, that gave him so many heart attacks. Personally, I have my doubts – all his life he remained playful, and involved in cultural pursuits and friendships.

Similarly and even more clearly, Brandchaft, Doctors, and Sorter (2010) have written of a form of what Leonard Shengold (1989) calls "soul murder." He described patients, unfortunately very common among us clinicians too, for whom a radical choice was early and long required. They had to decide between surrender to dominating caregivers and development of one's own soul, self, or path. The victim accommodates by passivity, rebellion, or some mad combination of the two to form almost all the pathologies we find in the manuals.

"Pathological accommodation" sounds less extreme than soul murder, but it is not. The patient is not the perpetrator of the crime. While Brandchaft intended to describe an intersubjective crime that the patient continues endlessly to memorialize, only a child born to (often unconsciously) exploitative parents suffers from this torture. The patient feels that the price of any significant attachment must be the sacrifice of her own soul, of her own path, of her own desire. Unconscious until it meets the analyst/therapist who can feel its terrible grip, this conviction keeps the patient in a depressive pit, a furious defiance, an obsessive terror, or a chaotic combination of all of these. Dante could not have imagined a hell worse than pathological accommodation.

In the face of such hell, I (2006) began to think and write some years ago, even before reading much of Levinas, about the absence of compassion discourse in psychoanalytic literature, musing:

> Psychoanalytic compassion is not reducible to moral masochism on the part of the analyst, nor is it to be contrasted with properly psychoanalytic work, usually seen as explicitly interpretive. It is, instead, an implicitly interpretive process of giving lived meaning and dignity to a shattered person's life by enabling integration of the pain and loss as opposed to dissociation or fragmentation. A compassionate attitude says to every patient: your suffering is human suffering, and when the bell tolls for you, it also tolls for me.
>
> (p. 16)

Over time, I believe, each clinician finds a way of working that ranks service to the other (Poland, 2000) first, but allows ongoing life including health, family, and those pursuits that make living precious. But each of us can lose our balance. If therapeutic work in the spirit of service to the patient becomes felt as submission, and it has sometimes felt so to me, it is time for consultation. Perhaps the therapist has idealized the patient, mistaking traumatic suffering for uncomplicated goodness. This patient may explode at the mere suggestion that he is less than perfectly benevolent.

Something, perhaps an absolutely needed rage in the transference–countertransference system, is occurring in the space between to evoke the therapist's (possibly traumatic) history of annihilation. When the therapist has regained calmness, and the capacity for passivity in the Levinasian sense, survival in Winnicott's words, or surrender in Ghent's terms, words like masochism no longer resound. Human dignity may be sought, modeled, and brought into conversation. Or at least, if relevant to the therapist and patient's experience, masochism will not be confused with ethical surrender and response, to which we now turn.

Ethical subjectivity and clinical humility

To conclude, let us revisit a now classic distinction by Emmanuel Ghent between masochism and surrender as well as the distinction between useless and useful suffering made by Emmanuel Levinas. Levinas (2003) wrote:

> Without introducing any deliberate seeking of suffering or humiliation (turning the other cheek) it [the prophetic text] suggests, in the primary suffering, in suffering as suffering, a hard unbearable consent that animates passivity, strangely animates it in spite of itself, whereas passivity as such has neither force nor intention, neither like it or not. The impotence or humility of "to suffer" is beneath the passivity of submission. Here the word *sincerity* takes all its sense: to discover oneself totally defenseless, to be surrendered. Intellectual sincerity, veracity, already refers to vulnerability, is founded in it.
>
> (pp. 63–64)

This text contains two of the three words compared by Emmanuel Ghent (1990), and refers to all three: masochism, submission, and surrender. Over the years I have often simply replied to colleagues worried about whether Levinasian ethics concealed masochism: "please read Manny Ghent." He claimed that masochism is a kind of false-self that longs for surrender to release the creative true self that Winnicott (1965) described. Such masochism, "which may be rooted in a deep quest for understanding, for undoing . . . isolation" (Ghent, 1990, p. 127), should never be confused with real surrender, or with the submissive compliance that is the behavioral expression of common masochism. Levinas, in the text quoted above, says much the same thing. Suffering without ego, without intention, with sincerity, does not seek pain; it simply suffers it for the sake of the other.

To surrender is not to seek pain or punishment. Ghent (1990) warned that analysts too may seek surrender but fall into masochism:

> Let us not overlook the role of masochism and surrender in being a member of our profession. What other occupation requires of its practitioners that they be the objects of people's excoriations, threats and rejections, or be subjected to tantalizing offerings that plead "touch me," yet may not be touched? What other occupation has built into it the frustration of feeling helpless, stupid and lost as a necessary part of the work? And what other occupation puts its practitioners in the position of being an onlooker or midwife to the fulfillment of others' destinies? It is difficult to find a type of existence, other than that of the psychoanalyst, who fits this job description. In a sense it is the portrait of a masochist. Yet I suspect that a deep underlying motive in some analysts at least is again that of surrender, and their own personal growth. It may be acceptably couched in masochistic garb or denied by narcissistic and/or sadistic exploitation. When the yearning for surrender is, or begins to be, realized by the analyst, the work is immensely fulfilling and the analyst grows with his patients.
>
> (p. 133)

It seems to me that rereading this article carefully can help us to sort out the residues of our history, which haunt our clinical lives, from the ethical spirit in which we attempt to respond to the other.

Mostly, I try to live my clinical life between two values, for my patients and for myself: basic human kindness, and restoration of dignity. Neither of these words, by the way, appears much in the psychoanalytic literature, or in the philosophers. Although kindness and hospitality are never simple, often they require immediate response, with reflection and theorizing later. Restoration of dignity, I think, begins precisely in this response to the naked and devastated face of the other, even though, as Jean Amery (1980) reminded us, "once tortured, always tortured."

When these values fail me, and I find myself faced by more trouble than my personal limitations can bear, I need the help of a third value, clinical humility. Ghent (1990) alluded to this situation: touch me, yet may not be touched. Just as I have always tried to hold theory lightly, now every so often comes a time to surrender to the vulnerability and passivity of my clinical limitations, and to say that this is beyond me. Consultation, referral to better-suited colleagues for the work at hand, slowing down the process of accepting new patients: all these and more form the practical content of clinical fallibilism and humility in one's early and middle working years. In the later years, humility in practice may include not only all of these, but also working less and considering retirement.

Unfortunately, young clinicians often receive the impression that they should be able to work with every patient who comes to them. Goodness of fit, and the sense that each of us has strengths and weaknesses to be welcomed, rarely appear in their training. Rarely do they learn how to estimate whether this patient fits the therapist's range of capacities, or to understand when this therapy has reached its limits. Instead, young therapists are assessed for their ability to keep patients in treatment. Combining this training bias with ethical desire to serve the other can create a trap for otherwise wonderful therapists. Remembering, however, that we work in service to the other in the context of a larger community can keep us humbler, and help us to surrender a certain hubris. Though my immediate *hineni* may be crucial, I am not the only person who can help, and must humbly realize that I work within a beloved community (Martin Luther King, Jr.'s term). Humility means, among other things, giving up the solipsistic ego.

What has all this to do with the question of ethics and masochism with which we began? Without humility, compulsive service to the other will indeed resemble superficially the classical story of the desire to suffer, or false-self compliance with patients whose needs come to rule our lives. With clinical humility, working within community (the third party, Levinas would have said), we will have a better sense – though never perfect – of whether we are still responding to the other, or whether it is time to turn to the resources of community.

Note

1 My thanks to Karen Starr for explaining to me that this Hebrew word contains nothing of "I" or "me." It simply expresses full willingness to respond to the call. It appears several times in Genesis. Levinas used it repeatedly to express his sense of ethical subjectivity without ego or agency.

References

Alford, C. (2007). Levinas, Winnicott, and therapy. *Psychoanalytic Review, 94*, 529–551.
Amery, J. (1980). *At the mind's limits: Contemplations by a survivor on Auschwitz and its realities*. Bloomington: Indiana University Press.

Berliner, B. (1958). The role of object relations in moral masochism. *Psychoanalytic Quarterly, 27*, 38–56.

Brandchaft, B. (2007). Systems of pathological accommodation and change in analysis. *Psychoanalytic Psychology, 24*, 667–687.

Brandchaft, B., Doctors, S., & Sorter, D. (2010). *Toward an emancipatory psychoanalysis: Brandchaft's intersubjective vision.* New York: Routledge.

Brooks, D. (2013, May 20). What our words tell us. *The New York Times.*

Ferenczi, S. (1949). Confusion of the tongues between the adults and the child: The language of tenderness and of passion. *International Journal of Psycho-Analysis, 30*, 225–230.

Freud, S. (1924a). The economic problem of masochism. *The standard edition of the complete psychological works of Sigmund Freud: The ego and the id and other works, 19*, 155–170.

Freud, S. (1924b). The economic problem of masochism. *The standard edition of the complete psychological works of Sigmund Freud, 19*, 155–170.

Ghent, E. (1990). Masochism, submission, surrender: Masochism as a perversion of surrender. *Contemporary Psychoanalysis, 26*, 108–136.

Herman, J. (2011). Posttraumatic stress disorder as a shame disorder. In R. Dearing & J. Tangney (Eds.), *Shame in the therapy hour* (pp. 261–276). Washington, DC: American Psychological Association.

Imber, R. R. (1995). Clinical notes on masochism. *Contemporary Psychoanalysis, 31*, 581.

Lansky, M. R. (1994). Shame. *Journal of the American Academy of Physician Assistants, 22*(3), 433–441.

Laplanche, J., & Pontalis, J. B. (1973). *The language of psycho-analysis.* London: Hogarth.

Levi, P. (1988). *The drowned and the saved.* New York: Summit Books.

Levi, P. (1996). *If this is a man: The truce.* London: Vintage.

Levinas, E. (1990). *Nine talmudic readings.* Bloomington: Indiana University Press.

Levinas, E. (1998). *Entre nous: On thinking-of-the-other.* New York: Columbia University Press.

Levinas, E. (2001). *Is it righteous to be: Interviews with Emmanuel Levinas.* J. Robbins (Ed.). Stanford, CA: Stanford University Press.

Levinas, E. (2003). *Humanism of the other.* (N. Poller, Trans.). Champaign, IL: University of Illinois Press.

Loewald, H. W. (1979). The waning of the Oedipus complex. *Journal of American Psychoanalytic Association, 27*, 751–775.

Morrison, A. P. (1999). Shame in context. *International Journal of Psycho-Analysis, 80*(3), 616–619.

Orange, D. (1995). *Emotional understanding: Studies in psychoanalytic epistemology.* New York: Guilford Press.

Orange, D. (2006). For whom the bell tolls: Context, complexity, and compassion in psychoanalysis. *International Journal of Psychoanalytic Self Psychology, 1*, 5–21.

Poland, W. S. (2000). The analyst's witnessing and otherness. *Journal of American Psychoanalytic Assocation, 48*(1), 17–34.

Racker, H. (1958). Psychoanalytic technique and the analyst's unconscious masochism. *Psychoanal Quarterly, 27*, 555–562.

Shengold, L. (1989). *Soul murder: The effects of childhood abuse and deprivation.* New Haven: Yale University Press.

Stauffer, J., & Bergo, B. (2009). *Nietzsche and Levinas: After the death of a certain God.* New York: Columbia University Press.

Sullivan, H. S., & Perry, H. S. (Eds.). (1953). *The interpersonal theory of psychiatry.* New York: Norton.

Winnicott, D. W. (1965). *The maturational processes and the facilitating environment: Studies in the theory of emotional development.* M. M. R. Khan (Ed.). London: Hogarth Press.

Wurmser, L. (1991). Shame: The underside of narcissism. *Psychoanal Quarterly, 60,* 667–672.

Chapter 5

Yale or jail

Class struggles in neoliberal times

Lynne Layton

Long before the Occupy movements began, I asked a friend why he was so concerned that his children go to law school, and he replied: "The US is well on its way to being like a third world country, where there's a tiny minority of rich people and the rest of the population in poverty, and I want my children to be among the rich." One could interpret his response as an expression of greed, and, indeed, it shows little concern for the poor. But I understand it also as an expression of anxiety, an anxiety that is being passed down daily to middle-class children – along with indifference, if not contempt, for the poor: "Yale or jail" is how one of my patients interpreted the parental message.

Our current social conditions of increasing income inequality, downsizing, outsourcing, high unemployment – extremely high in some groups – and generally precarious feelings about the economic situation have created much anxiety about class status and wellbeing in all classes. This has led, on the one hand, to split states of immense vulnerability and insecurity, and on the other, to public hatred of any signs of vulnerability and dependency. Dependency has come to signify "poor" and "failure." From a psychological perspective, however, we know that denying dependency leads to a kind of grandiose sense of omnipotence in which one feels that one needs nobody and nothing. As a result, it becomes hard to see how rich and poor, powerful and vulnerable, are connected to each other, how we are all part of the same social system and thus mutually interdependent (Layton, 2009, 2010, 2014a, 2014b). Grandiose states tend to be unstable and crash, precisely because we do need others. Fluctuations between grandiose omnipotent self-states and states of low self-worth are, in fact, symptomatic of the difficulties regulating self-esteem that clinicians refer to as narcissism, a dialectical disorder marked by oscillations between self-deprecation and grandiosity, devaluation and idealization of others, and longings to merge versus needs to radically withdraw from others. The form these oscillations take will differ depending on how the class inequalities that cause splitting intersect with the wounds of racism, sexism, and other social inequalities. I look here at some individual and large-group psychological effects of neoliberal social and economic policy, focusing particularly on the class inequalities these policies create. I argue that in all social groups, on both individual and large-group levels, the stark inequalities ushered in by neoliberal governance lead to sadomasochistic and instrumentalized relational scenarios marked by domination and submission – and by the eroticization of positions of power and weakness.

Neoliberalism, often referred to by critics as "free market fundamentalism," entails a fervent belief that markets can regulate themselves. Neoliberalism developed in the United States in reaction against the welfare state, including FDR's New Deal, LBJ's Great Society programs e.g., the War on Poverty, and Keynesian economic policies that advocate government intervention in the economy to ensure full employment and increase opportunity. All of this has been derided by neoliberals under the heading "big government," and welfare state policies have come to be reviled by large parts of the U.S. population. The first phase of neoliberalism in the US was ushered in during the mid-1970s crisis, years of high unemployment, high inflation, and high oil prices (Harvey, 2005; Peck and Tickell, 2002). In this period, a decline in capital accumulation caused rising anxiety among the capitalist elite. Besides high inflation and high unemployment, U.S. national identity in this era was battered and fragmented by the terrible losses of Vietnam, the humiliating defeat and ultimately unanswered question of what we were doing there in the first place, the unsettling of the social status quo brought about by race riots, student movements, several social justice movements angrily confronting racial, class, gender, and sexual discrimination, and the impeachment of a crooked president.

The elections of 1974 brought to the Senate Democrats such as Gary Hart and Paul Tsongas, who, like many Republicans of the time, embraced neoliberal principles of free market capitalism. But neoliberal principles of deregulation, privatization, and attack on the welfare state were most dramatically installed as social and economic policy in the Reagan and Thatcher era. By the late 80s and 90s, neoliberalism had become the new normal via the rise to power of the Democratic Leadership Council, which continued to dismantle the welfare state while also promoting the globalization and free trade agreements that led to the outsourcing of manufacture. And then came 9/11, which created even more feelings of vulnerability. Again, vulnerability was not acknowledged by government; in fact, vulnerability was publicly denied. We in the US were exhorted not to be afraid, to be strong, to go shopping. Meanwhile, the vast expansion of the wealth and power of multinational corporations and the finance sector created what would only recently, with the Occupy movements, be publicly named as the largest income gap between the very rich and everyone else since the Gilded Age of capitalism (Krugman, 2002).

Neoliberalism and social policy

In classical liberalism, the market was conceptualized as a sphere separate from government. Neoliberalism, on the other hand, is marked by a partnership between government and market, one in which government extends market values such as cost-benefit analysis and privatization into areas formerly understood to be part of the common good – e.g., health, education, social security. Whereas the welfare state shifted responsibility for market risks from the individual worker to collectivist solutions such as disability and unemployment insurance, neoliberal policies shift risk back onto the individual. As it retreats from providing a social safety net, neoliberalism promotes a particular vision of human nature: the individual is conceived of as an entrepreneur whose "nature" is competitive and based in self-care and self-interest.

Citizenship itself is re-defined as self-care rather than as interest in the public good (Brown, 2006, p. 695). Social problems are reconceptualized as individual problems that market forces such as privatization and consumer products can solve. Brown writes (2006):

> Examples in the United States are legion: bottled water as a response to contamination of the water table; private schools, charter schools, and voucher systems as a response to the collapse of quality public education; anti-theft devices, private security guards, and gated communities (and nations) as a response to the production of a throwaway class and intensifying economic inequality; boutique medicine as a response to crumbling health care provision; "V-chips" as a response to the explosion of violent and pornographic material on every type of household screen; ergonomic tools and technologies as a response to

the work conditions of information capitalism; and, of course, finely differentiated and titrated pharmaceutical antidepressants as a response to lives of meaninglessness or despair amidst wealth and freedom.

(p. 704)

The neoliberal reconceptualization of the individual rationalizes the radical split between those who have a chance of making it in the system and those who do not and cannot: social divisions, produced by neoliberal policies themselves, become understood not as system failures but as "failures of *individual* choice and responsibility" (Hamann, 2009, p. 50). This reassignment of blame encourages distinctions to be made between the deserving and the "undeserving" poor.

Neoliberalism is thus quite a bit more than merely an economic system or an ideology; rather, neoliberalism encompasses a whole way of living, that is, "a particular mentality, a particular manner of governing, that is actualized in habits, perceptions, and subjectivity" (Read, 2009, p. 34). The extension of market rationality into social life entails "marketing" the subjective practices that will turn subjects into entrepreneurs who rationally choose to maximize opportunity when possible and, at the same time, will agree to shoulder much of the responsibility formerly taken on by public agencies (du Gay, 2004). Read (2009) concludes that "The model neoliberal citizen is one who strategizes for her or himself among various social, political and economic options, not one who strives with others to alter or organize these options" (35).

All of us, no matter what our social class, have to contend with the current mainstream ideal that the most successful human is a rich human and not a dependent human. All of us have been enjoined to become entrepreneurial selves even if we belong to ethnic, racial, or class groups that offer contrasting norms to those of neoliberal individualism, for example, identities rooted in community and caregiving. Neoliberal policies have made many social groups, especially the poor, increasingly marginalized and denigrated; for some groups, neoliberal policies have severely damaged formerly tight communal bonds. For instance, as Michelle Alexander (2010) argues in *The New Jim Crow*, the decline in urban manufacturing in the 80s and 90s caused massive unemployment among unskilled and semi-skilled male urban African-American workers, up to 50% in some cities. Racist government policies, particularly the invention and execution of the war on drugs, combined with neoliberal economic policies to turn poor but formerly socially cohesive ghettos into wastelands. The mass incarceration of African-American men has led sociologist Loïc Wacquant (2001) to elaborate the systemic ties between what he calls neoliberal hyperghettos and neoliberal prisons, a complex that, he argues, is the most recent incarnation of four U.S. "peculiar institutions" forged from racism (slavery, Jim Crow, and the urban ghetto were the three preceding incarnations). Describing the prison-like conditions of public housing and inner city schools, Wacquant quotes an elderly resident of a DC housing project who said: "It's as though the children in here are being prepared for incarceration, so when they put them in a real lock-down situation, they'll be used to being hemmed in" (p. 108). What Alexander calls the New Jim Crow, a series of recently passed laws that obstruct or prevent those who have ever been in the penal system from voting, living in public housing, and receiving public assistance, operates alongside neoliberal economic changes that make it very difficult to get a job or have the means to get to a job. In neoliberal times, poor African-Americans are othered in ways that divide not only along racial but also along gender lines: the male criminal and the female welfare dependent. And yet even these extremely negative positions are subject to the demand to be an enterprising self. The options of "Yale or jail" between which my white middle-class patient felt she had to choose speaks a tragic truth about the deep social divides that mark everyday life in the US.

Psychological effects of neoliberalism and class inequality

To enable us to look more closely at some of what we know about the psychological effects on individuals of the kind of class inequality characteristic of neoliberal times, I present some clinical vignettes with two patients of white working-class and lower-middle-class origin. Both came of age in the post-1970s atmosphere of neoliberalism and neoconservatism and both of their families, conflictually to be sure, demanded that they show their worth by rising in class status. Sandy was born in the late 70s, the first child of a white mother who grew up in poverty and a white father who rose from blue collar to bureaucratic white collar. Father never let mother forget where she came from, and much of Sandy's specialness to father was wrapped up in his often-stated aspirations that she rise in class and status. Because she was so special, he asserted, she could do and have whatever she wanted. Intuiting this source of father's love, Sandy worked much harder academically than any of her peers, and she did indeed rise to become a professional in a high-income field. She thus secured her place as her father's favorite – which involved joining together in denigrating mother. What Sandy always knew, but couldn't really know until therapy, is that her father's capacities for love were rather damaged, and a part of her greatly resented what felt like a love contingent on performance. Her fragile sense of specialness was bolstered by her utter disdain for peers who didn't work as hard as she: "someday they'll be cleaning my toilets," she thought when she saw them out having fun while she studied.

Sandy fell in love with a working-class man who himself had risen to be bureaucratic white collar. As her therapist, I listened over and over again to her mocking denigration of his working-class ways. I surmise that Sandy thought she was bonding with me and my, in her view, exalted class position when she was denigrating the classlessness of her boyfriend. But, of course, it was her own anxiety about not being classy enough that she feared would be revealed – and her dreams did at times reveal it. At the point where I could no longer bear her contempt and could find a way to confront it calmly, I pointed out to her that she seemed to need to mock her boyfriend, a need to have close at hand an "other" deemed lower than she, and we ought perhaps to look at why. The first time I brought this up, she practically had an anxiety attack on the couch. She had an instant moment of recognition that, in fact, much of her sense of who she was rested on this defensive kind of class mockery, and she suddenly felt herself unraveling at the prospect of being shorn of this defense. It took much work to understand where her class grandiosity had come from, how it related to class dis-identifications with her mother and identifications with her father's disdain for what, in her mother, reminded him too much of his disowned class inse-curities. More importantly, she came to understand how the class grandiosity was a defense against recognizing that her father's love was contingent on her achievements – her mockery was aimed as much at hated parts of her-self that she had come to associate with classlessness as at her boyfriend.

Class wounds run deep. When it feels like love is contingent on perfor-mance, love itself gets tangled up in sadomasochistic enactments. Indeed, until she met this boyfriend, Sandy was entirely cynical about love. For years, she had been cheating on her previous upper-middle-class boyfriend with a lower-class man she had dated in high school – perhaps another way of externalizing and interpersonalizing her class struggle. But Sandy was aided in her denigration of love by a fairly new subject position offered to professionalizing women, one formed at the intersection of neoliberalism and a middle-class version of feminism. This is a subject position in which dependency is denied and caretaking capacities devalued in favor of a single-minded focus on career goals – and, indeed, before analysis Sandy occupied this position without apparent conflict (Layton, 2004a, 2004b). In her determination to rise in class, Sandy had become the kind of non-relational maximizer of self-opportunity described in neoliberal literature. She had come to hate her own vulnerability and to project it onto her boyfriend and lower classes in general. But we might guess that she fell in love with this boyfriend in part because he was comfortable with his class, with all she had come to call not-me, other, even though she would try to get me to laugh with her at him, for wearing a gold chain or showing some other sign of belonging to the white working class.

Another patient, Paul, was born in the early 70s and was the second child of a working-class mother from several generations of working-class and unskilled laborers. His father was a white-collar small business owner, but he left the family when Paul was three, plunging the family into poverty. His mother's grandparents had been proud working-class union people, but his maternal grandparents and his mother, the people who raised him, aspired, unsuccessfully, to rise in class (a generational shift perhaps due, in part, to the declining political and collective power of unions). Although he was only occasionally present in Paul's life, from time to time bestowing a bit of money and heavy doses of advice, his father stood as a family example of someone who had "made it" – but also as someone who was felt to be immoral, irresponsible, and an object of family derision. Paul, who did very well in school, seems to have been the target recipient in the family of the parental wish to advance in class. Like Sandy, Paul too had a vague feeling that the love of both parents was contingent on rising in class, on bringing the family a more legitimate social status.

The arena in which Paul chose to rise, academic science, was one that truly was dear and meaningful to him, but the rage at the almost desperate demand put on him to rise kept getting in the way of achieving what he hoped to achieve. The question "who am I doing this work for?" plagued him constantly, and because he perceived his parents as tyrannical and unloving, achievement always had the flavor not of self-fulfillment but rather of submitting to a rejecting, judgmental authority. An important basis of his sense of self involved a constant courageous fight against parental and other unjust authorities. But what we began to recognize was that part of the repeated transference scenario entailed a need to turn any authority perceived as "higher" than he into a potential immoral tyrant, and more than once Paul was fired from jobs after getting explosively angry at a superior.

For Paul, the very structure of analysis frequently and painfully evoked the feeling of unjustness, for while the caring attention of analysis promised love, each of its many limits seems to have been felt as unduly punishing and rejecting, although he rarely acknowledged that he felt hurt by them. Rather, from time to time, we became engaged in a struggle in which he defended the underdog world of patients against the injustices of arrogant analytic authority. Notable in Paul's case was a need to see me as powerful and punishing. On the one hand, that gave him a perch from which he could feel justified waging battle against the perceived (and real) injustices of the analytic situation. It also allowed him to keep me at a distance, so he would not be at risk of being overtaken by me, swallowed up, and destroyed. At the same time, his exquisite sensitivity to abuses of authority forced me repeatedly to examine the defensively grandiose aspects of my analytic stance.

Sandy and Paul's therapies illustrate how split states of grandiosity and self-hatred often ensue when children perceive that parental love is contingent on rising in class and economic status. The parents in these cases carried the intergenerationally transmitted trauma of being lower class and treated by multiple authorities in degrading and condescending ways. Their way of loving their children produced wounds that issued in split relations both to authority and to those lower in class. Sandy identified with professional class authority and generally denigrated those lower. Paul's relation to authority alternated between deference, rage, and panic. What crippled Paul was precisely an intergenerationally transmitted split relation to authority. It was only as sadomasochistic forms of relating began more clearly to define our own relationship that I was able to see that part of what gets in the way of his ability to work on his projects is inextricably tied to class inequality: feelings of illegitimacy and the impotent reverence for and hatred of power *were* and *are* his maternal family's way of living class.

As is so often the case, both Sandy and Paul had made a virtue out of the very place in which they were wounded: Sandy felt those who achieved middle-class status were better humans than those who had not, and yet, as in all cases of splitting, she had to keep the degraded other close so as to continue to feel special and perhaps also to stay close to some part of her that, in her class rise, she had lost. Unlike Sandy, Paul had made a virtue of refusing to comply with authority, of rebelling against rules, of *not* seeking accolades. The cost, however, was high: he could shake neither a pervasive sense of being unlovable nor a conviction that culturally sanctioned ways of doing things were the "right" way and the only way deserving of reward. Thus, he would repeatedly use his academic credentials to enter an upper-class world, and then he would fight with the boss about all the injustices he saw, thereby risking, and often incurring, either demotion or expulsion. For Paul, entering the middle-class world meant a loss of integrity. For both Sandy and Paul, the splits and projections resulting from the way class wounds were lived played out interpersonally in sadomasochistic relations, central to which were enactments of distinction between inferior and superior.

Sandy and Paul came of age in an era in which U.S. parents of all classes are anxious about whether their children would "make it." They grew up in a society in which being a "proper" human coincided more and more with being a rich and successful human. Their stories illustrate some of the psychic fallout that can arise from the demand to rise in class. What I want to highlight in particular is how class gets connected to particular ways of being, and how the demand to rise can cause one to hate those parts of self that are connected to the practices of what is deemed to be the inferior class (Layton, 2004c/2006). That self-hatred, and the connected sense that we are only loved when we enact certain "proper" ways of being, can cause us to try to distance ourselves from important parts of who we are and project those hated parts onto other people and groups. When, as in neoliberalism, vulnerable and dependent states are considered shameful, they are likely to become "not-me," other, associated with those others who are lower on the social scale (see Silva, 2013, whose interviews with white and non-white working-class young adults reveal how the class wounds caused by neoliberalism in fact create neoliberal subjects who draw sharp boundaries against those perceived as "other").

The psychic effects of neoliberalism on the white middle and upper middle class are in some ways different and in some ways similar to the experiences of Sandy and Paul. While Sandy's and Paul's parents demanded that their children rise in class, white middle-class parents, since the 90s, have become anxious about remaining middle class; seeing economic precariousness all around them, they harbor a fear of falling into a lower class (Ehrenreich, 1989). Their fear has led many of them to embrace neoliberal ideas about maximizing self-interest. In the early 1990s, long before I had ever heard the word "neoliberalism," I came upon a magazine cover I only later understood to be a horrifying example of the way neoliberal economic calculations have penetrated into the everyday life of the white middle class: a large picture of a baby was accompanied by a caption that read "Is Having Children Cost-Effective?" In neoliberalism, every aspect of private life is, as Read (2009) says, "charted according to a calculus of maximum output for minimum expenditure; [everything] can be seen as an investment" (p. 31). Many of my middle and upper-middle-class patients talk about maximizing effectiveness and optimizing just about everything. Most of them seem to feel a sense of virtue when they run themselves ragged, and a sense of shame and anxiety about just sitting around and experiencing what we used to call "downtime." When achievement is experienced as a demand for manic activity (Peltz, 2006), downtime – the split-off alternative – is experienced as shameful laziness.

There is a growing literature that focuses on the vast amount of work that middle-class parents, particularly mothers, currently put into assuring that their children get ahead and stay ahead in the world (what Lareau, 2003, has called 'concerted cultivation' – see, for example, Reay, Crozier, & James, 2011). A stark example of how practices of concerted cultivation embed within them an ideology of what it means to be a proper and successful human being appeared in an episode of the sketch comedy *Portlandia*, titled "Grover." A pre-school boy, Grover (his parents point out from the start that they have trademarked his name) sits at a kitchen counter as his parents try to engage him in understanding how important it is that he do well at his upcoming private pre-school interview. Holding up a flip-chart that shows the trajectory that follows getting into the pre-school, the parents first point to a symbol denoting Ivy League colleges; then, asking him if he can spell Ferrari, they point to a picture of the car he'll drive if he gets into the pre-school. As a cautionary tale, they then put up a flip-chart denoting failure: the commentary here is replete with denigrating comments about the lower-class children with whom Grover would be consorting in public school (the first icon is public school, figured as a prison), the dumb kids he'll be subject to in community college, and the guns and drugs that will lead to jail or to a life of shooting birds and squirrels for dinner. The crowning touch of the satire is when the father says, after one of his contemptuous comments about the lower classes: "Never judge." Grover, meanwhile, knows he is supposed to like the first flip-chart a lot better than the second one, and yet, with each new close-up of his face, we find him looking increasingly bewildered and depressed.

The demand to be an entrepreneurial self is conveyed not only by parents but also by other agents of the middle class as well. A former student who is now in her early 30s told me that in her upper-middle-class elementary school, lessons were taught that were designed to humiliate the children into striving for upward mobility: in 5th grade, one of her teachers asked his students where their parents had gone to college. As each child responded, it became clear that the predominant answers were Ivy League and elite schools. "Well," he concluded, "none of you is going to any of these schools because you don't work hard enough. You won't get your first choice." My student remembers that from that time forth she anxiously repeated to herself the mantra: "I must have my first choice, I must have my first choice." You can almost taste the invitation to a split state of grandiosity and feelings of low self-worth, and, indeed, this student suffered from depressions that had at their core a questioning of what she was doing, and for whom.

Sadistic and dissociative large-group responses to neoliberalism

Binkley (2009, 2011a, 2011b, 2014) and other Foucauldian theorists focus on neoliberal subjective practices that demand a shift from comfort with dependence to repudiation of dependence. In a psychoanalytic frame, however, which recognizes no possibility (or desirability) of overcoming dependence, the task is to comprehend the psychic effects of a cultural lack of attunement to dependency needs and a cultural encouragement to split off and project dependency needs and vulnerability – effects like intense shame about dependence and omnipotent versions of autonomy. Thinking along these lines, it seems to me that there have been two dominant large-group reactions to the changes wrought by neoliberalism, globalization, and then the attacks of 9/11. Beginning in the 1970s, social conservatives, largely white, launched retaliatory movements against the most vulnerable populations – gays, minorities, the poor, and women. Here, vulnerability and dependence are projected onto groups lower on the social scale. And yet, as on the individual level, I would argue that in groups, too, the split of vulnerable feelings continues to be held very near – for example, in the anti-abortion movement, the fetus holds all the vulnerability that its defenders cannot bear to hold.

Among privileged liberals the more prevalent reaction has been withdrawal from the public sphere. John Rodger (2003) described this withdrawal with the term "amoral familism," a retreat into an individualistic private sphere and a tendency to extend care only to those in one's family and immediate intimate circle.[1] The withdrawal response suggests that, at least unconsciously, the mainstream population does not want its privilege and its fantasy of American exceptionalism disturbed by awareness of their consequences. Those of us who were able to do so sought refuge from an increasing sense of precariousness and vulnerability in identifications that psychically distance us from more vulnerable populations. Over the past 40 years, empathy has become defined in such a way as to allow the privileged to feel distant and other from less privileged and suffering groups – obscuring recognition of our interdependence with vulnerable and dependent populations (Layton, 2006, 2009, 2010).

Whether on the individual or large-group level, retaliation and withdrawal are two typical reactions to trauma, reactions that reproduce trauma. I understand these large-group reactions in part to be responses to failures of accountability and responsibility in both the public and private spheres. There are countless ways that corporations and government have refused to be accountable for the inequalities they create and sustain by law and public policy.[2] The effects are everywhere. For example, Scanlon and Adlam (2013), clinicians who consult to caregivers of vulnerable populations, describe the vicious circle in which a lack of governmental accountability for poverty and social inequalities leads to situations in which privileged groups unknowingly inflict harm on those less privileged. The circle begins with neoliberal policies that create categories of people, like the homeless, who are socially excluded, pathologized, criminalized, and not deemed proper citizens. Caregivers tend to ignore or be unaware of the effect of these prior processes of social exclusion, and they often do not recognize the way neoliberal conceptions of subjectivity are embedded in their very caregiving practices (e.g., a rational actor theory that makes individuals responsible for their problems). Thus, their caring efforts are often met with hostility or indifference. The caretakers, who experience themselves only as giving something good, become enraged or disengaged, completing a vicious circle of sadomasochistic relating.

Friends who are educators familiar with failing inner city schools tell of another such vicious circle. This one begins in a neoliberal refusal to take responsibility for poverty levels not seen since before the 1960s War on Poverty. Instead of addressing poverty, recent policies hold teachers in inner city schools accountable for the poor performance of their students on high-stakes tests. In some inner city neighborhoods, very high percentages of students have witnessed or experienced violence. Poverty and violence can severely damage the capacity to learn. What these kids need, my friends asserted, is a safe environment that fosters creativity and a capacity to think (Archangelo, 2010, 2014). What they get instead is a sadistic regimen of teaching to the test, from teachers who themselves face punishment for not improving scores.

The perverse nature of such interactions seems to me to be endemic to neoliberalism (Layton, 2010). Perversion rests on the defense of disavowal and a form of lying. Freud (1937) wrote that when a perceived truth is too painful to take in, we substitute a more pleasurable or less painful lie. Bion (1962a, 1962b, 1970) elaborated on this insight, in part by distinguishing between suffering pain and feeling pain. Bion argued that when we are unable to suffer unbearable pain, we often inflict pain on ourselves, pain that is more under our control (Abel-Hirsch, 2006). One way of thinking about perverse states marked by domination and submission is to see them in part as a painful outcome of government and corporate abandonment, an outcome that we have refused to or been unable to suffer. When we can no longer rely on government and other public institutions to attend to our vulnerable, needy, and frightened selves, when we buy into the idea that the entrepreneurial self is the best self, we tend to go back and forth between a fantasy that we do not need anyone or anything outside the self, the omnipotent solution, and a fantasy that we will be loved and taken care of without having to make any effort, the helpless solution (Layton, 2010; for an elaboration of investments in neoliberal fantasies, see Glynos, 2014a, 2014b). The retaliation and withdrawal responses to the traumas of neoliberal governance are based in disavowal, and they are paralleled by an oscillation between these two fantasies.

Neoliberal subjectivity in the clinic

In 2011, I commented on a 1974 article by Lawrence Kubie. Kubie's clinical vignettes starkly demonstrated the way heterosexist ideologies of the

1950s and beyond were reproduced in clinical interpretations that, for example, pathologized female patients' wishes both to have a career and have children. Kubie diagnosed such wishes as a pathological drive to become both sexes. It was easy to express outrage at what analysts were doing back then to "normalize" their patients. It made me more uneasy, however, to contemplate what kind of collusions with today's social norms I myself might be performing in the clinic. Theorists of neoliberalism assert that the agenda of all different kinds of contemporary psychological practices is to create enterprising subjects in all classes, races, genders, and sexualities, subjects that reject collectivist moral values and instead embrace self-care and maximization of self-interest. Looking at self-help books, the field of coaching, and positive psychology, Binkley (2009, 2011a, 2011b, 2014) has identified some of the practices that experts encourage people to adopt to be successful, "enterprising" selves. Subjects, he found, are dissuaded from introspecting, dwelling on problems, putting their experience in a relational context, or looking into the past to understand the present; rather, they are exhorted to be forward-looking, optimistic, to set goals to maximize what is in their self-interest.

Psychoanalysts do not adhere to this agenda. They know that when dependency and vulnerability are denied, the self becomes fragile and relations to others become sadomasochistic. And yet, psychoanalysts, too, can fall prey to the neoliberal agenda. Two brief clinical vignettes illustrate how neoliberalizing processes can unconsciously enter the clinic and how hard it is for a therapist to resist colluding with these processes.

Vignette #1

No matter what class they come from, many of my patients are conflicted about what they are entitled to have. When they get something good, they often feel guilty about it, in some cases feeling they have coerced the other into giving it. A middle-class patient of mine had, at an early age, become ashamed of what she felt family members condemned as too much desire for attention. When I began seeing her, she was in fact quite constricted. Sometime during our work together I moved into a home office, which I had decorated in higher style than the office I had been renting. In our first meeting in the new office, the theme of entitlement and selfishness arose. The patient spoke about having just read Barbara Ehrenreich's (2001) book, *Nickel and Dimed*, and said she felt guilty and indulgent about having hired a maid for the first time. I said: "It's hard to acknowledge that you're privileged." She agreed and held out her hands to show me her nails, which she had recently had done in clear polish. She said, "I get my nails done, I have a therapist in Brookline in a place like this." My own privilege having been invoked, I think I felt anxious and did not know what to do with the guilt over privilege, hers, mine, ours. I remember having tried to normalize the privilege, saying something like, "You don't have to feel guilty for having nice things." I think this comment closed down something the patient was trying to say, something that went against the neoliberal grain because it attempted to connect her fortune to the misfortune of others. My first comment kept the question of privilege open; the second one closed it down. Of course we need to understand the patient's tendency to self-denial and guilt over wanting a better life, but I think there was also something significant to explore about our mutual discomfort about our privilege and its connection to the lack of privilege all around us. I'm suggesting that normalizing privilege is perhaps a neoliberalizing practice; it is a challenge to keep the fact of our privilege alive in our thoughts and feelings, not to close it down with either guilt or entitlement. We clinicians help our patients individuate; can we at the same time keep alive the question of what it means to be a citizen?

Vignette #2

A colleague presented a very familiar-sounding case in which a middle-class college student performed to perfection in one semester only to collapse into so much binging, purging, and alcohol abuse in the second semester that she could not complete any work and would find herself on the verge of expulsion. The student attempted to comply with parental and cultural demands to be an enterprising self but continued to fall sick from the attempt, rebelling in self-annihilating but powerfully signifying refusals. The therapist felt pulled to help

(continued)

(continued)

the student complete her work, a very understandable reaction given the student's apparent panic about not getting her work done. But I think such a pull entails an unconscious collusion with the perverse pole of non-caretaking and self-sufficient omnipotence to which so many of us, patients and therapists alike, have submitted ourselves in this neoliberal age. I think we need to see as symptomatic not only the patient's alcohol abuse and binging, but also the demand on the patient to achieve, a demand that, in most cases, is just accepted as normal. I think we need to help the patient look not only at the obviously self-destructive symptoms but also at her feelings about the demand to be an enterprising self. If we do not, we unconsciously contribute to sustaining the idea that such pressures for performance are normal (I have referred to such unconscious collusions as examples of normative unconscious processes, Layton, 2013a).

The more our current income inequality becomes entrenched and the more the measure of what it means to be a "proper" human rests on economic success, and the less government and business provide in the way of a safety net, the more anxiety about achievement we will find among those in the culture who have any hope of "making it." Such anxiety promotes dissociations between the privileged and the socially excluded others, on whose backs the privilege is sustained. It creates relations to power and powerlessness, marked by the oscillations between grandiosity and self-deprecation, characteristic of problems in self-esteem regulation – and thus to relational scenarios, in both individuals and large groups, of domination and submission.

Conclusion

In conclusion, I would suggest that arguments that blame the population for their greed and omnipotence (or argue that greed and omnipotence are "human nature") perhaps capture the appearance of what is happening culturally. In overlooking the fragility and vulnerability against which current forms of greed, grandiosity, and omnipotence defend, however, they do not offer solutions to our individual and cultural problems. Neoliberalism (along with the neoconservatism that marks the drive to Empire in the US) is primary to the production of various forms of vulnerability-denying grandiosity, and both movements are marked by ideological and policy assaults on dependency and interdependence. The Occupy movements finally brought attention to the shameful disparity between the 1% and the 99% in the US; I hope here to have illustrated a bit of the psychic fallout and problematic power dynamics spawned by increasing income inequality and the ensuing damage both to the self and to relations with others.

Notes

1 Very popular television shows like *The Sopranos* and, more recently, *Breaking Bad*, normalize amoral familism: their main protagonists wreak havoc on the general public while inhabiting, in their minds, the role of breadwinning family man. Until the final episode of *Breaking Bad*, Walter White claimed that his sole motivation in building his drug empire was to provide for the family.
2 One particularly egregious example is documented in Epstein (2013). Reviewing Markowitz and Rosner's 2013 book, *Lead Wars: The Politics of Science and the Fate of America's Children*, Epstein chronicles the way that the disastrous effects of lead paint on toddlers, effects known since the 1920s, were ignored in a 1990s Baltimore study that offered research subjects with toddlers, who had moved into apartments with lead paint, two forms of lead abatement known not to be effective. Although interior lead paint was finally banned in the US in the 1970s (many other countries banned it in the 20s and 30s), Epstein reports that, from the 20s onwards, the U.S. government repeatedly and knowingly supported industry interests over the welfare of children.

References

Abel-Hirsch, N. (2006). The perversion of pain, pleasure and thought: On the difference between "suffering" an experience and the construction of a thing to be used. In D. Nobus & L. Downing (Eds.), *Perversion: Psychoanalytic perspectives/perspectives on psychoanalysis*. (pp. 99–107). London: Karnac.
Alexander, M. (2010). *The new Jim Crow: Mass incarceration in the age of colorblindness*. New York: The New Press.
Archangelo, A. (2010). Social exclusion, difficulties with learning and symbol formation: A Bionian approach. *Psychoanalysis, Culture and Society, 13,* 315–327.
Archangelo, A. (2014). A psychosocial approach to neoliberalism, social exclusion and education. *Psychoanalysis, Culture and Society, 19*(1).
Binkley, S. (2009). The work of neoliberal governmentality: Temporality and ethical substance in the tale of two dads. *Foucault Studies, 6,* 60–78.
Binkley, S. (2011a). Psychological life as enterprise: Social practice and the government of neo- liberal interiority. *History of the Human Sciences, 24*(3), 83–102.
Binkley, S. (2011b). Happiness, positive psychology and the program of neoliberal governmentality. *Subjectivity, 4*(4), 371–394.
Binkley, S. (2014). *Happiness as enterprise: An essay on neoliberal life*. Albany, New York: SUNY Press.
Bion, W.R. (1962a). *Learning from experience*. Northvale, NJ: Jason Aronson.

Bion, W.R. (1962b). The psycho-analytic study of thinking. *International Journal of Psychoanalysis, 43*, 306–310.

Bion, W.R. (1970). *Attention and interpretation.* London: Karnac.

Brown, W. (2006). American nightmare: Neoliberalism, neoconservatism, and de-democratization. *Political Theory, 34*, 690–714.

du Gay, P. (2004). Against "enterprise" (but not against "enterprise", for that would make no sense). *Organization, 11*, 37–57.

Ehrenreich, B. (1989). *Fear of falling: The inner life of the middle class.* New York: Pantheon.

Ehrenreich, B. (2001). *Nickel and dimed.* New York: Henry Holt.

Epstein, H. (2013, March 21). Lead poisoning: The ignored scandal. *The New York Review of Books.* Retrieved from www.nybooks.com/articles/archives/2013/mar/21/lead-poisoning- ignored-scandal/

Freud, S. (1937). Analysis terminable and interminable. *Standard Edition, 23*, 209–253.

Glynos, J. (2014a). Neoliberalism, markets, fantasy: the case of health and social care. *Psychoanalysis, Culture and Society, 19*(1).

Glynos, J. (2014b). Hating government and voting against one's interests. Self-transgression, enjoyment, critique. *Psychoanalysis, Culture and Society, 19*(1).

Hamann, T. (2009). Neoliberalism, governmentality, and ethics. *Foucault Studies, 6*, 37–59.

Harvey, D. (2005). *A brief history of neoliberalism.* Oxford: Oxford University Press.

Krugman, P. (2002, October 20). For richer. *The New York Times Magazine.* Retrieved from www.ssc.wisc.edu/~scholz/Teaching_441/Richer.pdf

Kubie, L. (1974). The drive to become both sexes. *Psychoanalytic Quarterly, 43*, 349–426.

Lareau, A. (2003). *Unequal childhoods: Class, race, and family life.* Berkeley, CA: University of California Press.

Layton, L. (2004a). Working nine to nine: The new women of prime time. *Studies in Gender and Sexuality, 5*, 351–369.

Layton, L. (2004b). Relational no more: Defensive autonomy in middle-class women. In J. A. Winer & J.W. Anderson (Eds.), *The annual of psychoanalysis, 32*, 29–57. Hillsdale, NJ: The Analytic Press.

Layton, L. (2004c/2006). That place gives me the heebie jeebies. *Critical Psychology, 10*, 36–50. Reprinted in L. Layton, N.C. Hollander, & S. Gutwill (Eds.), *Psychoanalysis, class and politics: Encounters in the clinical setting.* New York: Routledge.

Layton, L. (2006). Retaliatory discourse: The politics of attack and withdrawal. *International Journal of Applied Psychoanalytic Studies, 3*(2), 143–155.

Layton, L. (2009). Who's responsible? Our mutual implication in each other's suffering. *Psychoanalytic Dialogues 19*, 105–120.

Layton, L. (2010). Irrational exuberance: Neoliberalism and the perversion of truth. *Subjectivity 3*(3), 303–322.

Layton, L. (2011). On the irreconcilable in psychic life: The role of culture in the drive to become both sexes. *Psychoanalytic Quarterly, 80*(2), 461–474.

Layton, L. (2013a). Normative unconscious processes. In T. Teo (Ed.), *Encyclopedia of critical psychology.* Retrieved from www.springerreference.com/docs/html/chapterdbid/307088.html

Layton, L. (2014a). Grandiosity, neoliberalism, and neoconservatism. *Psychoanalytic Inquiry, 34*(5), 463–474.

Layton, L. (2014b). Some psychic effects of neoliberalism: Narcissism, disavowal, perversion. *Psychoanalysis, Culture & Society, 19*(2), 161–178.

Peck, J., & Tickell, A. (2002). Neoliberalizing space. *Antipode, 34*(3), 380–404.

Peltz, R. (2006). The manic society. In L. Layton, N.C. Hollander, & S. Gutwill (Eds.), *Psychoanalysis, class and politics: Encounters in the clinical setting* (pp. 65–80). New York: Routledge.

Read, J. (2009). A genealogy of homo-economicus: Neoliberalism and the production of subjectivity. *Foucault Studies, 6*, 25–36.

Reay, D., Crozier, G., & James, D. (2011). *White middle-class identities and urban schooling*. Basingstoke: Palgrave Macmillan.

Rodger, J. (2003). Social solidarity, welfare and post-emotionalism. *Journal of Social Policy, 32*(3), 403–421.

Scanlon, C., & Adlam, J. (2013). Reflexive violence. *Psychoanalysis, Culture & Society, 18*(3), 223–241.

Silva, J.M. (2013). *Coming up short: Working-class adulthood in an age of uncertainty.* New York: Oxford University Press.

Wacquant, L. (2001). Deadly symbiosis: When ghetto and prison meet and mesh. *Punishment and Society, 3*(1), 95–134.

Chapter 6

Psychoanalysis in neoliberal times – a renewed dialogue with madness

Response to Lynne Layton

Sam Binkley

In what follows, I would like to present a critical response to the question of the contemporary role of psychoanalysis in the context of a broad set of cultural, social and economic transformations often grouped together under the rubric of neoliberalism. Considering some of the central questions brought up in Professor Layton's "Yale or jail: Class struggles in neoliberal times," I would like to pose some questions that emerge from the field of thought in which I spend much of my time, which has to do with the critical and theoretical legacy of Michel Foucault, and specifically, the rethinking of psychological discourses and practices that Foucault variously attempted in his own work (Binkley, 2014).

Specter of dependency

Let me first begin, then, by drawing out what I take to the be thrust of Professor Layton's chapter, which concerns the underlying emotional and psychological state, the desires, fears and anxieties that characterize a certain new kind of person – the subject of neoliberalism. With sensitivity and insight, Professor Layton describes what she terms the "psychic effects of neoliberalism on middle and upper middle-class whites" in a series of clinical portraits. These persons are quite interesting and unique for many reasons, not the least of which is the distinctive psychological dispositions they embody. These are subjects whose principal struggle is not, as is the case with classical psychoanalysis, the encounter with neuroses, persecutorial super-egos, residual guilt and sublimated or unrecognized desires. These problems, which preoccupied psychoanalysis since Freud, positioned the subject relationally, within a set of social attachments, however sublimated or concealed, which, it was believed, continued to play out under the surface of a seemingly individuated existence, and whose apprehension through therapy might resolve psychic conflicts in the indi-viduated self. For the subject of neoliberalism, however, the terms are reversed. It is instead the effort to sublimate the fact of dependency and relationality itself that defines the aim of a different therapeutic endeavor. As subjects of neoliberal discourse, the specter of dependency presents an affront to an idealized ego state, one which champions the strategizing, calculating disposition of a pure, sovereign subject, here inflated to the state of immense power. For the neoliberal subject, dependence on others is supplanted by a defensively overblown fixation on the autonomy and grandiosity of the subject herself, one that is so ensconced in neoliberal affirmations of her own authority as to be no longer able to come to terms in any meaningful way with her own implicitly social character.

Yet this is also a subject that is indirectly aware of the fragility and constructedness, and in a sense the disingenuous quality, of her own self-image. The disavowal of dependence, and the vulnerabilities it implies, often takes the form of a certain rage and contempt that moves in two directions. First there is an aggressive response, even rage against the other upon whom one depends, and upon oneself for expressing such dependence. But there is also an aggression directed against the other for the other's dependencies on the neoliberal subject herself. Where the other suffers structural disadvantage viewed through the lens of race or class, and where it is sensed that this disadvantage is what ultimately structures, in an undeclared way, the much-vaunted autonomy of the neoliberal sub-ject herself (transformed, as if by a certain social alchemy, into the unique qualities such a subject is believed to possess), the rage becomes all the more intense for the obfuscations it must manage. In other words, what seems to operate at the center of all of this is a sense of shame at the impossibility of the actual realization of neoliberalism's individualizing imperative, here transformed into rage and self-recrimination, directed against the dependency of the self upon others and against the dependency of others upon the self.

Given these circumstances, the therapeutic endeavor of the psychoana-lyst is clear. It is to bring about a recognition, a recuperation or a dialogue of sorts, with precisely that term that is displaced in the production of the stable, neoliberal subject – her sense of sublimated dependency. In other words, the dependencies we forge with others and that others forge with us are drawn out in the course of analysis. Social needs are made to speak, so as to quell the rage and ameliorate the guilt, and to render, in a sense, a sort of psychoanalytic cure. The voice of this dependency is precisely the other voice that psychoanalysis seeks to bring to articulation – it stands in for what Foucault (2006) called a "dialogue with madness," that is the implicit aim not only of psychoanalysis but of the psychological sciences that predate Freud's interventions. And of course, this concoction of rage and shame is not limited to the private rooms of psychoanalysis. One has only to Google "Obamacare + Fox News" to uncover its popular expression, mixed with a seething contempt for the inevitably dependent character of our own subjectivities. Try as we may, this dependence is one we cannot transcend, despite our most vigorous efforts.

A Foucauldian intervention

So what might a Foucauldian intervention into this program entail, and what might be its objectives? Let me begin by setting to rest what might be the anxieties that such a provocation might induce in any psychoanalyst who is told that her work is to be engaged from a Foucauldian perspective. In a very general and perhaps naïve sense, Foucault is often read as a critic of the psychoanalytic enterprise *tout court* – a stance he shaped for himself first with his criticism of the normalizing effects of the psychological sciences in *History of Madness* (2006), and later in his lectures of 1973, translated as *Power of Psychiatry*, and again, a third time, in his treatment of the "repressive hypothesis" in the first volume of *The History of Sexuality* (1976). In all cases, it is possible to interpret his engagements as hostile, as linking the endeavor to understand any effort, to interpret the inner movements of the psyche, and to induce the psychoanalytic subject to speak on behalf of these movements as a fundamentally disciplinary operation. According to a certain naïve Foucauldianism, psychoanalysis is a power that regulates, domesticates and conspires against other potentials of the subject by returning her to a set of inevitable and inescapable determinations. But this would be to mistake Foucault's historicization of psychoanalysis and the psychological enterprise to a total critique of its function. Missing from this account is the manner in which Foucault frequently called upon psychoanalysis as a counter strategy to these very tendencies, which are implicated in the more normatively laden fields of positive psychiatry. As Foucault (1994) wrote of psychoanalysis in *The Order of Things*, psychoanalysis has the potential to "traverse, animate, and disturb the whole constituted field of the human science . . . it would form the most general contestation of that field . . . threatening the very things that made it possible for man to be known" (p. 381).

This double function of psychoanalysis is precisely what Jacques Derrida (1994) meant to draw out when he wrote of Foucault's relationship with Freud that it resembled precisely the fort/da game itself. Just as Freud's 18-month-old grandson famously explored the dynamics of presence and absence by casting with a wooden toy on a string from the edge of his crib, pronouncing it gone (fort!) only to retrieve it a moment later with the exclamation "there" (da!), so Foucault, Derrida alleges, worked through his relationship with Freud, alternately banishing him to a function of power only to resurrect him as an agent of critique. Freud was for Foucault a hinge, a pivot that served alternately to impose a mechanism of control, but also to interrogate and subvert all such schemes. Psychoanalysis alternately inscribed a field of madness as the "unreasonable" object of a bona fide science, but also activated and opened up a dialogue with that field – a realm of "unreason" that was madness itself. What I am most interested in here, and what I think is more relevant to Professor Layton's approach, is the function of psychoanalysis, not as disciplinary technology but as counter-science, one that cuts against the hegemonic discourse of neoliberalism itself. And to get at that counter-hegemonic potential, it is worth spending another moment with Foucault, and with his reflection on the psychological professions as fundamentally social in character.

Foucault and the "psy" discourses

Psychoanalysis draws from a broad tradition of scientific, disciplinary and institutional discourse, which sought to inscribe in the very heart of the subjectivity of modern persons an irreducibly social character, a complex of agonistic relations, loosely derived from the family. An inquiry into the inner working of this subject already cuts against the grain of a neoliberal culture that strains to collapse this relational quality into pure opportunism, imposing instead the sovereignty of an entrepreneurial, self-interested individual. Thus, psychoanalysis already contains the kernel of something oppositional, something that seeks to break down a certain subject, to "desubjectify," in Foucauldian parlance. And this is a tendency evident in the dialogue Professor Layton opens up with her subjects. Now let me demonstrate this point in greater detail.

The social character of what Foucault (2003) called the "psy" discourses derives from the original functionality of the psychological professions, operating as an instrument of social regulation in the hands of nascent welfare states. In short, in the hands of early psychiatry, the family becomes the pin or the pivot, by which individuals are produced for their fit with disciplinary institutions – for cooperation, reciprocity and dependence on others. Indeed, dependency of sorts was at the heart of the disciplining objectives of psychology: in the name of social cohesion, the family was operationalized as a cell of interpersonal relations, one that could serve as a hinge, integrating the subject with others in society through the interpretation and manipulation of a deep psychic interiority – the inner residue of intra-familial relations itself. Foucault (2003) describes the "psy-function," a phrase he developed in his lecture course of the early 1970s, *Psychiatric Power*, to describe this effect. Within this function, the family is the place to which dysfunctional or abnormal individuals are sent when they are no longer able to serve within disciplinary institutions, owing to some psychological event of some sort. The family was the place, it was hoped, that such individuals could receive characterological rehabilitation to be readied once again for reintegration into the apparatuses of work, school, military service and the like. But the family was also the place from which individuals could shape a heuristic narrative of characterological development that could be called upon for corrective purposes. Foucault (2003) describes the method adopted in one asylum in Mettray, in which attendants reconstituted a "pseudo-family organization" (p. 108), adopting the names of father, elder brother and so on in the hopes of bringing about the cure that only the family could produce. This was a program of clinical treatment patterned on the interpersonal relations of family life with collective meals and the like. It is through this operation that a unique psychological interiority organized on the model of the family became a chief instrument of social government. The family motif was a technology for the fostering of a subject, examined and exercised for his capacity to integrate himself into a normative social order of a disciplinary society, with the capacity to relate productively to others at its center.

Given this, how, then, does the social character of psychoanalysis play out against the backdrop of contemporary neoliberalism and its inducements to enterprising subjectivity? Professor Layton has already acquainted us with the elements of neoliberal thought and policy, but let us take this a step further, and consider precisely what we mean by the neoliberal subject, understood in the light of Foucault's treatment of this question.

Governmentality and human capital

Neoliberalism, in contemporary Foucault scholarship, is frequently tied to the notion of self-government, or as Foucault (1991, 2008) famously invoked in one of his niftier neologisms, neoliberal governmentality. And at the heart of this neoliberal governmentality is the injunction not to sublimate one's drives or to sacrifice at the altar of civilization one's desires and attractions, but to cultivate one's capacities, to produce oneself as a unique presence within a field of competitive market actors. Neoliberal subjects look upon life as a competitive field emancipated from cumbersome social commitments and limiting social loyalties. No social contract, much less one mediated by the welfare state, imposes an obliging restriction upon us. Everything, including one's own mind, body, psychological state and interpersonal disposition, is a resource, a potentiality to be mobilized and leveraged for strategic advantage in a competitive market. Thus, neoliberal governmentality sets oneself to work not in the sublimation of complex and conflictual psychodynamic drives, but in the production of one's capacities, one's "human capital" as the bearer of unique differences that make one stand out from others (Foucault, 2008).

   In short, for the subject of neoliberalism, the very assumptions upon which psychoanalysis operate (that we are inextricably bound to others through desire and dependence) is anathema to the production of the enterprising self. The subject it proposes, the subject of interpersonal relations, mutuality and dependency, is precisely the subject neoliberal discourses instruct us to loathe and fear. A subject whose most inward experiences are premised on an internalized relation to others chafes against the imperatives to self-interest, self-optimization and calculated self-interest that are the kernel of neoliberal subjectivity itself. And it is by this token that psychoanalysis, and Professor Layton's psychoanalytic research itself, assumes its counter-hegemonic significance, its counter-science in an age of neoliberalism. This sociality, which once might have been a normalizing anchor in a social welfarist psychology of conformity, has now become a counterpoint to the dominant discourse of the enterprising individual. Psychoanalysis's intra-psychic dialogue fashioned on the model of the family now becomes a counter-hegemonic gesture, reminding us of our intrinsically social make-up. Psychoanalysis brings us back to the dependencies upon others, internalized as ongoing intra-psychic dialogues that are prohibited by the enterprising self. By inscribing the dynamism of relations between psychic agents at the core of the self, one fashioned on the family and its relations, the counter-scientific character of psychoanalysis assumes a new form in neoliberal times. The dialogue with madness that psychoanalysis opens up, in such times, is a dialogue with this fundamental sociality whose suppression occasions such rage, contempt, guilt and acrimony in our world today. Such psychoanalytic methodologies amount to a desubjectification of neoliberalism's subjectivizing effects.

References

Binkley, S. (2014). *Happiness as enterprise: An essay on neoliberal life.* Ithaca: SUNY Press.

Derrida, J. (1994). To do justice to Freud: The history of madness in the age of psychoanalysis. *Critical Inquiry, 20*(2), 227–266.

Foucault, M. (1965). *Madness and civilization: A history of insanity in the age of reason,* trans. R. Howard. London: Tavistock.

Foucault, M. (1976). *The history of sexuality, volume 1: The will to knowledge.* Paris: Gallimard.

Foucault, M. (1991). Governmentality. In C. Gordon & P. Miller (Eds.), *The Foucault effect: Studies in governmentality* (pp. 87–104). Chicago: University of Chicago Press.

Foucault, M. (1994). *The order of things.* New York: Vintage Books.

Foucault, M. (2003). *Psychiatric power: Lectures at the College De France 1973–1974.* New York: Picador.

Foucault, M. (2006). *History of madness.* New York: Routledge.

Foucault, M. (2008). *Birth of biopolitics: Lectures at the College De France 1978–1979.* New York: Picador.

Chapter 7

The complications of caring and the ethical turn in psychoanalysis

Elizabeth Corpt

Levinas (1969) uses the metaphor of opening the door as a way to capture what he calls our infinite responsibility to the other. He accompanies this hospitable gesture with the words "après vous" – after you – a linguistic acknowledgement of the other's overarching command that I care for him above me, a command not uttered directly but proclaimed by his very existence. Levinas's point is that the other person makes me aware of the fact that I am never apart from subjectivity. The other is always first. I am called to open the door to the "widow, the orphan, and the stranger". I use this metaphor as a stepping-off point from which to explore the complications of caring within a psychoanalytically informed relationship. Orange's (2010, 2011) recent attention to the ethical turn in psychoanalysis, the clinician's responsibility to the *suffering stranger*, and the relevance of thinkers such as Levinas to that turn challenge us to consider the ethical implications of our therapeutic care taking. In fact, for Levinas (1999), "to perceive that we come after an other whoever he may be – that is ethics" (p. 167). This radical ethics presents a particular challenge to the psychoanalytic practitioner who is obligated, by one's practice ethics, to continually plumb the depths of her own subjectivity to be fully present for the other.

Who, then, comes first? What does it mean to be infinitely responsible to one's patient whose developmentally younger self longs to be completely cared for as she had never been as a child? To push the 'après vous' further, how does one know when it is ethically more responsible to open a door, close it, or wait to reflect upon one's decision before speaking or taking action with a patient in our care? What does it mean and how does it feel for the therapist to cause a patient to suffer in the moment for potentially greater gains down the road? On what relationally ethical ground do we stand when we need to make a clinical judgment call? My intention is to address some of these challenges in what I am calling the complications of caring.

The ethics of care

The notion of the ethical turn is not original to psychoanalysis; it was introduced and influenced by Levinas, Gadamer, Derrida, and other post-modern thinkers. This movement has been rippling across many fields of study and practice since the 1970s, spawning serious academic considera-tion. In fact, psychoanalysis is arriving rather late to this discussion. But now, thanks to Orange (2010, 2011), Frie (2000, 2012), Shabad (2006, 2010), Riker (2010), Foehl (2010, 2011), Rozmarin (2007), and others, willing and able to take on the rigors of this particular philosophical chal-lenge, we are beginning to address what the ethical turn means for us. We can explore how it is lived, or not lived, in our everyday practice habits, our ways of being with our patients, and our ways of theorizing. Other philosophical discourses have impacted contemporary psychoanalytic dis-course: Hegel's influence on Benjamin (1990), for one. But this particular psychoanalytic discourse presents a unique challenge to the psychoanalytic clinician in that it calls forth a kind of ethical responsibility for care and a plea for vulnerability not typical to psychoanalytically informed practice.

All psychotherapeutic relationships are composed of forms and degrees of care that must be thoughtfully reflected upon and titrated with respect to the needs of each patient; elsewhere I have referred to this as a form of clinical generosity (Corpt, 2011b). Clinical generosity infers both the eve-ryday extension of the analyst's full emotional and intellectual resources and technical skill, and when necessary and appropriate, something beyond the usual and customary: a potentiality for a kind of care-full responsive-ness that may, at times, challenge the analyst's restraint, psychic comfort zone, or usual modes of relating. But to more fully explore the nature of care in psychotherapeutic practice, I first want to establish a link between the ethical turn and the previously well-articulated feminist ethics of care: a link that has been overlooked in our literature but will allow us to con-sider the ethical turn in and its relevance to therapeutic care.

The feminist ethics of care, first articulated in the 1970s and 80s, has since moved beyond its original gender binaries into a more universal care ethic (Held, 2005; Williams, 2001). But for my purposes, I want to retrieve something of the original spirit of these ideas that, at the time, was meant to give voice to the silent maternal subject whose subjectivity was seen as subsumed under the caring of others. By doing so, what I intend to capture here is something of the fate of the therapist's subjectivity as it responds to this ethical responsibility and care of her patient. What impact does this have on the analytic couple? Are both care giving and care receiving burdensome? How do mothers, therapists, or patients cope with the complexities of giving and receiving care?

Hollway (2006), in her book *The Capacity to Care: Gender and Ethical Subjectivity*, states that ethics "is another way of talking about the capacity to care" (p. 101). Her exploration begins with the feminist ethics of care (Gilligan, 1982; Noddings, 1984) and its beginnings as an exploration of maternal care practices. In doing so, she touches on the work of Simone de Beauvoir (1949/1972), Carol Gilligan (1982), Nancy Chodorow (1978), Sara Ruddick (1989), Joan Tronto (1993), and others, locating the capacity to care in early mother-infant and familial, particularly male-female, relations. The brevity of this chapter does not allow for a fuller explanation of the feminist ethics of care, a rich body of literature in and of itself, but some of its key aspects are as follows: feminist care ethics are more practice-oriented than theory-based. They are about what is moral in human relationships; caretaking is defined as an ethical practice (Gilligan, 1982). They encompass the wellbeing and experiences of the entire caretaking network (Tronto, 1993), both caretaker and care-receiver. Deeply humanist in orientation, they respect human vulnerability and dependency needs. In general, they assert a feminine voice of care as an equally legitimate alternative to the male-dominated justice perspective. Nell Noddings (1984), an instrumental feminist thinker, asserted early on that "the more natural and, perhaps, stronger approach would be through Eros, the feminine spirit. . . . It is feminine in the deep classical sense – rooted in receptivity, relatedness, and responsiveness" (pp. 1–3). Later, Noddings (1989) expanded this idea into a "relational ethics" (p. 222) as a counterbalance to the ethics of justice. Tronto (1993) identifies four aspects of the ethics of care: attentiveness, responsibility, competence, and responsiveness. Regarding responsiveness, her concern is for the moral complexity of care, particularly the vulnerability of the care-receiver.

We hear in this brief summary the linguistic and ideological ties to the current ethical turn in psychoanalysis through words like moral, vulnerability, care, dependency, dialogical relations, and humanism. The "voice of care" that is brought forth is the female voice. As I see it, therapeutic relationships embody the therapeutic voice of the "maternal", not literally as a maternal-ness defined by gender, but rather as that which makes up the various practices of care that unfold within a relational therapeutic matrix. Contemporary relational psychoanalytic practice is deeply rooted in attentiveness, responsibility, competence, and responsiveness.

Certainly, in psychoanalytic theorizing, the shadow of the maternal subject has consistently been present in terms of the far-reaching impact of early maternal relations on attachment, psychic functioning, transference phenomena, and relational dynamics. Yet according to Aron and Starr (2013) there has been a denigration of the concept of care in psychoanalysis. In their recent book, *Psychotherapy for the People: Toward a Progressive Psychoanalysis*, they devote an entire chapter to the split between treatment and care, tying this split to the gender binary. Of this, they say the following:

> As masculine scientific treatment and cure was increasingly contrasted with feminine care and support, psychoanalysis came to define itself as a scientific treatment that led to real cure, in contrast to psychotherapy, which provided only a comforting relationship. All that was associated with support, care, and dependence was split off.
>
> (Aron & Starr, 2013, pp. 76–77)

And although we consider the impact, over time, of the actual maternal object/subject on the evolving subjectivity of the patient, more rarely do we fully consider the actual complex subjectivity of the maternal subject beyond what she provided, or failed to provide. Benjamin's (1990) extensive work on mutual recognition has made a convincing and much-needed correction with respect to the importance of the mother's subjectivity in the developmental process. Contemporary feminist writers with strong psychoanalytic ties and leanings such as Baraitser (2009), Chodorow (1978, 2000), Featherstone (1997), Butler (1990, 1994, 2004), Frosh (1997), Hollway (2001, 2006), Kraemer (1996), Layton (2004), Parker (1997), and others have made our thinking about maternal caregiving more complex and nuanced. But we have yet to fully explore the complex maternal-ness of the analytic practitioner who functions not only as a recognizer, holder, container, metabolizer, mirror, and now caretaker, but also as punctuator of time, a closer as well as an opener of the door. Establishing the link between the feminist ethics of care and the ethical turn allows for a richer consideration of this complexity.

When an ethics of care is considered to be of equal importance to that of justice, such emotionally evocative ethical notions such as hospitality and responsibility for the other-as-patient, and the desires and resistances they engender, can be considered from within a broadened ethical framework. Both patient and analyst can be seen as organizing and negotiating, not only around the frame and other analytic guidelines of practice, but also around the complex experiences of care – both its potentialities and limitations.

The relevance of the maternal to psychoanalysis

It is through the threshold of the maternal that we enter the world and receive the gift of life, so it is no wonder that Levinas (1974) holds up the maternal – maternity and motherhood – as the primary and ultimate example of one's responsibility for the other. Of this he says: "Maternity is the complete 'being for the other' which characterizes it, which is the very signifyingness of signification, is the ultimate sense of this vulnerability" (p. 108). Several feminists, such as Brody (2001), Ziarek (2001), Sikka (2001), Irigaray (2001), Oliver (2001), and others, have strongly challenged Levinas on his metaphoric appropriation of the maternal body and his seeming disregard for the female subject. Sikka points out that "metaphors matter, and sometimes the concreteness of the letter – speaking, as it always does, of particular entities – signifies more than the superior spirit is meant to convey" (p. 107). She goes on to vehemently protest this use of a woman's body wholly for the affirmation of Levinas's masculine subject. Bueskens (2014), in her recent book *Mothering and Psychoanalysis*, agrees on the dangers of appropriation by metaphor, commenting on "the debt psychoanalysis owes to the mother as a key model who has been plundered for metaphorical significance and then abandoned when it comes to applying psychoanalytic insights to helping mothers understand their complex reactions to mothering" (p. 51). Her intent is to return to the sociologically and psychologically complex maternal subject.

The regressive nature of the therapeutic relationship is such that the mother-infant relation stands as the psychic template of psychotherapeutic care. Consequently, the maternal function of the analyst figures heavily in the thinking of numerous psychoanalytic theorists such as Bion

(1959, 1962), Ogden (1994), Loewald (1951), Winnicott (1965), Freud (1920), Balint (1968), Kohut (1971), and others. Slochower (1996), in her paper, "Holding and the Evolving Maternal Metaphor", refers to the maternal metaphor as "an evenly available, largely noninterpretive presence who brackets other aspects of his or her responses to the patient" (p. 195). Slochower calls particular attention to the more holding, containing, and metabolizing aspects of the maternal metaphor as it shapes the presence of the analyst. She also references the recent relational critiques of the maternal analyst. In an interesting twist, she notes concerns:

> The maternal metaphor places the analyst in an authoritarian, positivist position vis-à-vis the patient/baby. The maternal analyst would seem to *know* what the patient needs and also how to meet those needs. The analyst apparently does not experience conflict, either about meeting the patient's needs, or about the tension between those needs and the analyst's own.
>
> (p. 198)

This critique of the all-knowing mother-analyst, non-conflicted and quite comfortable with knowing and meeting the needs of the patient/baby, a position formally inhabited by the expert, all-knowing, interpreting, paternalistic analyst, portends some of what Stuart Pizer (2012) and Eyal Rozmarin (2007) have recently found difficult about a Levinasian-infused ethic of responsibility. This stance seems to suggest to them a kind of masochistically based over-investment in the other, a disregard for the "we-ness" of the dyad, the collapse of mutual influence, and a negation of mutual recognition and negotiation: some of the very cornerstones of relational psychoanalysis. The maternal analyst, or Levinasian-inspired analyst, as seen through their eyes, functions as a perverse kind of *mother knows best*: one who runs the risk, however well-meaning, of inadvertently appropriating those in her care, all for their own good. This mirrors some of the feminist critique of Levinas. Sikka (2001), coming at it from a different perspective, says the following: "The problem is that he has not *reached a conclusion* at the end of some process of dialogue and reflection. He has carelessly assumed his culturally engendered givens, without paying attention to any other that might question these givens" (p. 114).

Rozmarin (2007), in his paper, "An Other in Psychoanalysis: Emmanuel Levinas's Critique of Knowledge and Analytic Sense", concludes that this philosophy "does not fare well under the conditions of dyadic reciprocity" (p. 359). Pizer (2012), in his paper, "The Analyst's Generous Involvement: Recognition and the Tension of Tenderness", distinguishes generosity from responsibility and hospitality, seeing generosity as "elementally instinctual" (p. 18) while responsibility and hospitality are seen as "ethically obligatory". Pizer implies that ethical responses born out of obligation run the risk of being drained of their spontaneous subjectivity and mutuality, reading more as obedient, compliant, self-sacrificing, and lifeless; not lively, intuitive, actively responsive, and intersubjective. Rozmarin prefers that the analyst hold more of an ambivalent position rather than placing the other above one, suggesting that: "In a present and contemporaneous dyad, which is the founding event of psychoanalysis, self and other intermingle such that it becomes *ethically* impossible to give either of them primacy" (p. 359).

Are these responses, and Slochower's reported critiques of the maternal function of the analyst, a result of too narrow a reading of a maternally centered therapeutic ethics of care? On the one hand, it seems that the maternal function allows the analyst too much power (which, to my mind, actually reads as counter-Levinasian) and yet, on the other, not enough subjectivity to adequately decenter and make oneself as vulnerable and responsive to the other as one needs to be. Both Pizer's and Rozmarin's allegiances to Benjamin's work on mutual recognition clearly show their respect for the importance of the subjectivity of the maternal in psychoanalytic discourse. But perhaps this is where the problem of gender bifurcation figures large. Whenever we parse out what's maternal from what's paternal, there is the possibility of backing ourselves into a corner, unless a fuller reading of maternal-ness and paternal-ness can be found.

Levinas's marked tilt toward the maternal as "the ultimate example" of ethical responsibility for the other can, understandably, cause us to recoil if doing so negates the full subjectivity of the maternal (or paternal, for that matter) and the limiting of maternal possibilities to holding, metabolizing, mirroring, and containing functions. To the understandable horror of feminists, Levinas (1985/1999) only imbues paternity with transcendence; the possibility "of being able to escape the closure of your own identity and what is bestowed on you, toward something which is not bestowed on you and which nevertheless is yours – this is paternity. This future beyond my own being" (p. 70). Clearly, this bifurcation is problematic if read as Levinas's intention.

Lisa Baraitser (2009), British feminist theorist and psychotherapist, makes use of Levinas in her work, and is helpful here in offering a broader meaning. She says:

> In Levinas, it is not that the father recognizes himself in the son, but he discovers himself there for the first time. Paternity engenders the father as much as it does the son. In relation to his son, who is both himself and not himself, the father discovers his own subjectivity. As he discovers that his son is distinct, a stranger, he discovers that he too is distinct, even a stranger to himself.
>
> (p. 44)

Undaunted by the bifurcation that troubles some feminists, Baraitser goes on to assert: "I think it is possible, even desirable, to construct a reading of the paternal in Levinas as a figure for motherhood, and hence to reclaim this notion to think about aspects of maternal subjectivity" (p. 45). If we can look beyond the gender bifurcation in Levinas, and appreciate what, in his definition of paternity, he refers to as "the other in the same" – the stranger we are to ourselves – this re-establishes a space for two subjects. There is the potential to be stretched in relation to the stranger in oneself and in the other. As Butler (2004) asserts, the subject "is transformed through its encounter with alterity, not in order to return to itself, but to become a self it never was" (p. 286). For our purposes, the therapist and patient – strange both to themselves and to one another, and asymmetrical – can generatively exist in relation to one another. This retrieves a place for mutual influence, and helps us to broaden our understanding of the "maternal" in the analyst.

The dialectic of care and interruption

What becomes of my infinite responsibility to the other-as-patient and does this differ from my responsibility to the other-as-other? Is there a way to simultaneously hold a Levinasian ethic of responsibility and hospitality, while also assuming responsibility for one's own subjectivity and one's obligation to be the one who ends the session and closes the door? As therapists, we assume the obligation of responding to what Levinas (1988) refers to as:

> The evil of suffering – extreme passivity, helplessness, abandonment and solitude – also the unassumable, whence the possibility of a half

opening, and, more precisely, the half opening that a moan, a cry, a groan or a sigh that slips through – the original call for aid, for curative help, help from the other me whose alterity, whose exteriority promises salvation?

(p. 93)

But how does the therapeutic couple negotiate the call from the "half opening" behind the closed door?

Frosh and Baraitser (2003), who have made it their project to speak to the complexity of maternal subjectivity as well as that of the mother/analyst, say the following:

> The power of the mother/analyst . . . is derived from her or his capacity to "dip into" the mind of the patient, to become utterly connected, while also retaining a separate existence, coming out of a mental sharing in order, for example, to make an interpretation or bring a session – or an entire analysis – to an end.

(p. 780)

Although my patients and I "dip into" each other's minds, and in doing so, become "utterly connected", things become painfully complicated for my patient and me when it comes to my "retaining a separate existence, coming out of a mental sharing", but most particularly around my "bringing things to an end". I could fall back on the therapeutic ethics of justice – technique and the rules of the frame – to make clear-cut sense of this. It is my job, after all, to set limits and hold boundaries. But is there a more experienced way of understanding this in terms of the complications of caring and a maternal ethics of care?

Again, Baraitser (2009) is most helpful here in bringing in Lichtenberg-Ettinger's (2006) bridging of the inside and outside, and the maternal and paternal, with her notion of the matrixial. According to Baraitser, "[t]he matrix is a symbol Ettinger uses to propose another mode of human subjectivity linked to archaic traces of inter-uterine life in which the maternal and the unknown other within the mother coexist" (pp. 44–45). As Baraitser sees it, Lichtenberg-Ettinger's matrix suggests that it is:

> an encounter with what is fundamentally strange, as well as being the same, that establishes this relationship as ethical, and hence as one in

which we can begin to talk of the emergence of subjectivity. In recognizing the child as a stranger, as distinct, the mother also recognizes what is distinct about herself.

(p. 46)

Baraitser (2009) introduces "an ethics of interruption" that expands upon what Ruddick (1989) originally referred to as the "irregular, unpredictable, often mysterious" (p. 352); the interruptions built into an intense and sustained caring relation with an other, be it a child, or, for our purposes, the other-as-patient. The other-as-patient requires from the therapist both a deep knowing, what we think of as recognition, and an acknowledgement of mystery and the unrecognizable that makes itself known through interruption.

How does Baraitser define interruption?:

An interruption is an insertion of a break between or among something that is otherwise continuous, which has ongoing movement or flow. To interrupt is to perform a stop in this flow, to punctuate the flow thereby creating a "between" or "among" in an otherwise undifferentiated continuum.

(Baraitser, 2009, p. 68)

Although the analyst/mother is boundaried by technique and the frame, it is useful for us to hear more of what Baraitser considers the mother's experience of interruption, and then consider it in relation to the role of therapist/analyst. She refers to the "micros-blows . . . breaches, tears, puncturings" (p. 68) that continually and relentlessly communicate, "'respond to me', 'deal with me'; not later, and not because you've already dealt with me before, but now, and again now, and again now" (Baraitser, 2009, p. 68). Thus, we have two subjectivities in intense negotiation around care, each capable of interrupting the other in a multitude of ways, both consciously and unconsciously. Frosh and Baraitser (2003) comment: "It takes a mighty effort of ethical resistance, such as that found in Levinas's philosophy, to make the other primary in this, to hold on to the trajectory of recognition rather than revulsion" (p. 783). Both therapist and patient cause "breaches, tears, and puncturings" in the other and struggle mightily with the psychic costs of care, one in the seeking and receiving of it and the other in determining how best, ethically as well as technically and humanely, to provide it.

The analyst's extension of various forms of care can be seen as a kind of complex gift that places a demand on the patient. The person of the therapist and the care she promises invites – calls forth – the patient's fuller emotional presence, especially her deeply defended and sequestered needs for care. This calls up Derrida's (1992) notion of the aporia of the gift, that is, a gift that, by its very nature, negates its gift-ness by burdening the other to respond. This back-and-forth tension and necessary burdening is part of what catalyzes the therapy. Understandably, many of our patients are deeply ambivalent and shame-filled about needing, seeking, and accepting care, despite its necessity. No wonder: the very early care they received, or failed to receive, is likely the very thing that compromised their development.

What's compelling about Orange's (2010) introduction of a Levinasian ethics into the therapeutic conversation, and her particular focus on the notion of hospitality to the suffering stranger, is the way it addresses this vulnerability of needing care. In some way, to talk of hospitality works to mitigate some of the shame and humiliation of needing to enter the therapist's door. But hospitality itself, inevitably, becomes the very harbinger of interruption. Care itself does not always soften the felt sense of letting go of long-held and cherished ways of protecting and defending oneself against the Trojan horses of care. The more I open the door to the patient, the more the work becomes a site of interruption and potential loss. The deeper we go, the greater the stakes.

Clinical example

At the conclusion of every session, Sylvia slouches slowly toward the door. Leavings are excruciatingly painful for her. On better days, she jokes about wanting to develop a line of analytic shoes that would take a very long time to put on as a way to delay the inevitable. But her attempts to forestall prove futile. She often proceeds to the bathroom or her car for a pain-filled cry. Over the years she has railed at me for torturing her by throwing her out, despite my continual and dedicated extension of therapeutic hospitality and deep engagement. My work with her has, at times, rendered me shaken, psychically bleeding, vulnerable, and exposed. Sylvia is someone who was profoundly deprived of a consistent maternal presence in childhood and has found in me a good enough analyst/mother whom she unapologetically proclaims an unwillingness to ever give up. We both know a time will come when she will end her work with me and I will close the door for a final time, that is, as final as such closings these days can reasonably be. But there will be many difficult micro-interruptions and door-closings before that. My degree of emotional availability reminds her of my eventual absence. The very site of hospitality is the site of interruption. This is not unlike Baraitser's (2009) interrupted mother, whom she refers to as "the impossible subject par excellence" (p. 9). My patient and I are both interrupted and impossible subjects. How do we, within an ethics of care, avoid turning this work into an existential tragedy where care spirals in on itself, negating itself as it goes?

One Ash Wednesday, Sylvia, a devout Catholic, following her attendance at early Mass, came in for an appointment wearing the expected charred sign of the cross on her forehead. A difficult session ensued. Although still vulnerable after many years of work, Sylvia had managed to build some degree of resilience and managed to show some signs of it during this hour. But as the end of the session approached, Sylvia quickly digressed into another self-deprecating and attacking spiral, assuming her protracted slouch toward the door. As I watched her, I heard myself saying, without the benefit of reflection or pause, "Sylvia, get your ash out of here!" She turned to look at me, incredulous at what I had just said. I, too, was incredulous. What prompted such an un-careful outburst? What was my intention? Did I mean to jar her out of her regressive spiral with my blasphemous comment? Was it my way of saying *enough already*? Was it my inability to adequately cope with my own feelings of frustration and impatience, at her micro-regression and refusal to acknowledge her slow but steady progress? After a shocked pause, Sylvia suddenly seemed to shift out of her tragic place, no longer merely a wounded and soon-to-be expelled patient. With a hint of humor and some degree of triumph, she said: "You're a therapist! I can't believe you just said that to me! I'm going to report you!" And with that, she left, sporting the faint hint of a victorious smile. From this point on, partings never reached the same degree of regression. Even at the most difficult moments, something quite profound had shifted. And although Sylvia continued to suffer in various ways over the following years of our work together, this interruption marked an important turning point.

Discussion

What happened here and what does it have to do with the complications of care and the ethical turn in psychoanalysis? I must begin by saying that my response to Sylvia was outrageously and totally out of character for me. One could say it was an analyst's act of freedom per Symington (1983) or a form of emergent clinical improvisation in the spirit of Ringstrom (2001). I like to think it came out of a place of my deep care, affection, and empathic resonance with Sylvia, and a belief in her growing resilience. This all may be true. But it was also an unrestrained and rather aggressive interruption on my part, in response to Sylvia's constant microinterruptions and abrasions of my time and patience, an assault on my therapeutic hospitality. Perhaps we were both rebelling against the constraints of the kind of care and carefulness we had co-evolved, although understandable in the face of her suffering, but limiting and constraining over time. Perhaps we had lost a sense of mystery for each other by becoming too known and predictable, thereby needing a kind of jarring enactment that exposed fresh faces to each other and a new path for growth. I would say we had been sagging under the burden of an all-too-familiar and constraining kind of hospitality and responsibility that split off of ambivalence, hate, and exhaustion.

The work of Featherstone (1997), Hollway (1997), Parker (1997), and others on the psychic complexity and necessity of maternal hate and ambivalence, expansions of the earlier work of Klein and Winnicott, figures large here. Their work not only deepens and broadens the maternal ethics of care, but also attunes us to the full subjective experiences of caretaking. Although Levinas's project functions as an antidote to hate, as clinicians, we know this to be an important emotion that signals not only pain, but steps toward growth and self-definition. If left unacknowledged, misunderstood, and un-integrated, psychic and relational opportunities are lost. Of course, if my timing had been off, if I had misread the tenor of the session, if my aggression had not been so tenderly cloaked in humor, and if Sylvia had not yet been ready to receive my interruption, I could have deeply offended and truly hurt her. But the interruption rendered it otherwise.

Who was this stranger, not my usual therapist, who just said this ridiculous thing to me? Who is the stranger I hear myself becoming when I say these words? Critchley (2007), in response to Levinas's infinite demand, suggests that "the ethical subject is a split subject" (p. 63), meaning that one is confronted with an infinite demand from the other that is impossible to meet, regardless of whether the demand emanates from the other outside, or the other located within oneself. Critchley suggests sublimation, particularly sublimation through humor and the ridiculous, so that "we can come into contact with the dimension of the ethical demand without that demand crushing the subject" (p. 74). As I see it, his suggestion reads as a prescription for some form of interruption, a necessary playing with tragedy to make the infinitely demanding bearable.

As we engage the contemporary ethics of care, we need to do so with a willingness to acknowledge the burdens and complications that caring brings. This is the site of the complications of care, of hospitality, and interruption.

References

Aron, L., & Starr, K. (2013). *Psychotherapy for the people: Toward a progressive psychoanalysis*. New York: Routledge.

Balint, M. (1968). *The basic fault*. London: Tavistock.

Baraitser, L. (2009). *Maternal encounters: The ethics of interruption*. New York: Routledge.

Benjamin, J. (1990). *The bonds of love: Psychoanalysis, feminism, and the problem of difference*. London: Virago.

Bion, W. R. (1959). Attacks on linking. *International Journal of Psychoanalysis, 40*, 308–315.

Bion, W. R. (1962). Theory of thinking. *International Journal of Psychoanalysis, 43,* 306–310.

Brody, D. (2001). Levinas's maternal method from time and the other through otherwise than being: No woman's land. In T. Chanter (Ed.), *Feminist interpretations of Emmanuel Levinas* (pp. 28–52). University Park, PA: Pennsylvania State University Press.

Bueskens, P. (Ed.). (2014). *Mothering & psychoanalysis: Clinical, sociological and feminist perspectives*. Bradford, ON: Demeter Press.

Butler, J. (1990). *Gender trouble*. London: Routledge.

Butler, J. (1994). Bodies that matter. In C. Burke, S. Schor, & M. Whitford (Eds.), *Engaging with Irigaray*. New York: Columbia University Press.

Butler, J. (2004). *Undoing gender*. New York: Routledge.

Chodorow, N. (1978). *The reproduction of mothering: Psychoanalysis and the sociology of gender*. London: University of California Press.

Chodorow, N. (2000). *Reflections on the reproduction of mothering: Psychoanalysis and the sociology of gender*. Berkeley, CA: University of California Press.

Corpt, E. (2011a). The art and craft of psychoanalytic practice: A discussion of Orange's "speaking the unspeakable: 'The implicit,' traumatic living memory, and the dialogue of metaphors". *International Journal of Psychoanalysis Self Psychology, 6*(2), 214–227.

Corpt, E. (2011b). *Clinical generosity: A deeply embedded attitude of contemporary self psychology*. Paper presentation at the IAPSP Conference, Los Angeles, CA.

Critchley, S. (2007). *Infinitely demanding: Ethics of commitment, politics of resistance*. London and New York: Verso.

De Beauvoir, S. (1972). *The second sex*. Harmondsworth: Penguin. (Originally published in 1949).

Derrida, J. (1992). *Given time: Counterfeit money*. (P. Kamuf, Trans.). Chicago: University of Chicago Press.

Featherstone, B. (1997). Crisis in the western family. In W. Hollway & B. Featherstone (Eds.), *Mothering and ambivalence*. London: Routledge.

Foehl, J. C. (2010). The play's the thing: The primacy of process and the persistence of pluralism in contemporary psychoanalysis. *Contemporary Psychoanalysis, 46,* 48–86.

Foehl, J. C. (2011). A phenomenology of distance: On being hard to reach. *Psychoanalysis Dialogues, 21,* 607–618.

Freud, S. (1920). Beyond the pleasure principle. In J. Strachey (Ed.), *The standard edition of the complete psychological works of Sigmund Freud, 18,* 7–64.

Frie, R. (2000). Intersubjectivity and the philosophical tradition. *Journal of American Psychoanalytic Association, 48,* 684–686.

Frie, R. (2012). Psychoanalysis, religion, philosophy and the possibility of dialogue: Freud, Binswanger and Pfister. *International Forum Psychoanalysis, 21,* 106–116.

Frosh, S. (1997). Father's ambivalence (too). In W. Hollway and B. Featherstone (Eds.), *Mothering and ambivalence*. London: Routledge.

Frosh, S., & Baraitser, L. (2003). Thinking, recognition, and otherness. *Psychoanalysis Review, 90,* 771–789.

Gilligan, C. (1982). *In a different voice: psychological theory and women's development.* Cambridge, MA: Harvard University Press.

Held, V. (2005). *The ethics of care: Personal, political, and global.* Oxford: Oxford University Press.

Hollway, W. (2006). *The capacity to care: Gender and ethical subjectivity.* New York: Routledge.

Hollway, W., & Featherstone, B. (1997). *Mothering and ambivalence.* London: Routledge.

Irigaray, L. (2001). The fecundity of the caress: A reading of Levinas, totality and infinity, "The phenomenology of eros". In T. Chanter (Ed.), *Feminist interpretations of Emmanuel Levinas*. University Park, PA: Pennsylvania State University Press.

Kohut, H. (1971). *The analysis of the self.* New York: International Universities Press.

Kraemer, S.B. (1996). Betwixt and dark and the daylight of maternal subjectivity: Meditations on the threshold. *Psychoanalytic Dialogues, 6,* 765–791.

Layton, L. (2004). Working nine to nine: The new women of prime time. *Studies in Gender and Sexuality, 5,* 351–369.

Layton, L. (2014). Maternally speaking: Mothers, daughters, and the talking cure. In P. Bueskens (Ed.), *Mothering & psychoanalysis: Clinical, sociological and feminist perspectives*. Bradford, ON: Demeter Press.

Levinas, E. (1969). *Totality and infinity: An essay on exteriority.* Pittsburgh, PA: Duquesne University Press.

Levinas, E. (1974). *Otherwise than being, or, beyond essence* (A. Lingis, Trans.). Pittsburgh, PA: Duquesne University Press.

Levinas, E. (1985). *Ethics and infinity: Conversations with Phillipe Nemo* (R, Cohen Trans.). Pittsburgh, PA: Duquesne University Press.

Levinas, E. (1988). Useless suffering. *Giornale di Metatisica* 4: 13–26. Reprinted from Entre nous: thinking of the other, by M. Smith & B. Harshav, 91–101. New York: Columbia University Press. (Originally published in 1982)

Levinas, E. (1999). *Alterity and transcendence.* New York: Columbia University Press. (Original work published 1985)

Levinas, E., & Lichtenberg-Ettinger, B. (2006). What would Eurydice say: Emmanuel Levinas in conversation with Bracha Lichtenberg-Ettinger. *Athena Philosophical Studies, 1,* 137–145.

Loewald, H.W. (1951). Ego and reality. *International Journal of Psycho-Analysis, 32,* 10–18.

Noddings, N. (1984). *Caring: A feminine approach to ethics and moral education.* Berkeley, CA: University of California Press.

Noddings, N. (1989). *Women and evil.* Berkeley, CA: University of California Press.

Ogden, T. (1994). *Subject of analysis.* London: Karnac Books.

Oliver, K. (2001). Paternal election and the absent father. In T. Chanter (Ed.), *Feminist interpretations of Emmanuel Levinas.* University Park, PA: Pennsylvania State University Press.

Orange, D. (2010). *Thinking for clinicians: Philosophical resources for contemporary psychoanalysis and the humanistic psychotherapies.* New York: Routledge.

Orange, D. (2011). *The suffering strange: Hermeneutics for everyday clinical practice.* New York: Routledge.

Parker, R. (1997). The production and purposes of maternal ambivalence. In W. Hollway & B. Featherston (Eds.), *Mothering and ambivalence.* London: Virago.

Pizer, S. (2012). The analyst's generous involvement: Recognition and the "tension of tenderness". Paper presentation at the IARPP Conference, New York City.

Riker, J. (2010). *Why it is good to be good: Ethics, Kohut's self psychology, and modern society.* Lanham, MD: Jason Aronson.

Ringstrom, P. (2001). Cultivating the improvisational in psychoanalytic treatment. *Psychoanalytic Dialogues, 11*(5), 727–754.

Rozmarin, E. (2007). An other in psychoanalysis: Emmanuel Levinas's critique of knowledge and analytic sense. *Contemporary Psychoanalysis, 43,* 327–360.

Ruddick, S. (1989). *Maternal thinking: Towards a politics of peace.* Boston, MA: Beacon Press.

Shabad, P. (2006). To expose or to cover up: Human vulnerability in the shadow of death. *Contemporary Psychoanalysis, 42,* 413–436.

Shabad, P. (2010). The suffering of passion: Metamorphoses and the embrace of the stranger. *Psychoanalytic Dialogues, 20,* 710–729.

Sikka, S. (2001). The delightful other: Portraits of the feminine in Kierkegaard, Nietzsche, and Levinas. In T. Chanter (Ed.), *Feminist interpretations of Emmanuel Levinas.* University Park, PA: Pennsylvania State University Press.

Slochower, J. (1996). Holding and the evolving maternal metaphor. *Psychoanalytic Review, 83,* 195–218.

Symington, N. (1983). The analyst's act of freedom as agent of therapeutic change. *International Journal of Psycho-Analysis, 10,* 283–291.

Tronto, J. (1993). *Moral boundaries.* London: Routledge.

Williams, F. (2001). In and beyond new labour: Towards a new political ethic of care. *Critical Social Policy, 21*(4), 467–493.

Winnicott, D.W. (1965). The maturational processes and the facilitating environment: Studies in the theory of emotional development. *The International Psycho- Analytical Library, 64,* 1–276.

Ziarek, E.P. (2001). The ethical passions of Emmanuel Levinas. In T. Chanter (Ed.), *Feminist interpretations of Emmanuel Levinas.* University Park, PA: Pennsylvania State University Press.

Chapter 8

"Screams and shouts"

Trauma, uncertainty, and the ethical turn

Doris Brothers

Many psychoanalysts who rub elbows under the relational umbrella are wrestling with what Continental philosophers have called "the problem of the other." Having grown increasingly distant from our mythic, blank-screen, authoritarian predecessors who sought the causes of psychopathology within the self-contained psyches of their patients, we are ever more convinced that psychological life emerges and is sustained within the infinitely complex, constantly evolving context of relationships. Concomitant with our concern with otherness, and our skepticism about "abstract totality, universalism, and rationalism" (Bernstein, 1995, p. 57), is our growing preoccupation with the ethical dimension of clinical practice. The recent spate of publications on such topics as trust, gratitude, responsibility, promise-making, generosity, and forgiveness confirms that what philosopher/psychoanalyst Donna Orange (2010, 2011) has referred to as "the ethical turn" is gaining momentum.

As soon as analysts abandoned their search for authoritative, irreducible, transcendent explanations of human experience (which was linked to their focus on the intra-psychic) and turned their attention to the intricacies of relational life, a psychology of uncertainty began its ascendance in psychoanalysis (Brothers, 2008). Uncertainty, as a number of philosophers suggest (Anker, 2009), is also an essential constituent of the ethical.

The complex ways in which uncertainty and ethics are interrelated become more sharply focused when they are considered with respect to trauma. In what follows I offer a very brief and limited consideration of the dense relationships among trauma, uncertainty, and ethics as they relate to the therapeutic situation. To demonstrate how reactions to trauma may both compromise ethical relating and make it possible, I summarize a theory of trauma I have developed that places confrontations with what I call existential uncertainty at the heart of trauma; I draw briefly on Levinasian theory and Freud's concept of the "Nebenmensch" (see also Critchley, 2009, pp. 208–210); and I offer a clinical example.

Nowhere is the relationship between uncertainty and ethics more strikingly articulated than in the writings of Emmanuel Levinas. For Levinas, according to Simon Critchley (2007):

> The ethical relation begins when I experience being placed in question by the face of the other, an experience that happens both when I respond generously . . . to the "widow, the orphan, the stranger", but also when I pass them on the street silently wishing they were somehow invisible and wincing internally at my callousness.
>
> (p. 56)

Levinas's radical formulation of the problem of otherness involves the claim that the alterity of the Other is utterly irreducible. But it is not only the other who cannot be fully known; we cannot fully know ourselves. While we have long appreciated that much of our self-experience is unconscious, there is another striking reason for our uncertainty about ourselves. As Critchley (2007) suggests, "There is something at the heart of me, that arguably makes me the 'me' that I am, but which is quite opaque to me" (p. 62). As a relational analyst, I would say that "something" is, at least in part, my relation to the unknowable other (or others) upon whom my sense of differentiated selfhood is utterly dependent. Uncertainty, then, in the sense of not having complete access to one's own experience or the other's, stretches back through our intergenerational attachments.

Critchley (2007) makes the point that, for Levinas: "the ethical demand is a traumatic demand" (p. 61). In contrast to Critchley who examines trauma from the "economic" metapsychology that Freud (1920/1955) elaborated in *Beyond the Pleasure Principle*, I explore Levinas's assertion that the *traumatisme assourdissant* or the deafening shock of trauma enables the subject to become an ethical subject from the vantage point of my own understanding of trauma.

The traumatic meanings of the ethical demand

Levinas characterizes the relation of infinite responsibility to the other as a trauma (Critchley, 2007, p. 61). From his perspective, one's relation to the other is not a benign involvement but a weighty and persecutory responsibility. He claims that the other takes us hostage insofar as we must be prepared to substitute ourselves for any suffering and humiliation that they may undergo.

According to my way of thinking, trauma destroys the systemically emergent certainties that pattern psychological life (some writers, e.g. Atwood and Stolorow, 1984, prefer to think of these as "organizing principles"). Cognitively grasping the inescapable uncertainty that marks the human condition and experiencing the uncertainty of one's own psychological survival are very different matters. With the destruction of the previously unquestioned convictions that structure our experiential worlds, our relational systems are plunged into chaos. We are subject to the unbearably painful awareness that the relational exchange, on which a sense of differentiated selfhood depends, is not dependably available. Once we can no longer feel certain of our self-sustaining connections to others, we live as exiles in an unfamiliar world, filled with terror, dread, and what Heinz Kohut (1971) so aptly described as "disintegration anxiety." With this conceptualization of trauma in mind, I understand Levinas to mean that since our responsibility for the other is limitless, ethical relating means continually opening ourselves to the possibility of our own psychological annihilation on the other's behalf. In other words, we assume all the unbearable uncertainty of "going-on-being" (Winnicott, 1965) that torments the traumatized other.

I conceive of trauma as having two interrelated components: the shattering of a previously unquestioned sense of "going-on-being," and efforts, often desperate, to restore a sense of certainty about the continuation of psychological existence. Among these efforts is one that may well underlie a tendency that Levinas (1947/1987) has described as assimilating the other to what is the same. In our horror at having lost all that is known, familiar, and meaningful, we crave reassurance that we have not been stripped of what so powerfully reminds us of our connection to others – our similarity to them. Since the hope of emerging from the unbearably lonely exile of trauma depends, to a great extent, on finding that we are still welcomed into the human family, whatever confronts us with evidence of our difference from others may be dissociated from awareness or denied. In other words, among traumatized people, the search for sameness, which marks our development from birth, may be transformed into a denial of difference.

The sense of being a distinct, one-of-a-kind individual also emerges out of the relational give and take. When the availability of that relational exchange is thrown into doubt by trauma, the loss of one's very existence as a unique individual often seems imminent. At such times, a search for difference is also likely to become very intense. Finding differences, making sharp distinctions among that which is similar, tends to bring certainty to experience. Just as the search for sameness may become transformed into a denial of difference, the search for difference may be transformed into a denial of sameness.

It is probably obvious that feelings of uncertainty are increased by experiences that are complex and multifaceted. Likewise, these feelings are likely to decrease with simpler and more manageable experiences. In the aftermath of trauma, when the uncertainty of psychological survival seems close to unbearable, we tend to simplify experience by whatever means are available. Denials of sameness and difference are then often resorted to insofar as they rely on black-or-white thinking that reduces the complexity of lived experience. Moreover, these denials, which rest on dissociative processes, tend to be rigidly maintained and resist all appeals to reason. They tend to give rise to "us-them" dichotomies in which differences among those we consider "us" and our similarity to those we consider "them" can no longer be discerned. Once we consign others to the ranks of "them," we are disinclined to offer ourselves as substitutes for their suffering.

Clearly these complexity-reducing actions may compromise what Levinas deems the ethical bases of relating. Yet who among us has not undergone trauma? Few therapists in my acquaintance have been spared. I believe that a mutual desire to heal and to be healed is often what most compellingly draws patients and therapists into their therapeutic relationships. When faced with the danger of retraumatization in therapeutic encounters, therapists too may feel compelled to reduce complexity through denials of sameness and difference. The tendency to view patients in terms of diagnostic categories that obscure their irreducible uniqueness is all too common.

At the same time, it is the very fact that therapists have known trauma that makes for the possibility, not only of ethical relating, but also of healing for both therapeutic partners. Levinas's understanding of the ethical subject as traumatized calls to mind what Freud (1895/1950), early in his career, wrote about the Nebenmensch, the neighbor or fellow human being. The Nebenmensch complex, according to Freud, has two components:

one that makes an impression as a "Thing" which resists my attempts at comprehension (Lacan, 1992, places "als Ding" at the heart of psychoanalytic ethics), and the other which is made understandable by the activity of memory. That is, since the Nebenmensch "announces itself only if it screams, shouts, cries or screeches" it tends to "awaken the memory of his [the subject's] own screaming and at the same time of his own experiences of pain" (Freud, 1895/1950, p. 330). Thus, as Critchley (2009, p. 209), points out, the Nebenmensch is both incomparable and comparable. We are able to comprehend the suffering Other through our own suffering.

Traces of the notion that both patients and therapists contact one another through their screaming, their traumas, can be found in the writings of many analysts.[1] For example, Louis Sander (1995) posits a "recognition process" by means of which therapists and patients communicate their "fittedness" to one another. I would say that under certain conditions, both therapeutic partners communicate to each other, by nonverbal as well as verbal means, the understanding that as fellow trauma exiles, they are "fitted" to the task of reciprocal healing.

Tracy and my face

I have had many therapeutic relationships in which the screams of a patient have recalled memories of my own traumas, but occasionally it is my own silent screaming that has set off this recognition process with a patient. This was particularly true of my relationship with Tracy.

In December 2010 a severe case of Bell's palsy paralyzed half my face and contracted the features on the other half into a weird grimace. To say that the experience was traumatizing does not begin to capture the devastating effect my loss of facial expressivity had on my life (Brothers, 2012). I felt that I had become shamefully recognizable only as a member of a despised group of individuals – those with a disfiguring illness. Consigned to the ranks of Bell's palsy sufferers, and feeling interchangeable with all others similarly afflicted, I experienced firsthand what Levinas meant by the term "totalizing"; that is, being reduced to an object to be studied, categorized, or comprehended, which he contrasted with responding to the face of the other. And with that totalizing experience my own sense of differentiated selfhood seemed to dissolve and weaken.

It was just this sense of kinship with others who feel "hostage to the shaming gaze of others" (Stolorow, 2011, pp. 107–108) that, I believe, transformed my therapeutic relationship with Tracy, a dark-skinned and stocky African-American teenager. Severely depressed, given to cutting the skin on her thighs, and functioning well below her high capacity for academic achievement, Tracy had often bemoaned her difference from the thin, blond, and blue-eyed girls who were popular in her prestigious New York prep school. "My parents tell me to feel proud of being black," she once said, "but I don't." In fact Tracy had conveyed her feeling that being darker skinned than her younger sister and their mother was a source of unremitting shame. We had understood her cutting, in part, as her way of demonstrating her hatred of her dark skin as well as a secret way of spiting her mother who seemed obsessed with her daughters' perfection.

I had occasionally tried to initiate a discussion with Tracy regarding the effects of racial difference on our relationship. When I asked her directly what it was like to talk about her distress over her skin color to a white woman, Tracy dismissed my concern. "I know you're trained to help people who aren't the same as you," she said. Still, I suspected that my being white was partially responsible for the emotional distance she maintained from me, and the relatively small range of feelings that she expressed in our sessions.

It was only after she looked at my distorted face and broke into tears for the first time that I felt a wall between us dissolve. Neither of us said a word as she threw her arms around me, but her silent message seemed unmistakable: "Now that we're in the same boat, I can feel for you and with you." Needless to say, this sense of our fittedness to one another transformed our relationship. Tracy's sense of kinship with me seemed to embolden her to confront the most painful aspects of her difference from others in a deeply emotional way. But the healing this engendered was not only Tracy's. After discovering that neither my literal nor my metaphorical losses of face had estranged us – indeed it had brought us closer together – I too felt more whole.

Summary

To adopt a relational systems perspective in its most radical form is to accept the view that all human lives are interconnected and all traumas are shared traumas. Perhaps this explains why the shouts and screams of traumatized others relentlessly fill our ears. These harrowing cries place our ethical selves into question and confront us with profound uncertainty. Reminded of the deafening shock of our previous encounters with unbearable traumas and eager for reassurance that we will go on being, we may avert our gaze from the faces of our suffering neighbors. There are times, however, upon hearing echoes of our own suffering in their cries, when we feel called to respond with compassion, love, and care. I can only hope that, more and more, I will find the courage to heed these calls.

Note

1 See also the idea of bilateral healing in Brothers and Lewinberg (1999) and "radical engagment" in Atwood (2011).

References

Anker, M. (2009). *The ethics of uncertainty: Aporetic openings*. New York: Atropos Press.
Atwood, G. (2011). *The abyss of madness*. New York: Routledge.
Atwood, G., & Stolorow, R. D. (1984). *The structures of subjectivity*. Hillsdale, NJ: Analytic Press.
Bernstein, R. J. (1995). *The new constellation: The ethical-political horizons of modernity/postmodernity*. Cambridge, MA: The MIT Press.
Brothers, D. (2008). *Toward a psychology of uncertainty: Trauma-centered psychoanalysis*. New York: Analytic Press.
Brothers, D. (2012, April). *Losing face (literally) and finding creativity: The effect of the analyst's Bell's Palsy on the therapeutic process*. Paper presented at APA Division of Psychoanalysis (39). Santa Fe, New Mexico.
Brothers, D., & Lewinberg, E. (1999). The therapeutic partnership: A developmental view of self-psychological treatment as bilateral healing. In A. Goldberg (Ed.), *Progress in Self Psychology, 15*. Hillsdale, NJ: Analytic Press.
Critchley, S. (2007). *Infinitely demanding: Ethics of commitment, politics of resistance*. London and New York: Verso.
Critchley, S. (2009). *Ethics-politics-subjectivity: Essays on Derrida, Levinas, and contemporary French thought*. London and New York: Verso.
Freud, S. (1950). Project for a scientific psychology. *The standard edition of the complete psychological works of Sigmund Freud: Pre-psycho-analytic publications and unpublished drafts, 1*, 281–391. London: Hogarth Press. (Original work published 1895)
Freud, S. (1955). Beyond the pleasure principle. *The standard edition of the complete psychological works of Sigmund Freud, 18*, 3–64. London: Hogarth Press. (Original work published 1920)
Kohut, H. (1971). *The analysis of the self*. New York: International Universities Press.
Lacan, J. (1992). *The ethics of psychoanalysis*. In J. Miller (Ed.). (D. Potter, Trans.). London and New York: Routledge.
Levinas, E. (1987). *Time and the other*. (R. Cohen Trans.). Pittsburgh, PA: Duquesne University Press. (Original work published 1947)
Orange, D. (2010). *Thinking for clinicians: Philosophical resources for contemporary psychoanalysis and the humanistic psychotherapies*. New York and Hove, UK: Routledge.

Orange, D. (2011). *The suffering stranger: Hermeneutics for everyday clinical practice.* New York and Hove, UK: Routledge.

Sander, L. W. (1995). *Wholeness, specificity and the organization of conscious experiencing.* Paper presented at the meeting of the APA, Division 39, Santa Monica, CA.

Stolorow, R. D. (2011). World, affectivity, trauma: Heidegger and post-Cartesian *psychoanalysis.* New York: Routledge.

Winnicott, D. W. (1965). *The maturational process and the facilitating environment: Studies in the theory of emotional development.* New York: International Universities Press.

Chapter 9

Can one still be a Jew without Sartre?

Levinas, Jewish education, and the crisis of humanism

Claire Katz[1]

> *Learning is a good medicine: but no medicine is powerful enough to preserve itself from taint and corruption independently of defects in the jar that it is kept in. One man sees clearly but does not see straight: consequently he sees what is good but fails to follow it; he sees knowledge and does not use it.*
>
> Michel de Montaigne

> *I would like to suggest that our minds are swamped by too much study and by too much matter just as plants are swamped by too much water or lamps by too much oil; that our minds, held fast and encumbered by so many diverse preoc-cupations, may well lose the means of struggling free, remaining bowed and bent under the load; except that it is quite otherwise: the more our souls are filled, the more they expand; examples drawn from far-off times show, on the contrary, that great soldiers and statesmen were also great scholars.*
>
> Michel de Montaigne

In 1947, Jean-Paul Sartre gave a lecture sponsored by the Alliance Israélite Universelle that summarized the main ideas found in his book, *Anti-Semite and Jew* – a book that one might describe as a long meditation on "La Question Juive." Levinas (1946) wrote a short response to the lecture, which was then published in the *Cahiers d'Alliance*, along with passages from Sartre's talk (Levinas, 1999). Levinas opens with his praise for Sartre, noting how nice it is to hear someone who is not Jewish speak on these themes in this way. However, he is less impressed with Sartre's sympathetic response than he is with the new "weapon" Sartre deploys to identify the structure of anti-Semitism. Using existentialism and the structures of exist-ence in the modern world on which to base his response, Sartre is able to escape the trap of those who came before him – those who discussed our material condition but then advocated for anti-Semitism, the poets of blood and soil, he calls them. These he links to Nietzsche's legacy.

In the midst of this short response to Sartre's lecture Levinas comments on the awkwardness of Sartre's linking of Jewish destiny with anti-Semitism and he responds with a comment that refers to those whose Judaism was not the result of an anti-Semitism. The remark seems almost an aside, a glib joke, almost like he might add, "There was Hanukkah before there was Christmas, and Passover is not the Jewish Easter." Yet this comment appears to be the central motivation for his sustained response on ethical subjectivity over the next forty-five years. While Levinas praises Sartre's analysis of anti-Semitism, he disagrees with Sartre's proposed solution that the development of a Marxist state would be sufficient to bring an end to anti-Semitism – even as he appears to agree in later texts that this economic move might be necessary.

Sartre's relationship to Hegel, mediated by his classmates and friends who actually attended Alexandre Kojève's lectures on the *Phenomenology of Spirit*, inspires a view of intersubjectivity grounded not only in recognition, but also negation. Ironically, Sartre, the existentialist, appears to have no choice but to advance a view of the Jew that is contingent on the anti-Semite – the anti-Semite makes the Jew, regardless of how the Jew responds (succumbing to the stereotype or actively resisting it). In contrast to this Hegelian view of intersubjectivity, I read Levinas as taking Sartre's analysis of the Jew vis-à-vis the anti-Semite as a challenge to reclaim a Judaism that is not identified through the anti-Semite but rather finds its identity in pre-modern sources – that is, a Judaism that pre-dates modern anti-Semitism.

Twenty years after Sartre's lecture, in a 1966 radio interview published as "Education after Auschwitz," the critical theorist Theodor Adorno declared:

> the premier demand upon all education is that Auschwitz not happen again . . . the only education that has any sense at all is an education toward critical self-reflection. But since according to the findings of depth psychology, all personalities, even those who commit atrocities in later life, are formed in early childhood, education seeking to prevent the repetition must concentrate upon early childhood.
>
> (Adorno, 1998)

Adorno's comments, made in response to the atrocities of the Holocaust, imply that barbarism is not something that poses merely a threat of a relapse. Rather, Adorno insists, Auschwitz was the relapse. Adorno's solution lies in creating an environment that will prevent another Auschwitz by cultivating individuals who can resist authoritarian thinking.

Adorno's argument is compelling but I would add that resistance to authoritarian thinking will not by itself mitigate the danger that he fears. Although the critical thinking that Adorno advocates may help someone resist authoritarian thinking, critical thinking alone will not help someone become a person who resists authoritarian rule. Adorno's prescription is necessary but I do not believe it is sufficient. His warning nonetheless echoes the concerns Levinas began voicing soon after he was released from the POW camp.

Yet while Levinas and Adorno share the same concerns and, indeed, while both recognize the necessity of focusing on and radically changing the way we educate our children if we are going to prevent another Auschwitz, their respective views of education and what education should do differ in significant ways. I argue that for Emmanuel Levinas, the task of cultivating ethical subjectivity is two-fold: on the one hand, he focuses his attention on cultivating a subjectivity that will not breed the conditions that create a murderous self in the first place and on the other, this ethical subjectivity should have the courage to stand against such murderous conditions if they do appear. And to do this, he locates humanism in a Judaism that is pre-modern.

My chapter will proceed in two parts. I first briefly give an account of the limits of humanities education to make the case for why Levinas promotes Jewish education and not more generally a humanities education for his ethical project. I then turn to Levinas's account of Jewish education and show where and how it fits into his larger concerns regarding assimilation. But to be clear: what I find most interesting about Levinas's project is not simply that he promotes an educational method that he believes is significantly different from Western education, but also that he believes this education should be housed in communities within that Western culture. That is, Levinas does not move to Israel, nor does he implore his fellow Jews to do so. Quite the opposite. He believes the Jewish community has an obligation to itself and to the communities in which they exist to educate their children to stand up to injustice and hope that others might follow that example. And this view can be expanded to include his more general concern – how does the particular live with/in the universal?

Humanities education redux

"How does someone develop ethically?" This question occupies the 18th-century philosopher, Jean-Jacques Rousseau, in several of his writings. In his *Second Discourse* (1755), Rousseau offers two principles of human nature as a counter to Hobbes' claim that we have only the innate sense of self-preservation. If that were the case, Rousseau concludes, we would be monsters. But we are not. He offers then a second principle, which is "an innate repugnance to see his fellow suffer" (Rousseau, 1997a, p. 152). But having an innate repugnance to see my fellow suffer will not alone keep me from becoming a monster in a different sense. In this essay and later in his *Social Contract* (1997b), Rousseau expresses his concerns with the development of an intellect that is not anchored by a good character.

Several years after publishing his *Second Discourse*, Rousseau struggles with this same problem in *Emile* (1762), his treatise on education. Yet in this book, he offers an attempt at an educational project that will mitigate those concerns. In the voice of the tutor, Rousseau describes the problem of moral development. He repeats his claim that we are born with an innate repugnance to suffering and he warns us that as a result of this aversion there are different possible responses to another's misery: we can pity the other and then turn toward him in an attempt to alleviate his pain; or, we can compare ourselves to the other, silently expressing gratitude that "we are not like her." The latter response might lead us to position ourselves so that we do not have to see her suffering. For Rousseau's tutor, the task is to help the child develop the proper response to suffering so that, unlike the stereotypical image of the philosopher, Emile does not sit in his study while ignoring the cries outside of those who suffer.

Like Rousseau, nearly every major philosopher in the history of philosophy, extending as far back as Plato, either wrote an independent treatise on philosophy of education or included a version of it in his or her larger philosophical project. In his *Republic* Plato devotes two books solely to education, in addition to including the cave allegory, representing the education of the philosopher. Aristotle wrote the *Nicomachean Ethics*, which details the significance of the early formation of good character. In the modern period, Rousseau used *Emile* to complement *The Social Contract* and Kant included a catechism at the end of the *Metaphysics of Morals* in addition to writing a short treatise called *On Education*. In late modern philosophy, Hegel, influenced by Rousseau, uses *Bildung*, which provides a strong developmental focus to the *Phenomenology of Spirit*. Most significantly, we see philosophers in the history of philosophy use the role of education to incisively discuss women's subjugation. As John Stuart Mill observes in his "The Subjection of Women," it is not enough that women are kept in an inferior position to men – socially, personally, and politically – to men; through the educational process, they are taught that being a woman is to like the position in which they find themselves. It is not that Mill provides an educational model; rather, he argues that education is responsible for shaping who we are and how we see ourselves as political subjects. Writing almost one hundred years earlier than Mill and influenced by Locke's view that young children can reason at an early age and responding to figures like Rousseau (1977) who would deny women any serious education, the 18th-century philosopher Mary Wollstonecraft (2014) argues in her *Vindication of the Rights of Women* that we need to reshape the way we educate young girls and women to position them in society in a manner commensurate with their abilities, which are substantially greater than what has been granted them. This list, not meant to be exhaustive, simply names a few examples and they are all different in their ideas about the political and about education. However, what they do share is an understanding that a subject *develops* in relationship to the larger society in which the subject is situated and moral education is a fundamental component in this development. In most cases, this means the philosopher writes a political or ethical philosophy and then provides an educational philosophy to show how that end can be achieved.

When we approach the 20th century, the conversation between political philosophy and educational theory essentially disappears. With the exception of the classical American philosophers, e.g., John Dewey, Western philosophers no longer engaged questions regarding educational theory. Indeed with the rise of logical positivism and a rigid definition of what counted as "truth," and by implication, philosophy, finding philosophers interested in political theory was also a difficult task. This lack of interest, in turn, affected how the philosophical canon has been taught with regard to which philosophical themes are considered relevant. Scanning the course offerings in most North American philosophy departments, one might never realize that the philosophy of education, which is intimately related to core areas in philosophy (e.g., epistemology, metaphysics, and ethics, not to mention political philosophy), was given considerable attention by most figures in the history of Western philosophy. And to be fair, at this writing, the field of philosophy is changing, albeit ever so slowly. Yet even as it is slow, the change is also profound, as evidenced by the recent work of Philip Kitcher (2011), Jason, Stanley, and the new younger generation of analytic philosophers who see what was once on the margins as now central to the core areas of philosophy (Kitcher, 2011).

In addition to changes in the philosophical terrain, a multitude of other factors contributed to education's disappearance from the philosophical conversation, making it nearly impossible to hang the reason for its exile on one cause. In the late 19th century, we see the emergence of Normal schools, colleges specifically charged with training teachers. Kindergartens came into existence and the primary role of the elementary school shifted from a knowledge-based environment (like we might find in the old Latin schools) to one that emphasized nurturing children. And only in the 19th century did we see a movement toward public – as in state-funded – education in the United States. This shift, in turn, altered the role of the teacher. "Pedagogy" – a science of teaching – became far more important than imparting information or cultivating minds. With the shift in emphasis away from knowledge acquisition, the field of education also shifted from men to women in the role of the teacher. Additionally, the development of psychology into its own research discipline offered the field of education theories of learning and behavior that appeared far more useful than theories of knowledge had been. Philosophy appeared obsolete with regard to what it could offer education and, more importantly, what it could offer schools.

The reasons for the changes in the educational landscape are numerous and complicated, and most likely over-determined; it would be both impossible and irresponsible to locate these changes in one single cause. More important for my discussion here is that the effect was for contemporary philosophy to wash its hands, and its curriculum, of any philosophical interest in educational theory, thus removing its critical and reflective voice not only from the development of our current educational models but also from the connection educational theory might have to the development of moral subjectivity.[2] Thus, with few exceptions, philosophical moral theory describes, or applies to, adults, not children. Returning to Rousseau (1997a), we can recall that his suspicion of community led him to separate the education of the citizen from the education of the "man" qua male, the latter of which included moral development. Yet the development of the ethical person was central to the proper development of the political citizen, even if he saw the two tasks as separate.

Education and the suffering other

If the question I posed above, "How does one develop ethically?", occupies much of moral education, the more specific question, "How does someone develop so that they turn toward the suffering of another?", haunts Emmanuel Levinas's ethical project. The question, then, that guides my argument is: "Why does Levinas turn specifically to Jewish education?", an education that includes the Jewish sacred texts? Is it not the case, in light of certain beliefs about the humanities exerting a humanizing influence, that a humanities education can accomplish the task of cultivating humanity in the way that Levinas hopes? Is it not the case that Shakespeare's writings could just as easily replace the Jewish sacred texts? As we will see later, Levinas does not ignore this question but confronts it directly. In light of that, we can ask what it means that Levinas makes this case to the Jewish audience but does not offer a comparable discussion in his philosophical writing. That is, if this humanism is learned or cultivated, and if this cultivation is best done through Jewish education, what does it mean that it is offered only to Jews? Is the implication that Jews need this education and non-Jews do not?

Our current debates about the humanities and humanistic education return us to a more basic question about the aim of education: What is the role education plays in the cultivation of a self, and more specifically, in the cultivation of a moral self? James L. Jarrett's 1973 book, *The Humanities and Humanistic Education*, opens with an exploration of the crisis of the humanities. In this case, the sciences, feeling underprivileged and undervalued, were beginning to bear down on the humanities. The criticisms of the humanities Jarrett rehearses in 1973, the height of the explosion of university education, could easily be printed today without a date and no one would blink. Jarrett's book should be a signal that as academics many of us are nostalgic for a time when we believe the humanities were never under siege – but this is indeed nostalgia. Each epoch sees itself as "in crisis" – not recognizing that there has not been a time when the humanities have ever enjoyed unfettered respect, admiration, and support. We need only recall how Socrates' illustrious philosophical career ended to realize that when one asks too many questions, one might be invited to leave the community.

Responding to the current debates surrounding the humanities, Frank Donoghue, an English professor at Ohio State University, traces the roots of the corporate model of education back to the turn of the 20th century, the rise of industrialization, and the increased power attained by those with wealth. He argues in his 2008 book, *The Last Professors: the Corporate University and the Fate of the Humanities*, that it was not long before the newly moneyed were exerting power and influence over university education, while simultaneously expressing their suspicion of the very education they were funding. As Donoghue's analysis shows, education that did not aim to produce anything, that is humanities education, was rejected in favor or something – anything – utilitarian.

Recalling again Rousseau's (1997b) distrust of community, we are reminded that these more contemporary suspicions of community and education did not begin in the 19th century. Yet Rousseau was careful to separate the education of the citizen from the education of the "man" qua male, the latter of which included moral development. Indeed, for Rousseau, the development of the ethical person was central to the proper development of the political citizen, even if he saw the two tasks as separate. I do not have time here to cover this point in more detail, yet it is worth noting that, taken together, these two questions about moral and civic development lie at the heart of debates about the role, purpose, aim, and value of education.[3] My concern is that these attacks on humanities education may have backed humanists into a corner such that we believe our only defense is to describe or "sell" the humanities in vaguely utilitarian terms and/or to promise that the humanities can accomplish a feat that it neither can do, nor should we expect it to do – cultivate "better" human beings. We can pose the question in this way: What is the role education plays in the cultivation of a self, and more specifically, in the cultivation of a moral self?

With regard to the question of humanities education and its relationship to the cultivation of character and the development of civic responsibility, we find, on one side of the debate, Hannah Arendt, who argues that education is not political and is not intended to effect change. Rather, its aim is to introduce the child into the world in which he or she is born, thus enabling that child to participate in the public sphere when she is an adult. The role of a classical education then is to introduce the child to those traditions and ideas that inform the world in which the child now lives. Although Arendt's political philosophy is often viewed as unclassifiable by conventional categories in political theory, having positioned herself against progressive education, her own view of education is decidedly conservative.

The other side of the debate is represented most clearly by Martha Nussbaum in her 2010 book, *Not for Profit*, tellingly subtitled, *Why Democracy Needs the Humanities*. Where Arendt believed that education was not intended to mold in any particular fashion, Nussbaum takes up the mantle of progressive education and deploys it to promote an educational project that she believes will cultivate more people who are better suited to participate as democratic citizens. For her, this means creating more people who will live with each other in mutual respect and fewer people who will seek comfort in domination.[4]

Nussbaum and moral courage

In the chapter "Educating Citizens," Nussbaum (2010) explores the culti-vation of citizens with moral courage, those who would have stood strong in Milgram's experiment with authority and would have been immune to the position they were assigned in the Zimbardo prison experiment. She tells us in this chapter that "[w]e need to understand how to produce more citizens [who are prepared to live with others on terms of mutual respect and reciprocity] and fewer of [those who seek the comfort of domination]" (Nussbaum, 2010, p. 29). How do we achieve this goal? For Nussbaum, the answer is through an education in the humanities. In the chapter imme-diately following this one she outlines an educational process that is at once child-centered (Rousseau, 1997a) and based on a Socratic pedagogy, i.e., one that takes critical questioning as its point of departure. She cites progressive education as a means to accomplish this task and praises, for example, the *Philosophy for Children* program, developed by Matthew Lipman, which is based on Dewey's philosophy of education with an emphasis on developing critical thinking and reasoning skills. With this focus, Nussbaum's view of education directly opposes Arendt's.

We could approach Nussbaum's (2010) claim from several different angles, but the first one that comes to mind is to ask what it means to edu-cate for a democracy when one of the values that a democracy holds dear is precisely the plurality of voices within it. Yet Nussbaum seems only to consider democracy as a site where we are all like-minded with a similar set of values. But this is not true of either a democracy or of a humanities education. Indeed, we must consider that when we teach the humanities we explore all of humanity – the good side and the dark side. Additionally, we must consider that within a humanities education, the respective character of our students will influence how they filter both what they read and what their teachers say.

Nussbaum advances her argument by drawing on both Rousseau's *Emile* and Socratic pedagogy. These two models do not fit together neatly. Rousseau needs the kind of education he describes in *Emile* to lessen the power reason can have either to corrupt or provide power to an already corrupt soul. Rousseau needs to cultivate a man who will be immune to the corrupting forces of reason exemplified in particular by philosophical reason, which too frequently looks like sophistry. Reason at an early age is precisely the problem and "child-centered" for Rousseau would not mean the *Philosophy for Children* program, which Nussbaum mentions as an example of a promising educational model. I would argue that it is a promising educational model, but not for the reasons Nussbaum wants. And for those of you who have read *Emile*, you know that his educational project spectacularly fails.

In the end, Nussbaum's (2010) attempts to draw an easy line from Socratic questioning and democracy to humanities education and the morally cultivated create an argument that is remarkably deficient. If we know anything about Socratic questioning, it is the presumed integrity it displays in the pursuit of truth. Socratic questioning requires the participants to question everything including the future – or goodness – of an idea for which Nussbaum wants to install Socratic education to defend, namely democracy. True to his or her own mission, the Socratic gadfly pokes and prods everything, including those values that we might now believe to be true and right. And we must expect and allow our students at any age to do the same. The humanities education that Nussbaum promotes, which includes critical reasoning, not only runs the risk of creating people who are not concerned about others but also people whose greed, selfishness, and even brutality are now backed by reason to justify those actions.

As was pointed out by the political theorist Ryan Balot (2011), if Nussbaum is arguing that a humanities education is superior for achieving moral wisdom, then those of us with PhDs in the humanities are super superior, leading us down the path of the philosopher king, which is decidedly not democratic. Of course, the irony that Balot so astutely identifies is then betrayed by the fact that many with PhDs in the humanities are not morally superior and too frequently act in ways that realize Rousseau's worst fears about reason providing the moral justification for bad behavior. Nussbaum could argue in return that those who are using reason to justify greed or other forms of bad behavior could be shown through reason the error of their ways. But then we could find ourselves in a game of intellectual chicken, where each side refuses to yield to the other and nothing inherent in the argument for either side would tip the argument one way or the other.

This account of the humanities and its relationship to a democratic society carries its own set of questions. More importantly, it relies on an assumption about the role of the humanities in the creation of a virtuous or morally upright self that the 20th-century French philosopher, Emmanuel Levinas, finds questionable on multiple levels. The role of the humanities in the development of an ethical person is significant for my present discussion since Levinas turns to Jewish education and decidedly not to a classical humanities education to develop the ethical subjectivity he describes. This ethical subjectivity in turn provides a solution to what he identifies in his philosophical writings and his writings on Judaism as the crisis of humanism. Recalling my discussion of Sartre at the beginning of the chapter, I now turn to the second part of this chapter and consider the positive formulation of the Jew that Levinas offers through his essays on Jewish education.

Humanism and antihumanism

Levinas returned to Paris immediately following the murderous years of the Second World War, during which he served as an interpreter before his unit was captured. He then spent the duration of the war, 1940–5, in several POW camps in Germany (Caygill, 2010). Upon his return from the war and without delay, he went to work for the *Alliance Israelite Universelle* (AIU) and in 1947 he became the director of the *École Normal Israélite Orientale* (ENIO). At an event hosted by the AIU celebrating the occasion of his 80th birthday, Levinas made the following statement about his time immediately following his release from captivity:

> After Auschwitz, I had the impression that in taking on the directorship of the École Normal Israélite Orientale I was responding to a historical calling. It was my little secret . . . Probably the naiveté of a young man. I am still mindful and proud of it today.
>
> (Malka, 2006, p. 84)

This celebration brought together several of his former students from those years at the ENIO and issued in a small publication, *Levinas – Philosophe et Pédagogue*, which collected several short essays about Levinas as a teacher, Talmudist, and philosopher (Levinas, 1998). The collection comprises just a select few of the commentaries offered by Levinas's own students, yet even they provide a glimpse of Levinas as both a teacher and a philosopher of the highest order. One statement in particular stands out in its unique character.

Ady Steg, who was the President of the AIU at the time of the celebration, offered a fable speculating about the time when Levinas would stand before the Heavenly Throne (Steg, 1998). To summarize, the Eternal One asks Levinas what he did with his life. With each answer – "I believed in the Good, about which I wrote"; "I studied with Husserl and Heidegger"; "I studied with Chouchani" – the Eternal One replies – "And?" It is only when Levinas mentions that he directed the ENIO that the Eternal One is impressed and replies, "Director of the school, you, a prestigious philosopher?" After this response the Eternal One seems satisfied and sends Levinas on his way.

The response from the Eternal One, while it runs counter to the prevailing attitude toward education, also betrays a sense of surprise – a philosopher of such great prestige would direct a day school? While the Heavenly Throne considers this particular task to be of the greatest importance, this surprise reveals an awareness of the possibility that not everyone would see things in the same way, thus making Levinas's devotion to the school all the more admirable. The Eternal One's surprise indicated by his question – "You, a famous philosopher [directed a school]?" – clearly indicates that in spite of Levinas's academic accomplishments, he was not too proud or arrogant to devote himself to the education of the younger generation.

Nonetheless, the Eternal One's added question – "you, a famous philosopher?" – spoken with more than a hint of doubt or suspicion betrays the more common negative sentiment toward education and those who educate. The view that "those who can't, teach" is still prevalent today, and the attitudes toward education range from resentment – teachers are paid too much for jobs that appear to others as not very demanding – to outright cynicism and contempt regarding the educational system and what it promises. This range of negative attitudes creates a powerful force pushing against education, hindering any possibility of real reform: no one believes that education produces anything positive; only those who are not good at anything else would go into teaching; and teaching is so easy that teachers should not be compensated adequately for doing such a job. In contrast to the negative view about teaching, Levinas saw it as fundamental to any hope for the future, certainly for the Jewish people, and I contend for the rest of humanity. The future of the world rests on how we educate our young people. Ady Steg's fable is certainly written for effect. Yet it is clear to Levinas's students from the ENIO and to anyone who reads his essays on Judaism that education is not a side hobby in which he engaged.

The original publication venue of these essays on education indicates that at times they were intended for an audience of Jewish educators and at others they were directed at French Jewish intellectuals. Their purpose was, on the one hand, to convince their audience of the need to return to a traditional model of Jewish education, specifically a model that includes instruction in the Hebrew language and literature and, on the other, to reassure this audience that "returning" to Jewish education did not mean turning away from French culture and modern life – the original mandate of the *Alliance* (Steg, 1998).

Less than a year into his service in this position, Levinas penned a short essay on the reopening of the ENIO, whose operation had been suspended for the previous six years. He wrote the following:

> Our martyrdom, since 1933, gives us a more acute awareness of our solidarity across space but also across time, the need to find in the sources of our being, our reason for being and the mystery of our destiny, the meaning our hardships. Whether as a return to the land of their ancestors, or in a more general and perhaps more profound form, the recovery of mystical experiences and ethics, on which Judaism is based and from which it could never be banished – *there exists in Israel the need for a Jewish humanism. The ENIO must also take that into account.* There must be open access to this Jewish humanism . . . A long-term undertaking, certainly, and full of difficulties, but we must attempt a future worthy of the ENIO the past, creating in the old building on Rue d'Auteuil [the original site of the AIU] a center of Jewish Western spirituality [*spiritualité juive occidentale*] which will once again bring something new to the Judaism of the Orient.
>
> (Levinas, 1946, my translation)

Yet shifting this mandate required a gentle touch. In his 1956 essay, "For a Jewish Humanism," Levinas reassures his audience that the Jewish school does not betray the ideals of the secular school. By supporting what he calls "Jewish humanism" – "that which cannot remain indifferent to the modern world in which it seeks a whole humanity" – the Jewish school lends support to what gives meaning to Judaism in the modern world (Levinas, 1990b, pp. 273–276). The aim of the Jewish school, then, is not simply to bring a Jewish education to Jewish children to maintain Judaism as a religion; the aim of the Jewish school is to bring children into the kind of education that will reinforce the Jewish humanism he believes is found in and promoted by the Jewish sources.

Assimilation and Jewish uniqueness

Levinas identifies the problem with assimilation and the homogeneity that Jews desired and for the most part achieved as the loss of that which made them unique – "The unique nature of Judaism itself is that it consists in promoting as one of the highest virtues the knowledge of its own sources" (Levinas, 1990b, p. 276). Judaism's uniqueness consists not only in that it commands the teaching of itself, but also that this teaching has built into it the discovery, preservation, and enactment of a Jewish humanism. As a result, Levinas sees Judaism not as parochial, or as a mechanism for separation, but as precisely the opposite – as that which is indispensable to human harmony.

These themes continue ideas that Levinas (1990b) introduced early in these essays collected in *Difficult Freedom*, but they are poignantly expressed in his 1954 essay, "Assimilation Today," where he ties The Dreyfus Affair to the years of National Socialism, two events that are not only horrifying in the story of Jewish history but which also put into question the relationship Judaism had to the Principles of 1789. He painfully reminds his readers that assimilation failed:

> It failed because it did not put an end to the anguish felt by the Jewish soul. Assimilation failed because it did not placate the non-Jews, or put an end to anti-Semitism; on certain points, it stirred up heated reactions and arguments once more. Anguish and anxiety still surreptitiously alter apparently free behavior and every Jew remains, in the largest sense of the word, a Marrano.

(p. 255)

Referring to the Zionist Chaim Grinberg, who collected a set of essays on religion and the state, Levinas (1990b) cynically observes, "if Jews do not convert to Christianity, it is not because they believe in Judaism but because they no longer believe in anything religious" (pp. 255–256). He then astutely notes, "the fact that assimilation can succeed only in dissolution and that only irreligiousness slows down this dissolution, is the most serious crisis of assimilation" (p. 256). His discussion of the separation between church and state, between the private life of conscience and the realm of public life, could not be more pressing than it is today, here in the United States – and I might add on a personal note, right here in Texas! He reminds us that "the vice at the heart of a philosophy of assimilation is its forgetting, or ignorance of, the ways that secularized forms of religious life lie at the heart of the so called secular state" (p. 256). For many in the secular state, its religious framework need not be made explicit; indeed, it need not even be thought – "one breathes it naturally" (pp. 256–257). As we see only too well in the battle lines being drawn over public education, health care, and even our economic system, which is often cast in religious terms, "[this separation] does not simply vanish as a result of the juridical separation between Church and State" (p. 257).

In Levinas's view, the presence of Israel as a state presents an opportunity not available to the Jew previously – an opportunity for life in the state to converge with the life of conscience. But also, as a result of Israel's reality, "the error of assimilation becomes visible." What becomes noticeable to the Jew only after the state of Israel became a reality was the way she "breathed an atmosphere impregnated with Christian essence and that prepares them for the religious life of these states and heralds their conversion" (p. 257). The secular states which are founded on a Christian structure create a Christian atmosphere that is perceived as secular. It is to the Jew who resists being drawn into this pool, who tries to swim against this current, that the secular is revealed as religious. Thus, the Jew must make a decision, which will include reviving a Jewish science, and which must include returning to Hebrew. In this essay, as he does in every other essay on Jewish education, Levinas reminds his readers that this return, this reclaiming of Judaism, does not refute the principles of 1789. Rather, "these old texts teach precisely a universalism that is purged of any particularism tied to the land . . . . It teaches the human solidarity of a nation united by ideas" (p. 257).

"Antihumanism and education"

In 1973, almost 20 years after the publication of these early essays and only one year prior to the publication of *Otherwise than Being*, Levinas published "Antihumanism and Education" (Levinas, 1990b). He opens this essay by connecting the Western view of humanism with a conception of freedom that is protected by the liberal state. We see him struggling with the same questions about humanism and humanities education that continue to haunt most contemporary discussions of education. Additionally, this essay most explicitly invokes Jewish education as a response to the evil that the world saw unleashed in the 20th century.

Repeating many of the same themes from these earlier pieces, he argues that we are in a crisis of humanism for which Jewish education is ultimately the solution (Levinas, 1990b). With the emancipation and principles of 1789, he explains, Jewish education succumbed to the "hermeneutic methods of the west" (Levinas, 1990b, p. 270), which disqualified rabbinic exegesis and was sanitized of the very element that might have allowed it to contribute to modern culture in a meaningful way. It was precisely because Jews did not want to be seen as different that they – and Jewish education – lost any means to enact the distinctive ideas that precisely informed the humanism to which they attach themselves.

Thus, Levinas questions not only what Western liberalism promised and what modern humanism delivered, he also worries about the recent critiques launched against them. Thus, he finds himself positioned between these two poles – the fragility of a failed humanism on one side and the antihumanism that responded to it on the other. In these essays, Levinas calls for a new humanism, albeit one that does not allow those who promote it to become persecutors. For Levinas, it is unsatisfactory to support either the humanism that he has just described, a humanism that is sanitized of religion and devoid of everything that is in fact human, or the antihumanism that developed in response (Levinas, 1990b, pp. 280–286). More seriously, his mistrust of the prevailing humanism is a protest against appearances that cover over hypocrisy and conflation of revolutionary literature with being a revolutionary (Levinas, 1990b, pp. 282–283). That is, he worries that there is not a fundamental shift in the relationship to the other. Rather, there is a series of revolutions, of protests, each with its singular mission, and none getting at a fundamental responsibility. More significantly, he worries that intellectuals in particular have confused reading humanistic literature with being humanists, just as one might confuse or conflate reading revolutionary literature with being a revolutionary. In the same vein, one might worry that there is a confusion between reading Levinas and one being a Levinasian ethical subject.

When approached through the midrashic tradition, the biblical narratives teach us how to read carefully, critically, and sensitively. Is this not the kind of literacy that we want from students whom we hope will participate in the democratic process and, quite frankly, who will participate in the social structure? Is this not the kind of attention that we hope will translate into a responsibility for other people? Would it not be even more advantageous to teach our students that religious texts ask us to read them not only with sensitivity and respect but also with a critical eye? The Talmudic model of learning radically challenges the model we find throughout the history of philosophy. It not only resists an absolute truth; it also explicitly teaches this resistance.

Reading Jewishly

Levinas situates Jewish education as that which *simultaneously* inflames the mind and cultivates an ethical subject who is responsible for the Other. That is, Jewish education is not anti-intellectual, but nor does it simply rely on the intellect to cultivate an ethical subject. The aim, then, of Levinas's philosophical project is to employ an educational method that is informed by his understanding of Jewish education as that which cultivates intellectual acuity and also develops responsibility for the Other. His view of the ethical relation not only points to an educational model that includes reading biblical narratives Jewishly; it also relies on this model of education to cultivate an ethical subject. Levinas's insight reveals the role that alterity plays in midrash, since the role of midrash is to open up the text and allow voices that are otherwise muted to be heard.

Thus, for Levinas, reading Jewishly is precisely to read such that one is open to the Other. Although the process of questioning that we find in the Talmudic tradition is intended to teach students to question the material at hand, the Jewish tradition of learning recognizes something unique about the journey one takes in the educational process – it reveals an approach to education that is less concerned with the notion of absolute truth. Instead, its role is to engage the mind and to join the learners in a community of education. It might be that this role is what philosophy always intended – that philosophy was concerned less with a single truth than it was about identifying wisdom by inflaming the creative mind, and that this kind of learning was to be done communally. Unfortunately, this view is not the standard view of philosophy or of education.

Levinas demonstrates in his 1935 book, *On Escape*, that the seductive call of freedom presented to us by modern philosophy is a mythology (Levinas, 1990a/2003). First and foremost, our bodies require food, nurturance, and warmth. Our bodies betray us. Levinas's ethics, the response to the Other, which recognizes the possibility of sacrificing one's life for the Other, is prior to any sense of freedom or choice. And here he sees the mythology of freedom in the same way that he sees the mythology of autonomy. Even before the call of the Other, before any ethical response, we are not free. We can see, then, how a pedagogical model of education based on a view of learning that emerges from the Jewish tradition would be founded. And we can see that unless one is willing to step out of the tradition set forth by modern philosophy, and step out of it radically, this kind of pedagogy might not reveal itself. Levinas's implicit identification of the Talmudic approach to learning not only radicalizes his philosophical project. It also transforms how we think about education, our understanding of both teaching and learning (Levinas, 1990b). Education, and indeed a particular kind of education, is fundamental to the creation of the subjectivity that Levinas describes. If, as Levinas suggests, politics is derived from ethics, then it is the Jewish tradition from which Levinas's own ethical/philosophical project emerges that provides us with a more effective pedagogical model that encourages us first to engage with each other face to face. If we are not first mindful of Levinas's warnings, if the political, even as education, is not rooted in the radical ethics that he describes, we will simply leave ourselves vulnerable to becoming the perpetrators he warns against.[5]

Notes

1 This chapter is reproduced with permission from my 2013 book, *Levinas and the Crisis of Humanism* (Bloomington: Indiana University Press). The beginning argument, however, has changed slightly to emphasize the possibility that Levinas is responding also to Sartre's challenge regarding the identity of the Jew in relation to the anti-Semite. I wish to thank Indiana University Press for their permission to reprint.
2 There are of course exceptions to this claim, for example, most of the classical American philosophers including John Dewey and some European thinkers, e.g., Theodor Adorno.
3 Colleges of Liberal Arts, indeed even some particular programs (e.g., see the recent descriptions of how Women's and Gender Studies programs describe themselves),

prominently display the word "leadership" in the description of the education it provides their students.

4 There is large and ever-growing literature on this topic. The collection, *Debating moral education: Rethinking the role of the modern university*, stands out as particularly good. See Elizabeth Kiss and J. Peter Euben, eds. (Durham: Duke University Press, 2010). In particular, the essays by Stanley Fish and Ruth W. Grant. See Fish, "I know it when I see it: A reply to Kiss and Euben," pp. 76–91 and Grant, "Is humanistic education humanizing?," pp. 283–295. See also Peter Euben's essay, "Hannah Arendt on politicizing the university and other cliches," pp. 175–199, in Mordechai Gordon, ed., *Renewing our common world: Hannah Arendt and education* (Boulder: Westview, 2011).

5 Carl Cederberg wrote a lovely dissertation tracing the concept of the human in Levinas. At the end he discusses what is at stake politically in Levinas's concept. Like most recent political theory, he turns to philosophers like Agamben and Rancière. I do not know if either of these thinkers will be successful at offering a politics comparable to Levinas's ethics. Nor do I think that Bonnie Honig's work is immune to criticism. But it seems that any account of the political that will allow for the radical ethics Levinas suggests must also stretch beyond the tools in the Western philosophical toolbox. See Cederberg, *Resaying the human: Levinas beyond humanism and antihumanism* (Stockholm: Södertörn högskola, 2010) (p. 52). My thanks to Hans Ruin for introducing me to this work.

References

Adorno, T. (1998). Education after Auschwitz. In *Critical models: Interventions and catchwords* (pp. 191–204). (H. W. Pickford, Trans.). New York: Columbia University Press.

Balot, R. (2011, June 27). Socratic pedagogy. In *APT virtual reading group.* Retrieved from http://aptvrg2011.blogspot.com/2011/06/chpt-4-socratic-pedagogy.html

Caygill, H. (2010, July 27). The prison notebooks. In *Radical Philosophy, 160.* Retrieved from www.radicalphilosophy.com/issues/160-2

Cederberg, C. (2010). *Resaying the human: Levinas beyond humanism and anithumanism.* Stockholm: Södertörn högskola.

Donoghue, F. (2008). *The last professors: The corporate university and the fate of the humanities.* New York: Fordham University Press.

Euben, P. (2011). Hannah Arendt on politicizing the university and other cliches. *Renewing our common world: Hannah Arendt and education.* Boulder: Westview.

Fish, S. (2010). I know it when I see it: A reply to Kiss and Euben. In Kiss and Euben, eds., op cit.

Grant, R. (2010). Is humanistic education humanizing? In Kiss and Euben, eds., op cit.

Jarrett, J. (1973). *Humanities and humanistic education.* Boston: Addison-Wesley Educational Publishers.

Kiss, E., & Euben, J. (Eds.). (2010). *Debating moral education: Rethinking the role of the modern university.* Durham: Duke University Press.

Kitcher, P. (2011). Philosophy inside out. *Metaphilosophy, 42*(3), 248–260.

Levinas, E. (1946). La réouverture de l'Ecole Normale Israélite Orientale. In *Cahiers l'Alliance Israélite Universelle*, no. 9, juillet, pp. 1–2.

Levinas, E. (1990a). Reflections on the philosophy of Hiterism. Translated by Seán Hand. *Critical Inquiry, 17*, 63–71.

Levinas, E. (1990b). *Difficult freedom.* Translated by Seán Hand. Baltimore: Johns Hopkins University Press.

Levinas, E. (1998). *Levinas: Philosophe et pedagogue.* Paris: Les Editions du Nadir.

Levinas, E. (1999). Existentialism and anti-semitism (Denis Hollier and Rosalind Krauss, Trans.), *October*, *87*, Jean-Paul Sartre's "Anti-Semite and Jew" (Winter), pp. 27–31.

Levinas, E. (2003). *On escape* (Bettina Bergo, Trans.). Palo Alto: Stanford University Press.

Malka, S. (2006). *Emmanuel Levinas: His life and legacy.* Pittsburgh: Duquesne University Press.

Mill, J. (2010). The subjection of women. *On liberty and other writings.* Cambridge: Cambridge University Press.

Montaigne, M. (2003). *The complete essays.* New York: Penguin.

Nussbaum, M. (2010). *Not for profit: Why democracy needs the humanities.* Princeton: Princeton University Press.

Rousseau, J. (1979). *Emile; or on education* (Alan Bloom, Trans.). New York: Basic Books, Inc.

Rousseau, J. (1997a). Second discourse. *The discourses and other early political writings.* Victor Gourevitch (Ed.). Cambridge: Cambridge University Press.

Rousseau, J. (1997b). *The social contract.* Victor Gourevitch (Ed.). Cambridge: Cambridge University Press.

Rousseau, J., Kelly, C., & Bloom, A. D. (2010). *Emile, or, on education: Includes Emile and Sophie, or, the solitaires.* Hanover, NH: University Press Of New England.

Steg, A. (1998). A fable. *Levinas: Philosophe et pedagogue.* Catherine Chalier (Ed.). Alliance Israélite Universelle. Paris: Les Editions du Nadir.

Wollstonecraft, M. (2014). *A vindication of the rights of women.* Eileen Hunt Botting (Ed.). New Haven: Yale University Press.

Chapter 10

A wandering Jew with or without Sartre

Discussion of Claire Katz's "Can one still be a Jew without Sartre?"

Lewis Aron

While Sigmund Freud was anxiously waiting for an exit permit to flee Nazi-occupied Austria, he wrote to his son:

> In these dark days there are two prospects to cheer us: to rejoin you all and – to die in freedom. I sometimes compare myself with the old Jacob whom in his old age his children brought to Egypt. It is to be hoped that the result will not be the same, an exodus from Egypt. It is time for *Ahasverus* to come to rest somewhere.
>
> (as cited in Jones, 1957, p. 240)

Who is this *Ahasverus* with whom Freud so closely identified at this perilous time? He is perhaps the archetype of otherness and provides us with a primal typology of the psychology of the other. It is *Ahasverus*, the Wandering Jew, who embodies the figure of the Jew as nomad, stranger, outsider: the uprooted, and as Sarah Hammerschlag (2010) argues in *The Figural Jew*, *Ahasverus* represents the antithesis of the French nation, of the Enlightenment's Universal Man, and this is and remains the primal model for "the other" in Sartre's existentialist critique.

The legend of the Wandering Jew is thus highly relevant when focusing on the psychology of the other, and let me begin by expressing gratitude for the opportunity to engage this fine work by Claire Katz. In turn I want to say what a pleasure it has been to spend some months wandering from one area of scholarship to another, philosophy, education, biography, all subjects well outside my own expertise and yet all vaguely familiar – uncanny. The legend of the Wandering Jew began in Germany in the 17th century and then spread rapidly throughout Europe. In our book, *A Psychotherapy for the People*, Karen Starr and I describe Freud's exposure to his hero Charcot in his early studies in Paris as Charcot used this image in diagnosing his Jewish patients, hysterical Jewish men migrating from place to place with no home, limping from their ceaseless wandering (Aron & Starr, 2013). The tale of the Wandering Jew depicted a fictional Jewish shoemaker named *Ahasverus*, taunting Jesus on the way to the crucifixion and in response being castigated by him to "go on forever until I return."

Enflaming the popular and literary imagination, the image of the Wandering Jew quickly found its way into poetry and literature, including the works of Goethe, Heine, and Hans Christian Andersen. Jews were characterized by the larger society as unrepentant sinners who were doomed to roam without rest. Their seeming immortality as a people and their lack of a homeland were viewed as punishment for their repudiation of Christ. With the advent of the modernization of Europe, the traditional theological arguments were secularized, and the difference between Jews and Christians came to be defined in terms of race and biology. Jewishness was no longer a religious category but a racial one, a condition that was permanent, genetically inherited, and could not be modified by conversion. The Jews were now marginalized as the quintessential racial other, who had no homeland because they were incapable of it. They were considered fundamentally different, physically and psychologically, from non-Jews. In this racial model, the Jew was newly defined as everything the non-Jew "was not, nor would ever be" (Gilman, 1993, p. 9). Sartre (1948), drawing on Husserl, would make use of this "definition by opposition" in his book *Anti-Semite and Jew*.

Levinas (1999), like many critics, rejected Sartre's (1948) definition by opposition, that is the identification of Jewish identity in terms posed by anti-Semitism. Sartre's thesis was based less on a familiarity with Jews and Judaism than on an application of his concepts of alterity (or otherness), authenticity, and bad faith. For Levinas, this approach reduced Jewish identity to the product of the anti-Semite's gaze, thus confusing Judaism's "historical being" with its "metaphysical essence." But Levinas seems to have appreciated the attention that Sartre's book brought to the topic, especially right after the war when what would later be called the Holocaust was rarely mentioned. Judaken (2006) emphasizes how Sartre's penetrating work helped invigorate the discussion of anti-Semitism in postwar France, at a time when Jews and Gentiles alike were motivated to play down both the singularity of Jewish suffering and the pervasiveness of anti-Jewish hatred in favor of a comforting, even if illusory, memory of a France almost unanimously opposed to Nazism. This result occurred in spite of the fact that *Anti-Semite and Jew* itself contained almost no mention of the destruction of European Jewery.

Levinas could not have known much about Sartre's activities and choices during the occupation. Sartre had cultivated quite a compelling cover story so as to appear like he had been a hero of the resistance. But in her revisionist biography of Sartre and De Beauvoir, Carole Seymour-Jones (2008) exposes the postwar myth of the two brilliant lovers as impassioned heroes of the resistance. In 1941, Sartre had professionally profited as a teacher from Vichy racial laws, and Sartre never wrote a line to oppose the laws of Vichy or their implementation. The couple "barely noticed" when their Jewess lover, Bianca Bienenfeld, was forced to flee for her life in 1940. Bianca, one of numerous young female students who Beauvoir taught, seduced, and procured for Sartre, was tormented by their betrayal for the rest of her life, even as she maintained a relationship with Beauvoir. The biography documents numerous acquaintances and colleagues who accused Sartre and Beauvoir of collaboration, and indeed they appear to be strangely cut off, callous, even icy, and absorbed with themselves both during the war and later.

Levinas would not have known the truth, but as Seymour-Jones (2008) concludes, "the facts incriminate Sartre" (p. 263). Sartre took none of the risks to which he would later lay claim. "At every turn, Sartre rejected the chance to play a real part in the Resistance" (Seymour-Jones, 2008, p. 294). Sartre's friend Camus was truly a hero of the resistance, but Sartre and Beauvoir "glued together by their lies, colluded on an official version of events in which Sartre claimed parity with Camus" (Seymour-Jones, 2008, p. 288). Remarkably, with dazzling sleight of hand and within a month of liberation, Sartre became the principal spokesman for the resistance and was valorized as a fearless hero and fighter for the oppressed. If what you may know about Heidegger isn't enough to give you pause, then keep all of this in mind when reflecting on the existentialist principles of authenticity, freedom, and especially, bad faith. It does at the very least force us to consider and reconsider the benefit of higher education and the ideals of humanism and *Bildung* on a person's character. But Levinas, I imagine, could not have known much of this history.

Levinas (1999) championed Sartre's (1948) position against the analytic atomism of the Enlightenment as the basis for human rights. For Levinas, the individual is not only autonomously free for him or herself but has been thrown into the world with a history that makes a claim and a future that has meaning, and thus the Jew is responsible to community and tradition. For Levinas, it is Jewish particularity that leads to a universalist ethics. It is this tension between universalism and particularity that in my view was the central dispute, which continues to perplex us all. The issue that Sartre took up was whether the Jew should be legally respected specifically as a Particular Jew or as a Universal Person. The abstract, analytic thinker counsels, in effect, "You enjoy all the rights of a French Citizen, just don't be so Jewish." Sartre, on the other hand, argues "synthetically" for the rights of the Jew or the Arab or the woman (his examples) to vote *as such* in any election. In other words, their "rights" are concrete and not mere abstractions. One should not sacrifice the Jew (or the Arab or the woman) to the "man." The problem of Jewish emancipation coincided with an analytical vision of society . . . the human person as independent of his circumstances, his birth, his religion, and his social condition. Autonomous, that is, independent of his Judaism, his particularity, his community and tradition. This Enlightenment elevation of autonomous reason shifts the balance between autonomy or individuality and relationality or community all to one side, and leads in Freudian psychoanalysis to the privileging of the individual over the social, the intrapsychic over the interpersonal, and civilization over primitivity, which brings us back to the inter-related and entangled problems of racism, anti-Semitism, misogyny, and homophobia.

In *A Psychotherapy for the People* (2013), Starr and I argue that all of these binary terms call out for deconstruction, and so let's continue to examine the duality of particularism versus universalism. Our point is that in Freud's *fin de siècle* Austria, and this seems the case in Levinas's France, Jewish particularism *was* universalistic. The elimination of Jewish subjectivity – the drive to transform Jews into universal men and women who would be unmarked, uncircumcised, showing no trace of difference – was a powerful motivating force. Secular Jewish intellectuals were preoccupied with eliminating the supposedly Jewish traits that visibly separated them from their fellow countrymen. Secular Judaism was inherently universalist. To Freud, to be Jewish in the realm of ethics meant to be a humanist – as if Kant were the Jewish lawgiver or, a bit closer to home, perhaps Spinoza. Jacqueline Rose (2003) captures this well:

> Freud offers . . . one of the most striking self-definitions of the modern secular Jew – that is, a Jew for whom shedding the trappings of

linguistic, religious and national identity – paradoxically, by stripping away its untenable and, one might say, most politically dangerous elements – does not make him less Jewish, but more.

(p. 71)

The notion that universalism is derived from Jewish particularism is vividly captured in a joke often told by Rabbi Shlomo Carlebach, one of the foremost Jewish teachers and religious songwriters of the 20th century, and a frequent speaker on college campuses in the 1950–70s. Carlbach is currently in the news because he has become the subject of the play *Soul Doctor* (opened 2013), directed by Daniel S. Wise and now at Circle in the Square Theatre in New York. Carlebach, in real life one of my teachers, recounted that if he met a person who said, "I'm a Catholic," he knew he was a Catholic. If he met a person who said, "I'm a Protestant," he knew he was a Protestant. If he met a person who said, "I'm a human being," he knew he was a Jew! In telling this joke, Carlebach was drawing attention to the familiar theme of Jewish universalism. However, in contrast to Rose (2003), who applauds Freud's stripping away of Jewish particularism, Carlebach recognized the Jewish self-hatred, the internalized anti-Semitism, evinced in the disappearance of Jewish self-identification.

How and why was the particularity of Judaism transformed into universalism? The very idea of religion – what we mean by religion today – has largely been shaped by modern Protestant assumptions. Before the modern era, Judaism was not a religion. Batnitzky (2011) has illuminated that prior to emancipation and the acquisition of citizenship rights for Jews, it was impossible to distinguish between Jewish religion, nationality, and culture. The idea of conceptualizing Judaism as a religion emerged in a German-Jewish context that produced a highly intellectualized tradition of thought developed in response to the German Enlightenment, a historical context wherein Jews were promised, but never realized, full integration into German culture.

Batnitzky (2011) traces the origins of modern Judaism as a religion to German-Jewish philosopher Moses Mendelssohn's quest for a German-Jewish cultural symbiosis, in which he defined the Jewish religion as a matter of behavior rather than belief. In freeing Judaism from belief and dogma, Mendelssohn's definition allowed Judaism to exist in harmony with enlightened reason and universal ethics. By the early 20th century, German-Jewish philosopher Hermann Cohen, a founder of the *Wissenschaft des Judentums* movement, further advanced the German-Jewish synthesis, rejecting Judaism's particularistic features. Judaism became a universal ethical doctrine, a rational religion of inward faith and inseparable from German *Bildung*, the cultivation of individual character.

Freud's education at the gymnasium took place during the constitutional era in Austria, a time of political liberalism spearheaded by Enlightenment ideals. Jews eagerly anticipated social acceptance and integration into German society. Allegiance to German culture was equated with Enlightenment values, cultural assimilation, and the leveling of social differences. Jews tried hard to be German, which meant to be assimilated, universal, a part of the whole. They sought social integration rather than an assertive identity of their own. The assimilation of German Jews was so intense that they often believed they adhered to German culture more faithfully than the Germans themselves. Meanwhile, what it meant to be German was increasingly defined by opposition; to be German was to not be like a Jew. Tragically, the Enlightenment promise was never fulfilled – the doors to equality were opened only for a very short time during Freud's youth. Freud, like his contemporaries, could barely accept, and never really got over, the painful reality that the doors had so quickly shut. They held onto the hope that universal brotherhood of mankind was an attainable ideal.

Having survived the Holocaust, Levinas's universalization of his Jewishness was not exactly Freud's. But it is precisely here that I become eager to hear more from Claire Katz (2013). She argues that major philosophers developed treatises on education that reflected how people could acquire the good, beautiful, and moral life that they proposed. The question that pervades Katz's work concerns the *process of becoming* ethical: How does one develop ethically? How do we explain, concretely, how to build the face-to-face, the ethics of intersubjectivity? How do we link together "education, teaching, ethics, religion, and the political" (Katz, 2013, p. 161)? What are the educational conditions under which one becomes an ethical subject? As she quotes from Adorno's declaration, "the premier demand upon all education is that Auschwitz not happen again" (Katz, 2013).

Levinas was the head of a Jewish day school after the war. Focusing on Levinas's essays on Jewish education, no less than on his famous philosophical works, Katz (2013) demonstrates that his ethics calls for a "radically different educational system" (p. 13). Katz shows that, in Levinas's work, the recourse to "Jewish education" is meant to create a "new humanism" as an answer to the crisis of modern humanism founded on rights, that is, ultimately on individualism and egoism. Levinas (1997) contends that the cultivation of an ethical subjectivity constitutes the core of Judaism. As Katz indicates, the *particular* characteristic of Judaism, embedded in its classical texts (Bible, Talmud, and commentaries), is to comprise a *general* significance "indispensable to human harmony" (Levinas, 1997, p. 276; Katz, 2013, p. 111). Following Levinas, Katz advocates not an education along the lines of the classic humanities, but rather an education inspired by traditional Jewish learning rooted in Jewish sources. Yet she concludes by advocating an education based not only on dialogue (freedom) but on interdependency, namely, on responsible dialogue: "The children must learn to rely on each other and in turn they must also learn that they are responsible for each other" (p. 162). Particular or universal? Are these Jewish values, and if they are, what remains particularly Jewish about them once they are universalized?

The questions for me include the following: Are the values of interdependency and mutual vulnerability specifically Jewish? Are they even a universalization of Jewish values? And if they are and if we can generalize them as she does in her own educational examples, then is anything left of them that we can say continues to be Jewish? And if not, then how is Levinas's universalization of Jewish values any different from Freud's or from the Western European, Haskalah, *Bildung*, self-cultivation, and universal ethics? Is there something uniquely Jewish about maintaining the tension between individual autonomy, freedom, and agency on the one side and intersubjectivity, community, and mutual vulnerability on the other? How do we in our pluralistic country draw on particular religious traditions without enacting and promoting religious prejudice? How do we emphasize moral formation or ethical character development while respecting diversity? It is my intention here to call for ongoing discussion of these questions and encourage ongoing dialogue on these important matters.

Katz's (2013) thesis is particularly relevant today as educators argue about whether the university is the proper place for teaching morality or even citizenship. Stanley Fish (2008) argues that no form of moral or civic education can ever exemplify academic virtues of rigorous analysis, multiple perspectives, or commitments to truth. You can't make your students into good people and you shouldn't try (Kiss & Euben, 2010). Fish argues that the only thing we can teach our students is the acquisition of knowledge and analytical skills, but as Kiss and Euben (2010) ask, doesn't the more common professorial stance of moral detachment and ironic distance reinforce the fashionable forms of moral relativism and apathy? Think quite similarly of the contemporary psychoanalytic critique of analytic neutrality. Fish replies that he is teaching a value, namely the pursuit of truth, but he seems remarkably unaware of how this portrayal of truth implicates a complex system of values. Who is *Ahasverus*, the universal Other, the particular Jew? Claire and I share an interest in education, Jewish studies, and especially in the relationship between education and the development of character. As importantly, we share our continuing struggle with how to think about the particular within the universal and the universal within the particular.

References

Aron, L. & Starr, K. (2013). *A psychotherapy for the people: Toward a progressive psychoanalysis*. New York: Routledge.

Batnitzky, L. (2011). *How Judaism became a religion*. Princeton, NJ: Princeton University Press.

Fish, S. (2008). *Save the world on your own time*. Oxford: Oxford University Press.

Gilman, S. L. (1993). *Freud, race, and gender.* Princeton, NJ: Princeton University Press.

Hammerschlag, S. (2010). *The figural Jew: Politics and identity in postwar French thought*. London: University of Chicago Press.

Jones, E. (1957). Life and work of Sigmund Freud. *The Last Phase 1919–1939, 3.* London: Hogarth Press.

Judaken, J. (2006). *Jean-Paul Sartre and the Jewish question: Anti-antisemitism and the politics of the French intellectual*. Lincoln: University of Nebraska Press.

Katz, C. E. (2013). *Levinas and the crisis of humanism*. Bloomington: Indiana University Press.

Kiss, E. & Euben, J. P. (Eds.). (2010). *Debating moral education*. Durham and London: Duke University Press.

Levinas, E. (1997). *Difficult freedom: Essays on Judaism*. (S. Hand, Trans.). Baltimore: Johns Hopkins University Press.

Levinas, E. (1999). Existentialism and anti-semitism. *October: Anti-Semite and the Jew, 87,* 27–31. (D. Hollier & R. Krauss, Trans.). Cambridge: MIT Press.

Rose, J. (2003). Response to Edward Said. In E. Said (Ed.), *Freud and the non-European*. London: Verso.

Sartre, J. P. (1948). *Anti-Semite and Jew.* (G. Becker, Trans.). New York: Schocken Books.

Seymour-Jones, C. (2008). *A dangerous liaison: Simone de Beauvoir and Jean-Paul Sartre*. New York: The Overlook Press.

Chapter 11

The witnessing gaze turned inward

My Jewish history as the forgotten other

Judith Alpert[1]

For the last 40 years, I have been studying the wounds of others; my focus has been on sexual violence against women in wars, genocide, the military, families, schools, and in other institutional settings. I do research, see patients, and teach. In addition, I have served on a number of committees and Boards of the American Psychological Association concerned with women's issues, particularly violence against women and children. I have acted as an expert witness on a number of cases throughout the United States, testifying on behalf of victims. And I worked to create structures that would institutionalize this work. In this endeavor, my focus, as Donna Orange (2011) would put it, has been turned toward the "suffering stranger". I am inspired by what Freeman (2003) calls "the priority of the other"; to know and advocate for the other has given me a life infused with meaning and aliveness and passion. This position has closed the gulf of alienation that Freeman (2003) suggests is a feature of contemporary "me" culture. In this turn toward the other, I have always known that this other could be me, in some other time, and some other place. Still, I know the borders between the experience of the other and my own; I empathize but I always honor that distinction. And so, in some way, my witnessing gaze has never been turned on myself. Even in my Holocaust studies, I am pulled to witness that which is my own, insofar as I am Jewish. I am also witnessing a survival that is not my own, a history that is of me, and yet it is not my family's and it is not mine. Despite the inspiration I have derived from my work, one could argue as Grand (2000) does, that an excessive tilt toward the other can create an alienation from the self, and that this alienation from the self can actually limit our capacity to know the other. As Grand (2000) suggests, the capacity to know the other grows in an inter-subjective relation, in which self-knowledge enhances our empathy, and empathy with the other expands our knowledge of the self (Buber, 1970/1923; Benjamin, 1988). I had never been aware of the subtle alienation and limitation that can arise when our focus on the other constrains our look at the self. I became aware of this when I began to study the transgenerational transmission of trauma, and learned about the family legacy I have been carrying. Gradually, I have come to know myself, and my passions, through the forgotten other of my own Jewish history: the violence experienced by my grandmother during the Russian pogroms. Occluded by the larger atrocity of the Holocaust, the pogroms seem like a disappearing fragment of Jewish history. Insofar as they seem to exist in Jewish consciousness, they appear primarily as another exemplar of persecution, a precursor to the Holocaust. As with all atrocities, one monstrosity readily absorbs and displaces another: the specificity of human suffering is lost, and its victims are nameless. In the recent transgenerational turn in psychoanalysis, those ghosts emerge from that namelessness and enhance our knowledge of ourselves. In the matriarchal lineage of my family, the pogroms shaped the Jewish ethics and culture of our emigration and assimilation. The victims of these pogroms arrived unspoken, three generations later, in my dread of violence and my advocacy for abused women. In tracing this history, I have started witnessing myself. Now the "priority of the other" has led, also, to the priority of the self (Freeman, 2003). I have an enriched, internal, I–Thou relationship that carries the wounds of the other. And now I also know that other as myself. In this chapter I wish to trace my own story, in an effort to illuminate the inter-subjectivity of our conversation with these ghosts. And I hope to restore, and help metabolize, this lost Jewish history.

My dream

Last summer, I was invited to give a paper at a conference, and I did not know what to write about. Then, I had this dream. There was a perfect square, a two inch by two inch piece of glass in my left inner wrist. I could tell that it had been there a while. The longer it was in my wrist, the clearer the outline became. I knew that it was important to get the glass out and I knew that if I left it in my wrist, it would turn into a massive infection and eventually leave a lifelong scar. I remained calm but clear. It had to come out. I knew that once it was out and no longer inside me, I could look at the glass and see the world more clearly, as well as look through the other side of the glass and see me more clearly.

My story

I always knew that something terrible had happened to my mother. She was afraid of everything. She was afraid of dogs. She was afraid to stay alone. Lights had to be on at night, even when we were sleeping. Lurking strangers must be seen or frightened away. She was afraid of men she did not know. When there was a delivery, she would tell me to hide under the bed until he was gone. And when she opened the door to these unfamiliar men who delivered our groceries, she concealed a knife in her pocket, "just in case". There was little she was not afraid of and few possibilities of wickedness for which she was unprepared.

Before she married, she lived with her own mother as well as her sister and brother-in-law and their child. I have been told that there was a time when my mother participated in the family Sundays. At ten o'clock in the morning, all of those who lived with grandma would lay out tables in the foyer of grandma's apartment, and all the other family members would arrive. After eating, the work for the day began. The agenda was always the same. Every problem that arose over the week for each person was presented and discussed and some resolution or reassuring words followed. Everyone talked. Everyone helped. Decisions were not made and big items were not purchased without being evaluated by this powerful counsel. This was a strong family unit and the members were involved in each other's lives. I am told that my mother would participate at these events. At some point, though, she stopped participating. It was around the time that she became afraid of everything.

People let my mother be quiet. Perhaps they didn't even notice the change, her unusual silence. Perhaps they didn't know what to do about the sudden shift. Perhaps they knew and at the same time didn't want to know. Only later did I discover how much transgenerational history was distilled into my mother's silence and into my family's inability to ask, comment, and inquire. I have come to see that my mother's silence carried the echoes and reverberations of her own mother's tremendous suffering in the pogroms.

The family may have pushed my mother to marry because they thought that marriage was the solution to her withdrawal. She was twenty-eight. In the 1930s she was becoming an "old maid". She was fixed up with a man. Everyone at the family table said that he was a good catch. He was sweet and calm, and was described as the kind of person who wouldn't hurt a fly, the kind of person whose cheeks one would love to pinch. Marriage was not about love in my extended family. All agreed that he was perfect for my mother. He was not scary. He would be patient. He would be a good provider and, besides, it was time for my mom to be on her own. The family all agreed on this one Sunday afternoon.

One thing the family tribunal hadn't counted on: my mother did not like to be home alone at night and this man would be working many nights. To deal with this unspoken trauma, which was a nameless "it", the family had grandma move in with them. Somehow life moved on. I was born. Then I caught "it". It was as if I was invaded by her emotional state. "It", the fear that is, was transmitted to me. Within five years I had contracted many of my mother's terrors. I was afraid of dogs. I was afraid of men, and I was sometimes even afraid of my gentle father. I cried often. My mother did for me what all the wise family members never did for her: she put me in therapy and she got a therapist for herself. This was an enlightened move in 1949.

I remember my therapist. She didn't seem to be afraid. We met in a room full of colorful toys. There was a one-way mirror and my mother told me that she and her therapist would sometimes watch me play. While there were many play options, I repeated one of two activities. I hammered fat wooden round pegs into a piece of wood with round holes. Over and over again I did this. What was my play about? Was I announcing that I knew some secret about forbidden entry, of some fat round thing being hammered into a hole? Did I repeat the hammering in an effort to have control of some violation, which never should have happened? I wonder now. But then, I played.

I also played with the two-story dollhouse that opened on one side. I moved the mother in it. I kept putting her in different places until she was in just the right situation. And I moved the dollhouse furniture. I changed which rooms would be near the front door. I made the house safe. And then I made the house even safer. No one was going to enter who didn't belong. I was making sure of that. I don't remember talking in my childhood therapy, but I had found a way to tell my story, and I got better. My mother got better too. Over time her mind was freer. She was there. I believe that she faced her trauma to release me from inheriting it.

What happened to my mother? What made her so fearful? She was eighty-seven years old when she finally told me, many years after I had completed my own adult analysis. She was in hospice at the time. I had been with her for about five days. She was too tired to talk and I had talked so much. I had told her everything that I wanted to tell her. There were only truths and tears and deep love in that room. Finally it seemed that there was little else to say. I filled the space by singing songs that I used to sing as a child and that she used to sing to me. Mom listened, too weak to do anything else. Although dying, she seemed content. Right before she died, she asked for some chocolate. I had a piece in my pocketbook that was left on my hotel pillow the night before. I melted it in my hand and then I took a q-tip and scraped it in the chocolate. I put the chocolate covered q-tip in her mouth, her first food in five days. Her eyes opened wide. She told me it was delicious. I offered more. She said she was full. She smiled and then she died.

But something happened right before she asked for the chocolate. Before I gave her the treasured sweet, she gave me something. She gave me words and representation for her trauma story. It was a one-liner: "I was raped by the dress shop owner when I was fifteen." She had never told me this before. However, once she told me, I knew that she had told me what I had always known. I knew why I had been hammering fat wooden round pegs into a piece of wood with round holes. I knew why I had to make the house safe, and I knew why I had devoted my life to the abuse of women. But this knowing was only the beginning of a historical inquiry.

Intergenerational transmission of trauma: how there is knowledge and transmission

As a child, I felt the intergenerational force of her trauma. The transmission of her unresolved trauma was silent and the cargo was toxic. Several authors have noted that without this treatment, this trauma might have been passed on, leap-frogged across generations, or presented itself in new ways (Davoine & Gaudillière, 2004; Laub & Auerhahn, 1993; Grand, 2000; Apprey, 2003; Faimberg, 1988). In a discussion of the capacity to mentalize, Fonagy and Target (1996) state:

> when a parent is unable to incorporate and think about a piece of reality, and cannot then enable the child to do so safely through playing with the frightening ideas, this reality remains to be experienced in the mode of psychic equivalence. Neither child nor parent can "metabolize" the thoughts, and the "unthinkable" thoughts are passed from one generation to the next.

(p. 231)

Clearly, unconscious fantasies can emerge from events that were never actually experienced by the child. Different terms are used to describe this phenomenon. Faimberg (1988) speaks of the telescoping of generations, to describe the child's unconscious identification process with the dead selves of the parents' lost history.

While she did not tell me in words until the very end, my mother was not silenced. Her past was living in the present, in her affects and behavioral enactments. Her mind was not hers, not really. Of course I knew. And of course she knew. I believe she always had conscious memory and that she used dissociation to manage affective flooding and flashbacks. But when she saw her fear infecting me, she took action. She put us both in treatment, and faced her own demons. Mentalized by the witnessing presence of our therapists, our "unformulated" (Stern, 1997) ghosts found representation, and a degree of metabolization. In taking this risk, my mother was a frightened hero, who was able to look beyond her own suffering and focus on the suffering other as this other appeared in me, her daughter. Although, of course, trauma can linger, transform, and bypass generations, in this moment it seemed that she stopped the intergenerational transmission of trauma, and I internalized the ethic of the "priority of the other" (Freeman, 2003). But she also taught me something else that I have only begun to realize: the mutuality of empathic repair. This is the ethic I have learned from my mother's intervention: we repair ourselves by caring for the suffering other, and we repair the suffering other by knowing ourselves. This is a continual dialectic, a transgenerational I–Thou relationship between our ghosts, our loved ones, and ourselves.

As I reflect about this process, I have wondered what my normal baby and early childhood screams, demands, cries, helplessness, tantrums, and terrors triggered in my mother. How did she respond to them? What did they release in her? I wonder too what my mother's normal baby and early childhood behavior triggered in my grandmother. I have realized that my mother also inherited violent memories from previous generations. At the time of her own rape, my mother may have already been carrying the silent story of her mother's rape, during the pogroms. This is something I have deduced, but something I cannot ever really know.

Pogroms against the Jews

In the early 1900s, shortly after the tsar granted fundamental civil rights and political liberties, pogroms directed mainly at Jews broke out in hundreds of cities, towns, and villages, resulting in deaths and injuries to thousands of people, as well as damage and ruin to thousands of Jewish homes and businesses. While non-Jews maintained most of the wealth in Odessa, where my grandma lived at this time, Jews were seen as an economic threat and their growing visibility enhanced the predisposition of Russians to blame Jews for their difficulties. Clashes turned into pogroms and Russians indiscriminately attacked Jews and vandalized and looted their homes and stores. Weinberg (1987) writes:

> A list of atrocities perpetrated against the Jews is too long to recount here, but suffice it to say that pogromists brutally and indiscriminately beat, mutilated, and murdered defenseless Jewish men, women, and children. They hurled Jews out of windows, raped and cut open the stomachs of pregnant women, and slaughtered infants in front of their parents. In one particularly gruesome incident, pogromists hung a woman upside down by her legs and arranged the bodies of her six dead children on the floor below her.
>
> (pp. 63–54)

Where were the police? The literature is pretty consistent on this point. To facilitate attacks against Jews, policemen compiled lists of Jewish-owned stores and apartments. They participated in the looting and killing. They directed pogromists to Jewish-owned stores or apartments and prevented them from damaging the property of non-Jews. Protection for Jews was non-existent.

Like most Jews living in Russia in the late 1800s and early 1900s, my grandmother experienced anti-Jewish legislation and pogroms. My grandmother was beautiful and strong. When she lived with us, she had long white hair down to her knees, which she would wash, brush, make snarl-free, and put into a bun. She spent most of the day sitting on a big gray armchair in the second-floor living room seeming to look out the window of our quiet suburban neighborhood. When I would speak to her in the midst of her vigilant watch, she would jump up, as if I had frightened her. It would take a few seconds, too many seconds I always thought, before she responded. There wasn't much to see out the window. Mr. Casey would walk his dog. Mrs. Gilman would leave her house in her slippers to get mail. Occasionally cars would drive by. It was a sleepy street that didn't seem to warrant grandma's alert stare.

I often wondered why she looked at sameness and stillness for so long and why she kept her hair so very, very long. Unconsciously, I developed a fantasy related to the pogroms. I used to think about the German fairy tale Rapunzel and how the enchantress would say "Rapunzel, Rapunzel, let down your golden hair". Like Rapunzel in the fairy tale, my grandma was the most beautiful woman in the world. And as Rapunzel would drop her hair down to the rescuer who climbed up Rapunzel's hair to her tower room, I thought about my grandma dropping her hair out the window, so that we could climb down to safety. Somehow, I knew we might need to vacate in a hurry and that the stairs would not serve us well. Some man would appear, seeming innocent, and he would do something bad to us.

I think I sensed the fires set during the pogroms. I picked up on the insecurity of a police force that did not protect Jews, but instead rounded them up, stripped them naked and beat them mercilessly. My grandma was alive in Odessa for all three large-scale waves of pogroms directed at the Jews of Russia (1881–4, 1903–6, and 1917–21). Many women were violated in these pogroms. I don't know for certain if this was the case for my beautiful grandmother. But given the conditions, it is hard to imagine that she was spared this sexual violence. She escaped from Odessa after three of her children died in a fire, set during the 1905 anti-Jewish pogrom. While there were other pogroms before and after this one, the 1905 Odessa Pogrom is recorded as one of the most severe both in Odessa's history and across the Russian empire ("Jewish Virtual Library", 1995).

As a child, I sensed that men who were supposed to be good and protective were really bad and caused harm. I knew that we might need to escape. And grandma, by her alert stare from the second-floor living room, was watching out for us. Her long hair was the ladder that would provide an exit. How much did my mother know about the fires, the rapes, the murders in Odessa? What did she know about what happened to her mother? Was the family unable to help with my mother's rape because grandma was speechless and comfortless about her own history? Did grandma somehow know my mother's rape? And was grandma's trauma from the pogroms somehow transmitted to my mother? I think so.

So I read more about pogroms. I read about how this goes on for days and days and I know my grandmother was there. And I read about the rape of women in the pogroms. I read about the homes and businesses that were destroyed and looted, and about the men, women, and children being beaten, mutilated, and murdered. I read about women being gang-raped. I read about how the Russian police stood by, how local government officials ignored pleas for help, and I read about how the Russian police supported the violence by inaction. I read about how local government officials ignored pleas for help, and I read about how the postal service refused to deliver telegrams requesting that the central government intervene. I read about how people who were supposed to be good and protective were neither. I read about how this went on for days and days and I know my grandmother was there. I wonder what she witnessed and I wonder what happened to her.

The 1903 Kishinev pogrom was another ruthless and brutal event. Generations of Jews learned about it from reading Hayyim Nahman Bialik's 1904 poem, "In the City of Killing". How Bialik came to write this poem is significant. To gather survivor testimonies and to publish them in a book, Bialik was sent to Kishinev. While there he interviewed people, gathered eyewitness accounts, and corroborated them with other testimonies from other witnesses. He collected 150 testimonies in all, some as short as a paragraph and others as long as eight pages. While he was commissioned to write a book of survivor testimony, he abandoned the project for reasons he did not disclose. Instead, he wrote an indirect testimony: the poem.

It is not clear why he wrote the poem rather than the book of survivor testimonies. Was it because he believed a description of the rape of Jewish maidens by an acquaintance and his drunken friends was more powerfully portrayed by poetry than narrative? Was it because the treacheries of witnessing were too much? Was it because the testimonies reactivated his early sexual trauma? Was it because his exposure to the exposed resulted in vicarious traumatization?

The poem Bialik eventually wrote (Hadari, 2000) is about male witnessing. In it, he graphically describes some of the gruesome, sickening, and horrendous horrors he witnessed.

The second stanza was based on the testimony of Rivka Schiff, who was gang-raped by a business acquaintance and his drunken friends in front of everyone in the attic. After Rivka's gang-rape the other females in the attic were raped. In the second stanza, he mentions that women under and over age seven were raped. He also indicates that they were raped in front of their mothers and the mothers were raped in front of their daughters, and that they were killed before, during, and after the rapes.

I think about this. Then I remember my father telling me how groups of anti-Semitic youth would chase him and other Jewish boys on their way home from school. These bullies threw rocks at them, screamed epithets, and beat them. This was in Boston in the 1920s, prior to the Holocaust. My father was able to talk about this brutality. My mother's family was able to listen, and he was able to tell. Pogroms, rape, and the burning of children: this seemed unspeakable, beyond all capacity for listening. This kind of silence is often a memorial space for atrocity, but this silence also permits what Grand (2000) calls the "reproduction of evil" (p. 3).

In conclusion, in discovering this history and familial memory, lost Jewish souls began to speak. I entered a whole new relationship to persecution. I was witnessing my own story. I came to know my self and my mission on behalf of abused women, in an expanding dialogue with the lost generations of the pogroms. Once, I knew my mother's timidity and fear. Now, I can testify to my mother's courage. This courage reflected her mother's resilience and the resilience of women, as sexual violence recurs, silently, through persecuted generations. This knowledge has now opened up a new area of study for me: the rape of Jewish women, in the concentration camps during the Holocaust – another atrocity that has long been silenced. Knowing my own history and knowing my self has generated a new awareness of the other. Insofar as that other is also myself, I want to help name the rapes of our history and move toward healing and hope for people burdened by such histories.

Note

1 The author gratefully acknowledges the careful reading and insightful comments of Dr. Sue Grand and the library assistance of Ms. Natalie Ann Schaad.

References

Apprey, M. (2003). Repairing history: Reworking transgenerational trauma. In D. Moss (Ed.), *Hating in the first person plural* (pp. 3–29). New York: Other Press.
Benjamin, J. (1988). *The bonds of love.* New York: Pantheon Books.
Buber, M. (1970). *I and thou.* (W. Kaufman, Trans.). New York: Charles Scribner's Sons. (Original work published 1923.)
Davoine, F., & Gaudillière, J. M. (2004). *History beyond trauma.* (S. Fairfield, Trans.). New York: Other Press.
Faimberg, H. (1988). The telescoping of generations: Genealogy of certain identifications. *Contemporary Psychoanalysis, 24,* 99–118.
Fonagy, P., & Target, M. (1996). Playing with reality: I. Theory of mind and the normal development of psychic reality. *International Journal of Psychoanalysis, 77,* 217–233.
Freeman, M. (2003). The priority of the other: Mysticism's challenge to the legacy of the self. In J. A. Belzen & A. Geels (Eds.), *Mysticism: A variety of psychological perspectives* (pp. 213–234). New York: Rodopi.

Grand, S. (2000). *The reproduction of evil: A clinical and cultural perspective.* Hillsdale, NJ: Analytic Press.

Hadari, A. (Ed. and Trans.). (2000). *Songs from Bialik: Selected poems of Hayim Nahman Bialik.* Syracuse: Syracuse University Press.

Jewish Virtual Library (2016). 1995. Retrieved from www.jewishvirtuallibrary.org/jsource/History/time90s.html#1995

Laub, D., & Auerhahn, N. C. (1993). Knowing and not knowing massive psychological trauma: Forms of traumatic memory. *International Journal of Psychoanalysis, 74*(2), 287–302.

Orange, D. (2011). *The suffering stranger: Hermeneutics for everyday clinical practice.* New York: Taylor & Francis Group.

Stern, D. B. (1997). *Unformulated experience: From dissociation to imagination in psychoanalysis.* Hillsdale, NJ: The Analytic Press.

Weinberg, R. (1987). Workers, pogroms, and the 1905 revolution in Odessa. *Russian Review, 46*(1), 53–75.

Chapter 12

Gender and the Jew

The other within

Jill Salberg[1]

> Why can't a woman be more like a man? Men are so honest, so thoroughly square; eternally noble, historically fair. Why do they do everything their mothers do? Why can't they grow up, well, like their father instead? Why can't a woman behave like a man? . . . Why can't a woman be like me?
>
> (Henry Higgins in *My Fair Lady*)

Indeed, why *would* a woman be more like a man? I wonder if that is a fantasy that only men have about women or whether women also think this. In an interview in *The New York Times Sunday* magazine section Diane von Furstenberg (DVF) was asked about how, in the 1970s, she used to drive her Mercedes to Studio 54 alone at midnight. She replied: "That image of me driving the Mercedes and walking in alone is like the cowboy going to a saloon, you know? It was really a fantasy of mine, living a man's life in a woman's body" (Goldman, 2013). Is this the response Henry Higgins is longing for, a woman who fantasizes and plays with being a man? DVF uses the cross-dressing fantasy of the American cowboy – is this incubated within the Hollywood dream machine to "clothe" her sense of identity? Gender? I believe this particular kind of fantasy rests partially on an edge of otherness within gender. While there is recognition of how different the "other" gender is and acknowledgement of that, there is simultaneously a wish to collapse that difference into sameness: "why can't a woman be more like a man?", and with that movement eradicate otherness into non-difference. Is this a form of *passing* as a black might pass for white, or a Jew as a non-Jew? And is there even more to it? Why would a man need to fantasize this, or woman wish this since not everyone does?

Further in this interview DVF is quoted as saying, "Eighteen months before I was born, my mother was in Auschwitz. She weighed 49 pounds.

She always told me that God saved her so she could give me life. I was born out of nothing. My mother was nothing; she was ashes practically" (Goldman, 2013). It is not a leap for us to see how trauma is deeply implicated and formative in her life. Isn't it interesting then that she enlists a gender-bending fantasy to embody her desire to show up somewhere alone and not feel herself to be *other*? She is the child of a survivor and it is useful to wonder where we might discover the trace of the inter-generational transmission of trauma. Is she passing as a manly cowboy, a tough guy swaggering into the club using the Hollywood trope of masculinity to feel more powerful, to overcome the helplessness of trauma? If I am right, then "being girl" holds the unwanted stereotypical cultural threads of vulnerability and weakness associated with femininity.

Gender binaries and Judaism

I am interested in the way gender binaries – something that is a legacy of patriarchy, which has deep streams within Judaism and within Freud and psychoanalysis – still continue to infuse fantasy life. It is these kinds of questions and this enlistment of gender and its relationship with trauma that I will be using to explore the place of otherness within Judaism. As a psychoanalyst, I am interested in how someone carries psychically in their lives the histories of experiences – within their family, their culture, and the external world. In particular, I am drawn to stories about legacies of losses, triumphs, and sometimes traumas, and how these can unconsciously be carried, played with, and worked out using gender. While gender has always had a primary position within psychoanalysis, it has been in the past twenty-five years that there have been substantial reformulations. Relational psychoanalysis has recast Freud's singular ego, the seat of self-awareness, as multiple self-states each carrying affects, memories, and desires (see Bromberg, 2006; Davies, 1998; Harris, 1996). In this vein, Harris (1992, 1996, 2000, 2005) has written about gender, characterizing it as *soft assembly*, by which she means that many experiences, developmental levels, and self-other relationships cohere into a self that is gendered and an amalgam of these, all authentically true. She also believes that sometimes gender emerges to solve some intrapsychic, interpersonal, or intersubjective problem. Harris (2005) writes, "Genderedness is one particularly acute register of local trauma and of the more broad scaled traumas of social and historical change" (p. 35). She sees gender as a "creative solution" (personal communication, 2007) to types of difficult or even traumatic experiences that have led to dissociative responses encoded in distinct self-states and possibly gendered differently. As a consequence, there may be within one person both girl and boy self-states, each authentically true within certain family configurations and experiential contexts.

I had been told in my family that I was the son my parents never had. As an adult I learned from my mother about the difficulty she had giving birth to me, possibly even traumatizing to her. She had hemorrhaged badly and as a consequence I was the second child, the last child and younger sister in a two-daughter family. In some ways I was born into a kind of doubled alterity, girl but not daughter, son but not boy. Being tomboy was how I resolved this enigma, one of a few hidden traumas in my family, and it is how I lived in the world. I played more boy games than girl games, playing ball games with boys in the neighborhood and less dolls and house with girls. So it was never questioned by me that I would attend Hebrew school at the Reform congregation my family belonged to beginning in second grade through Hebrew high school while my older sister never did. By the time I was 11 years old, I was in classes with mostly boys having learned prayers for Shabbat and now for B'nai Mitzvah. I carry within me both daughter and son, girl and boy self-states so when I learned that I could not continue on, that at my Temple and this particular moment in the Reform movement, 1963, girls did not become Bat Mitzvah (literally translated as daughter of the commandments), I was at first surprised and confused. I know that I also felt deeply disappointed over being denied access to what up until then my peers, the boys, could engage in. (See Carol Gilligan, 2002 for how the voices of girls in adolescence become silenced.) I later came to see that I had been deeply upset and unsettled, and the seeds of my interest in feminism, gender, and psychoanalysis were an outgrowth of my personal response.

Seminal texts in Jewish feminism – my "go to books" where I could hear the voices of *othered* women questioning and exploring these issues – were Susannah Heschel's (1983) *On Being a Jewish Feminist* and Judith Plaskow's (1990) *Standing Again at Sinai.* What became clear to me in their work was how the feminist inquiry could be turned toward Judaism: how maleness and masculinity had been assumed as the normative order in Jewish life and if gender was to be considered it meant "women" since men were the unquestioned norm. Women were "other" and therefore downplayed in history, liturgy, and leadership and minimally present in Jewish stories.

Much of this paralleled for me the effects feminism had been having on psychoanalysis, an impact that led to new considerations and critiques of Freud and the phallocentric theories that had previously dominated psychoanalytic thinking. Specifically, Benjamin (1988a, 1998b) articulated how Freud's theories rested upon the patriarchal view of masculinity in the culture which valued hegemonic masculine traits such as strength, independence, and agency and devalued traits associated with and assigned to femininity – passivity, vulnerability, and dependency. Layton (1998) described how culture and psyche are in constant interaction and both become organized around these gender polarities with positive values attributed to males and negative ones to females. These streams of interest led me, for a few years, to study at the Jewish Theological Seminary. This is where – in classes on midrash, biblical women, and women in Jewish literature – I came upon stories of women that complicated gender in compelling ways.

Women who are more like men: stories of Beruriah and Yentl

Within Jewish literature there are two women whose stories capture for me a kind of gender binary paradox – being female and playing with being male or as Henry Higgins seemingly longs for, women who are more like men. These women are Beruriah from the Talmud and Yentl as written by I.B. Singer (1953). Each one poses a similar puzzle and I have often thought of Yentl as an eastern European shtetl *doppelgänger* for Beruriah. While most people know of Yentl, partly due to the Streisand film, many have never heard of Beruriah. Neither one has a full life story but I will try to synopsize the thrust of their stories here while also keeping in mind the historical context as it may affect how gender is rigidly held or fluidly played with. Beruriah is referenced only a dozen or so times briefly across a few different sections of the Talmud. Rachel Adler (1988) wrote an early feminist article on Beruriah and summarized the stories as follows:

> Once there was a woman named Beruriah, and she was a great Talmudic scholar. She was the daughter of the great Palestinian Rabbi Hananyah ben Teradyon, who was martyred by the Romans. Even as

a young girl, she far outstripped her brother as a scholar. It was said she had learned three hundred laws from three hundred teachers in one day. She married Rabbi Meir, the miracle worker and great Mishnaic sage. One time when Rabbi Meir prayed for some robbers to die, Beruriah taught him to pray that their sin would die, that they would repent. She also taught Meir resignation when their two sons died. Loving and gentle as she was with Meir, Beruriah could also be arrogant and biting. She ridiculed a Sadducee, derided an erring student, and made a fool of Rabbi Yose the Galilean when he met her on the road. Finally, she mocked the sages' dictum that women are easily seduced, and she came to a shameful end. Rabbi Meir set one of his students to seduce her. After long denial she yielded to him. When the plot was revealed, she strangled herself, and Rabbi Meir fled to Babylonia because of the disgrace.

(p. 28)

Adler (1988) suggested in this article that Beruriah, as a story character, may have resulted from the early Rabbi's imagining: "What if there were a woman who was just like us, someone learned, and dedicated to Torah?" This formulation has always interested me because I had not imagined the early sages having these kinds of ideas. And yet it is compellingly human to wonder just such a gender question; indeed, what if there was such a woman? Weissler (1998) suggests, "Each gender could symbolize to the other traits that it denied in itself, or that it feared, or abhorred or coveted, or desired" (p. 51). In this way the *otherness* of gender becomes like a Rorschach inkblot test; what one cannot accept in the self becomes projected onto and located within the other gender. The brief but intense scholarship that has ensued surrounding Beruriah reflects some of these questions: Did she exist? Were woman learned then, or how *other* was she? What can her story tell us about women, men, and early Israelite culture and religion? I will try to address some of this in what follows.

Although there are differences in Beruriah's textual appearance between the Palestinian and the Babylonian versions of the Talmud, consensus is that she most likely did exist even if some of the stories are elaborations or even a conflation of different females (Fonrobert, 2001; Goodblatt, 1975; Hartman & Buckholtz, 2011; Ilan, 1997, 1999). Goodblatt (1975) writes, "Several talmudic passages indicate that elementary education was open to women, but not advanced training. The uniqueness and importance of the Beruriah tradition is that it portrays a woman whose learning would require just such an advanced education" (p. 84). This was one of the first writings on Beruriah and highlights Beruriah's exceptional abilities – her speaking – which would mean her teaching as well, better than her brother or male peers. Tal Ilan (1999) agrees, "For a woman to know better than a man the *minutiae* of ritual purity, she would have had to be learned indeed" (p. 179).

All of this points to Beruriah's otherness from the category of most women whose main biblical function was as wife or mother. She has the intelligence and learning of a man but the body of a woman. Further, Ilan (1999) suggests that for Beruriah's sayings to have been written into the Talmud she would have had to state her opinions at the house of study, the ancient Beit Midrash, where these kinds of decisions were being discussed and debated. Ilan queries, "was she the only woman there . . . Were there any study-houses where women could be found . . . Did they study with men or did they study separately?" (p. 179). How "other" was this woman? On the one hand the Rabbis are attempting to allow for a different kind of woman. Perhaps this "new woman" is formed in *their* own image. This woman might then embody some desire on the part of the Rabbis, a wish that would then make Beruriah "other" to all other women. In fact there are no stories of her having interactions with women at all. Who would she interact with? Her mother is never mentioned, only that she learned from her well-regarded father and that she learned *better* than her brother.

Beruriah is a woman in a man's world, but I want to highlight that she is also living in a post-trauma era. Classical Rabbinic Judaism is considered to be established after the destruction of the second Temple was destroyed in Jerusalem, 70 C.E. Rabbinic Judaism was born from trauma, a direct result of the Roman overpowering and ending of the Jewish nation state. Rome was now fully in charge and all potential threats to Roman power were killed. A martyr's death awaited the sage Rabbi Akiva as well as Rabbi Hananyah ben Teradyon, Beruriah's father. Is Beruriah only to be seen as a woman who solely claims her father, a scholar, and followed in his footsteps? In losing and mourning him, does she more completely identify with him (a process Freud first details in *Mourning and Melancholia*, 1917)? Or, does she carry inside of her the trauma of witnessing the martyrdom of her father and fellow sages, the destruction of her world? I believe it is not *either–or* but *and*. Beruriah lives on as both witness and carrier of the torch of Jewish learning and life, something I believe the Rabbis wanted her to represent.

However, embedded within her story is the *other* story of trauma and loss. Given the feminist inquiry into the formation of gender binaries I agree with Benjamin (1998b) and Layton (1998) that the culture will infuse the categories of male and female with differing qualities and values. The very definition of one's gender suggests simultaneously what being male or female is and what it is not. The legacy of patriarchy is that maleness becomes associated with strength and independence while females are associated with dependency and vulnerability. Important cultural aspects of life inform these values and are also often split into the binary where aspects of power, hierarchy, and authority are riven from powerlessness and subordination. Therefore, I am suggesting that trauma – which I would define as the profound experience of helplessness, powerlessness, and subjugation – is more likely to be carried by that gender category that already is defined in a similar way: that is, women. In this way gender and trauma can be seen as inextricably entwined.

Boyarin (1995), in writing about the implicit gender hierarchy embedded within classical Talmudic Judaism, believes that "Both in the Palestinian and in the Babylonian text the dominant discourse suppressed women's voices in the House of Study" (p. 169). However, he doesn't believe it meant women never did study or learn, only that their opinions were suppressed. The greater harm, he feels, was the use that later European Jewish culture made of this, keeping women from ever entertaining the idea of studying Torah. Agreeing with Boyarin, Hauptman (2011) finds evidence that women did study Torah during the Rabbinic era and not just "household domestic" halakha, the obvious things girls might learn from observing their mothers. She believes that women growing up in Rabbinic families often learned Torah from men. Furthermore, Hauptman believes that the *beit midrash* of that era was "portable" and therefore locatable in homes, courtyards, under trees, or at a rabbi's table. These more porous settings allow for women to overhear discussions and even participate. She writes, "I am not suggesting that women were full-fledged students as were men, but that they were able to catch Torah 'on the fly.' This is still Torah study" (p. 3). What Hauptman describes fits Beruriah, daughter of a Rabbi, clearly comfortable discussing and being fluent with the laws, and now seen as not so "other."

Nonetheless, Beruriah is isolated in the text and not only from other women. In the Talmud, all teachings or sayings are placed in a tradition of who are one's teacher and one's student. Here, Adler (1988) sees how the unraveling of this Beruriah might begin. Despite her interactions with other Rabbis, Beruriah cannot enter the Talmudic web of authority. She cites no teachers and no students claim her as their teacher. She is effectively kept out of the chain of that tradition, its genealogical succession. The tradition she is steeped and learned in is one that sees women as intellectually inferior, "light-headed," and potentially "licentious." Additionally, sexuality was considered an essential characteristic of women, hence the need for prohibitions regarding speaking too long with a woman, hearing her sing, etc. In every way woman can distract and lead the male away from study into the erotic. Adler (1988) writes, "Were there a woman like Beruriah, schooled in and committed to a tradition that views her as inferior, how could she resolve the paradox inherent in her loyalty to that tradition?" (p. 30). As sharp and learned as she was, we cannot help but also discover and see played out the other negative pole of her otherness. A woman scholar must be *other* and so cannot exist. She is utterly alone, having been joined to a tradition that wouldn't have her as an equal member.

By that time of Rashi, the great Talmudic commentator in the 11th century, the gender binary was firmly established and study of these texts became solely the domain of men. The final Beruriah story is one that Rashi adds within a section of the Talmud dealing with sexual transgressions. In this story Meir and Beruriah argue with her, mocking the rabbinic dictum that "all women are light-headed," code for licentious. Meir, to prove his point, has a student seduce Beruriah. She resists and resists but finally gives in. I don't know if Beruriah gives in as a submission or out of any desire or agency of her own. This is interesting to contemplate as a further complication of her story. Where would Beruriah's desires lie? Does she submit to the seduction knowing on some level that her husband is behind it (the seducer is a student of Meir's)? Or is she rebelling against the tradition? We are told that after she learns of Meir's plan Beruriah commits suicide. It is this final story by Rashi that has tarnished Beruriah from being seen as the cross-gender lines female scholar extraordinaire back into the essentialist woman who is only a sexual object. The original attempt to undermine the gender binary, to imagine a woman embodying characteristics usually ascribed to men, is undone. Beruriah is "re-inscribed as girl" and this re-establishes gender conformity.

Yentl, the Yeshiva boy

I.B. Singer (1953), in his short story *Yentl, the Yeshiva Boy*, created a ficti-
tious woman who was not cut out for woman's work with her possessing
"the soul of a man in the body of a woman" (p. 149). Singer's 19th-century
story is located in an eastern European shtetl in Poland and opens with
Yentl's father dying. Yentl had secretly been learning Torah and Talmud
with her Rabbi father. All alone in the world, Yentl decides to refuse her
role as a woman and instead pursue studies as a boy. She cuts her hair,
dresses in her father's clothing, and assumes the name of Anshel, going off
to study at a Yeshiva. Once there she falls in love with her *havrutah* (study
partner) Avigdor. This friendship intensifies although Avigdor marries and,
upon his suggestion, Anshel/Yentl impulsively marries Avigdor's former
fiancée Hadass. After some time, no longer able to sustain the multiple
secrets of his/her transgressive cross-dressing lie/life, Anshel/Yentl invites
Avigdor to go on a trip together and reveals to Avigdor her true identity
as a woman. Avigdor offers to marry her but once again Yentl refuses her
female role, saying she wants to learn with him, not darn his socks. Avigdor
is bereft and confused while Yentl has firmly decided to leave and send
divorce papers to Hadass, disappearing from the story. The story ends with
Avigdor and Hadass marrying and having a son whom they name Anshel.

Beyond plucking feathers

Given the gendered underpinnings within Judaism, I will be looking at
how Beruriah and Yentl act to countervail the gender binary and in so
doing reveal a kind of complicated otherness of woman within Judaism.
There are many similarities between Yentl and Beruriah, and I have no
doubt that Singer was familiar with the Beruriah legends. Toward the end
of the story after Yentl undresses to prove to Avigdor that she is in fact a
woman, they argue over how she had violated the commandments against
cross-dressing. Yentl tries to explain how her nature was not cut out for
"plucking feathers" and goes back to their Talmudic conversation:

> A great love for Anshel took hold of Avigdor, mixed with shame,
> remorse, anxiety . . . In his thoughts he likened Anshel (or Yentl) to
> Bruria, the wife of Reb Meir . . . For the first time he saw clearly that
> this was what he had always wanted: a wife whose mind was not taken
> up with material things.
>
> (Singer, 1953, p. 165)

I consider Yentl as a "drash" on Beruriah, revealing a hidden piece of the legends making up the "text" on Beruriah. I wonder if Singer elaborated the "passing as a man" aspect of Beruriah by having Yentl dress and pass as a Yeshiva boy? Passing is a statement on rigid gender binaries, by highlighting, violating and even sometimes mocking them. Garber (1992) articulates this well:

> One of the most important aspects of cross-dressing is the way in which it offers a challenge to easy notions of binarity, putting into question the categories of "female" and "male," whether they are considered essential or constructed, biological or cultural.
>
> (p. 10)

Yentl does continue studying, but I also see her *passing* as a transgressive attempt to subvert rigid gender binaries by being the girl who can easily become a boy. In this way she embodies Butler's (1990, 1993, 1995) conceptualizations of gender as performance. Additionally, by defying Jewish law, i.e. the prohibition over wearing the clothing of the other sex, Yentl was undoing the subordinate status of woman. Harris (2005) has written, "The tomboy experience often simultaneously refuses conventions and gender coherences and swallows them wholesale. Gender conformist and gender outlaw" (p. 132). What Harris is characterizing is how gender gets used and misused, the very lawless behavior Yentl embodies. Yentl broke laws but also abided tightly to them, carefully dressing the part, determined to "pass" as boy.

This is not new to Jewish literature and Lefkovitz (2010) has written about how masculinity can at times also be the site of "passing." In her writing about the twins Esau and Jacob she notices how Jacob has to "pass" as his more stereotypically masculine brother to receive (and steal) his father's blessing. She writes, "Jacob, the son who is allied with his mother, dresses in animal skins to pass as Esau, and so, to pass as the kind of man who can inherit the patriarchy" (p. 48). In this way the biblical story riffs on what kind of masculinity, what type of man can be blessed and sanctioned to carry the patriarchy forward. In this story the complementary role of a son, identified with his mother, cross-dresses to "pass," to not be the "other" son.

The rigid gender binary inherent within patriarchy and woven into Judaism has a shadow side. The *other*, the shadow self of non-heteronormativity, can be seen in these stories of "passing," where regulatory anxiety prevails over gender fluidity. These are stories not only of girls passing as boys but as we see with Jacob, even boys may need to "pass" since the version of masculinity necessitated by the patriarchy may border on heroic versions of maleness. In discussing the ideal of the hero Grand (2010) writes, "In its most magical form, this ideal can actually sponsor rash acts *and* noble deeds. These actions appear to us as a source of inspiration, and they provide a bulwark against our anxiety" (p. 2).

Singer had left Poland and arrived in the United States, escaping the worst of Nazi Europe. He wrote Yentl post-WWII and the Holocaust, in the 1950s, and I wonder if we can see trauma lurking in this story as well. He locates his gender-bending heroine back in time, to a 19th-century Polish shtetl era, which pre-dated him and the Shoah that destroyed the world he had known. I want us to hold in mind the complicated ways that specifically a female is used to carry trauma. As with Beruriah whose father dies, Yentl's story also opens with death. Yentl's father, who is seen as nurturing her in an entire world of devotion to studying texts, dies in the opening page of the story. We also know that, in an instance, this world of shtetls and shteibls, of Rabbis and communities had been wiped out as part of Hitler's final solution. Singer brings this world back to life in many of his short stories but with Yentl we see how trauma and gender are interconnected. Both Beruriah and Yentl carry the trauma of death – the loss of their fathers and of vital Jewish communal life. Each of these eras – post-second-Temple destruction and 1930s Europe – saw the end of eras where Jews lived more independent, self-governing lives. I also believe it is a probable trope for Singer to use the category "woman" to carry any cultural trauma of oppression. It is Yentl who loses the most in this story; her father and family, her love of studying, her love for Avigdor and for Hadass, and ultimately her life, since she must disappear at the end of the story.

Concluding thoughts and questions

In many ways Judaism rests on stories. Each week a parsha, a section from the Torah, is read. Many of these sections are historical stories of the people and nation that became the Hebrews or Israelites, ancestors of today's Jews. We read about the children who descended from the first man Adam and the first woman Eve. Some of us have read about the woman who preceded Eve, Lilith. We read about the patriarchs, Abraham, Isaac, and Jacob, while some of us mightily read into the small fragments of the stories of the matriarchs, Sarah, Rebecca, Leah, and Rachel. There are so many stories we read and within them are the shadow stories, the back-story or the tale we imagine wasn't fully told. I feel trauma is one of those shadow stories. In many ways the history of the Jewish people is a history of trauma, oppression, victimization, and then triumph and freedom with later cycles of trauma, oppression etc. repeated again, and that is what gets transmitted across the generations. The moment of revelation itself follows a hard road from slavery to 40 years in the desert till freedom. We are often enjoined not to forget this journey where we were once strangers and slaves in Egypt, oppressed and denied our autonomy. This remembrance is to aid us in our duty to others, to safeguard ethical behavior toward the *other*, but it also keeps our own vulnerability and traumatization ever present. We were once *othered* and colonized and "*zakhor*" – we should never forget this. However, I do wonder if women will have to carry weakness and the spectral presence of trauma. The stories of Beruriah and Yentl are examples of how attempts to envision undermining the gender polarities may quickly dissolve and re-instatement of gender hierarchy and splits occurs. In this way they are cautionary tales.

Gender conformity is a prevailing aspect of the stories we are told, and a place where women became *othered*. Benjamin (1998b) has written, "Opposites are to some extent unavoidable because of the inherent psychic tendency to split; because in fact they allow the mind to think. It is the capacity to hold them in tension and overcome splitting that is at stake" (p. 24). I have also tried to show that "passing" is one way out of the gender split, in that it plays on binarity and refuses it. However, I wonder when passing allows for a kind of freedom for an "other self" to be expressed, and when it eradicates "otherness." When does passing carry what is permissible and when is it subversive? These questions further lead me to wonder about authenticity; who and what is an authentic Jew? Is Yentl authentically Jewish if she "passes" as a Yeshiva boy to study and express her authentically Jewish yearning for learning? Or was Beruriah more originally authentic since she imbibed her father's learning and the world around her, entering the discourse as she saw fit?

I do question if we ever fully transcend the legacy of gender binaries, of splits that allow for disowned parts of the self to be found in the opposite gender. Will men continue to own agency and dominance as a means to feel masculine? And can our models and expectations change enough to allow for authentic experiences to take root and grow? Henry Higgins ends his songful lament, asking, "Why can't a woman be like me?" This line reveals the narcissistic root that prevents us from experiencing the "other" as a full subject not to be colonized by our own subjectivity. Layton (1998) in her book and work on gender, culture, and postmodern theory believes that the cultural and the psychological are always interconnected and implicated in forming each other. Here is where the fulcrum may lie. We need to change ourselves while also needing to change our culture. Further, we allow for a constant interpenetration between self and culture to occur in lieu of colonization.

Note

1 This chapter was originally given at the Psychology and the Other conference, October 2013, on a panel entitled "The Otherness of Jewishness." I want to thank Rabbi Burton L. Visotzky for introducing me to midrash and Beruriah, Dr. Anne Lapidus Lerner for elaborating the feminist enterprise in the context of the Beruriah Legends, Rabbi Judith Hauptman for her thoughtful comments and encouragement on this chapter, and Dr. Adrienne Harris for her insights on gender, tomboys, and so much more.

References

Adler, R. (1988). The virgin in the brothel and other anomalies: Character and context in the legend of Beruriah. *Tikkun, 3*(6), 28–105.
Benjamin, J. (1988a). *The bonds of love: Psychoanalysis, feminism and the problem of domination.* New York: Pantheon Books.
Benjamin, J. (1998b). *Shadow of the other: Intersubjectivity and gender in psychoanalysis.* New York and London: Routledge.
Boyarin, D. (1995). *Carnal Israel: Reading sex in Talmudic culture.* Berkeley: University of California Press.
Bromberg, P. (2006). *Awakening the dreamer: Clinical journeys.* London & New York: Routledge.
Butler, J. (1990). *Gender trouble.* New York: Routledge.
Butler, J. (1993). *Bodies that matter.* New York: Routledge.
Butler, J. (1995). Melancholy gender-refused identification. *Psychoanalytic Dialogues, 5,* 165–180.
Davies, J. M. (1998). Multiple perspectives on multiplicity. *Psychoanalytic Dialogues, 8,* 195–206.
Fonrobert, C. E. (2001). The Beit Midrash which is not yet: Feminist interpretations of Rabbinic literature: Two views. *Nashim: A Journal of Jewish Women's Studies and Gender Issues, 4,* 7–14.
Freud, S. (1917). Mourning and melancholia. *The standard edition of the complete works of Sigmund Freud.* Trans: James Strachy. London: Hogarth Press. Institute of Psychoanalysis, 1953–74. Vol. 14, pp. 243–258.
Garber, M. (1992). *Vested interests: Cross-dressing and cultural anxiety.* New York & London: Routledge.

Gilligan, C. (2002). *The birth of pleasure.* New York: Random House.

Goldman, A. (2013, June 30). Like a cowboy going to a saloon. *The New York Times Sunday Magazine.*

Goodblatt, D. (1975). The Beruriah traditions. *Journal of Jewish Studies, 26,* 68–85.

Grand, S. (2010). *The hero in the mirror: From fear to fortitude.* New York and London: Routledge.

Harris, A. (1992). Gender as contradiction. *Psychoanalytic Dialogues, 2,* 197–224.

Harris, A. (1996). The conceptual power of multiplicity. *Contemporary Psychoanalysis, 32,* 537–552.

Harris, A. (2000). Gender as a soft assembly. *Studies in Gender and Sexuality, 1,* 223–324.

Harris, A. (2005). *Gender as soft assembly.* Hillsdale, NJ: The Analytic Press.

Hartman, T., & Buckholtz, C. (2011). Beruriah said well: The many lives (and deaths) of a Talmudic social critic. *Prooftexts, 31,* 181–209.

Hauptman, J. (2011). A new view of women and Torah study in the Talmudic period. *Jewish Studies Internet Journal, 9,* 249–292.

Heschel, S. (1983). *On being a Jewish feminist.* New York: Schocken Books.

Ilan, T. (1997). The quest for the historical Beruriah, Rachel, and Imma Shalom. *AJS Review, 22,* 1–17.

Ilan, T. (1999). Beruriah has spoken well: The historical Beruriah and her transformation in the Rabbinic Corpora. *Integrating women into second temple history.* Peabody, MA: J.C.B. Mohr Siebeck.

Layton, L. (1998). Who's that girl? Who's that boy?: *Clinical practice meets postmodern gender theory.* Northvale, NJ and London: Jason Aronson, Inc.

Lefkovitz, L. H. (2010). *In scripture: The first stories of Jewish sexual identities.* Lanham, MD: Rowman & Littlefield Publishers, Inc.

Plaskow, J. (1990). *Standing again at Sinai.* New York: HarperCollins.

Salberg, J. (2012). Reimagining Yentl while revisiting feminism in the light of relational approaches to gender and sex. *Studies in Gender and Sexuality, 13,* 185–196.

Singer, I. B. (1953). Yentl the Yeshiva boy. *The Collected Stories of Isaac Bashevis Singer.* New York: Farrar Straus Giroux.

Weissler, C. (1998). *Voices of the matriarchs: Listening to the prayers of early modern Jewish women.* Boston: Beacon Press.

Chapter 13

Trauma, Jews, and gender – how they are transmitted, imagined, and reconceived

Response to Judith Alpert and Jill Salberg

Susannah Heschel

How is trauma transmitted and experienced within the intimate relationships of a family? The chapters by Jill Salberg and Judie Alpert base themselves on the authors' reflections on the traumas experienced within their families, and ask how women's bodies, in particular, encapsulate traumatic experience.

Both chapters are also concerned with the link between private trauma and the trauma of recent Jewish history, including pogroms and the Holocaust. And both chapters continue a Jewish tradition that begins in the Bible, in which memory is always linked to action. Indeed, the most frequent passage in the Bible is God's injunction to the Israelites to remember that they were slaves in Egypt, and to treat the stranger properly (see, for instance, Deuteronomy 5:15). Remembering is linked to action and social justice.

Judie Alpert exemplifies this tradition magnificently. To her was transmitted, wordlessly, what happened to her mother: her mother was raped at the age of 15. Her mother never spoke of it until she was literally in her last moments of life. Somehow, though, Alpert knew what had happened. She did not have direct knowledge of that traumatic rape, but Alpert was unconsciously aware of what her mother had suffered. Alpert then responded to that unconscious memory with her own action and social justice. During the course of her career, Judie has devoted herself to alleviating the trauma of rape, and to efforts to stop it, to make known its horror, to establish rape as a war crime and human rights violation, and to offer help to those who have suffered rape. The link she discovered between her work and her mother's deathbed revelation is uncanny and remarkable. In her chapter, she calls to the attention of therapists the need to think, with patients, about unknown knowledge. She urges therapists to attend to memories that are not articulated in words, but that circulate along with the intimacies of family relationships, and that throb inside each of us.

My response to Alpert's chapter comes with three brief remarks. First, I would like to underscore the other remarkable quality about Alpert's mother that she emphasizes: her courage and resilience. The response to trauma may be not only suffering, but inner strength. Anna Ornstein (2003) has called our attention to resilience as a neglected aspect of Holocaust survival, and if Alpert's engagement as an analyst in treating victims of torture and as an activist on behalf of human rights is her unconscious enactment of her mother's experience of rape, surely she manifests her mother's remarkable resilience. Perhaps in addition to studying the rape of Jewish women, Alpert might help us understand the sources of the courage and resilience that were so important to women in surviving such trauma. Therapists must attend to the courage and resilience that function so fundamentally in the willingness of survivors to seek healing; resilience is as important to understand as trauma and suffering.

My second point concerns the much-vaunted intergenerational transmission of trauma. Deferred experience of childhood was recognized by Freud: *"The traumas of childhood operate in a deferred fashion as though they were fresh experiences; but they do so unconsciously"* (Freud 1896, p. 167, original italics). The question is whether parents' experiences function for us as if they were our elements of unconscious childhood experience, our own screen memories recognized only much later and then attributed meaning, in what Freud called "Nachträglichkeit"; James Strachey translated this as "deferred action" (Eickhoff, 2006) and Laplanche (2002) called it "après-coup." Laplanche (2002) explains the term as establishing "a complex and reciprocal relationship between a significant event and its resignification in afterwardsness, whereby the event acquires new psychic efficiency" (p. 121). This is not, as Carl Jung claimed, a retroactive fantasizing, but points instead, as Haydee Faimberg (2005b) argues, to profound "narcissistic links between generations" (p. 1). Surely parents transmit a great deal of unconscious material to their children, which is then assimilated in a unique fashion by each child, and historical events are also constantly reworked and given new meanings. Faimberg (2005b) speaks of a "telescoping of the generations," and the literary critic Marianne Hirsch (2012) speaks of the child's "postmemory" of the parents' memories.

What is crucial is the role of imagination: how do I imagine what happened to my parents, what they suffered, how they felt about it? This of course is not their trauma, nor is it my memory of their trauma; it is my intrapsychic imagination, woven by my own conscious and unconscious fantasies and desires, and this is precisely the domain of psychoanalysis. Moreover, the imagined suffering (or cruelty) we may attribute to our parents may well be a projected fantasy stemming from our experience of them. The difficulty, always, is distinguishing between fantasies about one's parents and the reality of what has happened to them and to us by them. The uncanny conjunction of Alpert's work against rape and her mother's own experience of rape is remarkable, but should not detract from the role of intrapsychic imagination, as Alpert wonders what might have stimulated her mother's enactment and disavowal, her paranoia and silence. Enactment and disavowal are precisely what constitute psychoanalytic treatment, affecting both therapist and patient, and the workings of intrapsychic imagination are delicate dynamics for the psychoanalyst to probe.

The very existence of Holocaust trauma and its transmission to the next generation has been called into question in recent years. In a forthcoming article, Robin Gomolin (2014) questions the validity of much of the psychoanalytic publications on second generation Holocaust survivors, since they seem to be based on very little empirical evidence and use Holocaust trauma as an interpretive "covering law" explanation that imposes a preconceived model. It is too easy to assert that an irrational fear results from a parent's years in a concentration camp, and too easy to bypass deeper analysis of the individual. Ultimately, a category of Holocaust trauma may give greater satisfaction to the analyst than the patient. The "intergenerational transmission process," Gomolin writes, "can also be viewed as an intergenerational imperative to record the trauma of the Holocaust in a way that maintains it as an active wound." That is, attributing trauma to the Holocaust experience of parents may lead therapists to neglect other problems faced by a patient. Indeed, the German psychoanalyst Tilo Held (2015) casts doubt on the empirical evidence of Holocaust trauma in survivors and their children: "Neither the general occurrence of major disability in the first generation nor the transmission of traumatic sequelae to the second generation have been verified in large non-clinical populations of survivors." Evidence of trauma in survivors was presented by psychiatrists on behalf of patients seeking financial compensation after the war, obscuring, Held (2015) writes, "the often astonishing 'recovery' of adult and child survivors." Gomolin (2014) and Held illumine for us that Alpert's mother was not unusual in her ability to recover and transmit to her daughter both her trauma and her recovery.

My third and final point concerns Jewish memory. The sociologist Maurice Halbwachs (1980) argued for an inseparable link between individual memory and collective memory: our individual memories are structured by the cultural and political imperatives of the groups in which we live. Scholarship on the Jewish past has not deviated significantly from the memories enshrined in Jewish holidays and prayerbooks: a lachrymose history that remembers persecutions and suffering as much in history books as in fast days and memorial prayers. Alpert places her mother's experience of rape into that larger context of Jewish history, a history replete with rape, murder, beatings, property destruction, and other horrors. Yet recent Jewish historians have regretted the lachrymose history that has become so popular, both because our history has been replete with joy and redemption, and because wallowing in a history of misery has had dangerous political and theological consequences. Strikingly, Alpert's narrative follows a common Jewish narrative of suffering that is then transformed into acts of social justice, from persecution to redemption.

More significant, however, is the repressed aspect of Jewish identity to which Alpert calls our attention: that of the emotional, often unconscious dimension of Jewishness. Recitations by historians of pogroms, expulsions, murders, and other atrocities committed against Jews do not convey the emotional dimension of the experience, its memory, and even the awareness that it occurred. Alpert's important contribution to scholarship in the field of Jewish Studies comes from her insights drawn from psychoanalytic theory, insights that lead her to uncover a new, emotional dimension of Jewish experience, and to argue that it is this emotional dimension (and not simply DNA, circumcision, or a taste for bagels) that transmits Jewishness from one generation to the next. Just as she herself did not "know" that her mother had been raped, but nonetheless "knew" and acted in response to that horror, Alpert is suggesting that we all bear within us dimensions of knowledge about Jewish experience, often unconsciously, that have enormous repercussions for the way we live our lives. This is a major contribution to Jewish Studies, and to the interplay between Jewishness and psychoanalysis, suggesting a new and important role of the Jewish in the origins of psychoanalysis.

Jill Salberg's chapter is linked to Alpert's at this important nexus of memory and trauma, and calls attention to the centrality of gender in Jewish experience. The Hebrew word for remembering, zachor, also means male,[1] thus rendering the biblical commandment to remember, "Remember the Sabbath day" to also mean "Make the Sabbath male." A central concern of Salberg's chapter is the role of women in traditional Judaism, with particular attention to attitudes toward women's bodies. As the child who was "supposed to be" a boy, not a girl, Salberg grew up experiencing denigrating attitudes toward female gender, and feeling encouraged to take an interest in male activities. Her physical presence as a baby girl, not a boy, seems to have inflicted trauma on her parents, whose disappointment was palpable to Salberg as a child even when not articulated verbally. In response to her parents' trauma over her "wrong" gender, Salberg became a tomboy and felt perfectly comfortable with that role, hoping to appease her parents. However, iteration of male gender found its limits in Jewish religious practice. Male roles in Judaism were closed to her, such as study of Talmud and prayer leadership in Reform as well as Orthodox settings, so in those realms she was "stuck" in a prescribed female role that was constricting because it was based on exclusion from the male realm. The dilemma was not hers alone; many Jewish women have felt similar constrictions, myself included. Salberg's chapter examines the responses of two Jewish women who rebelled against those strictures, according to stories about them told by male authors. These are Beruriah, whose life is known to us from brief references in the Talmud and its commentaries, written by male rabbis, and Yentl, who disguises herself in male clothing to study at a yeshiva, as related in the eponymous short story by I.B. Singer, which was turned into a film starring Barbra Streisand.

Salberg's observations are entirely correct, and I sympathize with her frustrations, many of which I have experienced in my own life. As a psychoanalyst, she goes further than the standard feminist analyses of Judaism, raising the issue of trauma and asking whether Judaism's divisions between male and female roles result in women becoming the bearers of trauma legacies within the family or even the wider Jewish community. This leads her to ask how women experience and somaticize trauma in the context of a religious community whose power and authority lies in the hands of men. Psychoanalytic theory enables deeper feminist analyses of gender within Judaism, as well as other religions.

For one thing, we learn that gender is not about polarities of men and women, male and female, but is far more fluid; I tend to think of gender in terms closer to Judith Butler's (1990) notion of citationality, that is, that gender is constantly under social construction and interpretation. For Butler, gender is neither innate nor static, but a performance that is constantly being recreated by reiterating previous performances of gender, so that gender is inauthentic, parodic, and an ongoing drag performance. The religious texts of Judaism add a material dimension by insisting that a proper understanding of Jewish sacred texts is only achieved by the circumcised penis, excluding women and Gentiles (Wolfson, 1995). Thus, the exclusion of women from Jewish memory occurs on several levels: the Jewish experience that is remembered is exclusively male; the construction of Jewish identity through the authority of history is resultingly male; the interpreters and the process of interpretation are inscribed as physically male. In the rabbinic context of the Talmud, men are in an exclusive domain that they define in contrast to the broader category of "women, slaves and minors," and worry constantly about hermaphrodites and others with unclear sexual organs, and yet these male Jews view themselves as women in relation to the male God. But where does all that leave women like Salberg (and myself) who long to participate in that male domain of study house and synagogue?

I would like to respond by suggesting that the problem is about both sex and gender. Women's sexuality has been at times demonized, and at other times respected and even valorized both in traditional and modern Judaism, but it is her mind that remains the constant problem for the rabbis. Traditional Jewish culture may have had a positive, even lusty attitude toward heterosexual relationships, but was stringent about maintaining boundaries excluding women's intellectual participation in the shaping of Judaism. At issue, as Leslie Adelson (1993) has described in a different context, is the meaning of a woman's mouth. If the vagina represents sex, then the mouth represents gender. The mouth is the portal of the mind, revealing knowledge, thoughts, and insights. In a famous essay by Hélène Cixous (1981), "Castration or Decapitation?", she points out that under patriarchy, women are undermined less through sexual disadvantage than by the rejection of their minds. However, the mind also plays a sexual role in Judaism, a religion increasingly reliant on the interpretation of texts, rather than in the mimesis of religious Jews (as Haym Soloveitchik, 1994, has pointed out). The exclusively male homoerotic setting for text study, itself viewed as a form of worship, creates a difficulty: how to evoke heterosexual pleasure when maleness has been cultivated in a homoerotic environment? Indeed, according to Rashi's commentary, Beruriah's husband gets his student to seduce her, after which she commits suicide and he flees. Yentl, in Singer's story, succeeds in gaining entry to a yeshiva, but in her male disguise she fails to integrate into Jewish society, which expects him (her) to marry a woman and father children.

Thus, when Salberg calls for women's access to Jewish learning, she encounters resistance. Women interrupt the homoerotic coziness of the rabbinical study hall; they might speak their minds, thus asserting their gender, and perhaps most worrisome is how women would react when studying texts that systematize the exclusion of women. For Beruriah and Yentl are not the same. Yentl simply wants access, whereas Beruriah demands change. It is hard to imagine a woman simply learning and repeating what the rabbis say; perhaps we are excluded because the rabbis know that once women are admitted, all hell will break loose!

Finally, I fully agree with Jill Salberg's concluding point about the psychological and moral dangers of gender passing as the only option for women in male-dominated societies, and the important search for authenticity both as a Jew and as a woman. The two chapters demonstrate that feminist scholarship on religion has much to learn from psychoanalytic insights regarding trauma, imagination, and resilience. As Judie Alpert makes clear, we should not look to the past for models of selfhood to imitate – that would be spiritual plagiarism – nor for trauma we need to reenact, but rather we should study the past to glean moral imperatives for the future.

Note

1 The two words are homonyms, but are not etymologically related, according to Willy Schottroff, who examined the word and its meanings within ancient Near Eastern cognates. Willy Schottroff, "Gedenken" im alten Orient und im Alten Testament; die Wurzel zakar im semitischen Sprachkreis (Neukirchen Verlag, 1964).

References

Adelson, A. (1993). Making bodies, making history. *Feminism and German Identity, 39.* Lincoln and London: University of Nebraska.
Butler, J. (1990). *Gender trouble.* London and New York: Routledge.
Cixous, H. (1981). Castration or decapitation. (A. Kuhn, Trans.). *Signs, 7*(1), 41–55.

Eickhoff, F.-W. (2006). On Nachträglichkeit: The modernity of an old concept. *International Journal of Psychoanalysis, 87*, 1453–1469.

Faimberg, H. (2005a). Après coup. *International Journal of Psychoanalysis, 86*, 1–16.

Faimberg, H. (2005b). *The telescoping of generations.* New York: Routledge.

Freud, S. (1896). Further remarks on the neuro-psychoses of defence. *Standard Edition 3*, 162–185.

Gomolin, R. (2014). *The intergenerational transmission of Holocaust trauma: A psychoanalytic theory revisited.* (Unpublished manuscript)

Halbwachs, M. (1980). *Collective memory.* New York: Harper and Row.

Held, T. (2015). *Child survivors of Nazi persecution: What did we understand and what not?* Paper presented at the American Psychoanalytic Association, New York.

Hirsch, M. (2012). *The generation of postmemory: Writing and visual culture after the Holocaust.* New York: Columbia University Press.

Laplanche, J. (2002). Après-coup. In A. Mijolla (Eds.), *Dictionnaire international de la psychanalyse.* Paris: Calmann-Levy.

Ornstein, A. (2003). Survival and recovery: Psychoanalytic reflections. *Progress in Self Psychology, 19*, 85–105.

Rothberg, M. (2009). Multidirectional memory. *Remembering the Holocaust in the age of decolonization, 15.* Stanford, CA: Stanford University Press.

Soloveitchik, H. (1994). Rupture and reconstruction: The transformation of contemporary Orthodoxy. *Tradition, 28*, 64–130.

Wolfson, E. (1995). On becoming female: Crossing gender boundaries in Kabbalistic ritual and myth. In T. Rudavsky (Ed.), *Gender and Judaism* (pp. 209–228). New York: New York University Press.

Chapter 14

Beyond betrayal

On responsibility in Heidegger, Loewald, and Levinas

Michael Oppenheim

I am deeply grateful for what I learned from him [Martin Heidegger], despite his most hurtful betrayal in the Nazi era, which alienated me from him permanently.

(Loewald, 2000, pp. xlii–xliii)

One can forgive many Germans, but there are some Germans it is difficult to forgive. It is difficult to forgive Heidegger.

(Levinas, 1968/1990a, p. 25)

Hans Loewald and Emmanuel Levinas were two of Martin Heidegger's many students of Jewish heritage[1] who felt betrayed by him when he both spoke and acted in strong support of the Nazi regime. While haunted by their teacher's treachery, they could not completely divorce themselves from his influence, or refuse to admit his important intellectual legacy. This complex, ambivalent stance is similar to what Richard Wolin (2001) found in his study of some of Heidegger's other Jewish students. As he wrote in *Heidegger's Children*, "his 'children' sought to philosophize *with Heidegger against Heidegger*, thereby hoping to save what could be saved, all the while trying to cast off their mentor's long and powerful shadow" (pp. 7–8).

This chapter will begin with a concise account of Heidegger's relation to Nazism, followed by a précis of his 1927 classic, *Being and Time*, focusing on the view of responsibility and the wider purview of human relations. It will then turn to discussions of the complex responses to Heidegger seen through Loewald's psychoanalytic understanding of intersubjectivity and responsibility, and through Levinas's philosophic rendering of these themes. The conclusion will widen the presentation to examine the importance given to responsibility in some post-Freudian psychoanalytic discussions.

Heidegger argued that a person's life is irrelevant to their philosophic legacy and his supporters add that, despite his activities in the early 1930s, his philosophy itself was unrelated and uncontaminated. His relationship to National Socialism has been well documented. The most overt acts of support occurred during the first year of the regime in 1933. Heidegger took over as Rector of the University of Freiburg and was vigilant in enforcing one of the earlier Nuremberg laws, the "law for the Preservation of a Permanent Civil Service," which banned Jews from government service, including at Germany's universities. In his inaugural address he lauded the new "spiritual" movement of the time and affirmed its ties to his own work as well as to the fate of the people, history, and Being. Jacques Derrida (1989) wrote of this, "[the *Rectorship Address*] capitalizes on the worst . . . the sanctioning of nazism and the gesture that is still metaphysical" (p. 40). Heidegger infamously declared in one speech of the time, "Let not ideas and doctrines be your guide. The *Führer* is the only German reality and its law" (Wolin, 2001, p. 10). Those Jewish students still working with him, including his intimate friend Hannah Arendt, were sent away. He prevented his famous mentor of Jewish descent, Edmund Husserl, from using the university library in his old age, and also withdrew the dedication to Husserl in the second edition of *Being and Time*. Although Heidegger remained as Rector for only one year, he had enough time to fully implement the regime's will. These were not isolated incidents. Heidegger gave earlier speeches that were blatantly anti-Semitic, and he never repudiated or apologized for what he had said and done. At the end of the war a university commission found him guilty of actively supporting the National Socialists and permanently took away his right to teach (Wolin, 2001).

As Wolin indicated, Hannah Arendt, Karl Löwith, Hans Jonas, and Herbert Marcuse, who were also some of Heidegger's Jewish students, responded to their teacher's treachery with, minimally, a critique of his work. They saw his flirtation with evil as an extension of themes in *Being and Time*, and were particularly interested in exploring deeper notions of human relationships and responsibility. In particular, in a study that compared Heidegger and the Jewish philosopher Franz Rosenzweig, Löwith (1942) insisted that Heidegger's fall was not accidental, but fully corresponded to his philosophy. As he stated it, "This political commitment . . . was not – as naïve people thought – a deviation from the main path of his philosophy" (p. 75).

Responsibility in Heidegger's *Being and Time*

It was around the time of the publication of *Being and Time* that Loewald and Levinas studied with Heidegger, and it was in relation to that text that their later responses should be understood. On the first page, Heidegger (1927/1962) affirms that the aim of the book is "to work out the question of the meaning of *Being*" (p. 19), which is the problematic of "fundamental ontology" (p. 227). For him Being cannot properly be comprehended by ferreting out some essence, as philosophy had insistently attempted throughout its history. Rather, Being should be understood as it shows itself, that is, in its acts or in time. In this context, he focuses on the one entity for whom "Being is an *issue* for it" (p. 32), that is *Dasein* or the existing individual. The issue of the meaning of its existence is not only distinctive to humans, but essential or constitutional. To understand this, one must explore Dasein "in its temporality and historicality" (p. 42).

The central issue for Dasein has to do with the authenticity of its own existence, whether it decisively chooses itself or just loses itself in the everyday world. Living in the world, humans are initially concerned with attending to things, doing things, making things. Humans do not just stand and observe things in an uninvolved manner, but turn to them with purposes. The first kinds of entities that Dasein finds, at hand as it were, are equipment or tools. This points to persons coming to be in a world of human-fashioned objects already there.

In understanding how humans exist in the world, it is to their principal emotions or moods that one must turn. Moods are in this way prior to and more definitive than ideas in disclosing the nature of human existence. The three most revealing moods are fear, evasion, and anxiety. These show Dasein as thrown into a world, not first choosing itself or the universe around it, and concerned with how it is to live in this given situation. One primary feature of Dasein is its ability to project itself into the future by assessing its possibilities within a world already there.

In the midst of the everyday, Dasein is cast into public life, lost in the "they" with its idle talk, superficial curiosity, and amorphous ambiguity. This is a fallen life of inauthenticity and alienation from itself. The sole escape from this is achieved by turning away from others – "all its relations to any other Dasein have been undone" (Heidegger, 1927/1962, p. 294) – and facing the reality of one's own death. In facing death a person comes to discover who he or she really is to be. As Heidegger writes, "Death is Dasein's *ownmost* possibility. Being towards this possibility discloses to Dasein its *ownmost* potentiality-for-Being, in which its very Being is the issue" (p. 307).

It is conscience that calls Dasein out of its fallenness into the they, to the possibility of choosing itself. This is also expressed in terms of guilt: "The call of conscience has the character of an *appeal* to Dasein by calling it to its ownmost potentiality-for-Being-its-Self; and this is done by way of *summoning* it to its ownmost Being-guilty" (Heidegger, 1927/1962, p. 314). Guilt refers to the state in which Dasein first finds itself, the default position of "irresoluteness," "of one's lostness in the 'they'" (p. 345). Still, Dasein has the ability to take over guilt with resoluteness.

Yet, authenticity requires more than resoluteness in the present about one's future living in the face of death. It also entails standing up to one's historicity or anchorage in the past. One must take up, even choose who one already is and where one already stands – fate, while being aware at the same time that this fate in which one finds oneself is actually unchosen. Heidegger (1927/1962) closes the penultimate section with an appropriate concluding statement for the whole work; "Resoluteness constitutes the *loyalty* of existence to its own Self" (p. 443).

What is the place of other persons in this scenario? Other persons do exist and they are significant features of living in the world. However, as we saw, before looking at others, *Being and Time* considers cultural things, tools, that are ready-at-hand. When others are encountered, it is always from a perspective of one's own interests. As Heidegger (1927/1962) states it, "in characterizing the encountering of *Others*, one is again still oriented by that Dasein which is in each case one's *own*" (p. 154). Still, other persons are not treated as things or tools, but are objects of a special kind of concern called "solicitude" (*Fürsorge*). Solicitude may be something superficial or significant. Superficial solicitude, which has many forms, helps the other evade their responsibility to themselves and the need for resoluteness. True solicitude aids or frees the other in recognizing their need to decisively make themselves in the face of death. Heidegger (1927/1960) writes, "it helps the Other to become transparent to himself *in* his care and to become *free for* it" (p. 159). However, he does not describe this type of positive solicitude further, and even notes that such an effort would be "beyond the limits of this investigation" (p. 159). Thus, while the author of *Being and Time* does present this dimension of "being with" others, it is dwarfed by the importance of the topic of being lost in the crowd. Further, this relationship is only an existential possibility, neither a responsibility nor a requirement for one's own authenticity.

Overall, in *Being and Time*, conscience, guilt, authenticity, and responsibility are not achieved in human relationships, but are clearly self-referential, although there is also a continuing refrain that the referent is not just the self, but the call of Being or one's own being. The preponderance of human relationships is alienating, and, most importantly, deceptively so. Only by breaking off relationships is authenticity achieved. The sole test of life is facing death, and this individualizes in the most extreme form. In Heidegger's (1927/1962) words, "The non-relational character of death, as understood in anticipation, individualizes Dasein down to itself" (p. 308). In essence, Dasein is constituted by a deep-seated concern for itself and its responsibility is solely to itself.

Finally, to say that *Being and Time* is a complex and ambiguous book is an understatement. There is no one "true" reading, but there are good and bad readings and I submit that this brief discussion is a balanced one. It follows a number of critics, in particular Löwith (1942), Martin Buber (1965), and some feminist theorists, including Tina Chanter (2001). Despite the many attempts to uncover, extend, or augment hints in *Being and Time* concerning the responsibility to others,[2] there is, at the least, no rejoinder to John Caputo's challenge that entirely missing is "the body in need, the body of the suffering, the bodies of those who lay claim to those who are well-off" (1993, p. 68).

Hans Loewald and interrelatedness

While I do not want to suggest that the complicated relationship of Hans Loewald with his teacher provides the single key to understanding his tremendously vital and original oeuvre, that relationship does highlight some of its essential features.[3] Loewald studied with Heidegger for three years until 1926. Stephen Mitchell (2000) wrote of the influence of Heidegger that, "In many respects, Loewald's life's work might be regarded as a kind of Heideggerian reworking of Freud's basic concepts" (pp. 11–12). Despite this, there are few direct references to Heidegger in Loewald's corpus. Two of the most extensive were written around the same period, in 1978–9, after many decades of virtual silence.

Loewald's deeply reflective essays, *Psychoanalysis and the History of the Individual* (1978), which were delivered as the *Freud Lectures* at Yale

University, include a long reference to Heidegger. This comes, fittingly, in his first lecture "Man as Moral Agent," in the context of the discussion of the developmental step of integrating the unconscious material of the id into the higher organization of ego. He calls this process "owning up"; that is, owning or personally taking up desires, fantasies, and memories that are embedded in the mind, but not originally chosen by or with the consent of the subject. Loewald writes:

> This appropriation, this owning up, integrating the id into one's life context as an individual self, is then a developmental task or, in a different framework, an existential task. I believe that Heidegger's concepts of *Geworfenheit* – man is thrown into the world, unplanned and unintended by himself – and *Entwerfen* – the taking over and actively developing the potentialities of this fact – have grown in the same soil.
>
> (p. 19)

A footnote follows these lines, which refers to *Being and Time* and notes that Heidegger's "philosophical elucidation of human existence" is different from Freud's psychoanalytic discourse, which includes "the differentiation of unconscious and conscious mentation [mental activity]." Still, both authors hold to the notion: "Become what you are" (p. 19).

Heidegger's name also appears in the "Preface" to *Papers on Psychoanalysis*, articles published between 1951 and 1979. A part of this passionate and revealing paragraph was already included at the beginning of this chapter:

> Philosophy has been my first love. I gladly affirm its influence on my way of thinking while being wary of the peculiar excesses a philosophical bent tends to entail. My teacher in this field was Martin Heidegger, and I am deeply grateful for what I learned from him, despite his most hurtful betrayal in the Nazi era, which alienated me from him permanently.
>
> (Loewald, 2000, pp. xlii–xliii)

This statement is followed by a reference to Freud as someone "who has remained for me, through his writings, that living presence" (p. xliii).

It is clear from the above citations that Loewald did not completely leave either philosophy or Heidegger behind when he took up his vocation as a psychoanalyst. The former, his "first love," was not totally spurned. This was explicit in his acceptance and interpretation of the challenge that the *Freud Lectures* (1978) entailed. In the "Preface" he said that he saw himself as being asked "to attend to and articulate some of the wider humanistic and philosophical implications of psychoanalysis and its influence on modern life and contemporary sensibility" (pp. ix–x). At the end of the *Lectures* he returns to this note, offering that they "turned out to be . . . tentative philosophical reflections on psychoanalysis" (p. 77). However, he also admits that this is not accidental, since "Some of the things I have discussed I have wanted to say for a long time" (p. 77). Anticipating what we will soon explore, it appears that he actually had been saying many of these things for a long time.

Two essential features of philosophy, which had important positions in *Being and Time*, were perennial concerns for Loewald. The first is that "love of truth or wisdom" which is built into the constitution of the Greek word itself, *philo-sophia*. For Heidegger, the goal of his book was to understand the truth of Being as revealed through the truth of human existence, Dasein. In the essay "Psychoanalytic Theory and the Psychoanalytic Process" Loewald (2000) discusses that "love of truth" which he saw animating all scientific endeavors, especially as practiced in psychoanalysis. He writes that, "In our field the love of truth cannot be isolated from the passion for truth to ourselves and *truth in human relationships*" (my emphasis, p. 297). It is this latter, relational aspect that was of overriding importance to him, while clearly peripheral to his teacher.

This departure from Heidegger is also evident in that goal of self-knowledge which has defined philosophy from its beginning, encapsulated in the famous Socratic maxim to "Know thyself." In *Being and Time* Dasein has as its distinguishing feature the solitary task of uncovering the meaning of its existence. Loewald's (2000) understanding of this quest highlights intersubjectivity or "interrelatedness," the view that the self cannot be known independently of its multifaceted relationships with others. He writes:

> Our object, being what it is, is the other in ourselves and ourself in the other. To discover truth about the patient is always discovering it with him and for him as well as for ourselves and about ourselves. And it is discovering truth between each other, as the truth of human beings is revealed in their interrelatedness.
>
> (pp. 297–298)

There is a haunting reference in Loewald's (2000) earlier cited comments about philosophy that cannot be left unaddressed: his statement about "being wary of the peculiar excesses a philosophical bent tends to entail" (p. xlii). It is not entirely evident what Loewald has in mind here, but there are hints in some of his reflections that we have just read. It might be a reference to the tendency of philosophic thought to become an end in itself, ignoring life concerns. More pointedly, in keeping with Loewald's dedication to the "truth of human beings . . . in their interrelatedness" (p. 298), it undoubtedly includes the idea that truth cannot be separated from care for or treatment of the other in her or his concrete life; that is, truth must be therapeutic.

Fundamental to Loewald's work are those twin concepts of Heidegger, *Geworfenheit* and *Entwerfen*, to which he referred earlier. The first points to Heidegger's insistence that philosophy could not start with an examination of the human abstracted from the tangible situation in which life is lived ("facticity"). Heidegger's account of Dasein, the being there of human existence, included such features as language, the cultural heritage, and, particularly the inevitability of death. Loewald also grounded his reflection and therapy in concrete life. The "thrown into the world, unplanned and unintended by himself" (1978, p. 19) for Loewald significantly added the Freudian legacy, which included the unconscious, repression, transference, and defense. He saw these processes as driven by one's "ghosts" from the past (2000, pp. 248–249), those repudiated dreams, wishes, fantasies, and memories, as well as the earliest relations with parents. Freud's "living presence" (p. xliii) was also felt in Loewald's insistence that the body in all of its material and sensible dimensions not be ignored. This aspect, which is one of the features that Loewald appreciated in Freud in contrast to his appraisal of Jung (pp. 413–416), is also a detail that his first teacher did not take up in *Being and Time*. While Heidegger certainly gave voice to the importance of the passionate nature of life, Loewald, following Freud, recognized that passions could not be detached from the body and gender (p. 125).

While there are significant differences between Heidegger and Freud/Loewald in portraying the situation into which one is thrown, we remember that *Entwerfen*, "the taking over and actively developing the potentialities of this fact" (Loewald, 1978, p. 19) of being thrown, was seen by Loewald as joining together his two teachers, under the precept, "Become what you are" (p. 19). Although no person has chosen the contents of her or his unconscious, Loewald held that a pivotal task of becoming a full person is to, as far as possible, take these up and integrate them into one's consciousness or reflection. This is his transformation of Freud's dictum; he calls it an "appeal" (2000, p. 95), that "*Wo Es war, soll Ich werden*; where id was, there ego shall come into being" (1978, p. 18). Loewald writes, "To own up to our own history, to be responsible for our unconscious, in an important sense means, to bring unconscious forms of experiencing into the context and onto the level of the more mature, more lucid life of the adult mind" (p. 21). The technical term he uses for this process is "sublimation," and he views it as a task both "evolutionary" and "moral" (pp. 75–76). Loewald clarifies this requirement by adding that it does not mean that unconscious contents are to be repudiated or repressed, for repression only galvanizes their disturbing power to haunt or overwhelm mature life. Such early wishes, fantasies, and memories are *us*, and one must draw upon them to live a fully personal, meaningful life.

The moral feature of this task is deepened through Loewald's translation of Freud's central notion of the super-ego. Classically the super-ego develops as the child, in the midst of a crisis torn by incest and aggressive passions in relation to his or her parents, repudiates these passions and appropriates parental codes as their own. Loewald sees this process, which Freud held was the key transformation of mental life, as unending, which brings one face to face with both guilt and, possibly, atonement. While the child's experience with parricide and incest are usually only in fantasy or dreams, there is real existential guilt. They symbolically tell of the child breaking off intense early identifications with the parents, to move toward more mature and reciprocal relations. Thus, there is an ending of something, a killing-off of something, but only through this process are more adult interactions (object relations) possible. If guilt is accepted for these symbolic crimes, then a reorganization of mental life ensues, and with it a richer life is opened up (Loewald, 2000, p. 394). In his dramatic words, "without the guilty deed of parricide there is no individual self worthy of that name" (p. 394).

The temporality of moods and the basic attitudes of *Dasein*

Despite the psychological nature of the material being addressed here, two additional philosophical elements, which Loewald may well have taken from Heidegger, add to this complex story. The first is the temporal dimension of existence as revealed in the temporality of moods. In this sense, Heidegger found that most moods are correlated with the past of Dasein. For his part, Loewald connected the three basic psychic structures or processes with time frames. The id is the projection of the past warded-off features into the present. The super-ego is the promised development or "voice of conscience" – in terms of standards, demands, ideals, hopes, reproaches, and punishments – for the future (1978, p. 23). The ego is the accessible present psychic performance of the person. In terms of owning up, the task is to make past features accessible, and to integrate the moral future into the present. As Loewald (2000) presented this, "That man can own up to his past and thus gain some measure of mastery of his present life and the shape of his future, is part of his experience of time and implicit in the whole undertaking of psychoanalysis" (p. 139).

Heidegger's impact can also be seen in the way that approach and object are connected. The nature of the objects Dasein encounters always corresponds to the basic attitudes that are taken. For Loewald, the development of the person and the engagement with objects, actually the very texture of the objects, are correlated. For example, in the first engagement with the world, since the infant is merged with the mother, no distinct object or objects are encountered. As the ego begins to differentiate from the mother, she begins to exist for the infant as distinct. Ego and object develop together. In terms of the process of owning up, integrating the moral dimensions of the parents transforms the ego so that it can relate to the parents as mature objects, rather than treating them in childish ways as just loving or, alternately, threatening extensions of the self.

How, then, does Loewald's treatment of responsibility differ from Heidegger's? For Heidegger, one is responsible to oneself and to Being for the nature of the life one chooses to live. That guilt has virtually the same referents is telling. This essentially closed circle of responsibility, the "to whom" and "for what," only notes other persons as those whom one is with; at most in solicitude there is the hint that the individual can help to free the other to choose their own life decisively.

Loewald also sees responsibility, at least partially, in terms of choosing, featuring the psychological dimension of owning up to the contents of the unconscious. The process of owning up is virtually synonymous with responsibility. As we saw earlier, for Loewald (1978), "to own up to our own history, to be responsible for our unconscious" delineates what it means to be "mature" or an "adult" (p. 21). Thus, to become a full person is to accept responsibility *for* the way one lives out what one has originally been given. However, others are not absent from this scenario. Choosing oneself has significant implications for relationships with others, because the human is essentially intersubjective. Mental development is a moral task, where guilt for the inevitable and necessary breaking of immature infantile bonds – shattering intimate ties with the other – must be atoned for. Thus, one is responsible *to* both the self and *to* others. Here other persons extend beyond the primary care-givers, since the earliest patterns of relationship continue to be salient for later interactions. In other words, if infantile approaches to the first significant persons are not transformed, then later relationships with other persons will be circumscribed by such alternating patterns as idealization or denigration.

This portrait of "man as moral agent" (1978, p. 1) must be augmented by Loewald's personal decision to become a psychoanalyst. This choice goes well beyond that possible "solicitude" in Heidegger's text, that helps the other to come to an authentic resolution about itself. For Loewald, the analyst's work with the patient is modeled on some features of the mother's crucial and loving care for her infant. He writes, for example,

> We note that the analyst's interpretation is a form of active mirroring, reflecting back to the patient his behavior in a different light, in terms of higher, more comprehensive and more articulate mental organization – analogous to the parental mirroring function in infancy and childhood.
>
> (p. 21)

Additionally, the goal of that psychoanalytic "truth of human beings . . . in their interrelatedness" (2000, p. 298), which Loewald so passionately sought, was a fundamentally therapeutic one. Thus, both in terms of theory and vocation, Loewald's approach to responsibility decisively departed from that of his teacher.

Emmanuel Levinas

Levinas's work in its entirety stands as a deep protest against the Holocaust. In his essay "Signature," he writes: "It [his intellectual development] is dominated by the presentiment and the memory of the Nazi horror"

(1990a, p. 291). The dedication to his second defining book, *Otherwise Than Being or Beyond Essence* (1974/1981), reinscribes this reflection:

> To the memory of those who were closest among the six million assassinated by the National Socialists, and of the millions on millions of all confessions and all nations, victims of the same hatred of the other man, the same anti-semitism.
>
> (p. x)

During the Holocaust Levinas was in a labor camp as a French prisoner of war from 1940 to 1945, and feared that this confinement was a mere way-station to the killing camps (Malka, 2002/2006, p. 262). At the same time, in Lithuania his father and brothers were murdered. His response to the Holocaust is to offer a scorching critique of the longstanding intellectual and political forces that led to that destructive caesura, and to fashion a counter-narrative about the binding power of human relationships, that could withstand those powers.

Levinas's compound, almost tortuous relationship to Heidegger reflects this theme. In 1928 he went to Freiburg to study with the creator of phenomenology, Edmund Husserl. However, once there he was captivated by Husserl's brilliant student, Martin Heidegger. Levinas was deeply influenced by this emerging star and continued to insist that no one could understand modern philosophy unless they went through the Heideggerian portal. Yet, Levinas was equally insistent that his teacher's reprehensible actions could not be ignored – "it is difficult to forgive Heidegger" (1968/1990a, p. 25). What Paul Ricoeur termed Levinas's "permanently polemical rapport" (cited in Malka, 2002/2006, p. 162) sums up those halting statements about Heidegger interjected throughout Levinas's writings, which are in the vein of: "when I pay homage to Heidegger, it is always costly to me, not because of his incontestable brilliance" (1986/1998b, p. 92), and "this is the case, whatever the debt of every contemporary thinker might be to Heidegger, a debt that he often owes to his regret" (1993/2000, p. 8).

Levinas believed that the basis for Heidegger's allegiance to National Socialism was cast early in his philosophy itself. He especially criticized such basic features of *Being and Time* as the elevation of Being over human existence, the pervasive denigration of everyday social life of the crowd or "das Mann," the discussion of encountering things before the meeting with other persons, the veneration of the legacy of "das Volk," and, finally, the complete lack of an ethics, despite a few peripheral asides to the contrary. Levinas's overall judgment is aptly captured in the statement, "The absence of concern for the other in Heidegger and his personal political adventure are bound together" (2001, p. 186).

Levinas's attitude toward philosophy was equally ambivalent. Personally, he saw himself as a philosopher, even though he worked most of his adult life as a school principal at the *Ecole Normale Israelite Oriental* in Paris. His philosophic writings span 60 years, while it was only in his fifties that an academic position at the University of Poitiers was offered, which eventually led to another at the Sorbonne. More significant was his complex stance toward the discipline itself. He lauded philosophy's rigor, clarity, and universality, that presupposition of the equality of humans, which accompanied the elevation of a common reason and a justice for all. Yet, there was a reverse side to this all-encompassing "wisdom." Permitting nothing outside of its grasp, philosophy was also synonymous with totality. Denying otherness and rejecting transcendence, it perpetuated a closed system where what was left mirrored itself, "the same." However, this did not mean that philosophy could not be redeemed. Levinas highly valued its ability to be self-reflective; that is, "to question itself, and ultimately to unsay itself" (1986, p. 22). More importantly, "Greek" or Hellenic *sophia* could be infused with "Hebrew" *ahava*, that love for the neighbor, the poor, orphan, widow, and stranger proclaimed by the biblical prophets. In this connection Levinas wrote, "My concern everywhere is precisely to translate this non-Hellenism of the Bible into Hellenic terms" (1986/1998b, p. 85). This infusion without synthesis would issue, again in Levinas's words, in a new definition of philosophy, substituting that traditional "love of wisdom" with "the wisdom of love in the service of love" (1974/1981, p. 162). Thus, with Levinas as with Loewald, the questioning of Heidegger's philosophy leads to a rethinking of the philosophic discipline itself.

Levinas with and against Heidegger

Actually, the whole course of Levinas's writings can be seen as a dialectical confrontation with Heidegger. It might begin with his first essay "On Escape" of 1935, which was later published as a book, and culminated in *Otherwise Than Being* of 1974. In terms of the first, the rejection of

Heidegger's view of the self that comes to rest ultimately with itself is seen in the note that "escape is the need to get out of oneself" (1982/2003, p. 55). There is also found in the last lines a sense of direction while the goal is yet unclear, of "getting out of being by a new path" (1982/2003, p. 73). By the time of *Totality and Infinity* of 1961, which marks Levinas's first signature philosophic book and his emergence as an important philosopher in France, the goal has been fully clarified. It is the Other, viewed through the optics of ethics, that breaks both the violence of philosophy's identification of thought with being and the *ennui* of the self given over to itself. Through the relation to the Other, which stands outside of thought as an Infinite, the decentered self finds its meaning. *Otherwise Than Being* (1974/1981) radicalizes this movement, quoting from Pascal's *Pensées*, "'That is my place in the sun.' That is how the usurpation of the whole world began" (p. vii), and finding authenticity for the individual in its "substitution" for the Other.

Over the course of this confrontation, or Ricoeur's "polemical rapport," the central features of Heidegger's philosophy are either contorted or totally refused. *Difficult Freedom* (1963/1990a) highlights one major contrast, "In the place of ontology – of the Heideggerian comprehension of the Being of being ... a relation with the Other" (p. 293). In place of the primacy of Dasein's self-concern, Levinas features the self obsessed with and hostage to the Other. Levinas accepts the truth of Heidegger's thrownness, but this original situation – unchosen yet inescapable – is described in terms of the overriding obligation to the Other. The treatment of death is especially telling. Rejecting the view that authenticity arises through facing one's own death, Levinas insists that the concern for the death of the other is the very definition of the human. Finally, in contrast to a text without an ethics, Levinas announces that "Ethics is First Philosophy" (1989, pp. 75–87).

The theme of responsibility is at the core of Levinas's sweeping break with Heidegger and with the whole tradition of the philosophy of being. For Levinas, human existence is bifurcated. There is first that aspect that ties the human to the rest of animal life. From this direction, each I or self is the center of the universe. The ruling principle is self-interest, that *conatus essendi* (self-preservation) of Spinoza, which most philosophers continue to regard as a natural given. The self seeks comfort, finds pleasure in life, and encounters others out of this approach. Regardless of how this attitude may be "tempered," or how solicitous one is for the other, in Levinas's view, where such natural egoism reigns, responsibility is banished. Put another way, he writes that "for ethical thought ... *the self*, as this primacy of what is mine, is *hateful*" (1986, p. 26).

This entrenched egoism cannot be escaped through the self's efforts, despite the hollowness and disgust that inevitably accompanies it. The self must be wrenched out of itself by another power for meaning and authenticity to ensue. This power comes from the encounter with the Other, a meeting not initiated by the self, but unwillingly undergone. This Other is neither my object nor my equal. Rather, the one beside me is totally outside of my designs, and ethically accosts me. This situation reveals the second dimension of human existence. According to Levinas, prior to or more original than human egoism is the concern for the Other. It is the very basis of *human* life. Thus, there is an aspect of the life of persons, a second register, that transcends natural life and Being. Not sought out of need and incapable of being fulfilled, there is a metaphysical "desire" for the Infinite. The situation out of which this desire is evoked is the face-to-face relation.

Responsibility and the face of the other

The face of the other opens the way to my responsibility. By the term "face" Levinas does not intend to point to or signify a specific part of the human body, but the full human presence of the one encountered. He writes, "A face is a trace of itself, given over to my responsibility" (1974/1981, p. 91). The face addresses oneself in two ways, as Levinas writes: "The transcendence of the Other, which is his eminence, his height, his lordship, in its concrete meaning includes his destitution, his exile, and his rights as a stranger" (1961/1969, pp. 76–77). By "height" Levinas is referring to the other's priority over the self's own interests, as well as the unavoidable obligation that the other confers. The term "destitution" relates to the vulnerability of the other that comes through the face. One is haunted by the lack of defense seen in the face of the other, in the presence of my "natural" instinct to be. For Levinas this is similar to the lack of legal protection of the stranger, abandoned in my land or country. The obligation or commandment not to kill expresses these two aspects of the encounter with the Other. "Thou Shalt Not Kill" is an imperative. It cannot be avoided and nullifies every other interest or concern. It is also a reminder that the Other's life is fragile. As obligation in the presence of fragility, "'Thou shalt not kill' signifies ... 'thou shalt do everything in order that the other may live'" (2001, p. 272).

Especially in his later work, Levinas uses hyperbole to accentuate the radical nature of, the surplus in, responsibility. He writes of being a hostage to the other, or alternately being persecuted. Responsibility for the neighbor is likened to an obsession, and the self finds itself substituted for the other. These expressions are reminders or reinforcements of a number of lessons, which directly clash with the way ethics is traditionally presented.[4] Responsibility is not taken up from out of one's freedom, and actually precedes any question of decision. Levinas also insists that responsibility has no limits, and incessantly quotes Dostoyevsky: "We are all responsible for everyone else – but I am more responsible than all the others" (1986, p. 31). Thus, no single action or group of actions fulfills one's responsibility. Additionally, one is responsible not just for one's actions, but even for those of the other person. In this regard, substitution "means, in the ultimate shelter of myself, not to feel myself innocent, even for the harm that another does" (1986/1998b, p. 91). While this last idea may appear unrealistic, it concretely means that if one person harms another, this is of real concern to me. Finally, reciprocity cannot be a consideration in this asymmetrical relation to the Other.

Of course, the command, "Thou shalt not kill!" is not itself without a reference. While Levinas insists that his ethics stands on its own, he acknowledges that it is inspired by the Jewish tradition. He also believes that the term "God" has a legitimate place in philosophy (1989, pp. 166–189), while vigilant in his effort not to allow it to be a theme appropriated into, that is subordinated to, a system. Levinas, thus, often just speaks of the "trace." At times he connects this to the face. In his words, "the trace is not just one more word: it is the proximity of God in the countenance of my fellow man" (1991/1998a, p. 57). At other times he finds that the term arises, that is, "God ... comes to mind" (1986/1998b, p. v), in the ethical response or open hands that one offers to the neighbor.

One of the most outstanding features of Levinas's discussion of responsibility, and again particularly pointed toward Heidegger, is its linkage with the topic of death.[5] For Levinas that subject is *not* connected to a concern about the self, but for the Other. He writes: "The fear for the other man does not turn back into anguish for *my* death. It overflows the ontology of the Heideggerian *Dasein*" (1986/1998b, p. 176). The facticity of death is revealed in the face of the other, which "in this nakedness is an exposure unto death: nakedness, destitution, passivity, and pure vulner-ability" (1991/1998a, p. 167). While the neighbor's death is inevitable, the requirement to not let her or him die alone still stands. Levinas writes that the Other "is alone and can undergo the supreme isolation we call death – and there is, consequently, in the Face of the Other always the death of the Other" (1991/1998a, p. 104).

Finally, while anxiety over the face of the other is so expressive of what responsibility means for Levinas, he is not reticent to speak of responsi-bility and love, especially in his later essays and interviews. For Levinas, these two terms are not opposites or incompatible. The response to the face that stands for responsibility is also the true meaning of love. With a reference to Pascal, Levinas writes that, "responsibility is the love without concupiscence" (2001, p. 108). What could be more a testament to love than to be with the Other when she or he is facing the ultimate challenge of death? In this case, Levinas's phrase "*me voici*" – French for the bibli-cal "*hineni*" (1993/2000, p. 188), refers to a *being there* that is a witness to responsibility, to a love that lingers beyond death.

Toward a recovery of the suppressed?

Responsibility as either for the self – in Loewald's words "owning up," or to the Other – the defining characteristic of Levinas's philosophy, is suppressed, as it were, within the history of psychoanalysis. It is missing in the explicit writings of the discipline's founder, although Freud does address issues concerning the therapist's relationship to the patient (Freud, 1915/1990). He also has an allusive statement that one is responsible for one's dreams, which Loewald characteristically uses as an imprimatur for his position (Loewald, 1978, p. 7).[6] Some of the factors behind Freud's attitude are well known. He saw himself battling some social conventions such as the moralistic stigmatizing of the mentally ill and the hypocrisy of late Victorian Europe in its attitudes toward sex. He also determined that the obsessive, crushing demands of what he called the super-ego had to be addressed, and not reinforced in therapy. Finally, Freud's accounts of the underlying processes of the psyche in terms of hydraulic, electric, and other mechanical-like forces left little room for personal responsibility. As Roy Schafer (1976) wrote, "the mechanistic and organismic language of metapsychology . . . by its nature . . . excludes concepts like responsibility from explanation" (p. 233).[7] Still, the original spirit behind Freud's new "science" was deeply ethical. It promised relief to patients experiencing years of overwhelming and inescapable suffering. He provided a method that eschewed both surgery and hypnotism, a "talking cure" that built up the conscious agency of his patients.

The topic of responsibility in relationships does appear in some of the first generation of post-Freudians. For example, there is an ethical feature in Melanie Klein's developmental narrative, in terms of the second, "Depressive Position." For her, the infant is at first overwhelmed by aggressive and destructive drives, fear, anxiety, and paranoia. It projects the drives onto the mother, and responds with destructive fantasies toward her (1935/1986, p. 40). Following this "Paranoid-Schizoid" foundation, the infant experiences remorse. In its feelings of guilt, loss, and reparation, there is something analogous to accepting responsibility for "the disaster created through its sadism" (1935/1986, p. 48). Erik Erikson's (1950/1963) unique examination of the later stages of the individual's "psychosocial" development brought him to highlight personal virtues important for a mature and fulfilling life, including responsibility. He describes the sixth of eight developmental stages, "Intimacy vs Isolation," in terms of the individual struggling with "the capacity to commit himself to concrete affiliations and partnerships and to develop the ethical strength to abide by such commitments, even though they may call for significant sacrifices and compromises" (p. 263). Of the seventh stage, "Generativity," he writes about "the concern in establishing and guiding the next generation" and of bequeathing something valuable that comes from the self (p. 267).

In light of the attention that the relational psychoanalysts give to issues of meaning and authenticity in their writings and therapy, coupled with the intersubjective basis for their approach, it is surprising that the topic of responsibility is virtually ignored in their literature. A perusal of the book indices of the major figures in the movement confirms the dearth of both "ethics" and "responsibility" as topics. This lacuna is evidenced in Stephen Mitchell's (2000) summary discussion of contemporary relational trends concerning what he labels, "Mode 4: Intersubjectivity," which focuses on recognizing and being recognized by another as a person. He writes, "Being fully human (in Western culture) entails being recognized *as a subject* by another human subject" (p. 64). Here at the conscious, intentional level is the notion that authenticity and fulfillment require mutual recognition of persons as subjects in their "own right" (p. 64). Still, the discussion does not explicitly acknowledge that one might owe the other this recognition, or that the patient's ultimate healing includes the realization of this responsibility to the other.

The reticence to speak of responsibility extends to the influential work of Jessica Benjamin, who Mitchell cited as an important theorist of inter-subjectivity. Benjamin has given recognition of the other's independence and inviolability a central place in her work. She writes, "we have a need for recognition and we have a capacity to recognize others in return, thus making mutual recognition possible" (1995, p. 30). However, she shuns using the term "responsibility" in conjunction with recognizing the other, because she believes that prescriptive language about normative ideals does not have a place in her psychoanalytic discourse (1995, pp. 20–21).[8]

Where contemporary psychoanalytic voices do feature substantial treatments of the patient's responsibility to others, these often reveal the influence of the main subjects of our treatment, Loewald or Levinas.[9] One of these theorists is Roy Schafer, who was a student of Loewald. Schafer's first book, *A New Language for Psychoanalysis* (1976), features a number of dimensions of responsibility as part of its central argument. He speaks of taking responsibility for one's life, even for events not chosen. He writes, "More and more, the analysand indicates a readiness to accept the responsibility of life as action . . . [However,] it does not imply a belief on one's part that one has caused one's whole life or can cause it from now on" (p. 146). This statement is reminiscent of Loewald's treatment of "owning up." Schafer also discusses one's responsibility for others as an important ingredient of the mature life. In *Tradition and Change in Psychoanalysis* (1997), he writes of "that well-developed sense of responsibility that takes into account the feelings of others and so recognizes that others do matter" (p. 102).

David Goodman's recent publication, *The Demanded Self: Levinasian Ethics and Identity in Psychology* (2010), is a fine example of the effort to highlight the topic of responsibility within the discourse of psychoanalysis. As the subtitle indicates, his work, and that of other theorists whom he notes (pp. 112, 186), reflects the impact of Levinas's philosophy on the discipline. Goodman extends Levinas's notion of "*hineni*" to speak of "The self lived as *hineni*," as "a self, first and foremost, forever responsive to the other" (p. 125). He sees this rendering of the meaning of a self as deepening and transforming the attenuated portrait of what constitutes the patient's health or an authentic human life that is currently the norm in psychology and psychoanalysis.

Following Goodman, I would suggest that Levinas's message is espe-cially relevant to the portrayal of what constitutes the ultimate *telos* of the analytic interaction, the patient's movement toward a full human life. While such a goal might be unreachable in the deepest sense, and especially difficult in the face of the complex details of any particular patient's life, it still can have a significant impact on how therapy is understood and conducted. The contemporary discourse of psychoanaly-sis often leaves such a goal underdeveloped, or presents it in a too narrow vein. Levinas's understanding of responsibility is significant for dis-cussing what might constitute that full life, or flourishing in the patient. Would we ever call a person healed or healthy in any deeper sense, who could not at times be responsible for the other? Responding to the other does not just fulfill an ethical obligation; it also provides the patient with a sense of competence, relevance, and meaning. Of course, there is a question of how the need for responsibility might be communicated by the therapist. Certainly not as a lesson, didactic or prescriptive – as Freud warned, but indirectly, and of course only incompletely, through the questions asked, the responses made, and the concern shown in the therapeutic dialogue. Put another way, Levinas is a significant resource for the problem that Stephen Mitchell (1993) believes brings patients to seek psychoanalytic treatment today, "a revitalization and expansion" of the "capacity to generate experience that feels real, meaningful, and valuable" (p. 24). Levinas holds that both authenticity and meaning can-not be reached directly, but arise when the self is forgotten, out of a life of responsibility for the other.

How does one move beyond betrayal? For Loewald and Levinas this included an honest expression of their feelings of hurt and abandonment brought about by the actions of their teacher, as well as the acknowledge-ment of the debt for what had earlier been received. However, they went further than this. Through their work in psychoanalysis and philosophy, they endeavored to fulfill some of the promise of their teacher's work and their respective disciplines' calling, while rejecting and correcting for those philosophical elements they saw contributing to their teach-er's pernicious political position. A major feature of this correction was to speak of the role of responsibility to others in a life of meaning and authenticity. As we have seen, their legacy has already had an impact on psychoanalytic theory and practice, and hopefully this influence will continue to grow.

Notes

1 Loewald's father was Jewish. Levinas was an Orthodox Jew, whose Judaism always occupied a central place in his life and thought.
2 Critics who find an ethical concern in *Being and Time*, in terms of the relationship to the other, focus on Heidegger's discussions of being with others, the call of conscience, and solicitude. For example, Jean Greisch writes, "one must keep in sight the breadth of the Heideggerian 'with,' which is capable of containing the moment of abandonment and of being delivered over to the other" (Raffoul & Pettigrew, eds., 102). Frank Schlow sees in conscience the experience of "the attunement that echoes the claim of the other" (Raffoul & Pettigrew, eds., 38), and in solicitude "a way of responding to the welfare of the other" (36).
3 Jonathan Lear's (2000) excellent introduction to Loewald's collected papers and monographs offers another approach to the question of responsibility, and his relationship to Heidegger.
4 Following Stanley Cavell, Hilary Putnam (2008) speaks of Levinas's philosophy, as well as those of Franz Rosenzweig and Martin Buber, in terms of "moral perfectionism." This type of moral theory recognizes that "it is only by keeping an 'impossible' demand in view" that the individual can realize their highest potentiality for living (p. 72).
5 Much of Levinas's last efforts focused on the twin subjects of Heidegger and death (2000).
6 There is also Freud's "fundamental rule," of the responsibility of the patient in analysis to say whatever comes into his or her mind.
7 Levinas's well-known hostility to psychoanalysis is a reflection of his view that the discourse about the unconscious did not break with the self, self-consciousness, and presence (1989, p. 93).
8 In Benjamin's work there is a brief note about responsibility, in terms of the importance of a subject's non-retaliatory response to the inevitable effort of the other to erase or destroy difference. However, she does not elaborate on the extent of or basis for this responsibility (1998, p. 99).
9 A little afield, the subjects of responsibility and ethics are fully manifest in the extensive writings of the French feminist philosopher and psychoanalyst, Luce Irigaray. In addition, she has authored two critical pieces on Levinas, which question his stereotyped view of the feminine, and insist that even intimate love relations include an ethics of *eros* (see Oppenheim, 2006, pp. 175–219).

References

Benjamin, J. (1995). *Like subjects, love objects: Essays on recognition and sexual difference*. New Haven: Yale University Press.
Benjamin, J. (1998). *Shadow of the other: Intersubjectivity and gender in psychoanalysis*. New York: Routledge.
Buber, M. (1965). What is man? In *Between man and man* (R. Smith, Trans.) (pp. 118–205). New York: Macmillan Publishing Company.
Caputo, J. (1993). *Demythologizing Heidegger*. Bloomington: Indiana University Press.
Chanter, T. (2001). The problematic normative assumptions of Heidegger's ontology. In N. Holland & P. Huntington (Eds.), *Feminist interpretations of Heidegger* (pp. 73–108). University Park, PA: Pennsylvania State University Press.
Derrida, J. (1989). *Of spirit: Heidegger and the question* (G. Bennington & R. Bowlby, Trans.). Chicago: University of Chicago Press.
Erikson, E. (1963). *Childhood and society*. New York: W.W. Norton and Company. (Original work published in 1950)

Freud, S. (1990). Observations on transference-love: Further recommendations on the technique of psycho-analysis III. In A. Esman (Ed.), *Essential papers on transference* (pp. 36–48). New York: New York University Press. (Original work published in 1915)

Goodman, D. (2012). *The demanded self: Levinasian ethics and identity in psychology*. Pittsburgh, PA: Duquesne University Press.

Heidegger, M. (1962). *Being and time* (J. Macquarrie & E. Robinson, Trans.). New York: Harper and Row Publishers. (Original work published in 1927)

Klein, M. (1986). A contribution to the psychogenesis of manic-depressive states. In P. Buckley (Ed.), *Essential papers on object relations*. New York: New York University Press. (Original work published in 1935)

Lear, J. (2000). Introduction. In *The essential Loewald: Collected papers and monographs* (pp. ix–xl). Hagerstown, MD: Norman Quist Book.

Levinas, E. (1969). *Totality and infinity: An essay on exteriority* (A. Lingis, Trans.). Pittsburgh, PA: Duquesne University Press. (Original work published in 1961)

Levinas, E. (1981). *Otherwise than being or beyond essence* (A. Lingis, Trans.). The Hague: Martinus Nijoff Publishers. (Original work published in 1974)

Levinas, E. (1986). *Face to face with Levinas*. Albany: State University of New York Press.

Levinas, E. (1989). *The Levinas reader*. Oxford: Basil Blackwell.

Levinas, E. (1990a). *Difficult freedom: Essays on Judaism* (S. Hand, Trans.). Baltimore: Johns Hopkins University Press. (Original work published in 1963)

Levinas, E. (1990b). *Nine Talmudic readings* (A. Aronwowicz, Trans.). Bloomington: Indiana University Press. (Original work published in 1968)

Levinas, E. (1998a). *Entre nous: On thinking-of-the-other* (M. Smith & B. Harshav, Trans.). New York: Columbia University Press.

Levinas, E. (1998b). *Of God who comes to mind* (B. Bergo, Trans.). Stanford: Stanford University Press. (Original work published in 1986)

Levinas, E. (2000). *God, death, and time* (B. Bergo, Trans.). Stanford: Stanford University Press. (Original work published in 1993)

Levinas, E. (2001). *Is it righteous to be? Interviews with Emmanuel Levinas*. Stanford: Stanford University Press.

Levinas, E. (2003). *On escape* (B. Bergo, Trans.). Stanford: Stanford University Press. (Original work published in 1982, and as an essay in 1935)

Loewald, H. (1978). *Psychoanalysis and the history of the individual: The Freud lectures at Yale*. New Haven: Yale University Press.

Loewald, H. (2000). *The essential Loewald: Collected papers and monographs*. Hagerstown, MD: Norman Quist Book.

Löwith, K. (1942). M. Heidegger and F. Rosenzweig or temporality and eternity. *Philosophy and Phenomenological Research, 3.1*, 53–77.

Malka, S. (2006). *Emmanuel Levinas: His life and legacy* (M. Kigel and S. Embree, Trans.). Pittsburg, PA: Duquesne University Press. (Original work published in 2002)

Mitchell, S. (1994). *Hope and dread in psychoanalysis*. New York: Basic Books.

Mitchell, S. (2000). *Relationality: From attachment to intersubjectivity*. Hillsdale, NJ: Analytic Press.

Oppenheim, M. (2006). *Jewish philosophy and psychoanalysis: Narrating the interhuman*. Lanham, MD: Lexington Books.

Putnam, H. (2008). *Jewish philosophy as a guide to life: Rosenzweig, Buber, Levinas, Wittgenstein*. Bloomington: Indiana University Press.

Raffoul, F. & Pettigrew, D., eds. (2002). *Heidegger and practical philosophy*. Albany: State University of New York Press.

Schafer, R. (1976). *A new language for psychoanalysis*. New Haven: Yale University Press.

Schafer, R. (1997). *Tradition and change in psychoanalysis*. Madison, CT: International Universities Press.

Wolin, R. (2001). *Heidegger's children: Hannah Arendt, Karl Lowith, Hans Jonas, and Herbert Marcuse*. Princeton: Princeton University Press.

Chapter 15

Changing the subject by addressing the other

Mikhail Bakhtin and psychoanalytic therapy

José Saporta

Lives change through conversation. Mikhail Bakhtin (1895–1975), and some subsequent dialogical theory, suggests some dimensions of how conversation or dialogue in psychotherapy, and the context in which it occurs, leads to change.

Consistent with the central theme of this volume, the other is central to Bakhtin's ideas. Speech, gesture, action, and even thought are always addressed to a particular or generalized other. The anticipated response of the other person or persons shapes the meaning of what we say and how we say it. At the same time, we are responding to the voices of others from past dialogues. We address the other in a position that is different from that of ourselves as subjects. The other's outside position, and the wider perspective this brings, is necessary for responsive understanding and change. The difference between dialogue and monologue turns on recognizing the consciousness of the other person, "with equal rights and equal responsibilities, another I with equal rights (thou)" (Bakhtin, 1984, p. 292). Internally persuasive discourse, a dialogue that leads to new and unanticipated meaning in new contexts, follows from mutual otherness. The word of the other is met with my own word and becomes "half mine and half someone else's" (Bakhtin, 1981, p. 293).

I propose that psychotherapy mobilizes dialogical processes within the self and between self and others, which leads to more complex and flexible meaning-making that is more responsive to unique local contexts. Rather than a limited number of fixed positions from which to address others and the world and to make meaning, rigidly and universally applied to all contexts, clients develop more rich and varied positions in varied relational contexts. This requires a capacity for some indeterminacy in meaning combined with stability. The goal of psychoanalytic psychotherapy is an enriched capacity to mean, an enriched meaning potential. Meaning potential includes the capacity to generate unanticipated and even surprising meanings in new contexts. The perspective of the therapist, similar but different from that of the client, mobilizes an internally persuasive discourse, as described by Bakhtin, which leads to a capacity for new and anticipated meaning in new contexts.

The dialogical perspective

Bakhtin (1984) thought that persons are fundamentally oriented to others through dialogue:

> The dialogic nature of consciousness is the dialogic nature of human life itself. The single adequate form for verbally expressing authentic human existence is the open-ended dialogue. Life by its very nature is dialogic. To live means to participate in dialogue: to ask questions, to heed, to respond, to agree, and so forth. In this dialogue a person participates wholly and throughout his whole life: with his eyes, lips, hands, soul, spirit, with his whole body and deeds. He invests his entire self in discourse, and this discourse enters into the dialogic fabric of human life, into the world symposium.
>
> (p. 293)

Bakhtin indicates here that dialogue is not just an intellectual or verbal process. His understanding of mind and discourse is that they are inter-subjective and embodied, suffused with intonation, gestures, and expressiveness. Scholars of dialogue following Bakhtin have emphasized the material, embodied, and affective nature of dialogue (Lannemann, 1998; Grossen & Salazar-Orvig, 2011; Shotter, 2008, 2012). Shotter (2008, 2011, 2012) in particular emphasizes mutual responding through the expressive body in conversation.

We come to know the world and each other through dialogue. Coming to know another person, such as in psychoanalytic therapy, is not passive reception or objective observation. We observe from a position or perspective. We engage the other person and answer his or her words with our own:

> The consciousness of others cannot be contemplated and analyzed and defined like objects or things – one must relate dialogically to them. To think about them means to converse with them; otherwise they

immediately turn their objectivized side to us; they fall silent and grow cold and retreat into their finalized objectivized images.

(Bakhtin, 1984, p. 56)

All listening, then, is responsive, and we respond with more than words. Even when silently listening, therapists respond to clients' words and expressive bodies with their own words and expressive bodies (Shotter, 2008, 2011).

Bakhtin's theory of the utterance

When we speak and act, and when we make sense of experience, we do so from a position or perspective. Positioning is related to Bakhtin's concept of voice. By voice, Bakhtin meant the speaking personality (Wertsch, 1991), the embodied position or perspective from which we speak.

The notion of position is complex and beyond the scope of this chapter to fully explicate.

Position entails an evaluative stance toward the object of reference and toward the listener (Leiman, 2002, 2011), a stance more of feeling and bodily experience than articulated cognition. Leiman (2002) quotes Shotter (1993a):

In the view explored here, then, the expression of a thought or an intention, the saying of a sentence or the doing of a deed, does not issue from already well-formed and orderly cognitions at the center of our being, but originates in a person's vague, diffuse and unordered *feelings*; their sense of how, semiotically, they are "positioned" in relation to the others around them.

(p. 63)[1]

Leiman (2002) adds:

When using the word "feelings" in this context, Shotter does not indicate emotions, as contrasted with cognitions. In a footnote (Shotter 1993b), he refers to William James, who used the term as a "feeling of tendency" or as "signs in the direction" of thought. In this sense, feeling is a semiotic threshold phenomena, uniting the person with his or her surroundings.

(p. 223)

One's position or stance orients and connects one in an affective and evaluative way to the person who is addressed and to the context – and it has a forward movement, orienting the subject toward future interaction (Salgado, n.d.).

Speaking and acting from a position is rooted in our earliest experience of location in space and time when moving and acting in the world and with others. Spatial and temporal position progressively extend to an experience of position in a space of signs and meanings. Harre (1998) argues that the personal pronoun "I" indexes the speaker's unique position in space and time and the speaker's position in relation to the values expressed or implied:

> To have a sense of self is to have a sense of one's location, as a person, in each of several arrays of other beings, relevant to personhood. It is to have a sense of one's point of view, at any given moment a location in space from which one perceives and acts upon the world, including that part that lies within one's own skin.
>
> (p. 4)

Benson (2001) extends the work of Harre and others to propose a theory of self as a system that locates the individual's position and orientation in space and time, and within a field of values.

Psychoanalytic field theories could be enriched through dialogue with the notion of position – an affective, embodied, and forward-moving place or orientation in a field of meanings. There may be some generative resonances between the notion of position and Bion's (1965) notion of the vertex, a term frequently invoked by those who write about the psychoanalytic field.

I think of voice and position as a complex gestalt – that includes verbal and non-verbal elements – from which one speaks and acts. This meaning system or gestalt can vary in its generality, from a particular position in a specific utterance to a more general orientation toward a wider field of meanings – a dominant orientation toward one's life. Life can look and mean differently from different positions in time and space, such as from different positions in one's life course, i.e. looking back or looking forward. For the purpose of this chapter, which is more orientation to a perspective rather than precision, I refer to position, perspective, stance, place, and orientation as loosely overlapping concepts.

An essential feature of position and voice, one relevant to the theme of this volume, is that they are relational rather than individual properties. They are partly defined by the person or persons we address and by the immediate context. Voice, speech, and gesture are always addressed to other voices and positions. The voices we address, and their anticipated response, shape the position from which one addresses the other and shapes the meaning that emerges from dialogue. Voloshinov (1973), a member of Bakhtin's intellectual circle, states:

> Orientation of the word toward the addressee has an extremely high significance. In point of fact the word is a two-sided act. It is determined equally by whose word it is and for whom it is meant. As word, it is precisely the product of the reciprocal relationship between speaker and listener, addresser and addressee. Each and every word expresses the "one" in relation to the "other" . . . A word is a bridge thrown between myself and another . . . A word is territory shared by both addresser and addressee, by the speaker and his interlocutor.
>
> (p. 86)

A person's voice, speech, and gesture are addressed to an other who we position reciprocally: "Each rejoinder, regardless of how brief and abrupt, has a specific quality of completion that expresses a particular position of the speaker, to which one may respond or assume, with respect to it, a responsive position" (Bakhtin, 1986, p. 72). The position from which we speak, and how we position the other, are influenced by our past experience of addressing others and being addressed. Bakhtin writes: "Any utterance is a link in the chain of communication. It is the active position of the speaker in one referentially semantic sphere or another" (Bakhtin, 1986). And:

> Every utterance must be regarded as primarily a response to preceding utterances of the given sphere . . . Each utterance refutes affirms, supplements, and relies upon the others, presupposes them to be known, and somehow takes them into account . . . Therefore, each kind of utterance is filled with various kinds of responsive reactions to other utterances of the given sphere of speech communication.
>
> (p. 91)

Words and gestures do not originate with the individual; they are taken from others: "Language is not a neutral medium that passes freely and easily into the private property of the speaker's intentions; it is populated – overpopulated –with the intentions of others" (Bakhtin, 1981, p. 294). The individual encounters others and their words in various social settings: "each word tastes of the context in which it has lived its socially charged life" (Bakhtin, 1981, p. 293). The individual makes the word his or her own, but the word is half one's own and half someone else's:

> language, for the individual consciousness, lies on the borderline between oneself and the other. The word in language is half someone else's. It becomes "one's own" only when the speaker populates it with his own intentions, his own accent, when he appropriates the word, adapting it to his own semantic and expressive intention. Prior to this moment of appropriation, the word does not exist in a neutral and impersonal language (it is not, after all, out of a dictionary that the speaker gets his words!), but rather it exists in other people's mouths, in other people's contexts, serving other people's intentions: it is from there that one must take the word, and make it one's own.
>
> (Bakhtin, 1981, pp. 293–294)

While the self is constructed inter-subjectively, each of us has a unique position in space and time and a unique life history, and thus we continue to be individuals. Salgado and Hermans (2005) argue that a Bakhtinian dialogical perspective restores individual subjectivity from its post-modern demise. We are the unique, embodied, continuous, and vital center for integrating the many voices in our lives (Grossen & Salazar-Orvig, 2011; Moore, Jasper, & Gillespie, 2011; Richardson, 2011).

When we address the person before us we are also responding to and addressing past voices that have responded to us. Bakhtin called this "double voiced discourse" or "the word with a side-ways glance". Double voiced speech:

> has a twofold direction – it is directed both toward the object of speech as in ordinary discourses, and toward another discourse, toward someone else's speech.
>
> (Bakhtin, 1984, p. 189)

The client addresses us and previous voices. The client anticipates our response based, in part, on previous responses. Transference is a form of what Bakhtin called double voiced discourse, or, the word with a sideways glance.

One of my patients speaks in a weak voice. She comes into the waiting room so softly that I barely hear a puff of air from the door. I ask, to whom is that puff addressed? It is addressed to me and to others – the word with a sideways glance. And from what position is she speaking? A single utterance is addressed. As I stated above, positions and meaning systems organize into wider gestalts. Aspects of a person's life or even an entire life can be organized as an address to an other or to the world. Another woman, in her 70s, complains bitterly that she cannot lose weight. She has had one raw deal after another in life. She might lose weight if she uses her recumbent exercise bike, but there it sits. She is angry that once again she has to adapt herself and do something. Her life is an address to the world that has cheated her. From this perspective the important questions are: which voice is speaking? From what position? And to whom? (Wertsch, 1991).

Even solitary thought, made possible from internalizing dialogues, retains a hidden dialogical structure. Thought is addressed to another, implicit consciousness:

> Imagine a dialogue of two persons in which the statements of the second speaker are omitted, but in such a way that the general sense is not at all violated. The second speaker is present invisibly, his words are not there, but deep traces left by these words have a determining influence on all the present and visible words of the first speaker.
>
> (Bakhtin, 1984, p. 197)

Self-reflection is dialogical. William James (1890) described it as the "I" reflecting on the "me". There is no view from nowhere; self-reflection is always from a position or perspective and is addressed to another position or perspective. In discussions of the observing ego, or in contemporary conversations about mentalizing, it can seem that there is some pure self-observing stance. American philosopher and social thinker George Herbert Mead (1934) argued that to know the self there must be a knower. Self-awareness emerges from seeing the self through someone else's eyes, from internalizing the perspective of another person or persons toward the self. One of the things that changes through psychotherapy is the dialogical position or perspective from which we regard the self. The therapist's perspective is internalized as an alternative perspective or position from which to make sense of ourselves. Other forms of psychotherapy, such as cognitive therapy, might be conceptualized dialogically. In cognitive therapy, maladaptive beliefs are regarded from a new perspective. These beliefs exist as monologue, with no opposing voice. The therapist's more rational voice, and the various reality testing procedures, come into dialogue with maladaptive beliefs. A monologue becomes dialogue.

A dialogical theory of change

In psychoanalytic therapy we allow ourselves to be addressed in different positions. This allows the client to speak from, elaborate, and deepen the position from which she or he addresses us. The client speaks more fully from that place. Much traditional psychoanalytic work assists the client to speak more freely and fully from a position that is addressed to the therapist. When we respond we do so also from a position that is different from where the patient has placed us. We respond from a wider perspective due to our position from outside the client. We will come back to the importance of our outside perspective. Our different response brings about some shift in the position from which the client addresses us and others.

Restricted sense-making occurs when there is a dominant monologue of a limited set of positions or voices, which leads to the inflexible application of the same meanings to varied circumstances. Alternative positions from which to make sense of things are insufficiently expressed and developed. Previously inhibited positions are allowed to speak. We facilitate dialogue between the client and us and between different positions within the self. This dialogue results in greater differentiation and integration of those different positions or perspectives. The availability of new positions from which to make sense of experience, and the ability to flexibly occupy different positions, allows for increased complexity and flexibility in making meaning.

Previous positions of the client are not eliminated in psychotherapy. They remain available as positions from which to address others, depending on the context and who we are addressing. This is consistent with research that shows how old transference positions are evoked long after psychoanalyses that were judged successful (Hurn, 1973). Rather than get rid of old positions, psychotherapy makes available other positions on which we can draw on in varied relational contexts.

If there is a dominant monologue of one voice or perspective in the psychoanalytic process, either the voice of the patient or of the therapist, there is a monotonous repetition of the same meaning. Bakhtin (1984) writes of monologue:

> Monologism, at its extreme, denies the existence outside itself of another consciousness with equal rights and equal responsibilities, another "I" with equal rights ("thou"). With a monologic approach (in its extreme pure form) another person remains wholly and merely an object of consciousness, and not another consciousness. No response is expected from it that could change anything in the world of my consciousness. Monologue is finalized and deaf to other's response, does not expect it and does not acknowledge in it any force. Monologue manages without the other, and therefore to some degree materializes all reality. Monologue pretends to be the ultimate word. It closes down the represented world and represented persons.
>
> (pp. 292–293)

New meaning results from dialogue between different voices. The repetition compulsion is a dominant monologue. It is, as I will describe later, the authoritative word as opposed to internally persuasive discourse. I would playfully suggest the goal of psychoanalytic therapy to be, "where monologue was, there dialogue shall be".

Psychoanalytic theories of change have been implicitly dialogical in the way described above, emphasizing a balance of sameness and difference. In Strachey's classic model (Strachey, 1934) the client views desire from a harsh and punitive position and expects a harsh and punitive response from the analyst. In the moment that the client directs desire to the person of the analyst, the analyst responds in a different way than expected, with empathy and curiosity. That is, the analyst responds from a different position from where the client has placed her to address her. The analyst's different response is internalized and modifies the position from which the client observes desire. It is a dialogical structure that is altered. Loewald (1960, 1971) distinguishes the passive repetition of the repetition compulsion from the active and transforming repetition that propels change in psychoanalysis. Transforming repetition occurs in communication and interaction with the analyst who responds from a position of increased differentiation and integration. Bakhtin would add that this is partly due to the analyst's position outside of the client. The act of addressing experience and meaning to the therapist – an outside perspective – allows for the client's experience and meaning to become more fully articulated, differentiated, and integrated. There must be some difference between the client and the therapist who is drawn into the repetition, which then changes the organization of that which is repeated. Loewald argued that in the psychoanalytic process internalized presences and processes, previously sequestered by repression, are evoked in the transference and once again brought into relation with a mediating other, which leads to transformation and growth. From a Bakhtinian perspective, previously sequestered voices are brought into dialogue with the voice of the therapist, leading to transformation of meaning.

In Sandler's (1976) notion of role responsiveness we unconsciously resonate with the role of others in the client's life. We embody the position in which we are being addressed. We answer from a position that is similar but different – containing elements of past and present. We sustain our difference through empathy, observation, and our attempt to understand. Greenberg (1986) reformulates the notion of analytic neutrality as occupying a position that is similar enough to others in the client's life to bring those voices to life in the present, but different enough so as not to repeat the past without change. Sandler's and Greenberg's models are consistent with allowing ourselves to be addressed in a position familiar to the client but providing enough difference for dialogue and new meaning to emerge.

Similarity and difference: the role of outsideness

These psychoanalytic models of change highlight a balance of similarity and difference. While empathy is important, difference is also necessary to stimulate dialogue and new meaning. Bakhtin (1990) writes:

> What would I have to gain if another were to fuse with me? He would see and know only what I already see and know, he would only repeat in himself the inescapable and closed circle of my own life; let him rather stay outside me.
> (p. 97; this is a slightly different translation found in Morson and Emerson, 1990, Kindle Edition, loc. 1128)

Without the therapist's answering word, without difference, there is only one voice, a monologue. Monologue repeats the same meaning in every context. When we occupy a position from outside the other person we have access to a surplus of meaning that is not available to the other because of his or her position from inside the self. We can see more from the outside. Bakhtin's ethics calls us to not finalize or complete the meaning of the other in our vision, but to allow the other to go on becoming in ongoing transforming dialogue (Bakhtin, 1986). Bakhtin writes of the importance of difference when one culture strives to understand the other. His comments are strikingly apt for the meeting of two individuals in psychotherapy:

> There exists a very strong, but one-sided and thus untrustworthy, idea that in order to understand a foreign culture, one must enter into it, forgetting one's own, and view the culture through the eyes of this foreign culture. This idea, as I said, is one-sided. Of course, a certain entry as a living being into a foreign culture, the possibility of seeing the world through its eyes, is a necessary part of the process of under-standing it; but if this where the only aspect of this understanding, it would merely be a duplication and would not entail anything new or enriching. Creative understanding does not renounce itself, its own place in time, its own culture; and it forgets nothing.
>
> (p. 7)

And:

> In order to understand, it is immensely important for the person who understands to be *located outside* the object of his or her understanding – in time, in space, in culture . . . our real exterior can be seen and understood only by other people, because they are located outside us in space and because they are others . . . . A meaning only reveals its depths once it has encountered and come into contact with another, foreign meaning: they engage in a kind of dialogue which surmounts the closed-ness and one-sidedness of these particular mean-ings, these cultures. We raise new questions for a foreign culture, ones that it did not raise for itself; we seek answers to our own questions in it; and the foreign culture responds to us by revealing to us its new aspects and new semantic depths.
>
> (p. 7)

Responsive understanding

When we listen and understand, from our wider perspective, we do not just passively take in the client's word. We respond. We meet his or her words with our own. This is the nature of how we understand each other – Bakhtin (1986) called it active responsive understanding. It is a dialogical response.

> Any understanding of live speech, a live utterance, is inherently responsive . . . . Any understanding is imbued with response and necessarily elicits it in one form or another: the listener becomes the speaker.
>
> (p. 68)

And, as I have discussed above, one does not just meet words with words. The speaker's words, intonation, expression, and gesture evoke the listener's own verbal and bodily response (Shotter, 2008, 2011).

Understanding and responding to another's suffering requires an active living in. It is empathy plus, as I do not leave behind my perspective or voice. As our voices meet, there is the possibility of new meaning:

> I *actively* enter as a living being into an individuality, and consequently do not, for a single moment, lose myself completely or lose my singular place outside that individuality. It's not the subject who unexpectedly takes possession of a passive me, but *I* who actively enter into him; *vzhivanie* is *my* act, and only in it can there be productiveness and innovation.
>
> (Bakhtin, 1984, p. 93)

Responsiveness and difference are essential to change through conversation and through psychotherapy. One includes the client's perspective from the inside but one does not renounce one's voice from an outside perspective. The therapist's outside position allows for similarity and difference from the position in which the client places and addresses the therapist. The therapist responds, with word and bodily expression, from that similar but different place. Difference allows for a kind of dialogue that Bakhtin called internally persuasive discourse and this leads to new meaning.

Authoritative discourse vs. internally persuasive discourse

If our words are met with the client's words an internal dialogue is mobilized in the form of internally persuasive discourse. If our words are taken in without modification, without the client's answering word, it is taken in as the authoritative word and authoritative discourse:

> The authoritative word demands that we acknowledge it; that we make it our own; it binds us quite independent of any power it might have to persuade us internally; we encounter it with its authority already fused to it. The authoritative word is located in a distanced zone, organically connected with a past that is felt to be hierarchically higher. It is, so to speak, the word of the fathers. Its authority was already *acknowledged* in the past. It is a *prior* discourse.
>
> (Bakhtin, 1981, p. 342)

The authoritative word, or authoritative voice, is taken in all-or-none, "a compact, indivisible mass" (Bakhtin, 1981, p. 342). One does not agree with one part and not the other. The persuasive power of that discourse comes from historical, political, or institutional power, as opposed to its assimilation into an internal dialogue:

> It is not a free appropriation and assimilation of the word itself that authoritative discourse seeks to elicit from us; rather, it demands from us our unconditional allegiance. Therefore, authoritative discourse permits no play with the context framing it, no play with its borders, no gradual and flexible transitions, no spontaneous and creative stylizing variants on it.
>
> (Bakhtin, 1981, p. 342)

The authoritative word does not acknowledge another consciousness or perspective. It repeats the same meaning without transformation. The authoritative word repeats itself in new contexts without change. The word with the authority fused to it, and the demand to be taken in whole, is reminiscent of projective identification.

As a boy, my client, Frank, idealized his father's word. His father's authoritative word went unquestioned, unmet by any word from the boy. There was one slight dissenting voice or position. He would sit on his father's garage and tear shingles off the roof, sending them flying like Frisbees into the woods. He moved away to college and met a girlfriend who voiced criticism of his father. He started to question his father's voice and to realize that his father was wrong about some things. According to Bakhtin (1981), the authoritative word does not allow for the distance necessary for one's own voice: "a playing with distances, with fusion and dissolution, with approach and retreat, is not possible here" (p. 342). By getting distance from his father's authoritative word, geographically and through his girlfriend's voice – as well as her permission – the young man was able to change his father's authoritative monologue into an internal dialogue. He met his father's word with his own responsive words. His father's voice continues to speak as a harsh internal critic, but he meets it with other voices in dialogue.

Internally persuasive discourse, in contrast, occurs when we take in the other's word and meet it with our own. Psychoanalytic interpretations, if presented not as an authoritative word, are internalized in the form of internally persuasive discourse:

> Internally persuasive discourse ... is affirmed through assimilation, tightly interwoven with "one's own word". In the everyday rounds of our consciousness, the internally persuasive word is half ours and half someone else's. Its creativity and productiveness consists precisely in the fact that such a word awakens new and independent words, that it organizes masses of our words from within, and does not remain in an isolated and static condition. It is not so much interpreted by us as it is freely developed, applied to new material, new conditions, and it enters into inter-animating relationships with new contexts. More than that, it enters into an intense interaction, a *struggle* with other internally persuasive discourses .... The semantic structure of an internally persuasive discourse is not *finite*, it is *open*; in each of the new contexts that dialogize it, this discourse is able to reveal ever newer *ways to mean*.
>
> (Bakhtin, 1981, p. 345)

The internally persuasive voice becomes a voice in our internal dialogue. It is a dialogized word, met with our own words. Internally persuasive discourse, when dialogized in new contexts, is able to mean new and unexpected things:

> the essence of the internally persuasive word, such as the word's semantic openness to us, its capacity for further creative life in the context of our ideological consciousness, its unfinishedness and the inexhaustibility of our further action with it. We have not yet learned

from it all it might tell us; we can take it into new contexts, attach it to new material, put it in a new situation to wrest new answers from it, new insights into its meaning, and even wrest from it new words of its *own*, (since another's discourse, if productive, gives birth to a new word from us in response).

(Bakhtin, 1981, pp. 346–347)

This idea, that internally persuasive discourse can yield new and unexpected meanings when in dialogue with new contexts, is very important. It relates to the notion of meaning potential (Morson & Emerson, 1990). It means that a psychoanalytic interpretation, or the internally persuasive voice of the therapist, has the potential to yield new and unanticipated meanings in new contexts. This is in contrast to the authoritative word that yields no new meaning in new contexts. The idea of new and unanticipated meaning – of indeterminate meaning – is a theme in Bakhtin's work. For example, the meaning of words is not coded hard and fast in abstract language. Words have meaning potentials; which of those potentials is realized when we use the word in a specific context and when we add intonation and accent. Bakhtin thought that great authors embed meaning potential in their work (Morson & Emerson, 1990). When the work comes into dialogue with new contexts, new meanings emerge that were unanticipated by the author.

Polyphony, the self, and emergent meaning

Bakhtin was particularly interested in Dostoevsky and the polyphonic novel. The characters in Dostoevsky's novels have their own voice, their own perspective or consciousness, independent of the voice of the author or narrator:

What unfolds in his novels is not a multitude of characters and fates in a single objective world, illuminated by a single authorial consciousness; rather a *plurality of consciousnesses, with equal rights and each with his own world*, combine but are not merged in the unity of the events he depicts.

(Bakhtin, 1984, p. 6)

There is a group of psychologists who have developed Dialogical Self Theory (Hermans, 1996; Hermans & Dimaggio, 2004; Leiman, 2011), in which the self is analogized to the polyphonic novel. There are multitudes of voices within us, existing in an imagined space and more or less in dialogue. Voices struggle for dominance and suppress and marginalize other voices.

The aspect of Bakhtin's work on the polyphonic novel that I want to use has to do with indeterminacy of meaning and meaning potential (Morson & Emerson, 1990). Dostoevsky's creative process used literary devices to set up dialogue between voices, to set dialogue in motion. The meaning that emerged was not guided by preconceived plot or abstract structure. The emergent meaning was a surprise even to the author. Psychoanalytic therapy also sets dialogue in motion, between internal voices and with the voice of the therapist. The meaning that emerges is indeterminate and unpredictable. An older psychoanalytic psychotherapy might suggest that if we knew all we needed to know about a patient's life and inner world, and with a reasonably objective analyst, we could identify the internal meanings that need to change and we could predict the new meanings with a successful outcome. From the dialogical perspective, meanings that emerge from inter-subjective dialogue are not determined. They can surprise us. The voice of the therapist, when it becomes part of an internally persuasive discourse, has the potential to mean in new and unanticipated ways in new contexts. Psychoanalytic process cultivates a more rich meaning potential for the individual. By mobilizing dialogical processes we enrich the person's capacity to mean in new and unanticipated ways in new contexts. We cultivate the capacity for surprise. This is in contrast to fixed positions applied universally to all relational contexts, leading to the same repetitive meaning.

Indeterminacy and stability of meaning

A unique moment of dialogue contains aspects of meaning that are unique and unpredictable (Shotter & Billig, 1998). Speakers orient themselves to the uniqueness of each other and to the unique immediate context. And there are aspects of meaning that are more repeatable and stable. The wider context of dialogue is more stable and repeatable, and thus brings stable and repeatable influence to the meaning of the moment. In his book, *Rethinking Language, Mind, and World Dialogically*, Linell (2009) describes uniquely situated dialogue where participants draw on resources that transcend the immediate context and use these to make meaning. These resources stabilize the meaning of the uniquely situated moment. They include shared language, the symbolic resources of culture, and our personal histories. As therapists we draw from the wider context of theories and professional dialogues. The shared history of the psychotherapy is also context that stabilizes and shapes the meaning that emerges in a moment of dialogue. Context can be thought of as a field of interacting meanings that shapes and stabilizes the meaning that emerges from dialogue.

Meaning emerges from the intersection of the indeterminate, unrepeatable and the stable, repeatable. Bakhtin (1986) thought that with every utterance and social act there was tension between centrifugal tendencies, which pull toward the indeterminate and unrepeatable, and centripetal tendencies, which pull toward stability and repetition. Shotter's (2008, 2011) theory of conversation and meaning-making, inspired by Bakhtin and Wittgenstein, also emphasizes the unique first-time nature of every conversation which co-exists with more stable, repeatable elements. I propose that a complex, dynamic, and self-organizing system emerges from the interaction of stable-repeatable and unstable-unrepeatable aspects of meaning-making. Local indeterminacy and more generalized stability is a feature of physical and biological systems. The balance allows the system to be sensitive and adaptive to unique local contexts – a survival advantage in a world of varied contexts. Theoretical biologist and researcher of complex systems, Stuart Kauffman (1993), writes, "Selection achieves and maintains complex systems poised on the boundary, or edge, between order and chaos" (p. xv). The same is true of communicative systems and systems of meaning. Relational contexts are varied and require a similar balance of local indeterminacy and flexibility with more generalized stability.[2]

According to dialogical theory, meaning does not exist in the speaker's mind to be transmitted to and decoded by the receiver (Linell, 2009). What a speaker means is worked out in the process of conversation. Meaning emerges from the interaction of speaker, addressee, and context. Speakers bring to the conversation stable and repetitive potentials and vulnerabilities for certain kinds of interactions and meanings (Shotter, 2008). For example, speakers color their addressee according to previous formative dialogues. But enduring potentials and vulnerabilities interact with unique aspects of the listener/addressee and the context.

If the meaning that emerges from the therapeutic dialogue is partly unique and indeterminate, what changes that generalizes to other contexts? Rather than changing stable internal meanings, we change our relationship to meaning. Shotter (2008, 2011), following Wittgenstein, suggests that helpful conversation changes one's orientation within a set of meanings. I would add that psychotherapy mobilizes the meaning-making process. Psychotherapy cultivates a potential for complex and flexible meaning-making which is adaptive to varied relational contexts. Psychoanalytic treatment makes possible not just a change in orientation, as described by Wittgenstein and Shotter, but ideally helps a person develop multiple and varied orientations or positions for varied relational contexts. A dialogically based psychotherapy cultivates the potential to mean in new and unanticipated ways in new contexts through mobilizing dialogue and internally persuasive discourse.

Valuing otherness as cultural context

Transforming dialogue depends on the context or field in which it takes place. Jaan Valsiner's (2003) theory of enabling social representations describes an aspect of the wider context that guides meaning-making toward change. These are generalized, even vague, culturally shared meanings and values which act as "promoter signs" (Valsiner, 2007; Branco & Valsiner, 2009), guiding the direction of meaning-making toward the future and change. They are a silent background that shapes dialogue and the meaning that emerges. The ethical value of recognizing the legitimacy of the other is a generalized cultural value that can shape dialogue and meaning-making. Valuing the other, acknowledging the other's legitimate difference, is a cultural meaning and value that shapes dialogue and meaning-making between persons and between communities. The generalized value of otherness makes possible dialogue that leads to new meaning.

Therapeutic goals as meaning shaping context

The agreed-upon goals of psychotherapy are part of the background context that orients the participants. They are one of the resources that transcend the immediate context and that stabilize and shape meaning-making in the immediate context. The goals of the work are part of the background field to which speakers consciously and unconsciously orient themselves. They shape and guide the trajectory of meaning-making in a future direction, toward change – much like the function of "promoter signs" in Valsiner's (2003) semiotic theory. I work with an obsessive man who has been in therapy with one therapist or another for his entire adult life. He comes out of ritual, but there is nothing he wants to change or work on or change.

I feel disoriented; don't know what to do with what he tells me. I often think, "why are you telling me this?" There are many possible dynamics here: his anxious need to evacuate himself, projective identification. But there is also the absence of any orienting context of meanings to guide and shape the direction of our dialogue. We have no sense of direction.

Curtailed dialogue and constricted subjectivity

Psychotherapy ideally cultures the individual's capacity for inter-subjective dialogue – we become more open and responsive to the voice of the other. Inter-subjective dialogue – or internally persuasive discourse – makes possible new meaning in new contexts. Monologue and repetition are closed to the voice of the other. There are many ways in which we restrict communication and through this we limit our recognition of the other. Benjamin's (1993, 2004) work on dominance and lack of recognition is relevant and has been applied by social psychologist Sandra Jovchelovitch (2007) to recognition between communities. By restricting conversation we restrict who the other is to us, in the service of our needs. This is common in relationships. I see conversation patterns in couples where opportunities to expand conversation are responded to in ways that curtail further communication and elaboration. I frame this for them as conversation enders versus conversation extenders.

Consider another form of conversation restriction by my client Tom. Tom had multiple affairs with married women who were professionally subordinate. He described intense connections and conversations in which he was acutely in tune with his partner's subjectivity. But they never talked about, and he never thought about, a dimension of meaning – what it meant for his partner, in the context of her life, her relationship to her spouse, and her career, to engage in a secret romance with him. His partners participated in the restricted communication and meaning. Each molded the meaning of the other in ways that met their needs and they restricted the range of their conversation to preserve that reality. This occurs between communities. Edward Said (1978) described the essentialist images of the Oriental by the West that met colonialist needs for wealth and power. A culture's image of the other is sustained by ways of speaking of and with the other. There are relative restrictions of the other's subjectivity, a continuum on the range between dialogical and monological ways of communicating and relating, a continuum between I–thou and I–it ways of communicating, in the service of need and desire. Restricted communication is a means by which the other's restricted subjectivity or meaning is constructed and maintained. Unfinished and ongoing dialogue, as advocated by Bakhtin, open to the ever-evolving difference of the other, leads to new meaning. For Tom there was little new meaning. It was the same love story over and over.

Conclusion and summary

Bakhtin's dialogical theory of meaning suggests the outlines of a dynamic and inter-subjective model for change through psychoanalytic psychotherapy. Psychoanalytic psychotherapy is a dialogical process that mobilizes dialogical processes within the self and between the self and others. The client addresses the therapist from different positions. This allows the client to elaborate, deepen, and thus speak more fully from those places. The therapist responds from a position that is similar to but also different from where the client is placed her to address her. This difference mobilizes dialogue and new meaning. The therapist's different voice becomes an alternative position or perspective from which to regard the self. The client develops more varied positions or orientations from which to make sense of experience. Old positions remain available depending on the context but there is more flexible access to alternative positions or perspectives.

Dialogue leads to new and more complex meanings. The dominant monologue of a single voice leads to the repetition of the same meanings without change. Repetition without transformation – the repetition compulsion – is the dominant monologue of authoritative discourse. Interpretations, or the therapist's voice, become part of the client's internally persuasive discourse which yields new meaning in new contexts. Internally persuasive discourse finds new ways to mean in new contexts.

Psychoanalytic process does not replace one set of fixed meanings with another, even if more benign. We seek to mobilize meaning-making processes that yield more complex and flexible capacities to mean, to mean in new ways in new contexts. Rather than the same meanings and positions applied universally to all contexts, more varied meaning-making is more responsive to varied local, relational contexts. Such meaning-making balances indeterminacy of meaning and stability. Psychotherapy cultivates the capacity for unanticipated and surprising meanings.

Transforming dialogue depends on the wider context that shapes dialogue and meaning. The goals of psychotherapy are an orienting context that guides and stabilizes the meaning that emerges. The wider context of cultural meanings and values, such as valuing the legitimacy of the other, promote dialogue and meaning change between persons and communities. Persons and cultures more or less restrict the meaning and subjectivity of the other through restricted dialogue.

Notes

1 Bakhtin's and Shotter's notion of the expressive body and an embodied stance resonates with Merleau-Ponty's thought. For a discussion of Merleau-Ponty and Bakhtin see Gardiner (1998).
2 The value of vagueness and indeterminacy in language and conceptual understanding is a central feature of the language theory of Karl Bühler (1990/1994) (Branco & Valsiner, 2009).

References

Bakhtin, M. M. (1981). *The dialogical imagination: Four essays.* In M. Holquist (Ed.) (C. Emerson & M. Holquist Trans.). Austin, TX: University of Texas Press.

Bakhtin, M. M. (1984). *Problems of Dostoevsky's poetics.* In C. Emerson (Ed. and Trans.). Minneapolis: University of Michigan Press.

Bakhtin, M. M. (1986). *Speech genres and other late essays.* Austin, TX: University of Texas Press.

Bakhtin, M. M. (1990). *Art and answerability.* Austin, TX: University of Texas Press.

Benjamin, J. (1993). *The bonds of love: Psychoanalysis, feminism, and the problem of domination.* London: Virago.

Benjamin, J. (2004). Beyond doer and done to: An intersubjective view of thirdness. *Psychoanalytic Quarterly, 73*, 5–46.

Benson, C. (2001). *The cultural psychology of self: Place, morality, and art in human worlds.* London: Routledge.

Bion, W. R. (1965). *Transformations: Change from learning to growth.* London: Heinemann.

Branco, A., & Valsiner, J. (2009, September 25). *Values as signs: The role of field theory in semiotic understanding of feelings.* Paper presented at the 9th World Congress on Semiotics, LaCoruña, Spain.

Bühler, K. (1990/1994). *Theory of language: The representational function of language.* Amsterdam: John Benjamins.

Gardiner, M. (1998). "The incomparable monster of solipsism": Bakhtin and Merleau-Ponti. In M. Bell & M. Gardiner (Eds.), *Bakhtin and the human sciences.* London: Sage Publications.

Greenberg, J. (1986). Theoretical models and the analyst's neutrality. *Contemporary Psychoanalysis, 22*, 87–106.

Grossen M., & Salazar-Orvig, A. (2011). Dialogism and dialogicality in the study of the self. *Culture and Psychology, 17*, 491–509.

Harre, R. (1998). *The singular self: An introduction to the psychology of personhood.* London: Sage Publications.

Hermans, H. J. M. (1996). Voicing the self: From information processing to dialogical interchange. *Psychological Bulletin, 119*(1), 31–50.

Hermans, H. J. M., & Dimaggio, G. (2004). *The dialogical self in psychotherapy*. New York: Brunner-Routledge.

Hurn, H. T. (1973). On the fate of transference after termination of analysis. *Journal of the American Psychoanalytic Association, 21*(1), 182–192.

James, W. (1890). *The principles of psychology*. Cambridge, MA: Harvard University Press.

Jovchelovitch, J. (2007). *Knowledge in context: Representations, community, and culture*. New York: Routledge.

Kauffman, Stuart (1993). *The origins of order: self-organization and selection in evolution*. New York: Oxford University Press.

Lannemann, J. (1998). Social construction and materiality: The limits of indeterminacy in therapeutic settings. *Family Processes, 37*, 393–413.

Leiman, L. (2002). Toward semiotic dialogism: The role of sign mediation in the dialogical self. *Theory and Psychology, 12*(2), 221–235.

Leiman, M. (2011). Mikhail Bahktin's contribution to psychotherapy research. *Culture and Psychology, 17,* 441–461.

Linell, P. (2009). *Rethinking language, mind, and world dialogically: Interactional and contextual theories of human sense-making*. Charlotte, NC: Information Age Publishing.

Loewald, H. (1960). On the therapeutic action of psychoanalysis. *International Journal of Psychoanalysis*, *41*, 16–33.

Loewald, H. (1971). Some considerations on repetition and the repetition compulsion. *International Journal of Psychoanalysis, 52*, 59–66.

Mead, G. H. (1934). *Mind, self, and society*. Chicago, IL: University of Chicago Press.

Moore, H., Jasper, C., & Gillespie, A. (2011). Moving between frames: The basis of the stable and dialogical self. *Culture and Psychology, 17*, 510–519.

Morson, G., & Emerson, C. (1990). *Mikhail Bakhtin: Creation of a prosaics*. Stanford, CA: Stanford University Press.

Richardson, F. C. (2011). A hermeneutic perspective on dialogical psychology. *Culture and Psychology, 17*(1), 462–472.

Said, E. W. (1978). *Orientalism: Western conceptions of the Orient*. London: Penguin.

Salgado, J. (n.d.). *The heart in-between: Feelings as dialogical movement*. Unpublished manuscript.

Salgado, J., & Hermans, H. J. M. (2005). The return of subjectivity: From a multiplicity of selves to the dialogical self. *Electronic Journal of Applied Psychology, 1*, 3–13.

Sandler, J. (1976). Countertransference and role responsiveness. *International Review of Psychoanalysis*, *3*, 43–47.

Shotter, J. (1993a). Vygotsky: The social negotiation of semiotic mediation. *New Ideas in Psychology, 11*, 61–75.

Shotter, J. (1993b). Bakhtin and Vygotsky: Internalization as a boundary phenomenon. *New Ideas in Psychology, 11*, 379–390.

Shotter, J. (2008). *Conversational realities revisited: Life, language, body and world*. Chagrin Falls, OH: Taos Institute Publications.

Shotter, J. (2011). *Getting it: Withness-thinking and the dialogical . . . in practice*. New York: Hampton Press.

Shotter, J. (2012). Ontological social constructionism in the context of a social ecology: The importance of our living bodies. In A. Lock & T. Strong (Eds.), *Discursive perspectives in therapeutic practice*. Oxford: Oxford University Press.

Shotter, J., & Billig, M. (1998). A Bakhtinian psychology: From out of the heads of individuals and into the dialogues between them. In M. Bell & M. Gardiner (Eds.), *Bakhtin and the human sciences*. London: Sage Publications.

Strachey, J. (1934). The nature of the therapeutic action of psychoanalysis. *International Journal of Psychoanalysis, 15*, 127–159.

Valsiner, J. (2003). Beyond social representations: A theory of enablement. *Papers on Social Representations, 12*, 6.1–6.16. Retrieved from http://psych1.lse.ac.uk/psr/

Valsiner, J. (2007). *Culture in minds and societies*. New Delhi: Sage Publications.

Voloshinov, V. N. (1973). *Marxism and the philosophy of language*. Cambridge, MA: Harvard University Press.

Wertsch, J. V. (1991). *Voices of the mind: A sociocultural approach to mediated action*. Cambridge, MA: Harvard University Press.

Chapter 16

I got grand things in me and America won't let me give nothing

Constructing and resisting a standard American identity

Donna San Antonio

In her book, *Ethnic Options*, Mary Waters (1990) documents evidence of shifting identities in immigrant families, adaptations that continue for generations as descendants of other nations embrace and resist an "American" identity while creatively integrating distinctive language, symbols, and ways of being into everyday life. Recently, while visiting relatives in Italy, I was acutely aware of the way ethnic identities are created within a social context. I had always had a sense of myself as Italian-American – the *Italian* part decidedly first. The older I get, the more I am aware of the nuanced and deep influences of my working-class childhood and my *southern* Italian, dialect-speaking, peasant ancestry. While in Italy, I went to get my Italian citizenship card in my grandfather's village. Ironically, it was on this visit, rejoicing in my long sought-after dual citizenship and speaking Italian every day, that I had a surprising shift: I have no idea of what it means to be "Italian." Cultural identity is socially influenced, nuanced, and unstable, even more so when, out of need or curiosity, we let ourselves consider the multiplicity of our identities, rejecting some aspects of cultural ideals that we previously embraced. Psychoanalysis is, in part, an iterative process of undermining the cultural ideals with which we identify.

Sigismund Schlomo Freud was himself an immigrant, born in Freiberg, Moravia in 1856. When his father's business failed, he moved with his family to Leipzig and then to Vienna, Austria in 1860. At the age of 19 he changed his name to Sigmund. He was apparently never fond of Vienna and longed for the countryside of his childhood (Gay, 1988). In 1938, facing increasing anti-Semitism and hardship, including the temporary arrest by the Gestapo of his daughter and son, Anna and Martin, Freud and his family moved to England. About his departure from Vienna he wrote to a friend saying, "the feeling of triumph at liberation is mingled too strongly with mourning, for one had still very much loved the prison from which one had been released" (Gay, 1988, p. 9). I am struck by the lasting impact of Freud's childhood experience of emigration and how Freud spoke about the ambivalence he (and we) feel about liberation, often longing for our familiar prisons instead.

In *Hermeneutics and the Voice of the Other* James Risser (1997) wrote:

> What is at stake in understanding is the otherness of the text and its ability to assert its truth against one's own fore-meanings . . . . The openness to experience means that one does not overlook the claims of the other, whereby one must accept some things that are against the one who seeks to understand.
>
> (p. 15)

In this chapter, I consider how immigrant and non-immigrant people opened to the assertion of the other, or not, during a period of rapid cultural and demographic change. I am particularly interested in how identities are pushed and pulled into shape, in social, political, and cultural contexts, in which we are, simultaneously, players in establishing ethnic identity and being played, toward contradictory ends. Then and now, whether encounters among people of different ethnicities and classes evoke curiosity, repulsion, sympathy, suspicion, indignation, or deference is dependent upon the lens through which people view one another and their willingness to accept some things that go against their fore-meanings.

At the end of the 19th century, as immigrant populations grew, schools were called upon as the institutional avenue for the project of Americanization and cultural assimilation. Sustaining this agenda, Hirsch and other cultural literacy proponents supported cultural essentialism and called upon schools to teach "what every American needs to know," the subtitle of Hirsch's 1987 book. Each new generation of immigrant children has worked to get a foothold in U.S. society through schooling. However, children suffer the social and emotional harms, cultural losses, and educational consequences when schools become the battlefield for discriminatory national and local policies, such as Arizona's HB 2281 which bans ethnic studies.

In this chapter, I present several distinct, historical standpoints that support particular interpretations of immigration and create multiple narratives that weave through U.S. society and schooling in curricula, formal and informal laws, structures of civic engagement, and norms of interaction.

At their core, these interpretations question responsibility and loyalty: To whom and to what is the immigrant person responsible? This is a particularly salient question because the vast majority of people emigrate to the United States during adolescence and young adulthood, at precisely the time when drives are pressing, when the subject challenges the demand of the other, and when there is an irrepressible hunger for something not yet identifiable. Considering the experience of immigration from a Lacanian standpoint gives rise to these questions: What might be happening *in* the body, *to* the body, and to gender and skin color when someone leaves his or her ancestral land, comes to the US, and faces both hostility and promise?

For this chapter, I reviewed historical documents, contemporary retrospective texts written by immigrants, training manuals for teachers, and citizenship primers, most of them written from 1890 to 1920. My four grandparents came to the US between 1909 and 1911. The contemporary political debates, and the activism of immigrant people and allies, such as today's "Dreamers," are resonant with that period. It is during those decades that the nation constructed a narrative on immigration, filled with inconsistencies, fantasies, wishes, and distortions, that persists today. Most of the texts I analyzed were written during a period of migration from Southern and Eastern Europe of poor, Catholic, Orthodox, and Jewish young adults who did not speak English. It is important to be clear that when immigration is framed as a "crisis" today, it is specifically a reaction to a population that is predominantly young, black, brown, and poor or low-income. There are many pointed similarities in the experience of immigration groups of today and those of 100 years ago; however, the differences, particularly in terms of entrenched racial biases that continue to operate, cannot be superficially overlooked.

In analyzing texts, I discerned three, distinct interpretive standpoints with regard to individual psychology and the role of the other: critical theory, which Gallagher (1992) summarizes as a social and political critique that calls for a "suspicious interpretation of those ideologies and institutions which support and maintain ruling power structures" (p. 240); humanistic constructivism, a hermeneutics of faith that acknowledges the inescapable distortion of interpretation but that strives to meet the other through an inter-subjective and reflexive process (Levinas in Peperzak, 1993; Ricoeur, 1981); and Lacanian psychoanalysis, radically suspicious of "morality" based in the norms of the social link, committed to deconstructing one's relationship to the pleasure of the other as his/her *raison d'être*, and invested in an ethic that takes the side of desire that is often counter to social norms and ideals (Apollon, Bergeron, & Cantin, 2002).

The immigrant stories in this chapter aim toward describing the ethical tension in these conceptualizations of the other in a way that avoids the dualism of an ethic of responsibility toward others vs. an ethic of responsibility toward becoming a desiring subject.

In responding to an earlier iteration of this chapter, Kristine Klement of York University suggested: "Perhaps the place to start is not with theory, but with the ethics of psychoanalysis – an ethics that takes the side of the desiring subject, but that recognizes that the only place that the subject can express their desire is on a social scene which is hostile to it" (personal communication, June 5, 2013). As a counselor and as someone who trains counselors, I offer this question: How can community and school counselors make a space for children and adolescents to speak about themselves fully, even when it defies societal and cultural ideals? I am particularly interested in how school and community counselors might listen to immigrant children in a way that opens the possibility of the child's speech attesting to his or her *singular* experience, while simultaneously acknowledging the struggle of the subject imposed by cultural values and norms.

In the next section, I underscore this pivotal struggle using two case examples. Then, I describe the way assimilation attempted to appropriate a specific American identity through socialization projects implemented in schools and communities. Next, I consider language as the medium of authority creating a rupture in psychic and communal structures, followed by a discussion of the role of paternalism and seduction as tools of control. Finally, I give three examples of individual and collective resistance to the paternalistic work of objectification.

Becoming teenager-America

American culture and identity is perpetually narrated as something true, universal, stable, and self-evident. A young Haitian woman[1] told me of her mother's playful mocking when she wanted to do things like her American peers. "Are you being teenager-America now?" her mother would challenge, drawing a line between cultural identities within and outside of the family. American identity is so well marketed that we might guess what she means by "teenager-America," but we would still not know anything about what is at stake in this comment for both mother and daughter. The pull toward peers during adolescence almost always sets up a conflict between the demands of significant others within the family and the demands of the others within the peer group. In immigrant families, there is often great loyalty to parents and siblings because of the narrative of sacrifice and the responsibility to "give back" that is woven into daily discourse in immigrant homes. What is notable in my work with young people is that they tell me over and over again, "There is no one helping us" as they sort these conflicts out. To quote this young woman:

> I feel as though I have a better understanding of what goes on at this age because of the time I take for introspection but I find myself just as confused at times about life expectations of me . . . and the identity struggle that comes with the transition into a more independent adult. What I want and what my parents want for me in terms of goals and desire: Is it the same, parallel, or opposite?

Like so many first and second-generation adolescents today from the Caribbean, Central America, Asia, and Africa, she does a lot of soul-searching about her own desire and her position to the other as represented in secular vs. religious norms, peer vs. family relationships, self vs. community goals, American vs. Haitian cultural identities. She is beginning to be aware of the risk of misidentifying herself with the desire of the other; yet, there is no one making space for this exploration. What might it mean, individually and collectively, for her singular experience to be expressed in a bold, unapologetic voice?

A personal story comes to mind that illustrates how we come into being in relationship with the other; how race, social class, gender, and culture matter; and how, even as children, we are actors, literally *performing* within a social link. I hope this story illustrates how the "I" of who one is is inextricably connected to the "eye" (E-Y-E) of the other in the construction of the imaginary self, who is always under surveillance (Lacan, 1978; Sturken & Cartwright, 2009).

When I was 13 and in the 8th grade at Holy Rosary Grammar School, I was elected May Queen by my peers and vested with the honor of crowning a statue of the Blessed Mother in the May procession. For a good Catholic girl like myself, this was about the best thing that could happen. The procession looped through the tenement-lined streets of the Italian neighborhood where I grew up. I was a particularly devout, quiet, and shy 13-year-old and this was my very first foray into having a public identity.

We could pick our attendants – primary-grade students that would walk with us in the procession and, as the May Queen, I got first "pick." A tiny Dominican first grader rushed to me when I entered the classroom and begged me to pick her. I was resistant. I had an image of something "perfect" for the procession and that persistent dark-skinned little girl rattled me and my image of "perfect." I was too shy and unassertive to actually say "no," so she was chosen.

A couple of months before this, I wrote a letter to the editor of the *Lawrence Eagle Tribune* about civil rights. The letter called for racial equality and an end to violence. Conflating sameness with justice, my 13-year-old self argued, "Beneath our skin, we are all the same." I told my father I was uneasy about having a black girl as one of my attendants. Thankfully, he quickly and firmly pointed out the contradiction between my written words to the editor and my discomfort. I wish I could say that I was ashamed to realize the inconsistency of my stated values and my uneasiness but it took me several more years before I grasped the moral issue of that moment.

By the age of 13, I had absorbed both messages of racial equality and justice and also racialized messages of the "undesirability" of darker-skinned people. There was an "otherness" about this first grader that was informed by the attitudes and images of the day, both subtle and overt. In some way, I had also absorbed the negative attitudes of others from outside my neighborhood about us, and I was reacting to a sense of others as powerful judges of my worthiness. I wanted to create an image beyond reproach – to be as white as possible in this public spectacle. Simultaneously, I had an image of others in the crowds of people that would line the streets of my neighborhood to see the May procession. I imagined this audience to be kind and admiring. In a vague sense that I can only articulate now, 50 years later, I wanted to know, "What do those others want from me?" I wanted to do everything in my power to fulfill whatever it was the others might expect of me. It is important for us to create a space for young people to deconstruct the meaning of these stories, how the stories are told, the way they make us who we are, and the way these stories, imbued with political and cultural significance, lead to both possibility and limitation.

Anglo-sizing America

Between 1905 and 1908 more than a million immigrants arrived each year, most of them young adults from Eastern and Southern Europe. Total immigration exceeded 27,500,000 by 1920 and many cities in the US had immigrant populations exceeding 50%. Prejudice and fear were exploited to frame immigration as a crisis and the immigrant as a threat, paving the way for more restrictive immigration laws, particularly aimed at reducing immigration from Southern and Eastern Europe. In the last two decades, people have again been immigrating to the US in numbers exceeding 1 million a year.

Doris Lessing's book, *Prisons We Choose to Live Inside* (1987), discusses the powerful draw of human beings toward primal fears and suspicions, demarcating insider and outsider, creating an imaginary enemy, and then a narrative, imbued with urgent morality, about the need to defeat that enemy. Throughout the history of immigration in the US, conceptualizing immigration and the immigrant as either a commodity or as an economic, social, cultural, and national security threat has had powerful sway. Legislative consideration of immigration unabashedly places business and political interests as the rationalization for immigration reform, a blatant contradiction to the mythical and powerful narrative of America as a safe haven for those seeking safety, freedom, and opportunity.

The manipulation of skin color was a subtler but equally powerful deception. Early 20th-century immigrant people were positioned in a racialized, social status hierarchy, lower than English-speaking white people, but higher than Africa-descendant people. The "one drop rule" determined that someone was black if they had *any* black ancestors and, therefore, subject to Jim Crow segregation. This is important because of the immigrant's position in the social hierarchy as a tool of social control and of oppression. The unspoken message of assimilation in the United States is, "Act more like us or you will be treated like them." Darker-skinned ethnic groups, such as Italian-Americans, became more and more "white" over the course of the 20th century.

Ellwood Patterson Cubberley (1868–1941), well-published and influential Professor of Education at Stanford University, wrote:

> About 1882, the character of our immigration changed . . . these southern and eastern Europeans are of a very different type from the north Europeans who preceded them. Illiterate, docile, lacking in self-reliance and initiative, and not possessing the Anglo-Teutonic conceptions of law, order, and government, their coming has served to dilute tremendously our national stock, and to corrupt our civic life . . . the problems of moral and sanitary conditions, honest and

decent government, and proper education have everywhere been made more difficult by their presence. Our task is to . . . implant in their children . . . the Anglo-Saxon conception of righteousness, law and order, and popular government, and to awaken in them a reverence for our democratic institutions.

(Cubberley, 1909, pp. 14–16)

Cubberley both reflected and fueled a widespread sentiment that immigrant parents were unwilling or incapable of providing the moral, religious, and civic education needed by children to become responsible members of American society. Cubberley (1909) argued, "If our schools are to become more effective social institutions our teachers must become more effective social workers" (p. 66).

The 1918 manual, *First Steps in Americanization*, impressed on Boston teachers the urgent nature of the "immigrant problem":

The presence in our country of such a large number of persons unable to speak the language of the country would constitute, even in times of peace, a problem of deep national interest . . . [the immigrant] becomes in wartime a threatening liability unless government action or patriotic initiative weld him into a splendid asset.

(Mahoney & Herlihy, 1918, pp. 2–3)

In this conceptualization of the immigrant as a national security threat, schools must not encourage ethnic pride, multiculturalism, or critical thinking for fear that such teaching would fuel dangerous anti-American sentiments.

Language and authority

Addressing the power structure in which language thrives or fails, Gallagher (1992) commented, "The acquisition and use of language are always conditioned in some degree by the social conditions and power relations in which they happen. Language, in effect, serves a larger master, a cultural and social system that tends to reproduce itself" (p. 242). We construct what we take to be "reality" through language, and the speech of the immigrant – muted as it may be by more dominant rhetoric – often testifies to a very different reality.

Discourse on immigration is fixated on the story of people *entering* the United States from other countries. There is little attention to the subjective experience of *emigration*. How might exiting be filled with hope, grief, and split loyalties and identities? What did migration mean for the family left behind and what resentments and regrets are there? In southern Italy, these stories are still very much alive. A mural in Piano Viale depicts the emotional departure of a young man leaving a young woman and his family behind; a monument stands in a tiny piazza in remembrance of people who left and then fought and died in a war conducted by their adopted country; second and third cousins eye each other trying to imagine the life they almost had. There are volumes of feelings and experiences that make their way imperceptibly but influentially into the lives of immigrants and the people and places they left.

"I know the day when America as a world entirely unlike Polotsk lodged in my brain, to become the center of all my dreams and speculations," remembered Mary Antin (1881–1949) (Antin, 1911/1969, p. 142). The pain and confusion of adjustment were clear in her book, *The Promised Land*:

> Chaos took the place of system; uncertainty, inconsistency under-mined discipline. My parents knew only that they desired us to be like American children . . . never doubting that the American way was the best way. In their bewilderment and uncertainty . . . they must step down from their throne of parental authority, and take the law from their children's mouths, for they had no other means of finding out what was good American form. This sad process of disintegration of home life may be observed in almost any immigrant family . . . it is part of the process of Americanization.
>
> (p. 271)

In Toni Morrison's (1993) searing and profound Nobel speech on language as both politically and personally defining, she speaks about language "as agency – as an act with consequences." She speaks about the way language can "surge toward knowledge" as well as "lock creative people into cages of inferiority and hopelessness" (pp. 13–18). Language is capital; it is power; and it is contested. What divides immigrant children and their parents is not only that they use different words but, also, that language profoundly changes identity, experience, and ways of interacting with others.

Chinese-American author, Amy Tan (1989), described in *Joy Luck Club* what is lost in the relationship between mothers and daughters, commenting on the fear of immigrant parents that the authority, meaning, and significance in their narratives of loss and hope will be entirely lost on their children and grandchildren. In a society that demands assimilation, children quickly learn to be impatient or embarrassed by "broken English" and their parents' awkward attempts at learning a new culture. Language, authority, and identity are tightly and insidiously intertwined. For immigrant parents, one of the most disturbing aspects of schooling is that language often creates a rupture in the family in which the children have more language capital than their parents. Parents are compelled to extinguish their authority to allow society, through the school, to interpret rules, norms, and ideals. Children learn implicitly who has authority and who does not.

Paternalism and seduction

Journalist-photographer Jacob Riis (1849–1914), himself an immigrant from Denmark, did a great deal to expose the health, housing, and working conditions of immigrant tenement-dwellers and to arouse a sentiment of sympathy and concern. However, these responses were often born out of paternalistic pity and without economic or cultural analysis of the causes and persistence of these conditions. Unlike the ignorant, immoral, predatory immigrants in Cubberley's writing, the immigrants that Riis (1892) described were more "quaint" than evil. Paternalistic representations portrayed immigrant people as helpless victims of their circumstances without psychological and intellectual complexity, and without the power, knowledge, and ambition to change their circumstances.

Immigrants to the US were generally seen as people in need of remediation. Civics texts taught that U.S. citizens believe in a benevolent, organized government, law and order, and the value of gender role differentiation in the home. For example, *Civics for Americans in the Making*, a widely used 1912 text for new immigrants, described the way work is divided in the American home: "The father works to buy food, clothing, and fuel for his family . . . the mother works in the home" (Plass, 1912, p. 3). This fantasy is accompanied by a drawing of a smiling woman and three young girls energetically making a bed, sweeping the floor, and dusting in an affluent home (Plass, 1912). Not only were these texts out of touch with immigrant lives, they were out of touch with the lives of the majority of American citizens. Along with concern about hygiene, anarchy, prostitution, and the dilution of Anglo-Saxon culture, there was worry that politically active, working women would threaten the gender role balance so important to the "American way of life."

The first lesson of a 1904 reading text for non-English-speaking children teaches students much more than how to get ready for school:

> The teacher asks, "What will you do to get ready for school tomorrow?"
> I shall get ready for school at eight o'clock.
> I *shall wash* myself.
> I *shall comb* my hair.
> Miss White will say that I am a *clean* boy.
> She likes the boys to come *early*.
> I do not wish to be *dirty*.
> I do not wish to be *late* for school.
> Is this a *neat* paper?
> Miss White says that it is a neat paper and that I am a neat boy.
>
> (Harrington & Moore, 1904; no page numbers; emphasis in the original)

Along with learning to read, the students in this class learned that their teacher, aptly named Miss White, would like them if they were clean and on time. It also taught the more subtle message that it is the *teacher's* authority to appropriate the qualities of "clean" and "neat" and that a boy who is "liked" by the teacher is a boy who wishes himself to be what the teacher wishes him to be. The teacher as social worker, who was herself an instrument of a paternalistic system in which she had little voice, was instructed to inculcate values of punctuality, cleanliness, respect for authority, and proper understanding of one's place in the social-economic caste (Dexter & Garlick, 1905, pp. 10–11).

But these transactions involved the fantasies of both the teacher *and* the student. Some children will want to create themselves in the image of the other by becoming all the teacher wishes him to be; some will respond with disdain for the authority of the school and, perhaps, drop out or be pushed out; some will wish to *be* the teacher and begin to deride other children for not being good enough; some will vow to create a new school ethic by becoming progressive school leaders, and so on.

Willy Apollon referred to the "masquerade of seduction" – the ruse of the ego to ask the imaginary other to be seen, heard, and recognized (May 2012, Yearly Training Seminar of *Groupe Interdisciplinaire Freudien de Recherche et d'Interventions Cliniques et Culturelle*). I learned very well as a child that the "bargain" of working-class immigrant families with society was this: "We will behave in a way that does not ask much and does not challenge your norms and customs in exchange for being allowed to live and work here." This compromise was reinforced over and over again at home, at school, at work, and in the community. In this construction of a person as the object of the other's pleasure, the goal is to "obtain love and protection from the other who can kill you," Danielle Bergeron said in her lecture (May 2012, GIFRIC Yearly Training Seminar). Caught between the other that can kill you and the other that can love you, the hope of seduction is that one can be pleasing to the other by never asking for too much and by accommodating the imagined and real demands of the other.

Appropriation and resistance

Acts of resistance work toward abandoning the appropriation of the other and the fantasy that seduction will succeed. In this section, I highlight three forms of resistance that emerge from different psychoanalytic and ethical standpoints, and the efforts to repress this resistance: first, a response ignited by critical consciousness and collective action in the form of a labor strike; then, the work of progressive-humanistic educators and social workers in the settlement house movement; and, finally, the insistent, solitary voice of a young immigrant woman staking a claim on her own life.

Critical consciousness: the "bread and roses" strike

A year after my grandparents came to Lawrence, Massachusetts, they participated in an historically significant textile strike. On January 12, 1912, thousands of workers shut down or damaged looms in the woolen mills and called for a strike, after receiving paychecks in which their hours were reduced from 56 to 54 hours a week, deducting needed pennies from their paychecks. The strike lasted three months and involved more than 20,000 immigrant people, from at least 30 nations, speaking 45 languages (Cahn, 1954/1980). The strikers were vilified but also received broad support from around the country and the world. Harvard College excused students from exams to serve with the militia against the strikers in Lawrence

(Cahn, 1954/1980, p. 174) but Professor Vida Dutton Scudder (1861–1954) of Wellesley College wrote, "I would rather never again wear a thread of woolen than know my garments had been woven at the cost of such misery" (Cahn, 1980, p. 194).

The 1912 strike is an extraordinary chapter in U.S. history for many reasons. People from dozens of ethnic, linguistic, and religious backgrounds left their isolated neighborhoods and organized for a successful outcome together. The strike empowered an increasingly relevant labor movement and propelled important changes in labor legislation. However, perhaps the greatest significance of the strike is that workers overcame systematic censorship of their lived experience. They overcame the physical and emotional exhaustion of subjugation. They surmounted their own fear that "biting the hand that feeds you" will only make matters worse, and the worry that ethnic prejudice would manipulate their call for justice and lead to further suspicion, discrimination, and hunger for their families.

However, this is also a story about silencing. In an attempt to raise fear and suspicion, a mill contractor and a member of the school board planted dynamite in a business on Oak Street just steps away from where my family lived (Cahn, 1980, p. 144). Strike organizer, Angelo Rocco, was from the same southern Italian community as my paternal grandfather. But my grandparents and parents never mentioned the strike. Nor did my teachers. I did not hear about the strike until I was in college. As an example of the way language can be used to define and control, the mill owners, assisted by the media, politicians, educators, clergy, and the legal system, discredited the strike and the strikers by creating a narrative that the strikers were manipulated by outside anarchists that did not care about the workers but used them toward their goal of creating a socialist system.

American Woolen Co. President, William Wood, appealed to strikers using the language of a protective father:

> Last Friday many of you left our mills and have since remained away. This action was wholly a surprise to me . . . you stated no grievance and made no demand . . . I have looked after your interests pretty well in the past. Why should I not have your confidence for the future? You are being advised by men who are not and never have been employees of this company . . . . They do not know the history of your relations as employees with this company . . . I, therefore, as the head of this

organization of which we are all members, appeal to you to return to your work and faithfully discharge your duties.

(The Evening Tribune, January 20, 1912)

The Strike Committee quickly responded:

You have had ample time to consider the demands of the men, women and children who have made what the American Woolen Co. what it is today. You speak of men who are from out of town and know nothing of the textile industry . . . . We would like to know if the militia, the special policemen and the Pinkerton detectives, recently brought into the city, know anything about the textile industry.

(Cahn, 1980, p. 141)

Progressive humanism: the settlement house movement as a subjective necessity

Jane Addams (1860–1935) and other key leaders of the settlement house movement created places in which immigrant people were seen as neither morally and intellectually inferior, nor as needy victims, but as complex people with cultural heritage, beliefs, values, and skills, capable of reflection and taking action on behalf of themselves and others. The challenges of education and social reform were analyzed in the context of broader economic, political, and cultural realities. They conceptualized adaptation as a reciprocal process, not a unilateral one in which the immigrant alone adjusts to a predetermined culture (Addams, 1912).

In her 1902 book, *Democracy and Social Ethics*, Addams warned about the damaging impact of capitalist interests in schools and communities: "It is possible that the business men whom we in America so tremendously admire, have really been dictating the curriculum of our public schools in an effort to insure a willing and inexpensive work force" (pp. 190–191). In the introduction to her 1922 book, *Peace and Bread in Time of War*, Addams wrote about the inevitable relationship between war and bread.

Feminist activist, social scientist, and educator Grace Abbott (1878–1939) rejected the notion of a singular American culture: "There are those who find that one of the greatest lessons of the war has been to demonstrate the need of 'molding' immigrants into true Americans as fast as possible.

But this cannot be accepted as an educational end either for children or for adults" (1917, p. 236). Instead, she argued, "The fundamental challenge of education for all Americans" is successfully adapting "our school system to meet the needs of the community" (1917, p. 223).

On every educational and social issue of the day, Addams and Abbott offered an analysis that contrasted sharply with mainstream social and educational analysis. Abbott urged that teachers must know the parents of their students and become familiar with immigrant communities. She warned about the dangerous reversal of family relationships when immigrant children are asked to guide their parents in understanding and adapting to their new country (1917, p. 227).

The visionary work at Hull House did more than respond to the outward, physical struggles of poverty; they addressed what Italian immigrant, Constantine Panunzio (1884–1964), called "the inner conflict, the soul struggles" of immigrant life – the desires, anxieties, hopes, and cultural disconnections (1921, p. xii).

The activism of women on behalf of immigrants came out of their awareness of their own inferior political and cultural status. They understood that their lives and the lives of the immigrants who came to the settlement houses were inextricably connected. Jane Addams (1892/1912) stated that her work on social reform was a "subjective necessity." While these early 20th-century women were dedicating their lives to improving educational, social, economic, and civic opportunities for immigrants, they were themselves restricted in all these areas.

The body, trauma, and the voice of desire

In writing, speaking, and photojournalism, the immigrant is represented as a body – a laborer, a prostitute, a person with poor hygiene, a wetback, a farmer etc. – and these representations are experienced subjectively in the body. The way bodies are viewed, felt, used, and controlled has far-reaching subjective and societal implications that are often not discussed. The body carries the trauma of oppression.

When girls such as Anzia Yesierska (1880–1970) arrived at school, they found that education for menial jobs was their only option. The work of their bodies was in high demand; their other ambitions were met with indifference or opposition. Teaching manuals and vocational schools for immigrant students prepared children of the lower classes for jobs as "common wage earners" and prepared children of the upper classes for "business life or the professions" (Seller, 1978). Yesierska's voice is filled with uncompromising indignation when she confronts these restrictions in an encounter with the benefactor of a school for immigrant girls, as recounted in her 1920 book, *Hungry Hearts*:

> "I'm crazy to learn!" I gasped breathlessly, and then the very pressure of the things I had to say choked me.
>
> An encouraging smile warmed the fine features. "What trade would you like to learn – sewing machine operating?"
>
> "Sewing machine operating?" I cried. "Oi weh!" I shuddered. "Only the thought 'machine' kills me. Even when I only look on clothes, it weeps in me when I think how the seams from everything people wear is sweated in the shop."
>
> Mrs. Olney stood abashed a moment. "Well, my dear," she said deliberately, "what would you like to take up?"
>
> "I got ideas how to make America better, only I don't know how to say it out. Ain't there a place I can learn?"
>
> A startled woman stared at me. For a moment not a word came. Then she proceeded with the same kind smile. "It's nice of you to want to help America, but I think the best way would be for you to learn a trade. That's what this school is for, to help girls find themselves, and the best way to do that is to learn something useful."
>
> "Ain't thoughts useful? Does America want only the work from my body, my hands? Ain't it thoughts that turn over the world?"
>
> "Ah! But we don't want to turn over the world," her voice cooed.
>
> "But there's got to be a change in America!" I cried. "Us immigrants want to be people – not 'hands' – not slaves of the belly! And it's the chance to think our thoughts that makes people . . . I came [to America] to give out all the fine things that was choked in me in Russia. I came to help America make the new world . . . . They said, in America I could open up my heart and fly free in the air – to sing – to dance – to live – to love . . . . Here I got all those grand things in me, and America won't let me give nothing."

"Perhaps you made a mistake in coming to this country. Your own land might appreciate you more." A quick glance took me in from head to foot. "I'm afraid that you have come to the wrong place. We only teach trades here."

(Yesierska, 1920)

Immigrant people want adequate jobs that provide for the health and happiness of their families. They want opportunities for cultural and intellectual stimulation. They want to be, as Yesierska so powerfully asserted, more than a body. And they want a say. Max Frisch famously quipped, "We asked for workers. We got people instead."

Ethical shift in practice

It is to the other that we address our hopes, fears, and expectations. All people and, perhaps, particularly those who have experienced exploitation and oppression, pay a hefty price for abating their needs with the hope of a reciprocal return on their sacrifice, miscalculating the possibility that their desire will be joined by the other. How do we therapists and school counselors act to encourage what Lacan calls "full speech," speech that is not constrained by societal and cultural ideals and that takes the side of the desiring subject? How do we hold a place for the inspiring stories of resistance while also making room to explore the contradictions – the part of being human that hates repression but also colludes with it? How can we work ethically to uncover the injustices that build the prisons we are forced to inhabit *and* to know something about the prisons we build for ourselves?

Some years ago I counseled a student when she was 14 and 15 years old. Her dad was not present and her mom worked hard to make ends meet. She was struggling with her Latina, working-class identity in a predominantly Caucasian, middle-class school. She tried to please her mother by getting excellent grades in school and taking care of her younger siblings. She said often that her most cherished aspiration was to get a good job and contribute to the household financially, even hoping to buy her family a house. She was determined and hard-working. I joined her in her fantasy, reinforcing cultural ideals, becoming another person whom she could please by speaking about her generous hope to take care of her family by subjugating her own desire. I reasoned that at least this aspiration of providing for her family might get her through high school and maybe motivate her to go to college. This wish on her part continued for some time but ended quite suddenly later in high school when she became completely estranged from her family and entered an abusive relationship.

I've now witnessed this sequence repeatedly. When our clients bring us problems with the other, it is essential for us to know where we ourselves stand in relation to cultural ideals, norms, and values, so that we can listen for the person's quest for freedom and desire. This is particularly relevant when working with people whose position in society is under attack and for whom pleasing the other is a matter of survival. When we are not aware of how our clients' stories resonate with our own values, experiences, and longings, and when we collude with someone to try to meet the demand of the other, missing that tiny, unsure voice trying to speak his or her own truth, we are inevitably heading for trouble.

Having grown up in a collectivist-oriented family and neighborhood, my ears were tuned to a single story – the story of a young girl's admirable concern for her family. I heard and valued what was familiar: a story of gratification in seeing herself as useful to her mom and siblings, a cultural story of responsibility and sacrifice. But there is also a story of an adolescent girl responding to the demands of family and culture, seeking to figure out, and then fill, the desire of the other. There is a story of an obligation that is too heavy for a child to carry, resulting in resentment and rage, a story of impossibly filling the role of an absent father, a story of sacrifice of self for the good of the family or community. These multiply layered narratives are shaped, told, and heard differently depending on the situatedness of each person in the counseling dyad.

Multicultural counseling and cultural competence literature offers a useful perspective and skill set for working effectively and ethically across cultures. It is important to be able to recognize the variable emphasis on collectivity, individuality, authority, democracy, and so on. However, multicultural counseling can paradoxically encapsulate people within a culture and risks holding them there. I worry that the individual goes missing when multiculturalism becomes ideology. Almost always, people come to us hoping we might offer something different, but they are also afraid we might offer something different. We might offer the somewhat frightening possibility of a different relationship to the other that might catalyze a new way of living.

According to the Pew Research Center analysis of Census Bureau data, the 2014–15 school year was expected to be the first time "minority" children would be the majority in public schools in the US. Counselors must learn to listen deeply for that tiny, uncertain, fledgling voice of desire – the words that immigrant children choke on and cannot "say out," as Anzia Yesierska said so beautifully. A lot of counseling with low-income and immigrant adolescents is a linear, practical process: identify interests and strengths, set specific goals, take the right courses, identify and remove financial and logistical barriers, take SATs early, learn skills to get a job, know how to present yourself on college applications, and so on. These are important tasks and I do not mean to dismiss them; I spend dozens of hours every year doing this kind of work. However, what gets sidelined in the process, what I have realized is missing in the lives of many adolescents, is an opportunity for introspection, an uncensored space that welcomes challenges to the established curriculum. Even in schools, we can make room for the unconscious by paying attention to things like missing or "forgetting" deadlines, sickness and symptoms, speaking in platitudes, contradictions, etc. We can say, for example, "You've missed our last couple of meeting times. Let's talk about the part of you that perhaps does not want to go to college." Or, "You forgot to go home after school to take care of your younger brother and sister while your mom worked late. Is there something that this act of forgetting is saying that you have not said out loud?"

The ethical shift is this: we must focus on examining barriers, not only on removing them; we must support passion and desire, not only employability; we must encourage liberation, not only adjustment; and we must listen, not only guide. I believe we cannot truly have a worthwhile and sustainable sense of responsibility to a collective unless we have a full sense of our singularity. Likewise, we cannot be ethically autonomous without a sense of how our lives contribute to, or rob from, the collective. In overcoming the contradict of Levinas and Lacan, I see the possibility of loosening opposing perspectives of "the other," one expressed by Lacan as the imaginary other, whose perceived demand propels us toward an unethical disregard for our own freedom and desire, and the second perspective by Levinas, whose "ethics is an ethics of an inescapable responsibility for the other" (Harasym, 1998, p. ix). We need to find ways to sustain work at the intersection of faith *and* suspicion, conformity *and* resistance, the collective *and* the individual, cultural traditions *and* challenges to those traditions.

Note

1 Details of identity are changed throughout this chapter to protect the confidentiality of research participants and clients.

References

Abbott, G. (1917). *The immigrant and the community.* New York: The Century Company.

Addams, J. (1902/1964). *Democracy and social ethics.* Cambridge, MA: The Belknap Press of Harvard University.

Addams, J. (1912). Subjective necessity for social settlements (c. 1910). *Twenty years at Hull House.* New York: Macmillan Co. (First delivered as a lecture in 1892.)

Addams, J. (1922). *Peace and bread in time of war.* New York: McMillan Co.

Antin, M. (1969). *The promised land.* Boston, MA: Houghton-Mifflin Co. (Originally published in 1911 by Atlantic Monthly Company.)

Apollon, W. (2012, May). *Training seminar lectures.* L'Ecole Freudienne du Québec.

Apollon, W., Bergeron, D., & Cantin, L. (2002). *After Lacan: Clinical practice and the subject of the unconscious.* Albany, NY: State University of New York Press.

Bergeron, D. (2012, May). *Training seminar lectures.* L'Ecole Freudienne du Québec.

Cahn, W. (1980). *Lawrence 1912: The bread and roses strike.* New York: The Pilgrim Press. (Originally published as *Mill Town* 1954. University of California, Berkeley: Cameron & Kahn.)

Cubberley, E. (1909). *Changing conceptions of education.* Cambridge, MA: Riverside Press.

Dexter, T. F. G. & Garlick, A. H. (1905). *A primer of school method.* New York: Longmans, Green, and Co.

Frisch, M. (2013, November 17). Retrieved from www.goodreads.com/quotes/31843-we-asked-for-workers-we-got-people-instead (Accessed 2.24.16).

Gallagher, S. (1992). *Hermeneutics and education.* Albany, NY: State University of New York Press.

Gay, P. (1988). *Freud: A life for our time.* New York: W. W. Norton & Co.

Harasym, S. (Ed.). (1998). *Levinas and Lacan: The missed encounter.* Albany, NY: State University of New York Press.

Harrington, W. L. & Moore, A. C. (1904). *A second book for non-English speaking people.* Boston, MA: D.C. Health and Co. (Pages not numbered. Emphasis in original text.)

Hirsch, E. D. (1987). *Cultural literacy: What every American needs to know.* New York: Houghton-Mifflin Co.

Lacan, J. (1978). *Seminar XI: The four fundamental concepts of psychoanalysis.* London: W. W. Norton and Co.

Lessing, D. (1987). *Prisons we choose to live inside.* New York: HarperCollins.

Mahoney, J. & Herlihy, C. (1918). *First steps in Americanization: A handbook for teachers.* Boston, MA: Houghton-Mifflin Co.

Morrison, T. (1993). *Lecture and speech of acceptance upon the award for Nobel Prize for Literature, delivered in Stockholm on the seventh of December, nineteen hundred and ninety-three.* New York: Alfred A. Knopf.

Panunzio, C. (1921). *The soul of an immigrant.* New York: MacMillan.

Peperzak, A. (1993). *To the other: An introduction to the philosophy of Emmanuel Levinas.* West Lafayette, IN: Purdue University Press.

Pew Research Center. (2014, August 18). *Department of education predicts public schools will be "majority-minority" this fall.* Available at: www.pewresearch.org/fact-tank/2014/08/18/u-s-public-schools-expected-to-be-majority-minority-starting-this-fall/ (Accessed 1.2.15).

Plass, A. A. (1912). *Civics for Americans in the making.* Boston, MA: D.C. Health and Co.

Ricoeur, P. (1981). *Hermeneutics and the human sciences.* (J. B. Thompson, Ed. & Trans.) Cambridge, MA: Cambridge University Press.

Riis, J. (1892). *The children of the poor.* New York: Charles Scribner's Sons.

Risser, J. (1997). *Hermeneutics and the voice of the other.* Albany, NY: SUNY Press.

Seller, M. (1978, May). The education of the immigrant woman, 1900–1935. *Journal of Urban History, 4*(3).

Sturken, M. & Cartwright, L. (2009). *Practices of looking: An introduction to visual culture.* Oxford: Oxford University Press.

Tan, A. (1989). *Joy luck club.* New York: Penguin Group. *The Evening Tribune* (1912). Retrieved from www.marxists.org/history/usa/unions/lawrence-strike/index .htm (Accessed 12.7.13).

Waters, M. C. (1990). *Ethnic options: Choosing identity in America.* Berkeley, CA: University of California Press.

Yesierska, A. (1920). How I found America. *Hungry hearts.* Cambridge, MA: Houghton-Mifflin Co. Retrieved from http://digital.library.upenn.edu/women/yezierska/hearts/ hearts.html (Pages not numbered) (Accessed 11.17.13).

Chapter 17

Creativity and hospitality

Negotiating who or what is known in psychoanalytic psychotherapy

Brian Smothers

What are we to do when the other standing before us wishes to become known, yet the act of being known reminds her of traumatic intrusion? For such patients, being known represents a paradox, as each encounter with another person is full of both exciting and horrifying potentialities. How are clinicians to remain at a level of evenly suspended attention without either invalidating the patient with our knowing or remaining so disconnected that we feel unknowable? Starting with enactments as a point of inquiry, this chapter aims to explore a model requiring evenly suspended attention between seemingly dichotomous polarities: knowing and unknowing. Case material will be used to illustrate an application of clinical hermeneutics that seeks to remain at tension, without foreclosing prematurely in either direction. Such a model of being in-between two positions requires an ability to play and create without becoming disorganized by uncertainty. A clinical stance of hospitality can provide relative theoretical and technical grounding amid the apparent groundlessness of what is occurring. Gadamer (1960/1989) suggests that hermeneutics is based on polarity, in his words, a "polarity of familiarity and strangeness . . . the true locus of hermeneutics is this in-between" (p. 295). For Gadamer, hermeneutic work resides in a place of in-between-ness, a space that is always in the process of becoming and becoming again (Laing, 2012). The concept of in-between-ness resonates deeply with Winnicott's ideas regarding transitional space, and the creative playing that restores one's sense of going on being (Winnicott, 1960, 1971). It is therefore appropriate to consider both play and creativity as occurring in this in-between-ness, moving within the medians of the known and the unknown, and serving as a technical guidepost for clinicians in moments of uncertainty (Laing, 2012). While this space of in-between-ness is ripe with new possibilities, it is also a space of uncertainty that can quickly cause one to relinquish emerging possibilities, collapsing moments of creativity into restricted knowing. Despite this conflicting tension, a stance of hospitality (Derrida & Dufourmantelle, 2000; Kearney, 2003) to the emerging moments within psychotherapy may restore a sense of creativity within both participants.

In psychotherapy, often such moments of in-between-ness are situated within enactments, when the patient's and therapist's histories and sensitivities are comingled. In a 2006 paper, Jessica Benjamin, owing to Winnicott (1971), suggested that enactments are essentially known by the presence of the unknowable. She states:

> The patient needs to come up against her actual otherness to explore new ways of being. The therapist also moves between periods of knowing and not knowing his or her own otherness, while moving between similar positions of knowing and not knowing the client.
>
> (p. 377)

In the moment of enactment, the therapist loses perspective, and finds herself feeling less free to move between her own story and her client's, bound to be trapped within time, as if this way of being together will remain forever. Such moments collapse in-between-ness, the sense of shared possibility and potential, essentially draining the moment of new and novel possibilities found within play and creativity (Ruti, 2011). From my perspective, these moments of collapse all too often revolve around issues of certainty and blame.

For a greater understanding of the collapse of in-between-ness that occurs within an enactment it is important to examine the collapse in openness involved in traumatic impingements (Winnicott, 1958, 1960). While definitively not equating the two situations, there is an essential quality of familiarity within both situations. One potential outcome of trauma is the ossification of self and self-boundaries, a collapse in creative playing with identity, agency, and knowing (Slavin & Pollock, 1997). Similarly, enactments often call upon the participants to surrender their sense of certainty, essentially allowing what is known to become again unknown, or, at least, up for reinterpretation. The subject allows, through the giving over through surrender, novel moments of thought and being to be again covered, uncovered, and discovered (Ghent, 1990).

Enactments at the threshold

The term "enactment" has entered the psychoanalytic lexicon with such force and omnipresence that clear definitions are flecting and perhaps overly reductionist. Jacobs (1986) suggested that an enactment, or reenactment, involved the meeting of desires and behaviors on the part of the therapist and patient that are elicited by the ongoing relational closeness of the work together, but are related to the individuals' past conflicts. More recently, enactment has been defined by Maroda (1998) as:

> an affectively driven repetition of converging emotional scenarios from the patient's and the analyst's lives . . . not merely an affectively driven set of behaviors, it is necessarily a repetition of past events that have been buried in the unconscious due to associated unmanageable or unwanted emotion.
>
> (p. 520)

Recent movements within relational and intersubjective psychoanalysis have valorized the process of enactment as a reified relational technique that distinguishes the relational model from less participatory ones (Jacobs, 1986; Nahum, 2005). While the concept of enactment remains varied across differing schools of analytic practice, there is general agreement as to the inevitability of its occurrence (Chused, 2003; Maroda, 1998).

For the purposes of this chapter, I do not seek to define an enactment. Instead, I aim to describe some of the phenomenological aspects of the encounter relevant to what I believe it requires of the therapist. Enactments are threshold moments, moments of in-between-ness. Enactments in the clinical encounter are known by the presence of polarized events represented by the meeting of two distinct minds with their distinct demands; these demands are often experienced subjectively as a sense of restriction. In an enactment, the therapist may feel unable to occupy her normal therapeutic role; her ability to feel free to play and create may feel restricted by the demands and desires arising in the clinical moment. Enactments contain both regressive and progressive possibilities. Due to the closeness of the encounter, there is the invitation to regress into old conflicted ways of being, yet there is also the possibility to create novel ways of being together not reliant on harmful conflict-laden configurations. This inherent tension between progression and regression has likely influenced the technical and theoretical divergence around the concept, leading some analysts to refrain from pursuing enactments and others to approach them (Chused, 2003; Nahum, 2005).

Within an enactment, both participants stand attentively in waiting within the liminal space of the threshold, the space between inner and outer, doer and done to (Benjamin, 2004; Kearney & Semonovitch, 2011). What can be said about these threshold moments? Perhaps they call for and await a response, and the other in front of us awaits our response before committing to hers. They are moments of in-between-ness, neither in nor out, guest nor host, hospitable nor hostile (Kearney, 2003). They may be what Winnicott (1971) referred to as transitional moments, or even allude to Freud's (1912/1958a) evenly hovering at tension. Returning to the works of Jessica Benjamin, she notes (2009) that in contemporary relational thinking, an important marker of repairing the analytic space that has been closed within an enactment "is being restored to the capacity to hear multiple voices" (p. 442). To her astute assessment, I would add that such a re-opening restores one's in-between-ness, neither all-in nor all-out, but evenly suspended between a multiplicity of possibilities, reminiscent of Winnicott's restored capacities (1965a, 1958). The space between the foreclosures at the poles found within an enactment is ripe with possibility, creativity, and ingenuity, a place where imagination is free to play and be played. These moments require hesitation, discernment, and creativity from both therapist and patient. Enactments beckon us to hesitate before prematurely committing to a stance of either knowing or not knowing. They invite a collaborative discernment with the other regarding what is known and, through this way of being, create something new. While these moments may seem ungrounded, the transitional moment, which Bromberg (2003) states is more akin to dream than reality, "permits the coexistence of opposites" (p. 570). The grounding in-between is no less real. In fact, according to Winnicott (1965a, 1971), it may be more real.

From my clinical experience, there are two essential features relative to the in-between-ness of an enactment: initiation and identity. It is my assertion that these two features overlap with similar ruptures to those found in instances of traumatic impingements. Through case material, I will describe how the collapse caused by these two issues surrounding initiation and identity may hinder the creativity required within the therapeutic process.

Initiation

The issue of initiation, or "who started it," within an enactment is a matter of uncertainty, situated in rather unstable and shifting arrangements (Kearney & Semonovitch, 2011; Maroda, 1998). The source of an enactment is a matter shrouded in conflict and finger-pointing. Even in those instances when the matter of who started it is clear, there may be private uncertainty about its source that is steeped in conflict (Davies, 2004). Despite this ambiguity regarding initiation, the issue of cause is always present within our minds during an enactment. By attempting to exclusively place the blame within the self or the other, the tension of the enactment presses forward, collapsing other possibilities and avoiding the acceptance of the in-between-ness of not knowing. While I am certainly not suggesting that each individual shares equal ownership of responsibility, I am suggesting that the issue of initiation invades our thoughts, holding them hostage. The mental restriction occurring within an enactment results in constriction within our judgment and analytic functions. Through the preoccupation with blame, the essential in-between-ness that opens our mind to novel ways of being within the enactment collapses. It is precisely these matters of who initiated what during an enactment that saturate our private thoughts, and have implications for our sense of identity and role. What does it mean about me if I started this conflict? What does it say about my therapeutic identity?

Identity

One of the clearest indicators that I am caught up in an enactment occurs around issues of my identity. This happens when the therapist I want to be feels somehow out of reach or held hostage by the demands of the situation. While this issue is certainly connected to matters of blame, it is likely experienced through both internal and external conflict between roles and identifications. In therapy, the therapist's identity is usually associated with aspects of the therapist's role or function (Rifkin, 2013). Often in an enactment, our private desires and urges clash with our desired role of being the good therapist, or the good object (Davies, 2004). The arising self-criticism and shame that can accompany such moments very often keep us silent and in private turmoil, feeling as if our current thoughts, impulses, and reactions are incongruent with our better therapeutic selves. Such experiences of incongruence very often lead to self-blame and shame, experiences that may keep us caught up in our own inner responses to the moment while not taking a more process-reflective approach (Aron, 2003). Being experienced so concretely as the one responsible for the current predicament may threaten our therapeutic identity even in the most seasoned analyst. For young clinicians, such incongruent experiences might easily threaten their developing identities.

Issues of identity and initiation are, in essence, situated somewhere between the realms of the intrapsychic and the interpersonal, always creating mutually influencing loops of reference. Neither all inner, nor all outer, but somewhere in the middle, the matters of identity and initiation quickly become complicated in the minds of participants caught up in an enactment. The forces at play within an enactment can too quickly push each participant to arrive at a certain answer to the questions of initiation and identity. For a point of reference and clarification, I turn now to examine similar processes involved in traumatic intrusions. While not equating the gravity of the two concepts, I will suggest that there is an air of familiarity across the constructs that results in a collapse in the creativity required to live reflexively. In response, a clinical stance of hospitality can serve to restore what has been lost.

Traumatic intrusion

What is enacted in experiences of traumatic impingement? If enactment involves a collision of desires and possibilities, traumatic impingement might bear phenomenological kinship to an enactment without the aspect of hope. In my clinical experience, there is a commonality among many trauma survivors' injuries to their sense of self: these injuries are within the domains of initiation and identity. It should be noted that I am not discussing only moments of actual aggression to another, but also recurring impingement and deprivation experienced within the caregiving environment. Early psychological trauma can be experienced as an existential disruption to the child's developing self (Kohut, 1971; Winnicott, 1965a). This disruption impacts his or her views of self, others, and society at large. Two such ruptures to the trauma survivor's self-representation revolve around issues of initiation and identity.

Initiation

While to outside observers and witnesses, the matter of initiation of trauma is quite clear, those in the midst of the emotional turmoil delivered at the hands of the other are often confused by initiation. The psycho-analytic literature has had much to offer in this regard and has aided our understanding of the dynamics at play regarding self-blame. Two of the more relevant ideas that have addressed this can be found in the works of Fairbairn (1943) and Anna Freud (1936). Anna Freud discussed the ego's use of the defense of identification to provide a sense of mastery in situations where the subject is stripped of agency. Her work was an early attempt to deal with issues of self-blame and confusion about initiation. Within this conceptualization, one can see that the trauma survivor, in a time of intense anxiety and forced objectification, might identify with the aggressor or initiator of the aggression to provide a sense of mastery. The memory traces of this identification live on through narrative means of constructing the stories of self and other, victim and abuser, and so forth (Davies & Frawley, 1994).

Fairbairn (1943) also mentioned the individual's ability through the splitting of the ego to internalize the bad object as if it resided within oneself, making it seem as if matters of badness originated within the vic-tim rather than outside. While, according to Fairbairn, this internalization opens individuals to the possibility of redemption and the preservation of hope, it also places a considerable burden upon their psyche through the private preoccupation with thoughts that might lead them to assume responsibility for the horrors that have befallen them. Both of these theo-retical concepts suggest to me that issues of blame, initiation, and cause are of extreme importance to the trauma survivor, and my clinical experi-ence with many survivors of sexual trauma has confirmed this belief. I am reminded of a six-year-old girl who had been horribly subjected to child pornography and believed that she had caused the abuse because she so desperately wanted her picture taken. She reported in one of our sessions that she had never had her picture taken by anyone, and that she felt so special having someone want to take her photograph.

Identity

Another rupture to the individual's ongoing self-structures caused by trau-matic intrusion resides within the area of identity (Gobodo-Madikizela, 2003). Trauma collapses the individual's adaptive capacity to negotiate one's sense of self through taking in aspects of others (Slavin & Kriegman, 1998). Because the initial transgression against the subject robbed him of his sense of subjectivity, agency and autonomy, the subject inevitably wrestles with issues of blame and initiation, as well as how these concerns will shape whom he is becoming. Countless young male survivors of sexual abuse have stated to me that they were frightened about the impact of the sexual assault on their sexual orientation, as if being aggressed upon from the outside would rob them of the ability to discover their own sexual identity for themselves. They feared that this act would make them become something outside of their control.

Due to the traumatic intrusion of the other, many survivors of trauma may need to control relational closeness, to titrate the level of relational vulnerability felt at any moment (Bromberg, 2003; Slavin & Pollock, 1997). Vulnerability to the other requires a loosening of control and an openness to experience without knowing the outcome. Following the traumatic inclusion of the victimizing other, the individual closes borders to most others and becomes deprived of the permeability and flexibility – the in-between-ness – required to live reflexively in a world that often requires shifting identities and roles. The ability to take in the other and allow moments of creative un-integration, when one's self can be found and affirmed, is ruptured through the traumatic introduction of the other's desires in the traumatic scene (Ruti, 2011; Winnicott, 1971).

One outcome of trauma is the calcification of identity and self-boundaries (Davies & Frawley, 1994). To regain a sense of control in a world experienced as chaotic, and to provide a stable sense of oneself through the construction of an identity, the subject must quickly negotiate how much she will be influenced by the outside world. In my experience, the decision is one of all or nothing (Slavin & Kriegman, 1998). The constructed identity is experienced as an effigy that must by all means remain intact and unchallenged. It is as if the subject says to the world, "this is who I am," while privately hiding the scars that this public identity conceals from themselves and the world, the questions they are afraid to entertain. The self-representation is rigid, yet brittle. While this is an adaptive act of self-assertion, the public identity can become increasingly traumatic. As the world will begin to adopt the persona/identity of the individual, the subject will foreclose on the possibility that he can be anyone else, depriving him of ongoing creative efforts at adaptation. The individual may feel confined by his public identity, especially when analytic inquiry opens and reignites his movement toward greater self-discovery.

Clinical example

In his commentary on the Scherber case, Freud (1911/1958b) referred to trauma as a "world catastrophe" (p. 69). The subject is overtaken by the desires of the other. The subject feels overridden and re-written, her desires are (con)fused and re-situated into a story that was largely not authored by her. The situation results in confusion and fusion of desire and identity with the aggressing objects. In the case that follows, issues of identity and initiation that were ruptured early in my patient's life became central to the ongoing work of treatment and helping her to free herself from these painful feelings.

Naomi is a 23-year-old, Asian American female. At the time of our therapy, she was beginning a degree in philosophy. She is the oldest of three daughters born to an intact family. Both of her parents are evangelical Christian ministers, often involved in building new churches in Asian countries. Naomi is ethnically Vietnamese, though since her family moved frequently throughout her life, she feels as if her identity is more of a product of her many transitions rather than her place of origin. When she was 14 years old, Naomi developed difficulties with attention and concentration. She was subsequently diagnosed with Attention Deficit Hyperactivity Disorder (ADHD) and was treated with varying medications and behavioral interventions.

Naomi originally sought therapy for help with the symptoms of ADHD and for adjustment-related concerns. She felt alone and isolated, and reported periods of mental confusion, attention and concentration difficulties, and persistent feelings of lethargy. Speaking with rapid sentences and loosely connected fragments of thoughts, she reported that she was prone to procrastination and forgetfulness. Therapy, she hoped, would address underlying beliefs and feelings that might be contributing to her current experience of being stuck and having a deep sense of dissatisfaction from life. Naomi stated that she felt chronically misunderstood and isolated. She reported a series of conflicted relationships and long-standing experiences of discrimination and marginalization, especially in her close relationships. Near the close of our first session, Naomi reported feeling very "scattered" and "shut off," and presented as frustrated and hyperactive. She spoke rapidly, often with tangential associations. Her speech was appropriate and clear, and her thoughts were non-delusional, but she was nevertheless difficult to follow.

As I explored her history, I began to get a sense of the ways in which Naomi's identity had been constructed through assimilating many disconnected fragments of others' desires for her. Naomi was born in Canada and lived there until she was six years old. At this point, the family relocated to Vietnam, the first of many subsequent relocations. Growing up, Naomi never lived in one place for more than two years.

Naomi's father was an energetic and charismatic leader, and a strict, rule-bound man. His personal charm attracted many followers, yet his public persona was remarkably different from his private life with the family. Naomi's father also had a temper that often escalated to physical assault. She reported one incident that occurred soon after the family's move to Vietnam. Naomi had gotten into trouble at school. After receiving several lashes at school, she was sent home to her father's assault. Naomi remembered falling to the ground, while her father remained on top of her continuing to hit her and to verbally belittle her. As this show of force continued, Naomi recalled that her mother and younger sister watched in horror, but did little to intervene. Naomi's mother has been described as passive and permissive, allowing her husband to dominate much of their family life. Her references to her mother are best described as impoverished and shallow. She believes that her mother was depressed for most of Naomi's childhood, and lived in the shadow of her husband.

Naomi always arrived to session with an overwhelming number of associations and ideas to explore. I routinely felt both excited and left out of her stream of associations, as they were both tantalizing and restricting. My awareness of this dynamic only developed over time, however. As our work progressed, Naomi slowly began to explore her fears of transitions, especially in regard to how her family's many relocations contributed to her feelings of alienation. As our exploration of this dynamic progressed, the "uprooting" she experienced with her family became noticeable. I began to privately wonder how her stream of associations might be contributing to a similar feeling of alienation in our work, especially as I began to become more aware of my own moments of uprooted-ness within our time together. My confusion during her associations became somewhat disorienting for me. This might have been the beginning of an enactment, as I worked harder and harder to understand her, hiding my private feelings about not being able to understand her.

Issues of identity had become traumatic for Naomi. She routinely felt as if she were a stranger in her surroundings. During her early years in

Canada, she recalled being one of the few children of Asian descent in her religious community. In the various communities in Vietnam, she felt that she was perceived as an outsider, despite the fact that her parents were Vietnamese. In what might be seen as her homeland, she was thought to be too Westernized. In the West, she felt that she was too Eastern and exotic. This sense of strangeness resulted in profound feelings of dislocation, and longing for recognition and merger. Naomi deeply desired to fit in with those around her, although throughout all of her transitions her differences seemed to betray her, marking her as a stranger. Much of Naomi's struggle was between competing desires to assimilate and to be recognized as unique and special, to fit in for the sake of survival while also creating a sense of private and certain knowledge of herself that continued across time and location. Her survival skills were remarkably adaptive. At home, she learned to anticipate her father's moods and quickly changed her behavior to avoid his assaults. She learned to be demure and non-questioning of his authority. In school, she described herself as a "social sponge," quickly absorbing the social trends and preferences of her peer group to reduce the likelihood that her differences would be noticed and exploited.

This trend continued through the transition from her family to college. In college, Naomi gravitated to energetic spiritual leaders and social crusaders. She often surrounded herself with charismatic people who had strong opinions about whom she should be. Their sense of knowing and naming her was captivating and touched upon her longing for recognition. Alongside these strong merger needs, she was slowly becoming aware of an unarticulated sense of lacking direction in her life. She would routinely defer to another's authority and desire for her. During this period of our work, she would often blame herself for this predicament, that her lack of self-direction brought such distress upon her. As our sessions became more overtly related to her experiences of being the recipient of the others' desire/demand, I began to invite some exploration of the ways that she might experience the therapeutic relationship as possibly imposing. The more that my interventions took a relational, process-centered focus, I noticed that she would become more disorganized. Her speech would become more tangential and difficult for me to grasp.

As our work began to deepen, and Naomi's desire began to become disentangled from the desire and demands of others, she began to uncover feelings of being objectified regardless of her attempts at self-definition. During this phase, she would often comment on how she felt sickened by others' "constructed image of [her]," yet she would continue to move toward them despite her emotional alarm system. During one of these sessions, Naomi said something that struck me as both strange and certain, a statement that I would often turn over in my mind. She said that she is "afraid of the minds of others." Much of her life had been determined by the minds and decisions of others, by minds that were beyond her control and participation, depriving her of a sense of agency and recognition. She feared not having control over the thoughts and impressions of others. At the insistence of others, she had moved multiple times, her attachments had become temporary, time had become a luxury she was not afforded, and she had become dislocated from her sense of self.

A creative hermeneutic

The therapist's endeavor is one of creative suspension of knowing to access novel possibilities hidden from our mind when we are restricted by our own sense of certainty. Our task is to keep a sense of hospitable in-between-ness alive and open amid experiences of restriction. Mari Ruti (2011) suggests that this creative approach invites therapists "to surrender [their] habitual psychic boundaries so as to allow nonhabitual modes of thought and being to emerge; in this sense, it is only by relinquishing the ordinary that the extraordinary can be discovered" (p. 366). Such an approach calls for more than technique, but a therapeutic stance, and I believe, a stance informed by an ethic of hospitality (Derrida & Dufourmantelle, 2000; Kearney, 2003; Levinas, 1969).

An ethic of hospitality to the unknown calls for a freedom to play with possibilities, a regression in the service of the other (Kris, 1936; Olinick, 1969). A stance of hospitality to emerging possibilities might serve a restorative function, allowing both participants to entertain new and more adaptive ways of being with themselves and with others. Returning to Gadamer (1960/1989), one might consider that his understanding of play alludes to the restorative function of hospitality. Gadamer's notion of play frees the subjects from their role of either initiator or respondent, allowing the two players to be lost within the play, emerging within iterations of "to" and "fro," bouncing within and between positions of actor and acted upon (Laing, 2012). This ungrounded, standing in-between poles is essential to Gadamer's (1960/1989) understanding of play as back and forth, "to and fro motion" (p. 104), where play occurs in the movements between the poles not through achieving or having achieved either pole itself

(Gadamer, 1989; Laing, 2012). Play resists foreclosure and certainty. The creativity required in moments of play is less of an activity that someone performs, and more of a movement with emerging intentions. Only when losing oneself within the play is play achieved (Laing, 2012; Winnicott, 1971). Thus, a stance of hospitality suggests giving oneself over to the possibility of love, hate, and play within the bounded-ness of ethical practice. In his writing, the philosopher Richard Kearney (2003), following Paul Ricoeur (1970), suggests that a position of hospitality to emerging possibilities enables one to come into contact with basic insights into the human condition without foreclosing into certainty. Hospitality, thus, acts as a therapeutic ethos or way of approaching an openness to others and the clinical moment ripe with possibility, unpredictability, and uncertainty, without reducing these events to the same, the known.

The therapist must sustain an internal position of creative hospitality to unknowing and its accompanying vulnerability, especially to those times of confusion and uncertainty, when not knowing provides relatively more grounding than knowing (MacKendrick, 2011). The hospitality to the unknown allows for moments of spontaneous creation, where the meeting of minds is not felt as violent knowing but as welcoming and waiting for the moment to gradually take shape and become reshaped. The regression in service of the other (Olinick, 1969) found within a hospitable stance harkens back to Winnicott's thoughts about a period of primary maternal preoccupation (Winnicott, 1965b), which allows the mother to prepare a space within her own mind for another to inhabit. The parent – or therapist – allows for moments of regression away from their own certainties of experience and being so that an openness for the creation of the other is made possible. Through the process of giving over she creates the space necessary to allow the child to maintain his place in the process of becoming. Returning to the clinical material will demonstrate a stance of hospitality to the unknown and emerging possibilities.

As previously disowned aspects of Naomi's desire began to emerge, I began to allow myself to notice the increasing sense of disconnection from her and from my experience in the room. Her words began feeling more hollow and difficult to follow and I found myself routinely asking for more information or trying to clarify my understanding of her content. On the surface, each association seemed fairly straightforward, yet when strung together they took on the appearance of a collage with infinite linkages. As I grew more uncomfortable with the lack of knowing, my sense of competence as a therapist began to falter. I desperately wanted to understand her, to be the one who might hear her voice, yet the more I tried the more confused I felt and the more frustrated she became. Was my curiosity causing me greater confusion, or was she simply distancing herself from me? As I became more aware of emerging aspects of my experience, I began to disclose how I often felt confused and alone during the early moments of our session. As previously mentioned, Naomi often began the session with a fifteen to twenty-minute bombardment of meaningful events and insights during the time since our last meeting. Much more than a laundry list of details, each statement could be potentially explored until a deeper degree of shared understanding could be found. In session, as I am becoming aware of my growing curiosity into the content of her speech, she has already moved on, leaving me lost in the transition. Using the metaphor of a mosaic, I suggested to her that each piece of her story was rich on its own and while we could probably spend a good deal of time talking about those ideas, it seems as if we both have to move on quickly before we can get an understanding of how this special piece might fit into a larger picture.

She looked at me somewhat surprised and confused and said, "Well, we have fifty minutes so you'll just have to try to keep up." Feeling as if she were reproducing an early experience of herself within my current experience of her in the room, I pointed out how time had been a luxury for her growing up, but that understanding and deeper connections may take time, time that she never felt that she has had. She responded quickly, "I don't want you to understand me." She went on discussing how she was feeling tired and stressed by her relationships, adding that therapy is a burden at times. She noted that my attempts to understand her cause her further distress. At that moment it seemed certain that I was the one doing this to her. After inviting Naomi to explore how my attempts to understand her are experienced, I became aware of a loss of freedom, a strange awareness of my inner stuck-ness in this dialectic. My feelings of blame and shame at not understanding began to trap my creative flexibility. Naomi deeply desired to be understood, but my attempts to understand caused her to feel distressed, even possessed, objectified by my knowing. While the care that I had for her moved me to understand this dilemma, my attempts at understanding further injured. I felt locked and unusually alienated from the better parts of my therapeutic self.

Following this moment, I began to actively experiment with being hospitable to moments of not knowing without seeking the foreclosure that can accompany understanding. These moments freed me from my own experiences of shame and blame for not being able to understand what was emerging. Through our shared moments of play with uncertainty we were able to create a new awareness of the adaptive quality of Naomi's speech and interpersonal behaviors. We came to see that the exciting energy of her speech and the contents of her communication were likely very attractive to others, myself included. Naomi's ideas were very complex and compelling, just the sort of ideas that most therapists and interested individuals of a creative sort would find enticing. Her approach to interaction drew individuals in while also keeping them at a distance. The disconnection of her ideas served to protect her from being possessed by the knowledge of the other who always sought to know her and define her identity but was never allowed complete entrance. The disconnection protected more fragile aspects of her identity, and while this had been adaptive, it had also kept her from being understood in less possessive ways, where moments of mutual recognition could serve to reinforce her fragile identity.

Following this playful phase of our work, she came to session with a dream of watching herself standing at a bus depot. In the dream she knew that her family and friends were on the bus, pleading and begging, in fact instructing, her to board. Somewhat confused, but empowered, Naomi would decline their offers by saying "No thanks, I think I'm going to stay here for once." It felt to both of us that she had awakened her desire and agency, in her words, "opening to a new experience of myself."

Slavin (2007), in comparing Freud and Loewald's work on transference love, suggests that Loewald's loving vision of his patient in the process of becoming is akin to a parent's loving sense of her child's emerging possibilities. The hospitality found in this loving mind, ripe with potentials, opens up liminal spaces for the patient that had been previously restricted. This hospitable mind, while certainly capable of becoming imprisoning and stifling to the patient when the analyst's mind is fixed only on her known vision for the patient, can be free to move in-between possibilities by remaining hospitable to the unknown aspects of becoming. While many clinical moments, especially those that might be understood as enactments, serve to impinge and restrict our creativity, we might try to allow for more moments of disruption. By being hospitable to emerging possibilities within ourselves and within our patients, we might stall moments of restricting foreclosure, opening us to new ways of being with ourselves and with others.

References

Aron, L. (2003). The paradoxical place of enactment in psychoanalysis. *Psychoanalytic Dialogues, 13*(5), 623–631.

Benjamin, J. (2004). Beyond doer and done to: An intersubjective view of thirdness. *Psychoanalytic Quarterly, 73*(1), 5–47.

Benjamin, J. (2006). Crash: What we do when we cannot touch: Commentary on paper by Meira Likierman. *Psychoanalytic Dialogues, 16*(4), 377–385.

Benjamin, J. (2009). A Relational psychoanalysis perspective on the necessity of acknowledging failure in order to restore the facilitating and containing features of the intersubjective relationship (the shared third). *International Journal of Psycho-Analysis, 90*(3), 441–450.

Bromberg, P. M. (2003). Something wicked this way comes: Trauma, dissociation, and conflict: The space where psychoanalysis, cognitive science, and neuroscience overlap. *Psychoanalytic Psychology, 20*(3), 558–574.

Chused, J. F. (2003). The role of enactments. *Psychoanalytic Dialogues, 13*(5), 677–687.

Davies, J. M. (2004). Whose bad objects are we anyway? Repetition and our elusive love affair with evil. *Psychoanalytic Dialogues, 14*(6), 711–732.

Davies, J. M., & Frawley, M. G. (1994). *Treating the adult survivor of childhood sexual abuse.* New York: Basic Books.

Derrida, J., & Dufourmantelle, A. (2000). *Of hospitality* (R. Bowlby, Trans.). Stanford: Stanford University Press.

Fairbairn, R. D. (1943). The repression and the return of bad objects. *British Journal of Medical Psychology, 19*(3), 327–341.

Freud, A. (1936). *The ego and the mechanisms of defense.* London: Hogarth.

Freud, S. (1958a). Psycho-analytic notes on an autobiographical account of a case of paranoia (dementia paranoids). In J. Strachey (Ed. & Trans.), *The standard edition of the complete psychological works of Sigmund Freud, 12*. London: Hogarth. (Original work published 1911)

Freud, S. (1958b). Recommendations to physicians practicing psycho-analysis. In J. Strachey (Ed. & Trans.), *The standard edition of the complete psychological works of Sigmund Freud, 12*. London: Hogarth. (Original work published 1912)

Gadamer, H. G. (1989). *Truth and method* (Rev. ed.). (J. Weinsheimer & D. G. Marshall, Trans.). New York: Continuum. (Original work published 1960)

Ghent, E. (1990). Masochism, submission, surrender: Masochism as a perversion of surrender. *Contemporary Psychoanalysis, 26*(1), 108–136.

Gobodo-Madikizela, P. (2003). *A human being died that night: A South African woman confronts the legacy of apartheid.* New York: Mariner.

Jacobs, T. J. (1986). On countertransference enactments. *Journal of the American Psychoanalytic Association, 34*(2), 289–307.

Kearney, R. (2003). *Strangers, gods and monsters: Interpreting otherness.* New York: Routledge.

Kearney, R., & Semonovitch, K. (2011). At the threshold: Foreigners, strangers, and others. In R. Kearney & K. Semonovitch (Eds.), *Phenomenologies of the stranger: Between hostility and hospitality.* New York: Fordham University Press.

Kohut, H. (1971). *The analysis of the self.* New York: International Universities Press.

Kris, E. (1936). The psychology of caricature. *International Journal of Psycho-Analysis, 17*, 285–303.

Laing, C. M. (2012). In play, at play. *Journal of Applied Hermeneutics, 2*, 1–10.

Levinas, E. (1969). *Totality and infinity: An essay on exteriority.* Pittsburgh: Duquesne University Press.

MacKendrick, K. (2011). The hospitality of listening: A note on sacramental strangeness. In R. Kearney & K. Semonovitch (Eds.), *Phenomenologies of the stranger: Between hostility and hospitality.* New York: Fordham University Press.

Maroda, K. J. (1998). Enactment: When the patient's and analyst's pasts converge. *Psychoanalytic Psychology, 15*(4), 517–535.

Nahum, J. P. (2005). The "Something More" than interpretation revisited: Sloppiness and co-creativity in the psychoanalytic encounter. *Journal of the American Psychoanalytic Association, 53*(3), 693–730.

Olinick (1969). On empathy, and regression in the service of the other. *British Journal of Medical Psychology, 42*(1), 41–49.

Ricoeur, P. (1970). *Freud and philosophy: An essay on interpretation.* (D. Savage, Trans.). Oxford: Yale University Press.

Rifkin, M. (2013). Toxic impasse: Loss and recovery of the analysts mind. *The Round Robin Newsletter of Section I of the Division of Psychoanalysis of the American Psychological Association, 28*, 1–7.

Ruti, M. (2011). Winnicott with Lacan: Living creatively in a postmodern world. *American Imago, 67*(3), 353–374.

Slavin, J. H. (2007). The imprisonment and liberation of love: The dangers and possibilities of love in the psychoanalytic relationship. *Psychoanalytic Inquiry, 27*(3), 197–218.

Slavin, J. H., & Pollock, L. (1997). The poisoning of desire: The destruction of agency and the recovery of psychic integrity in sexual abuse. *Contemporary Psychoanalysis, 33*(3), 573–593.

Slavin, M., & Kriegman, D. (1998). Why the analyst needs to change: Toward a theory of conflict, negotiation, and mutual influence in the therapeutic process. *Psychoanalytic Dialogues, 8*(2), 247–284.

Winnicott, D. W. (1958). The capacity to be alone. *International Journal of Psycho-Analysis, 39*, 416–420.

Winnicott, D. W. (1960). The theory of the parent-infant relationship. *International Journal of Psycho-Analysis, 41*, 585–595.

Winnicott, D. W. (1965a). *The maturational processes and the facilitating environment.* Madison: International Universities Press, Inc.

Winnicott, D. W. (1965b). *Through pediatrics to psychoanalysis.* London: Routledge.

Winnicott, D. W. (1971). *Playing and reality.* Oxford: Penguin.

Chapter 18

The disabled

The most othered others

Christina Emanuel

I found my way to thinking about otherness unexpectedly. I feel like it found me, actually. In this chapter I will discuss how that occurred and how my work with autistic patients raised my awareness of what it means to be disabled in our culture. I will discuss the main themes in the disability studies literature, suggest reasons for the absence of these ideas in the psychoanalytic literature, and offer a case that illustrates these themes. There is much to be gained when we add a disability studies sensibility to psychoanalytic theory and practice.[1]

About 15 years ago I was accruing hours toward licensure as a therapist and serendipitously ended up working in a special education school serving students with autism. This was the late 1990s, so Asperger's disorder, having been added to the DSM in 1994, was a newly chic diagnosis. The huge and unprecedented increase in the prevalence of autism was just beginning at that time. The economy had not yet tanked so there was funding for treatment. The school I worked for couldn't hire therapists and teachers fast enough to meet the increasing demand for services, so, for better or for worse, I had plenty of job security. And I became utterly fascinated with minds so different from mine, on the edges of society, with a view that those of us in the middle just don't have.

However, I also didn't know what I was doing. Most days as a psychoanalyst I still feel the same way, although I have come to appreciate that such epistemological wobbliness is a sought-after state, as too much knowledge interferes with understanding my patients' experiences in the world. So, because I knew nothing about how to work with an autistic person, and because the training I received was really inadequate, I decided just to go full-Kohut, listening and understanding, as well as I could. Since then I've spent tens of thousands of hours with autistic people – mostly young adults these days – and their families, listening and understanding, first in the special education school and later in my private practice. People with autism have taught me what it is to be the ultimate other in a culture in which the dominant group is a highly social majority.

The autism experienced by these individuals, I've learned, has little to do with the autism we are asked to consume as a society, defined by the medical model, the idea that autistics cannot read social cues, and that they are always and only and permanently autistic. These mainstream approaches to autism dictate that autistics require lots and lots of expensive remediative treatment to cure their incurable, tragic, and miserable impairment and become more "normal."

I don't mean to say that people with autism don't need services or don't have any relevant impairment. My critique has to do with how we think about this group, how we other them, and how some treatment providers exploit by over-pathologizing autism. And to the extent that I have profited from my work with this group of people, I'm part of this exploitative system too, something I feel I ought to disclose. My point here is that my autistic people have a *different* experience of their condition. Importantly, many individuals on the spectrum consider themselves to be disabled. And many do not. In either case, the notion of what it is to be disabled – to have a disability – was put on my radar by this group, something I personally hadn't thought about much because I am not disabled, at least not yet.

Separately from my thinking about autism, seven years ago I found myself drawn to contemporary psychoanalytic thought and entered psychoanalytic training. My institute, The Institute of Contemporary Psychoanalysis in Los Angeles, has a very significant commitment to diversity issues, supporting our community in examining our individual and collective minds for hidden biases, inevitable prejudices, and the tendency to totalize individuals in our overt actions and our more insidious microaggressions. This is how thinking about otherness found me at my psychoanalytic institute as well.

Perhaps naïve about politics in psychoanalytic institutes, a few years ago I requested to join my institute's diversity committee because of my interest in disabilities. I was rebuffed and told, "Disability is not relevant to our institute. There is no one with a disability here." Given that 20% of the population has a disability, either mild or more severe, at any one time (Brault, 2012), I was incredulous. And I was angry. My request to expand the diversity category to include disabilities was put to the bottom of the Board agenda, repeatedly tabled until next month, pushed out by more important or allegedly relevant issues such as budgets, curriculum, and programs.

Motivated by my irritation and my curiosity, I started reading the disability studies literature. I owe a debt of gratitude to one of my patients for introducing me to this discourse, as I likely would never have known to look for it. Disability studies comprises a very considerable body of scholarship, but most people have never even heard of it, even those of us sensitive to and aware of identity politics. Conferences and journals are loaded with papers taking up the experience of the other in terms of race, class, gender, and religion, including those marginalized through political oppression, trauma of all sorts, and postcolonialism. But where is there mention of those with disabilities? I have never seen a presentation on this topic and have found scant reference to it in the psychoanalytic literature. To the extent that individuals with disabilities – particularly mental disabilities – have been excluded from our discourse, they comprise a group of most othered others. Lennard Davis (1995), one of the most important figures in the disability studies world, notes the "strange and really unaccountable silence when the issue of disability is raised (or, more to the point, never raised)" (p. 5) in academic and intellectual circles. He continues:

> The silence is stranger, too, since so much of left criticism has devoted itself to the issue of the body, of the social construction of sexuality and gender. Alternative bodies people this discourse . . . But lurking behind these images of transgression and deviance is a much more transgressive and deviant figure: the disabled body.
>
> (p. 5)

Disability studies

Disability studies as an academic discipline developed parallel to the disability rights movement, that in turn following on the heels of the civil rights and women's rights movements in the US and abroad. The first wave of the disability rights movement began in the 1960s and 1970s, with activism and passage of the landmark Rehabilitation Act of 1973, prohibiting discrimination against individuals receiving federal aid on the basis of handicap. The disability rights movement in the US gained greater visibility in the 1980s, culminating in 1990 with passage of the Americans with Disabilities Act, or ADA, and the Individuals with Disabilities Education Act, or IDEA, sweeping legislation guaranteeing accessibility and civil rights protection for people with disabilities, as well as free and appropriate public education for children with disabilities. Interestingly, these were both enthusiastically – and with broad bipartisan support – signed into law by George H.W. Bush. Modeled after the provisions of the ADA, The United Nations Convention on the Rights of Persons with Disabilities came into force in 2008. Perhaps a sign of our shifting political climate, the US, ironically, is one of very few UN member states that has voted against ratification of the Convention, with many on the right objecting to its provisions, the same ones they supported when creating the ADA.

Now well into its second wave (Davis, 2010b), disability studies has three key ideas. The first is to point out the ubiquity of *ableism* in our culture, that is, discrimination against individuals with disabilities (Linton, 2010; Watermeyer, 2013; Davis, 1995), which continues despite the legislation I mentioned above. In some parts of the world the term used is *disablism* (Watermeyer, 2013), and which term is preferable is debatable. The second key idea notes the transition from a *medical model* of disability to the *social model*. This reflects a shift in thinking about disabilities not as pathology experienced in individual bodies with the goal of cure or, if that is not possible, sequestration (Straus, 2010), but rather as "a social creation – a relationship between people with impairment and a disabling society" (Shakespeare, 2010, p. 266). The aim of social model thinking is to remove barriers to accessibility and to view all bodies as acceptable, with no one body type privileged (Shakespeare, 2010; Longmore, 2003; Goodley, 2011; Watermeyer, 2013). Interestingly, the revolution in the disability studies discourse from the medical model to the social model has parallels in the contemporary psychoanalytic literature, in our relational turn, the move from a one-person medical model approach to a two-person psychology, the emphasis on social construction, context, and culture.

The third key insight is the idea that *"normal" is a construction* (Davis, 1995; 2010a). Normalcy – the idea of measurable norms – was a creation of pioneers of statistics in 19th-century Europe. They created the famous bell curve, its mean and standard deviations categorizing people along lines of normal vs. deviant. Prior to these ways of categorizing people, no culture had the concept of "normal" as we use it now; instead, the prevailing trend had been to compare a human ideal against everyone else, with no one reaching the ideal. This was a remarkable shift that coincided with the development of Darwin's ideas of fittedness. I was both surprised and not to discover that these statisticians were actually eugenicists, interested in identifying and eradicating deviance. We use the term "normal" all the time without realizing its sinister implications (Davis, 1995, 2010a; Longmore, 2003). Few people would say now that a particular race, gender role, or sexual orientation is "normal" but this loaded term is frequently used with impunity in discussions about disability (Davis, 2013).

Interestingly, the disability studies literature is in conversation with scholars in the areas of feminist theory, queer theory, studies of race and class, postcolonialism – in short, they talk to all the other identity politics scholars, the same ones with whom the psychoanalytic literature talks. Even more, many of the disability studies theorists engage psychoanalytic theory (e.g., Goodley, 2011; Marks, 1999a, 1999b; Watermeyer, 2001, 2013). Most of this writing about psychoanalysis takes up Lacanian theory, exploring the symbolic foundations of ableism (Goodley, 2011), the extent to which the sense of bodily wholeness is an illusion (Watermeyer, 2013), and the idea of "disability's role as messenger from the *real*" (Watermeyer, 2013, p. 90). Theses writers also take up how our culture engages in defense mechanisms to disavow our feelings of vulnerability when considering the disabled body (e.g., Watermeyer, 2013). As Tom Shakespeare (1994) puts it, people with disabilities are "dustbins for disavowal" (p. 283).

Psychoanalysis and disability studies

The contemporary psychoanalytic canon, however, very specifically excludes the disability studies literature, a curious oversight. For example, Lew Aron and Karen Starr (2013) argue that "psychoanalysis is situated in the midst of a hierarchical division of binaries into male/female, heterosexual/homosexual, white/black, and gentile/Jew. This is why we find racism, misogyny, anti-Semitism, and homophobia to be surprisingly relevant to the fundamentals of psychoanalysis" (p. 5). When discussing these and other binaries, though, Aron and Starr leave out the disabled/non-disabled binary, even as they make a strong case for enacting Freud's ideal, that we should be "a psychotherapy for the people" (Aron & Starr, 2013, p. xiii; Freud, 1918), which I presume includes all people, not just the non-disabled. Freud was writing in Europe at the height of the eugenics movement, so surely the notions of normalcy and deviance, disability and non-disability, were on his radar, making the absence of this binary in Aron and Starr's writing that much more curious.

This is an oversight shared by myriad psychoanalytic writers, including those writing about embodied subjectivity (Aron & Anderson, 1998; Anderson, 2008). Much is written, about how our body sense is constructed relationally, how embodied experience is brought into the analytic dyad (Aron & Anderson, 1998), how our subjectivity is inextricably linked to our "bodily grounding" (Anderson, 2008, p. x), how we use our bodies to register subtle aspects of intersubjective relating (Anderson, 2008), and how our bodies are an irreducible aspect of our vulnerability (Anderson, 2008). These writers discuss how bodies are raced, sexed, and gendered, though across the board they leave out that our bodies are also "abled." There is no mention of our status as disabled or non-disabled subjects anywhere in this writing, and our participation in the system of non-disabled privilege is left not theorized. There is mention of the analyst's body when she experiences an illness (e.g., Gerson, 2001), but that writing never takes it as far as discussing disability and the politics therein.

When our literature does take up disability, the medical model is privileged. This is ironic, given the supreme value we place on contextuality, social construction, and embodied subjectivity, as well as our rejection of a medical model of psychology (Watermeyer, 2013). We see this in the ableist tone and language in this writing, and in the lack of reference to society's role in a disabled person's experience; instead, we locate the so-called tragic pathology in the individual and end our thinking there. These writers refer, for example, to patients' deficits, the experience of being abnormal, and one autistic individual's "unmanageable" and "alienating" behaviors (Gould, 2011). As a patient of mine recently commented, if we were to use words like these – "deficit," "abnormal," "unmanageable," "alienating" – to describe an African American person we would be considered racist, but in the context of a person with a disability this language is not questioned. The tone of much psychoanalytic writing about disabilities is often unintentionally condescending and patronizing too, such as one writer suggesting the importance of helping these patients set "realistic goals," to find "occupation[s] . . . suited to [their] talents and abilities," (Dasteel, 2012, p. 252), and for the therapist to "feel pleasure with small gains and minimal changes" (Dasteel, 2012, p. 259).

Cathy Hannabach (2007) writes:

> Many disability, queer, transgender, postcolonial, and feminist theo-
> rists have been understandably suspicious of psychoanalysis for its
> complicities with a medical model that constructs a normative body
> and pathologizes all of the embodiments, identifications, and desires
> that exceed such a norm.
>
> (p. 256)

This is highlighted in a case described by Lynne Jacobs[2] (2008). She
announces her patient: he was "born with an obvious deformity" (p. 410).
She then – apparently unwittingly – continues to use ableist language, stating that her patient feels "paralyzed" when required to consider others'
feelings, and referring to his "blindness to the otherness of the analyst"
(p. 421). Disability studies scholars strenuously object to language linking
physical impairments to negative human tendencies (Kleege, 2010), such
as describing people as metaphorically lame, paralyzed, or blind. When
talking about metaphorical blindness, Simi Linton (2006) asks, "how can
the culture get away with attaching such an absurd proliferation of meanings to a condition that affects, simply, visual acuity?" (p. 213).

Jacobs (2008) draws us into her difficult experience with her patient.
Her writing is beautiful, vulnerable, and intimate. She writes:

> My desire to be recognized and affirmed surged like waves on our
> relationship. The more he ignored my subjectivity, the stronger my
> desire surged. My work with him was messy, continually being infil-
> trated by my reactions to feeling disregarded and negated.
>
> (p. 411)

Although recognition is a tall order in any case, I'm wondering, how much
of Jacobs' specific struggle has to do with unrecognized ableism being
enacted in the dyad? To what extent is she enacting her own disavowed
non-disabled privilege? Knowing how sensitive she is to structures of
power and privilege – indeed, she is a leading theorist in the areas of social
location and white privilege – I know Jacobs would never consciously
overlook this aspect of the work.

Psychoanalysis is interested the hidden meanings in things (Watermeyer,
2013). Although I am gratified to have found our non-disabled bias hidden

in what seems like plain sight, I remain perplexed: if we really care about these types of ideas, how did we miss this one? I will briefly highlight a few possible explanations for our oversight. First, the language of ableism is insidious and slippery, the narratives ubiquitous yet very well hidden in both our psychoanalytic culture and the culture at large. A recent short film, popular on social media websites such as Facebook, shows a poor little boy with tattered clothes and shoes who covets the nice clothes and shoes of another boy he sees sitting on a bench nearby (Page & Raoofi, 2012). Then we discover that the little boy on the bench uses a wheelchair. The explicit message in the video is: be happy with what you've got! The grass isn't always greener! But the hidden ableist message is loud and clear too: being disabled is worse than being poor; being disabled is most definitely something tragic that you don't want.

This leads to my second observation, the extent to which we may unconsciously rank individuals with disabilities against those in other marginalized groups. A patient of mine, a young white man with cerebral palsy and mild intellectual disability, states unequivocally, "society treats me worse than a black person." This is a provocative comment that says as much about the perceived ranking of marginalized groups as it does about how the black man has become the quintessential other. Even within the disability population there is a hierarchy of disabilities, with the physically and sensory impaired at the top, and those with mental disability at the bottom (Docherty et al., 2010). Perhaps even more telling is another patient who recently fell, broke her hip, and is struggling to take care of herself. She stated, "if I don't take better care of myself I could die – or worse! – I could become permanently disabled." Being disabled is apparently even worse than being dead, and you can't get much more marginalized than being dead.

Perhaps more relevant is the role of our own vulnerability. I am never going to be a Latina woman or a gay man, for example, but there's a really good chance that at some point I am going to become disabled. The literature makes frequent reference to our status as "Temporarily Able Bodied" (Davis, 1995). This scares us, because on some level we know how society feels about people with disabilities. For the other categories of identity we can safely say that each represents a "me" or "not-me" attribute, but for disability that does not apply. The neoliberal trend (Layton, 2009) to disavow both our own vulnerability and our interdependence with others' vulnerabilities might be at play here (K. Gentile, personal communication, November 2013), and in turn ableist attitudes may solidify neoliberal ones as well.

We can gain further insight from such writers as Steven Botticelli (2004) who demonstrates that as psychoanalysts we do have political concerns, though we often do not act on them outside the consulting room, unwitting participants in a system of "ameliorative projects" (p. 635) rather than true social transformation. He cites Philip Cushman's (1995) insistence that we not overlook the extent to which political structures may cause psychological suffering in our patients. Whereas we may be aware of this when it comes to race, gender, and so on, we have been slow to include the experience of being disabled.

I would also say that, despite our oversight, our collective psychoanalytic heart is in the right place. There are many examples of how we theorize other areas of identity extraordinarily well, and we can borrow some of these themes as we begin to theorize disability. For example, Lynne Layton's (2006) seminal idea of normative unconscious processes, as demonstrated in racial identity and racial enactments in the consulting room, is a natural fit with the disability studies theme of constructing normalcy. "Normative unconscious processes refer to that aspect of the unconscious that pulls to repeat affect/behavior/cognition patterns that uphold the very social norms that cause psychic distress in the first place" (p. 242), she explains. And writers such as Adrienne Harris (2009) frame questions about, in her case, gender, that could be asked of disability as well, such as: can we question psychoanalytic accounts of disability? To what extent is disability a stable category? And how does a person come to participate in the disability/ability system? She implicitly asks us to take up the able-normative body that inhabits our theories and practices.

In any case, much is to be gained if we add a disability studies sensibility to our discourse. First, we can recognize the irreducibly political aspect of our work, understanding our own implicit ableism, how we co-construct the system of non-disabled privilege in which we participate. Harris (2009) writes, "we cure with contaminated tools. We are embedded in structures of money, hierarchy, and power, and we must keep a double vision in play. Psychoanalysts practice subversion and hegemony in every hour" (p. 16). Thinking about ableism – keeping this "double vision in play" – allows us better to understand our patients when they experience disabilities, particularly the mental disabilities that we as mental health clinicians are very likely to encounter. We can analyze the extent to which we may subtly discourage people with disabilities from coming to our practices. And we can appreciate how in our professional ranks we exclude people with disabilities, either by implicitly requiring them to pass or hide their disabilities, or by just not making our institutes accessible or truly inclusive.

Medical model autism

In the specific case of mental disability, Foucault (1964) notes that madness was considered special – a mad person was a wise person – prior to the age of reason, after which the warehousing of these others began. This was followed by construction of categories for "normal" and "deviant" bodies, as theorized by Davis (1995, 2010a). In our contemporary world we can see how a disability studies sensibility shines a light on our construction of diagnostic labels too, particularly the diagnosis that fills me with endless fascination: autism. I will identify several trends.

First, when we apply the medical model to autism we mistakenly conceive of this condition as a cluster of allegedly measureable behaviors comprising the DSM criteria, rather than considering it in terms of an individual's subjective experience in the context of the social environment (Emanuel, 2015). Behaviors fail to capture what is essential about autism. By way of example, if I were to take a Tylenol and then put my hand on my forehead you might imagine that I have a headache, but those behaviors would not *be* the headache. The same is true for autism – the behaviors are not the autism. Part of medical model autism consists of the metaphor of an autism spectrum "that fades into normality at one end" (Solomon, 2012, p. 257). A spectrum implies that someone's behaviors can be measured and the person's condition located somewhere along the spectrum of normal to deviant.

Furthermore, there is also no one-to-one correspondence between these behavioral criteria and the diagnosis of autism. Lots of things look like autism behaviors but are not (e.g., schizoid phenomena, some aspects of narcissism, certain presentations of fetal alcohol spectrum disorders, and the behaviors of some highly gifted individuals), and autism itself can have many different behavioral manifestations. My patient Lexi puts it best: "I could have two of these diagnostic criteria and you could have the other three criteria that I don't have, and we'd still be given the same diagnosis and treatment. How absurd is that?" Furthermore, professionals frequently conflate autism with the other diagnoses that often accompany it.

The behavioral criteria also fail to consider that autistics are sometimes not autistic, and I, to the extent that I may not read someone correctly, am sometimes autistic. Even the best readers of others do so far less than

100% of the time. For example, when building Legos with my autistic patient Ryan a few years ago, I noticed that I wished I could find Lego wheels to buy, just the wheels, for the vehicles my patients liked to make. I kept this wish to myself, though the very next week Ryan came in with an entire box of Lego wheels he had bought for me. "How did you do know I wanted these?" I asked. He responded, "I just knew." This led to my conviction that autism is a state, not an always/only/forever trait. The medical model literature, though, treats it as an all-or-nothing phenomenon, even when it offers data suggesting otherwise. For example, when describing one of his studies Hobson (2002) writes, "Ten of the thirteen children with autism *never* referred to emotional states, whether correctly or incorrectly" (p. 56). He makes no comment, though, about the three of thirteen autistic children who *did* refer to emotional states.

Medical model autism also does not include the role of context in making the diagnosis. This is extremely ironic, given that autism is an impairment of poor social engagement. In the right environment, autism is not an issue, with autistic minds highly valued in many circumstances. Autism is not like the chickenpox or a broken arm, where no matter the context you'd still have a legitimate impairment.

So, medical model autism has too many moving parts and too many undecidable, equivocal cases, and even too many undecidable moments in an individual who has legitimate autism. At best we can think of autism as a metaphor that applies to some people some of the time, depending upon the situation. A social model autism shifts the focus from the impairment to the context, and the case I will present below illustrates that. Aron and Starr (2013) use Derrida's concept of "undecidables" (p. 47) to bust the binaries – the artificially sharp distinctions – that plague psychoanalysis. We can use this concept as well to deconstruct the medical model of autism. Instead, we can see that autism is an unstable category (see Davis, 2010b), with more variation within groups than between, that is only problematic to the extent that the context considers it to be such. Stuart Murray (2012) emphasizes, and I agree, that we cannot assume that autism always represents an illness.

Lexi, a human subject

Lexi, a Japanese-American young woman I see, was diagnosed with autism during her early elementary school years when her teachers noted that she had no friends and tended to drift off into her own world, replaying scenes from Star Wars and the anime Sailor Moon verbally and in her imagination over and over again. She would flap her hands and spin, also known as "stimming," when excited. She did not pay attention in school. Lexi was excluded by peers and bullied. It was assumed that she was intellectually disabled.

Her parents were stunned to learn, when she was evaluated at UCLA, that she was both autistic and highly gifted. She was reading at an 11th-grade level even as her peers were just beginning to sound out words. The evaluators also noted her extreme sensory sensitivity, something I consider to be at the core of autism. Lexi subsequently received an IEP – an Individualized Education Program – in which she was sequestered in special education programs. This involved her being pulled out of the regular classroom for speech therapy and other services. All the children knew where she was going, causing Lexi to feel even weirder than she already did. Lexi was placed in social skills groups where she learned that there was something wrong with how she communicated with other kids. She was instructed to adopt the social skills of the highly social, extroverted majority, who sat in clusters of desks at school and were expected to complete collaborative group projects.

Her parents were ashamed of Lexi, wanting desperately for her to be normal. Filled with anxiety from the pressure at home and at school, Lexi would stim frequently. Her parents punished her for that, attempting to extinguish this so-called inappropriate behavior. Lexi later described to me that her chronic anxiety was, at times, terrifying.

Lexi's parents took her to psychiatrists beginning in her 3rd-grade year, where she was given medication to help her focus, though it was not clear that she actually had ADD. When she was older, she was prescribed medication for the mood symptoms that were often made worse by the ADD meds. These interfered with her sleep and so Lexi was given medication for sleep. Groggy in the mornings, her ADD meds were increased. This went on for years, a sort of pharmaceutical death spiral, culminating in a series of excruciatingly traumatic hospitalizations where Lexi was restrained and forcibly medicated. Stripped of her dignity, Lexi was grossly misunderstood to be a cluster of maladaptive behaviors rather than a human subject.

The most important factor in Lexi's recovery has been the realization that the dominant, highly social majority culture has been unfairly imputing to her the requirement to adopt its social skills and be "normal," rather than giving her the *choice* whether and how to join the social environment.

I didn't try to change anything, but rather she helped me see – and I then helped her see – how she was being misunderstood. More than anyone I've worked with, Lexi exemplifies that the culture's response to her autism has been much worse than the autism itself. She was assumed to be more impaired than she really was, over-medicated, and taken advantage of by care providers who gave the impression that they were more expert in the area of autism than was truly the case.

Lexi, who knows I am writing about her in this chapter, would like you to know how angry she is to have been repeatedly harmed by the medical model system, othered by the very system designed to help her. She would also like you to know the advantages that autism offers while at the same time emphasizing that it represents, for her, an impairment and a disability. She has told me many times, "Just because I'm not reading as many social cues as you are doesn't mean I'm reading *nothing*." Lexi has shown me that the view from the margins can be interesting. She takes great comfort in organizations such as the Autism Self Advocacy Network (ASAN), a community supporting a neurodiversity agenda, very much in line with disability studies thinking, and madinamerica. com, an online forum for mental health advocacy that is stridently anti-psychiatry.

There are many treatments that are extremely helpful, if not essential, for autistic people, including psychiatry for some. I want to make it very clear that I don't question that. Rather, it is the ableist tone and attitude toward autism, seen in both the mainstream and the psychoanalytic literature, that troubles me to no end. Lexi once told me, "You want the missing part of the culture and so do I." When we add a disability studies sensibility we do construct a better autism, one that captures what is essential about this condition while at the same time appreciating the extent to which it is constructed.

A disability studies sensibility helps me think about the exquisite care and thoughtfulness we should take when applying normative data to an individual person in the service of cure. It also helps me think of diagnostic labels such as autism as potentially helpful starting points when understanding individual people, though not good endpoints. It helps me realize how, in treating individuals with disabilities, the psychoanalytic profession may inadvertently harm these patients with our ableist biases, our normative unconscious processes. And it helps me unhinge autism and other disabilities from categories of normalcy and deviance.

I don't want to end without acknowledging how controversial it is for me, a non-disabled person, to be writing about disability. I experience the unearned privilege that comes from being non-disabled, and, in the case of autism, neurotypical. I'm part of the disability/ability system, as I construct it and am constructed by it. This chapter is a call better to theorize the body that shows up in psychoanalytic discourse. But beyond that, there are significant limits to my position (Linton, 2006). Therefore, with deep respect I call on disabled persons to speak with more authority about their experience than I can, as I attempt to honor their important slogan: "nothing about us without us" (Linton, 2006).

Notes

1 In this chapter I alternate between person-centered language (i.e., "person with autism") and the more contemporary language that places the disabling condition first (i.e., autistic person, or autistic), recognizing that the disability is an integral aspect of the individual's identity (Linton, 2010). This is consistent with language used in the disability studies literature.
2 The author wishes to express gratitude to Lynne Jacobs, both for her helpful comments in writing this chapter and for her permission to discuss her writing.

References

Anderson, F. (Ed.). (2008). *Bodies in treatment: The unspoken dimension*. New York: The Analytic Press.
Aron, L. & Anderson, F. (Eds.). (1998). *Relational perspectives on the body*. New York: The Analytic Press.
Aron, L. & Starr, K. (2013). *A psychotherapy for the people: Toward a progressive psychoanalysis*. New York: Routledge.
Botticelli, S. (2004). The politics of relational psychoanalysis. *Psychoanalytic Dialogues, 14,* 635–651.
Brault, M. (2012). Americans with disabilities: 2010 household economic studies. *U.S. Department of Commerce, Economics and Statistics Administration, U.S. Census Bureau*. Retrieved from www.census.gov/prod/2012pubs/p70-131.pdf on October 14, 2013.
Cushman, P. (1995). *Constructing the self, constructing America*. Reading, MA: Addison-Wesley.
Dasteel, J. (2012). Full of feelings, disabled, and treatable: Working psychodynamically with special-needs adults. In Berzoff, J. (Ed.), *Falling through the cracks: Psychodynamic practice with vulnerable and oppressed populations* (pp. 241–260). New York: Columbia University Press.
Davis, L. (1995). *Enforcing normalcy: Disability, deafness, and the body*. London: Verso.
Davis, L. (2010a). Constructing normalcy. In Davis, L. (Ed.), *The disability studies reader* (pp. 3–19). New York: Routledge.
Davis, L. (2010b). The end of identity politics: On disability as an unstable category. In Davis, L. (Ed.), *The disability studies reader* (pp. 301–315). New York: Routledge.

Davis, L. (2013). *The end of normal: Identity in a biocultural era.* Ann Arbor, MI: University of Michigan Press.

Docherty, D., Hughes, R., Phillips, P., Corbett, D., Regan, B., Barber, A., & Izzidien, S. (2010). This is what we think. In Davis, L. (Ed.), *The disability studies reader* (pp. 432–440). New York: Routledge.

Emanuel, C. (2015). An accidental Pokemon expert: Contemporary psychoanalysis on the Autism spectrum. *International Journal of Psychoanalytic Self Psychology, 10,* 53–68.

Foucault, M. (1964). *Madness and civilization: A history of insanity in the age of reason.* London: Routledge.

Freud, S. (1918). Letter from Sigmund Freud to Oskar Pfister, October 9, 1918. In psychoanalysis and faith: The Letters of Sigmund Freud and Oskar Pfister. *International Psychoanalysis Library, 59,* 61–63.

Gerson, B. (2001). *The therapist as a person.* New York: Routledge.

Goodley, D. (2011). *Disability studies: An interdisciplinary introduction.* London: Sage Publications.

Gould, K. (2011). Fantasy play as the conduit for change in the treatment of a six-year-old boy with Asperger's syndrome. *Psychoanalytic Inquiry, 31,* 240–251.

Hannabach, C. (2007). Anxious embodiment, disability, and sexuality: A response to Margrit Shildrick. *Studies in Gender and Sexuality, 8,* 53–261.

Harris, A. (2009). *Gender as soft assembly.* New York: Routledge.

Hobson, P. (2002). *The cradle of thought: Exploring the origins of thinking.* New York: Oxford University Press.

Jacobs, L. (2008). Dialogue, confirmation, and the good. *International Journal of Psychoanalytic Self Psychology, 3,* 409–431.

Kleege, G. (2010). Blindness and visual culture: An eyewitness account. In Davis, L. (Ed.), *The disability studies reader* (pp. 522–530). New York: Routledge.

Layton, L. (2006). Racial identities, racial enactments, and normative unconscious processes. *Psychoanalytic Quarterly, 75,* 237–269.

Layton, L. (2009). Who's responsible? Our mutual implication in each other's suffering. *Psychoanalytic Dialogues, 19,* 105–120.

Linton, S. (2006). *My body politic: A memoir.* Ann Arbor, MI: University of Michigan Press.

Linton, S. (2010). Reassigning meaning. In Davis, L. (Ed.), *The disability studies reader* (pp. 223–236). New York: Routledge.

Longmore, P. (2003). *Why I burned my book and other essays on disability.* Philadelphia, PA: Temple University Press.

Marks, D. (1999a). *Disability: Controversial debates and psychosocial perspectives.* London: Routledge.

Marks, D. (1999b). Dimensions of oppression: Theorising the embodied subject. *Disability and Society, 14*(5), 611–625.

Murray, S. (2012). *Autism.* New York: Routledge.

Page, A. (Producer) and Raoofi, N. (Director). (2012). *My shoes* [Motion picture]. Australia: Media Arts Production. Retrieved from www.youtube.com/watch?v=SolGBZ2f6L0

Shakespeare, T. (1994). Cultural representation of disabled people: Dustbins for disavowal? *Disability and Society, 9*(3), 283–299.

Shakespeare, T. (2010). The social model of disability. In Davis, L. (Ed.), *The disability studies reader* (pp. 266–273). New York: Routledge.

Solomon, A. (2012). *Far from the tree: Parents, children, and the search for identity.* New York: Scribner.

Straus, J. (2010). Autism as culture. In Davis, L. (Ed.), *The disability studies reader* (pp. 535–559). New York: Routledge.

Watermeyer, B. (2001). Blindness, attachment, and self: Psychoanalysis and ideology. *Free Associations, 9A,* 152–167.

Watermeyer, B. (2013). *Towards a contextual psychology of disablism.* London: Routledge.

Chapter 19

What fascinates

Re-reading Winnicott reading Blanchot

Peter August

As a kid I loved to watch things go backwards, especially when they really didn't, like the wagon-wheels on TV westerns whose spokes rotating out of sync with the film's frames created the illusion of wheels going one way while wagons went the other. I also looked at things that were not moving at all and imagined them re-tracing their steps from nowhere. Studying the Brooklyn Bridge on my subway rides to and from high school, I watched the real bridge fade into the blueprint of a bridge that was there before.

Beyond optical illusions and flashbacks to physics class, more recently I've grown mistrustful of metaphor. A nine-year-old boy walks into my office with his hands in his pockets and stops in the middle of the room. He takes his hand out of his pocket and drops a piece of lint onto the floor. As if like Orpheus, to turn and look, I begin to wonder "what's he up to?" but the scene slips out of any conceptual grasp and slides back to what it always already was. "When we are face to face with things themselves" (p. 255), writes Blanchot (1955), in one of the short appendices he wrote to *The Space of Literature* called "Two Versions of the Imaginary":

> If we fix upon a face, the corner of a wall – does it not also sometimes happen that we abandon ourselves to what we see? Bereft of power before this presence suddenly strangely mute and passive, are we not at its mercy? Indeed, this can happen, but it happens because the thing we stare at has foundered, sunk into its image, and the image has returned into that deep fund of impotence to which everything reverts.
>
> (p. 255)

To think what disappears and to write backwards

It happens that we "abandon ourselves to what we see" and that what we look at "sinks into its image" (or as I sometimes experience it, moves backwards), that the thing disappears to right where it is, standing before us in resemblance with itself alone. When this happens to me, as it still does in the world and the playroom, I am compelled to ask: What do I say, and how can I write? Or as Blanchot puts it: "Finally, in order to be silent, it is necessary to speak. But with what sort of words?" (The Unavowable Community, 1988, p. 56).

My writing begins when I meet that which I cannot describe. Returning to the boy walking into my office, this is one of the countless performances of the story of Orpheus turning to look at Eurydice that takes place in my office every day. Except, turning, I see what disappears standing before me, "suddenly strangely mute and passive" in resemblance to itself alone, accepting neither explanation nor comparison and leaving me fascinated.

When we take our seats at the little table a moment later, I try to scribble something on a piece of paper but only manage: "his dropping the piece of lint will never be to me what it is to him." Fascination dislocates my thinking, and my speech. How can I think what has disappeared? How do I write backwards? And what does this have to do with what might come next? How do I play with him now? All my questions come back to play. Thinking, writing, and playing are all pursuits of some actual and must find ways to follow what vanishes to where it was already.

The patient comes to love the therapist and the therapist goes on to write

Although neither Winnicott (1971) nor Blanchot (1955) tells me exactly what to say, or how to write about a boy standing in the middle of the room, who's taken a piece of lint out of his pocket and dropped it on the floor, Blanchot's thoughts about the imaginary and Winnicott's about transitionality offer a kind of theoretical trampoline. Dislocated, however, by the experience of fascination, theory doesn't find a foothold and when it speaks it is likely to slip genre and become part of something like a poem, theory becoming poem, becoming theory. Fascination interrupts how we think and use language. Blanchot (1955) says: "To write is to let fascination rule language" (p. 33). "Re-reading Winnicott reading Blanchot," although not exactly poem or essay, is my response to the boy who comes into my office who knows how to go backwards. Blanchot continues: "Whoever is fascinated doesn't see, properly speaking, what he sees. Rather, it touches him in an immediate proximity; it seizes and cease-lessly draws him close, even though it leaves him absolutely at a distance" (p. 33). Fascinated and dislocated, I write to keep up. The patient comes to love the therapist and the therapist must go on to write.

The two versions of the transitional

As much as it looks like this is about us – his pausing in the middle of the room as if to abandon one temporality for another, hands in his pockets looking for me, dropping a piece of lint and hoping I will catch him – these metaphors seem not only useless to me but besides the much larger point. Sometimes it is the case that with certain patients, psychotherapeutic work cannot be interpretative until a communicative self has had the opportunity to emerge. Winnicott's (1971) introduction of the concept of transitionality is helpful because he describes what is a half-step back from the symbolic, shifting the focus from meaning to the ways meaning can come into being:

> When symbolism is employed," he writes, "the infant is already clearly distinguishing between fantasy and fact . . . between primary creativity and perception . . . the term transitional object . . . gives room for the process of becoming able to accept difference and simi-larity . . . there is a use for a term for the root of symbolism in time.
>
> (p. 6)

But to read Winnicott's (1971) theory of the transitionality as merely a prequel to our acquisition of a symbolic capacity, a preface to the story of story, is to leave out something essential. It is obvious, but to my mind still not adequately acknowledged, that by the time we are talking about Winnicott's theory of the origins of symbolic thought we are using symbols, we are already story tellers, and tend to recognize the transi-tional object as its not so strange precursor. The scene, however, of the boy walking into my office, hands in his pockets, stopping in the middle of the room, taking his hand out of his pocket and dropping a piece of lint on the floor possesses a density and self-sufficiency that rejects interpretation not only because it is pre-symbolic. One version of transitionality would imply a forward path toward symbol while what I would call a second version (inviting Blanchot to take over where Winnicott may have had to leave off) feels like the sensation of being tugged backward toward being.

This "second version of the transitional" is not the precursor to the symbolic, but the thing that moves backward and "sinks into itself". Blanchot (1955) tries to describe it this way:

> When concealment appears, concealment, having become appearance, makes "everything disappear", but of this "everything has disappeared" it makes another appearance. "Everything has disappeared" appears. This is exactly what we call an apparition. It is the "everything has disappeared" appearing in its turn.
>
> (p. 253)

Every appearance of the transitional is an entering of the realm of representation as well as a return to a kind of dwelling that knows nothing of realms. The boy who walks into my office with his hands in his pockets, who stops in the middle of the room, takes his hand out of his pocket, and drops a piece of lint on the floor, is "transitional" and "apparition". The movement is still "transitional" but now in two directions. To make reference to the act of making reference is the pre-symbolic moving forward toward making metaphor; the boy, his hands in his pockets, the lint, and my office head off to becoming any one of a number of other things, all according to my previous understandings, as well as to the structure which is understanding. When the event is allowed to speak for itself, however, it takes a half-step back, returning to being itself, and is the "'everything has disappeared' appearing in its turn" (Blanchot, 1955, p. 253).

Not my being a little less myself

In "The Essential Solitude and Solitude in the World," Blanchot (1955) explains that being is that which we abandon when we accept identity, and what we discover when that identity disappears:

> When I am alone, it is not I who am there, and it is not from you that I stay away, or from others, or from the world. I am not the subject to whom this impression of solitude would come – this awareness of my limits; it is not that I tire of being myself. When I am alone, I am not there. This is not a sign of some psychological state, indicating loss of

consciousness, the disappearance of my right to feel what I feel from a center that I myself would be. What approaches me is not my being a little less myself, but rather something which there is "behind me," and which the "me" conceals in order to come into its own.

(p. 251)

When Blanchot speaks of "essential solitude," I think of Winnicott's (1971) description of the relation before relation that precedes and coexists within the transitional. In the "transitional area" Winnicott imagines between "the subjective and the objectively perceived," things move backward as well as forward. Going backwards, however, there is no such thing as a "subjective" that comes before the "objectively perceived". In fact, the projection of that notion is a function of our attachment to category and dialectic. The subjective does not exist prior to the objective. What does? Blanchot (1955) imagines that "when I am alone, I am not there" (p. 251) and that "what approaches me is not my being just a little less myself" (p. 251). I can imagine that prior to what we know, there is a world of objects which in their backwards transitionality recall themselves before their own being, where each object possesses the essence of those conditions that preceded it and "is not being a little less itself".

The boy who walks into my office with his hands in his pockets and stops in the middle of the room, who takes his hand out of his pocket and drops a piece of lint on the floor, who is not yet or is no longer the representation of something else, a metaphor, invites in his pause a world of objects that recall themselves before their own being. What is present in that absence of the meaningful and singular is a polysemy, which I understand as the "many not composed of many ones". The event of his not being there becomes a reenactment of the Kabbalist story of the origin of the cosmos, which goes something like this: the Divine, that which was everything everywhere all the time, before creating the world, needed to contract or recede back into itself to make room for the world. In doing so it became possible to create the world and simultaneously introduce into this world the idea of an everything-all-the-time in each-thing-at-anytime.

I can now imagine, as a psychotherapist, what exists behind or before the things I see in my patients' play as something other than the precursor of symbol and self. In Winnicott's transitional and in Blanchot's imaginary, both of which have two versions, I experience this intersecting of world and worlds, things moving forward toward the symbolic and things moving backwards toward their origins that existed before their beginnings.

This movement implies infinite degrees

What happens when, as therapists, we understand the transitional in this way? Or to ask the question another way: What is Blanchot's theory of playing? Which he puts this way, "What happens when one lives an event as an image?" (p. 262). And responds:

> To live an event as an image is not to remain uninvolved, to regard the event disinterestedly in the way that the esthetic version of the image and the serene ideal of classical art purposes. But neither is it to take part freely and decisively. It is be taken: to pass from the region of the real where we hold ourselves at a distance from things the better to order and use them into that other region where the distance holds us – the distance which then is the lifeless deep, an unmanageable, inappreciable remoteness which has become something like the sovereign power behind all things. This movement implies infinite degrees.
>
> (p. 262)

It is with the idea of a movement of "infinite degrees" that I begin to fantasize Blanchot's theory of playing. I will have more to say about this later.

When the boy who walks into my office with his hands in his pockets stops in the middle of the room I also stop. I'm used to it. It's how we almost always begin. In a sense, it is all to do with how we measure our togetherness; and it is a beginning without a future since nothing happens next that is related to what happened before. So really, there is nothing to get used to. In the absence of time and theory I am dislocated and fascinated, again. Blanchot (1955) would say:

> It is the time in which nothing begins, in which, before affirmation, there is already the return of affirmation. Rather than a purely negative mode, it is on the contrary a time without negation, without decision, when here is truly nowhere, when each thing recedes into its image and when the "I" that we are recognizes itself dissolving into the neutrality of a faceless "He". The time of the absence of time is without a present, without presence.
>
> (p. 30)

To be fascinated is to be dislocated in thought, is to be dislocated in language, is to be dislocated in time.

Knowing pivots on the idea of fascination

If fascination is the conceptual center of this presentation, then the center of fascination is to stop in the middle of a room when a nine-year-old boy stops with his hands in his pockets, takes his hand out of his pocket, and drops a piece of lint on the floor. It is a situation of the event explaining the idea. It is the vividness of the absence of any interpretation, or metaphor, which is the thing we are finally able to see. Knowing pivots on the idea of fascination. We are listened into the world, which requires, ultimately, that we speak, but "with what sort of words?"

When the boy who walks into my office with his hands in his pockets stops in the middle of the room, takes his hand out of his pocket, and drops a piece of lint on the floor I don't say anything. When I speak it is not to the boy but to you, the reader. This is the crucial point and the beginning of my response to the question: "But with what sort of words?" Orpheus says nothing to Eurydice. What has happened goes backward and cannot be analyzed or interpreted but only written into a series of stories. Eventually play like this happens in the room and the scene becomes Blanchot's (1955) second version of the image. The patient comes to love the therapist and the therapist must go on to write. Fascination, in dislocating my speech, interrupts it into "infinite degrees". Writing follows the real when it is representational, but writing is also that sense of interruption or dislocation that enters our discourse, whether in person or on the page, whether we write or not. In its fundamental disruptiveness, writing invites polysemy and the possibility of play: "Here meaning does not escape into another meaning, but into the other of all meaning" (Blanchot, 1955, p. 263).

Unburdened of the demand to communicate

In the end things do move forward again. Something always happens after the boy drops the piece of lint, after I scribble my thoughts sitting at the little table. But the question implied throughout this chapter, and put off once already, has been and is still: What do we call playing? It is what I hear when I read Winnicott, when I read Blanchot, and that which I hear differently again when I re-read Winnicott reading Blanchot.

According to Winnicott (1971), all psychotherapy moves in the direction of playing, and playing – ultimately – "backwards" in the direction of nonsense. "Perhaps," writes Winnicott:

> It is to be accepted that there are patients who at times need the therapist to note the nonsense that belongs to the mental state of the individual at rest without the need even for the patient to communicate this nonsense . . . without the need for the patient to organize nonsense . . . The therapist who cannot take this communication becomes engaged in a futile attempt to find some organization in the nonsense, as a result of which the patient leaves the nonsense area because of hopelessness about communicating nonsense.
>
> (p. 56)

To write about play is inevitably to play with the ways one writes. The ideas of Maurice Blanchot and D.W. Winnicott are, in the end, less explanatory than they are invitational. What forms can suffice to respond to the "incessant interruption" that is the encounter with the other? Unburdened of the demand to communicate univocally, play is free to respond to what fascinates polysemously. Every idea is relentlessly dismantled and meanings are eliminated by "infinite degree," leaving us, in the end, at the beginning, with the nonsense of the everything-that-was-everywhere-all-the-time.

References

Blanchot, M. (1955). *The space of literature* (A. Smock, Trans.). Lincoln, NE: University of Nebraska Press.
Blanchot, M. (1988). *The unavowable community* (P. Jorie, Trans.). Barrytown, NY: Station Hill Press.
Winnicott, D.W. (1971). *Playing and reality*. New York: Routledge.

Index

parshas 174–5
particularity 148–52
partings 111–12
passing 172, 173–4, 175
paternalism 241–3
paternity 107–8
pathological accommodation 57, 68–70
patriarchy 24, 28–9, 165, 170
"Paul" 81–3
pedagogy 130
performance pressures 89–90
Perkins, C. 52
permeability 36, 37
perversion 87
phenomenology 7–9, 58–61
philosophy: and education 128–30; ethical turn 2–3
Philosophy for Children program 133, 134
Pizer, S. 106, 107
Plaskow, J. 166
Plass, A.A. 241
Plato 128
play 264–7; fascination 16, 286–93
pogroms 154, 158–62
Poirier, J.-F. 59–60
police 159, 160–1
political positioning 6–7
political structures 278
political theory 2
polyphonic novels 223–4
polysemy 290, 292
Pontalis, J.B. 61–2
Portlandia "Grover" episode 84–5
position 211–13; previous positions 216–17
poverty 87
primary maternal preoccupation 265
primitivity 26, 28, 29–31
privilege 88–9
process focus 45–6
product focus 45
progression 255–6
progressive education 133
progressive humanism 245–6
pseudo-family organization 98
"psy" discourses 97–9
public housing 79
Putnam, H. 26

Rabbinic Judaism 169; rabbinic law 27–8
racial equality 237
racism 24, 28; social policy 78–9
Racker, H. 65–6

rage 95
Rand, A. 52
Rangell, L. 24
ranking of marginalized groups 277
rape 153, 157, 158, 159, 160, 161, 162, 178–9
Rapunzel tale 160
Rashi 171
rational influence 29
Read, J. 78, 84
reading Jewishly 141–2
recognition: mutual 37, 104, 204, 227; process 121
regression 255–6
Rehabilitation Act 272
relational psychoanalysis 4–5, 44
religion 30; *see also* Christianity; Jews
repetition compulsion 217–18
resilience 179
resistance 243–8
Resistance 147
responsibility 14, 103–4, 106–7, 186–208, 250; and the face of the other 200–2; Heidegger 14, 188–200; Levinas 14, 101, 196–202, 204–5, 250; Loewald 190–6; recovery of the suppressed 202–5
responsive understanding 220
responsiveness 103–4
restoration of dignity 71
restricted communication 227–8
retaliation 85–6
Riis, J. 241
Risser, J. 233
Rocco, A. 244
Rodger, J. 86
role responsiveness 218
Rose, J. 148–9
Rousseau, J.-J. 128, 130–1, 132, 134
Rozmarin, E. 106–7
Russian pogroms 154, 158–62
Ruti, M. 264

sadistic large-group responses to neoliberalism 85–7
sadomasochism 33–4
Said, E. 227
Salgado, J. 212, 214
sameness 119–20
Sander, L. 121
Sandler, J. 218
"Sandy" 79–81, 82–3
Sartre, J.-P. 125–6, 146–8